D0758041

DATE DUE

The Kennedy Round in American Trade Policy

The Twilight of the GATT?

Written under the auspices of
The Center for International Affairs
Harvard University

John W. Evans

The Kennedy Round in American Trade Policy

The Twilight of the GATT?

Harvard University Press, Cambridge, Massachusetts, 1971

Contents

Tables

Abbreviations

AAA — Agricultural Adjustment Act
ASME — American Society of Mechanical Engineers
ASP — American Selling Price
BISD — GATT, *Basic Instruments and Selected Documents*
CAP — EEC, Common Agricultural Policy
CARIFTA — Caribbean Free Trade Association
CCC — Commodity Credit Corporation
CIF — cost, insurance, freight
CXT — EEC, Common External Tariff
ECSC — European Coal and Steel Community
EEC — European Economic Community
EFTA — European Free Trade Association
EPU — European Payments Union
FOB — free on board
GATT — General Agreement on Tariffs and Trade
GNP — Gross National Product
IBRD — International Bank for Reconstruction and Development
IGA — International Grains Arrangement
IMF — International Monetary Fund
ITO — International Trade Organization
IWA — International Wheat Agreement
LTA — Long-Term Cotton Textile Arrangement
MFN — most favored nation
OECD — Organization for European Cooperation and Development
OEEC — Organization for European Economic Cooperation
SITC — Standard Industrial Trade Classification
TIAS — Department of State, *Treaty and International Agreement Series*
TVA — tax on value added
UNCTAD — United Nations Conference on Trade and Development
UNTS — *United Nations Treaty Series*
USC — United States Code
UST — *United States Treaty Series*

Preface

The original purpose of this study was to compile a contemporary case history of the most important negotiations in the history of the US Trade Agreements program in order to provide future administrators and students with an appreciation of the issues and the negotiating techniques involved that could not be obtained from official reports.

Like most plans that take several years to materialize, this simple concept was drastically modified before the book was completed. The Kennedy Round did not end until nearly two years after the study was begun. This delay provided an opportunity to expand on the original plan and, as background for the case history, to explore the origins and evolution of the complex issues in intergovernmental commercial relations that the negotiators had been called upon to unravel.

The scope of the study was still further enlarged when my experience conducting a graduate seminar in international commercial policy convinced me that there was a serious deficiency in the literature bearing on that subject. There were excellent works on the theory of international trade and a considerably smaller number of authoritative, but often outdated, works on limited aspects of international trade relations and agreements. But anyone who wanted a general survey of commercial policy was forced to piece the picture together from many sources, not all of equal merit. The plan of the present book, therefore, evolved around the dual purpose of providing a text which, while maintaining its central focus on the Kennedy Round and its place in history, could also serve as an introduction to the general subject of commercial policy for use both by students and by those with practical problems to solve.

There is no escaping the necessity of asking the reader to accept on faith some of the statements I have made that are based on personal experience. Where I have been aware, however, of the existence of any published sources against which my accuracy may be checked, I have cited them. That this has often been impossible is accounted for by a problem that is more or less peculiar to trade negotiations. Because of the natural aversion of governments to conduct their bargaining in public, most internal documents bearing on a negotiation are restricted to a limited audience within the government concerned, and those documents submitted to the international organization concerned (in this case the GATT) are often similarly restricted. When the latter have eventually been released, they have usually ceased to be of sufficient interest to justify publication for general use. As for the internal documents of the US government, none involving the Kennedy Round have as yet been released.

The contents of US classified documents available to me during this study have, of course, not been divulged. And, while many GATT documents now in the public domain have been cited, it is regrettable that readers will not find copies readily available unless they have access to the files of the GATT secretariat or the files of government departments in Washington or other capitals.

It may be helpful to the reader to have an advance view of the way in which the general framework of the book has been fitted to its dual purpose. Part One follows the economic and legal development of the issues, emphasizing their relevance to the internationally accepted rules of commercial policy incorporated in the GATT.

Part Two examines the political and economic climate that inspired the Kennedy administration to seek from Congress the extraordinary delegation of authority that was contained in the Trade Expansion Act of 1962 and the changes in that climate that occurred between the passage of the act and the inauguration of international negotiations. It analyzes the influence of the growing realization in the United States that the European Economic Community had become a fact and of the rise and subsequent decline of the concept of "Atlantic Partnership."

The prolonged preliminary bargaining over the negotiating rules for the formal negotiations is the subject of Part Three. Although the reader may conclude that the space devoted to this phase is as excessive as the extraordinary length of time consumed by the prenegotiations, the case can be made, however, that the preliminary phase justifies more detailed treatment than the formal negotiations. The Kennedy Round was the first multilateral trade negotiation that attempted to substitute an automatic procedure for haggling over individual tariff rates; the effort to translate that aspiration into a formula is in itself of historical interest. But the more persuasive reason for the length of Part Three is that there is more to be learned about the possibilities and pitfalls for future negotiations from this period than from the more formal phase of the negotiations that followed. The reader should not, however, be misled by the word "period" into assuming that the rule-making phase ended on a single date and was then succeeded by the negotiation proper. For the four major objects of negotiation — industrial tariffs, agriculture, nontariff barriers, and the trade of less developed countries — the progression from the first to the second phase occurred at widely differing points in time. Thus, the division between Part Three and Part Four is, of necessity, functional rather than chronological.

Part Four examines the formal period of each of these conceptually separate negotiations and seeks to show the manner in which the issues that proved too intractable to be settled separately were carried forward and resolved in a compromise that was multifaceted as well as multilateral.

While the treatment of Parts Two, Three, and Four is imperfectly chronological, each at least enjoys a natural terminal date. By contrast, Part Five suffers from the inexorable tendency of present to become past and future to become present. Its arbitrary cutoff date, imposed by the exigencies of publication, is roughly mid-1970. Its two chapters appraise the results of the Kennedy Round from the vantage point of that time and examine not only their in-

fluence but the influence of external developments on the prospects for future rounds and, indeed, for the future of the multilateral trading system established after the Second World War. It is
the contemplation of these post-Kennedy Round developments
that raises the specter of GATTerdammerung, suggested in the
title of the book.

I have received help above and beyond the call of duty from so
many people in the United States and abroad that it will be impossible to name them all. There is no difficulty, however, in knowing where my thanks should begin. If it had not been for Professor
Raymond Vernon my study would not have been begun and, if
begun, would have been far less successful. He persuaded me to
undertake the project, was largely responsible for the hospitality
proffered to me by the Center for International Affairs of Harvard
University during the early stages of my research, and read and
criticized with care and penetration the entire first draft. Also, the
Rockefeller Foundation gave me valuable financial assistance during the initial year, and the Center for International Affairs financed
a visit to the site of the Kennedy Round during the final weeks of
the negotiation.

Others who read and gave me their most useful criticism of selected chapters were Professors Isaiah Frank, Gottfried Haberler,
Charles Kindelberger, Raymond Mikesell and Gardner Patterson,
as well as Dean D. Gale Johnson, William B. Kelly, Jr., G. Maggio,
Margaret Potter, and Oscar Zaglits. My special thanks go to William Diebold, Jr., who read the entire manuscript in its penulti-
mate form. His keen eye and his superior knowledge of some of
the less familiar territory into which I ventured have spared the
final version a number of errors that might have escaped even the
keen eyes of the editors at the Center for International Affairs and
Harvard University Press.

Those in and out of the United States government who went to
unusual effort to provide me with essential information and docu-
ments include, in addition to Mr. Maggio and Mrs. Potter in the
GATT secretariat, Mr. F. A. Haight of that organization and Sir Eric
Wyndham White, then its Director General; William Hart, John
Boyd, and John Howard of the US Tariff Commission; Walter Hol-
lis and Lucille Thompson of the US Department of State; Theodore
Gates and Caroline Jahn of the Office of the Special Representa-

tive for Trade Negotiations; and Paul Luyten, Leonard Tennyson, Alessandro Silj, and Pierre Malvé of the Commission of the European Communities.

Among the typists who at one stage or another labored to produce a legible copy, my special thanks are extended to Margaret Thompson, Louise Richards, and Pearl Clark.
Clark.

No one, of course, expended more time and effort on the enterprise than the editors. Mrs. Marina S. Finkelstein of the Center for International Affairs had the more difficult task of forcing my reluctant steps to follow the path of scholarly citations and of suggesting a more economical and intelligible organization of the text. And, Miss Rita Howe of the Harvard University Press provided a sympathetic and workmanlike polish to the final product. To both of them, my sincere thanks.

My wife, Avis, gave almost as much to this book as did the author. From the typing of first drafts, through the search for elusive sources, right down to the galley slavery of proofreading, she provided practical as well as moral support.

Introduction

Ten months after John F. Kennedy's inauguration, his administration launched the campaign that culminated in passage of the Trade Expansion Act of 1962.[1] The act has been described both as the most sweeping delegation of tariff negotiating power in the thirty-year history of the Trade Agreements Program and as the most extraordinary legislative accomplishment of Kennedy's presidency.

It is possible to quarrel with both of these claims. On two earlier occasions Congress had authorized the President to cut existing tariffs in half. It is true that the act did contain the unprecedented authority to reduce certain tariffs all the way to zero in an agreement with the European Economic Community (EEC). But what in 1962 had seemed to be the most powerful of the weapons provided was to prove unusable in practice. What did make the Trade Expansion Act unique, however, was the fact that, to some extent in the provisions of the law itself but more importantly in its legislative history, Congress demonstrated a willingness to allow the President unprecedented latitude in using the authority that it granted him.

Why and how this revolution in congressional attitudes was achieved is the subject of a later chapter. At this point it is enough to recall that the spark that set it off was the unexpected speed with which the European Common Market was being achieved. Recognition of that success brought unprecedented unanimity as to the need for new negotiating tools and techniques that would permit the United States to deal effectively with its first near equal in the history of the Trade Agreements program.

The product of this short-lived unanimity was the Kennedy Round, with its notable successes — and its failures if measured against the optimism that dominated Washington during John F. Kennedy's short term. But "success" and "failure" have little meaning except as they relate to known ends and to obstacles overcome. To appreciate the ends that motivated the actors in the Kennedy Round is as important to an understanding of their achievements as is an examination of the processes by which they managed to reconcile their differences.

Some of the objectives of the negotiators had origins that were no older than the European Economic Community. Thus, "Atlantic Partnership," if it was in fact an objective of the American administration, could not have been conceived until the successful negotiation of the Treaty of Rome. No previous trials or errors could provide a clue to the road blocks that stood in its way.

But most of the aims of the protagonists were simply the latest manifestations of efforts that had begun soon after the end of World War II. Though some took on new forms or heightened visibility as a result of the emergence of the Common Market, each had a history upon which negotiating plans could draw. In all GATT tariff negotiations "reciprocity" had played its contradictory roles. The Kennedy Round simply presented a unique opportunity for remolding it into a more consistently constructive force. Nor were the problems presented by domestic farm policies, by non-tariff barriers, or by the frustrated aspirations of developing countries inventions of the 1960's. The solution of these and other issues had simply taken on a new urgency in the context of European integration.

It is for reasons such as these, rather than a zeal for history as such, that the first six chapters of this study have been written. By tracing the evolution of the problems faced in previous negotiations, we may be able to understand the successes and failures of the Kennedy Round.

Part One: The Issues

1

Tariff Negotiations, 1934-1962

When the US Trade Agreements program was launched in 1934, alternative methods of achieving its objectives were considered. The method finally chosen, that of negotiating reductions in individual US tariff rates in exchange for reciprocal concessions by other countries, was pursued with no essential change for the next thirty years.

By 1933, the Smoot-Hawley Tariff of 1930 — the highest in American history — had accentuated the reduction of US imports and exports that accompanied the depression. In that year, imports fell to 33 percent of their 1929 value.[1] During the 1920's exports of capital by the United States had supported a large net export of merchandise. Even when loss of confidence curtailed the capital flow, an export surplus continued, financed largely by imports of foreign gold. But gold transfers could not continue to support that surplus indefinitely, even at the disastrously low level to which exports had fallen. Only a massive increase in imports would permit a major recovery in US export trade.[2] The quickest way to accomplish this would have been for the United States to reduce its tariff unilaterally, and this possibility was favored by some. But a number of considerations led to the Roosevelt administration's decision to seek reduction in the high

Smoot-Hawley rates, but only in exchange for "reciprocal" reductions by others.[3]

This decision to negotiate tariff reductions on a reciprocal basis, combined with the equally fundamental decision to continue the existing policy of avoiding discrimination among sources of supply, led inevitably to other decisions that were to establish the basic technique of tariff negotiations for the next thirty years. Cordell Hull had considered the possibility of a broad, horizontal tariff cut, in concert with other countries. But he abandoned this plan when he became convinced that neither the US Congress nor the governments of other countries would agree to "a worthwhile multilateral undertaking" of this kind.[4] This meant that tariffs would be negotiated piecemeal, item by item. And, since conducting such a negotiation simultaneously with many countries was, at the time, regarded as impossible,[5] separate, bilateral negotiations were inevitable.

From 1934 until the postwar period, this bilateral pattern for trade negotiations severely restricted the choice of articles on which tariff reductions could be granted. The Trade Agreements Act of 1934 reaffirmed the policy of extending "Most Favored Nation" (MFN) treatment to virtually all countries. Thus, any tariff reduction granted in a bilateral negotiation had to be "generalized," leading to the practice of limiting such reductions to tariffs on products supplied principally by the negotiating partner in order that "unrequited benefits" to other countries might be avoided. That they should be avoided insofar as possible followed from one of the expressed purposes of the Trade Agreements Act — namely, to obtain foreign markets for US exports in exchange for reductions in the United States tariff.

Another practice that became a common feature of tariff negotiations, especially between 1934 and 1947, was a direct result of the same dilemma: the separation or "ex-ing out" of portions of a tariff item for negotiating purposes. For example, many countries produce and export chinaware; but the United Kingdom had a virtual monopoly on expensive bone china. By reducing the duty only on bone china sold at more than a stated minimum price, the benefit of the reduction could be denied other china exporters without technical violation of MFN. This practice broadened the scope of bilateral negotiations, but it also resulted in a tariff structure that was unduly complex and sometimes irrational. The negotiating partners of the United States operated under similar handicaps insofar as they, too, either were bound by existing treaties to extend MFN treatment to third countries or followed a unilateral policy of tariff nondiscrimination.

In addition to the limitations imposed by reciprocity, the US administration was further restricted by inhibitions against granting tariff reductions that might result in serious injury to a competing domestic industry. Although this restraint was not spelled out in the prewar legislation itself, it was implicit in the decision to negotiate on a selective, item-by-item basis and was explicit in the legislative history of the Trade Agreements Act.[6]

Under the circumstances, it is remarkable that US administrations managed to expend as much of their negotiating coin as they did. In 1934 the President was authorized to reduce any tariff by 50 percent of its 1934 level. From 1934 until 1945, when the authority of the original act was replenished, bilateral negotiations were concluded with twenty-seven countries.[7] The concessions granted by the United States in these bilateral agreements involved tariff reductions on approximately 64 percent of all dutiable imports.[8] These rates were reduced, on the average, by 44 percent of their base date level. This appeared to be a substantial accomplishment.

Measured solely by the statistical results, these bilateral agreements taken together went further toward correcting the excesses of the Smoot-Hawley Tariff than did even the most far-reaching of the subsequent multilateral negotiations until the Kennedy Round. But these gains were aided by some circumstances that no longer existed in later negotiations. The negotiations of the 1930's began from a level of tariffs that was widely recognized to be exorbitant. And, except for two supplementary agreements with Cuba, which affected only preferential rates of duty, and one supplementary agreement with Canada, each bilateral agreement was the first of its kind between the partners involved and presented a unique opportunity to reduce those tariffs with which the partner was especially concerned, including many that exceeded even the demands of the protected industries themselves.

Comparable statistics do not exist to measure the benefits achieved for US exports in these bilateral negotiations. Were they available, they would tell only part of the story. As was pointed out by the US Tariff Commission in its evaluation of the prewar negotiations, a substantial part of the benefit to US export trade was derived from the "general provisions" of the agreements entered into, including the guarantee of MFN treatment and the agreement of the signatories not to impose quantitative restrictions on imports from each other of products for which tariff concessions had been granted.[9] From the incomplete statistics available, however, it would seem that, in terms of the number of items, a larger proportion of the tariff concessions granted by others consisted of the "binding" of existing duties than was true of concessions granted by the United States.[10] Unless the total trade covered by the concessions of others was greater than that covered by United States concessions, which does not appear to be the case, this fact suggests that the United States did not insist on complete reciprocity in a statistical sense. Its negotiating goals were evidently tempered in part by recognition of the extraordinarily high US tariff levels which it brought to the bargaining table and, in the case of negotiations with less developed countries, by broader policy considerations.[11]

The First GATT Negotiation: 1947

By the time the end of World War II was imminent, only a relatively small part of the authority granted the President in the Act of 1934 remained. Tariffs on 40 percent of US dutiable imports had already been reduced by the full 50 percent permitted under the act,[12] and many others had been substantially reduced, though by less than the maximum permissible amount. President Roosevelt therefore asked for and obtained the first authority to reduce tariffs to below the levels authorized by the act of 1934. The new act, signed into law in 1945, authorized the President to reduce tariffs by 50 percent of their level on January 1, 1945.[13] Rates that had in previous negotiations been reduced to the maximum allowable could now be cut to as little as 25 percent of the level established in the 1930 tariff act.

Except for some minor concessions resulting from a bilateral agreement concluded with Paraguay in 1946, all of this new authority was available to the administration when, in November

1946, it invited other countries to join it in the first multilateral conference for the mutual reduction of tariffs. But other provisions of the original act of 1934, as well as its legislative history, remained unchanged. In spite of the unprecedented task it faced, the administration was therefore still constrained to select tariffs for negotiations only after a study of the possible effect on individual US industries and then to barter concessions, item by item, in exchange for reciprocal advantages for American exports.

The 1947 tariff negotiating conference in Geneva was but one of several preparatory steps intended to lead to the creation of an International Trade Organization (ITO), which was to perform, for international commercial relations, a role parallel to that of the International Monetary Fund (IMF) in the field of exchange rates and controls. The General Agreement on Tariffs and Trade (GATT), created by the Geneva negotiation in 1947, was to have been absorbed into this broader institutional structure. It was not foreseen that the GATT would prove to be the only lasting product of the Geneva Conference.[14]

Confronted with the problem of organizing a tariff negotiation among twenty-three countries while adhering to the item-by-item method, the original GATT partners undertook a task that had been judged impossible by the United States government in the 1930's. In some ways the problem was more difficult in 1947. Nine of the twenty-two countries at Geneva already had bilateral agreements with the United States, and they accounted for 83 percent of all US imports from the group.[15] Thus, many of the tariff reductions that could be exchanged with these major negotiating partners without risk of injury to "sensitive" industries had already been granted.

On the other hand, some factors favored the Geneva negotiations. Except for the United States, Canada, and certain Latin American countries, the negotiating countries seriously needed dollars. Their active participation was ensured by the prospect of improved access both to the United States market and to the few other markets able to pay for imports in hard currency. But, because they were to be permitted to maintain quantitative restrictions against imports while their monetary reserves were still dangerously low, their own tariff concessions on imports from the dollar area would not become fully effective until some later date.

In the meantime, their domestic industries were not likely to be jeopardized by undue exposure to US competition.

This did not mean, of course, that the United States was bound to "lose" as a result of the Geneva negotiations. The tariff concessions it received would acquire value when its partners emerged from their payments difficulties and discharged their obligation to dismantle their import controls. Meanwhile, if, through reduced US tariffs, other countries could earn dollars with which to pay for American exports, the danger of a serious slump in US employment could be averted. Furthermore, both the political and economic interests of the United States lay in the restoration of more normal economic relations within the Western world. The immediate compensation for tariff concessions granted by the United States at Geneva would be the contribution those concessions, themselves, could make toward that objective.

The Geneva negotiating techniques and those used in later GATT negotiations were not, and could not have been, truly multilateral. For the most part, they followed closely the procedures that had been developed in bilateral bargaining. Each pair of negotiators exchanged "request lists," followed by "offer lists." Initial offers, as before, were largely limited to the items of which the country receiving the offer was "principal supplier" to the country proposing to reduce or bind its tariff. But when pairs of countries exchanged offers, the lists were made available to all other participants, who were then able to take them into account in their own bilateral negotiations. Where two exporting countries stood to benefit substantially from a tariff concession, the offer could be, and often was, made contingent on the receipt of "compensation" from both. At the end of the day, when the concessions of each negotiating partner were consolidated into its GATT "schedule," all contracting parties[16] acquired contractual rights even to those concessions which they had had no part in negotiating.[17] Thus, within the limits imposed by "reciprocity" and by item-by-item bargaining, the Geneva negotiations achieved some of the benefits of multilateralism.

The results of Geneva were respectable indeed, even though, in both scope and depth, they fell appreciably short of the combined results of the bilateral agreements of the preceding twelve years. This was not surprising, given the fact that tariffs of the United

States and of many of the other participants in 1947 started at a considerably lower level than they had in 1934. About 54 percent of US dutiable imports were affected by tariff reductions granted at Geneva, as compared with 64 percent in all the previous bilaterals. The weighted average reduction of those rates that were reduced was 35 percent, as compared with a 44 percent average for the combined prewar bilaterals.[18] Tariffs on US dutiable imports as a whole were reduced by an average of 18.9 percent. This reduction, of course, is calculated from the levels prevailing in 1945, which were substantially lower for most products than the negotiating base for prewar reductions.

Reports by the US Tariff Commission on the Geneva negotiation do not provide comparable data concerning the concessions obtained by the United States from others. But they do summarize the combined concessions obtained in all negotiations, including the Geneva Agreement. From 1934 to 1948, the United States received tariff concessions from its negotiating partners on products that accounted for 62 percent of their total imports from this country.[19] Of these concessions, less than half were tariff reductions; the rest involved the binding of existing duties or of duty-free status. On the other hand, about 17 percent of the duty reductions involved tariff elimination.[20] United States negotiators were not permitted by legislation to make similar concessions.

Diminishing Returns: 1949-1962

Measured either in terms of volume of trade directly affected by tariff concessions or of average depth of tariff reductions achieved, after 1947 no negotiation until the Kennedy Round produced results approaching those of the first Geneva Agreement (see Table 1). The most far-reaching of these negotiations, held at Torquay in 1950-1951, resulted in an average reduction of 26 percent in the ad valorem equivalent of those duties that were reduced, but achieved little more than a 3 percent reduction in US tariffs on dutiable imports as a whole.

There were reasons for these diminishing returns. In 1961, when the Trade Expansion Act was proposed by the Kennedy administration, it was a common belief, reflected in the congressional hearings, that the item-by-item form of negotiation had outlived its usefulness. There was much to support this judgment, especially under conditions that have prevailed since the formation of the European Economic Community (EEC) in 1957. But the assertion

Table 1.   United States duty reductions in GATT negotiations.

GATT Conference	Imports of items on which tariff was reduced as a percentage of total dutiable imports[a]	Average reduction of tariffs that were reduced[b] (percent)	Weighted average reduction of all duties
First Round, Geneva, 1947	54	35	18.9
Second Round, Annecy, 1949	5.6	35.1	1.9
Third Round, Torquay, 1950-1951	11.7	26	3.0
Fourth Round, Geneva, 1955-1956	16	15 (approx.)	2.4 (approx.)
Fifth Round, Geneva, 1961-1962	20	20 (approx.)[c]	4.0 (approx.)

Source: US Tariff Commission, *Operations of the Trade Agreements Program:* First Round, *June 1934–April 1948,* pt. IV, Table 6; Second Round, *Third Report,* Table 7; Third Round, *Fourth Report,* Table 1; Fourth Round, *Ninth Report,* Table 1 and p. 60; Fifth Round, *Fourteenth Report,* Table 1 and p. 19.

[a]1939 imports in the case of the First Round. For subsequent Rounds, import data are for latest year available at the time of the Tariff Commission's postnegotiation report.

[b]From rates in force immediately before negotiation.

[c]No authoritative figure available. Most US reductions were by 20 percent. Those that were less may have been offset by reductions of more than 20 percent in very low rates and in rates that were over 50 percent and reduced to that level.

concealed more than it revealed as it blanketed under a single cover some causes that were, in fact, related to negotiating methods and others that would have ensured slim results no matter what techniques had been employed.

Meager Results

Limited objectives at some of the conferences were no doubt responsible for their meager results. Neither the Annecy negotiations in 1949 nor the Torquay negotiations, for example, involved an exchange of tariff concessions among all the GATT contracting parties. The sole purpose of the Annecy Conference was the negotiation of agreements with eleven countries then seeking accession to the GATT. The ten countries with which agreements were actually reached provided only 8.2 percent of the dutiable imports of the initial GATT countries.[21] The negotiations at Torquay in 1950-1951 were more ambitious. For the United States, they involved not only agreements with seven newly acceding countries, the largest being the Federal Republic of Germany, but also supplementary agreements with an important group of existing contracting parties as well, including the Benelux Customs Union, France, Italy, and Canada. Countries with which the United States negotiated accounted for about 35 percent of US dutiable imports.[22]

The Fourth Round of multilateral negotiations, in 1955-1956 at Geneva, involved a large number of contracting parties, including most of the more significant trading countries. But the resulting concessions by the United States affected only a small percentage of its dutiable imports from any country except the United Kingdom, which had failed to conclude any agreements during the preceding negotiating round, at Torquay. Although the countries with which agreement was reached accounted for almost 60 percent of those imports,[23] as shown in Table 1, the resulting tariff reductions affected only 16 percent of US dutiable imports. The net effect was to reduce the average tariff level of US dutiable imports by around 2.5 percent.

The Fifth Round of trade negotiations under the GATT, popularly known as the "Dillon Round," was convened for two quite distinct purposes. In order to establish a customs union as an essential feature of the European Economic Community, the Treaty of Rome,[24] had set the level of the Common External Tariff (CXT) for most products by an arithmetical average of duties in force on January 1, 1957, in the four customs territories of the member states.[25] Where the CXT involved an increase in any rate previously bound in GATT by a member state, it was required under Paragraph 6 of Article XXIV of the General Agreement to negotiate a release from the other contracting parties that had been beneficiaries of that binding. The first phase of the negotiations in 1960-1961 was devoted to this operation. As will be seen later, the "XXIV: 6 negotiations" left certain difficult problems unsolved, which later added to the complications of the Kennedy Round.

The second task of the conference was a reciprocal reduction of the tariffs of all the participants. Within the modest limits of available authority, the principal US objective was to obtain a reduction in the CXT of the Common Market in order to lighten the adverse effect on US exports of the gradual adoption of free trade among the six.[26] But the Dillon Round also engaged the United States with most of the largest among the other contracting parties, negotiations being concluded with twenty-three countries, including the members of the EEC and the European Free Trade Association (EFTA),[27] as well as Canada and Japan—countries which provided about 60 percent of total US imports. The United States granted concessions which consisted mostly of tariff reductions but also included the binding of some existing duties on about 20 percent of US dutiable imports.[28] The reductions granted constituted about a 2.4 percent weighted average tariff cut for dutiable imports taken as a whole.

Reduced Negotiating Authority

As has already been pointed out, the limited objectives and scope of the Second and Third Rounds of negotiations could account in large measure for their meager results. But other reasons need to be found for the relative sterility of the Fourth and Fifth Rounds. The tremendous influence of the United States immediately following the war, as well as its ability to obtain ready international acceptance for its commercial policy objectives, had, by 1955, been partly eroded. Also, most European countries were approaching the point at which they could no longer invoke balance of payments difficulties as a reason for forestalling, through quantitative restrictions, the trade effects of tariff concessions previously granted. At the same time, after some twenty years of whittling away at tariffs, many contracting parties were finding further reductions more difficult politically. In the case of the United States, this growing political resistance was expressed in the inadequate bargaining ammunition that was provided US negotiators after the initial round of GATT negotiations in 1947.[29]

During the 1949 and 1950-1951 conferences, the President had available for negotiating purposes only that part of the 1945 grant of authority—to reduce a tariff rate to 50 percent of its 1945 level —that had not already been expended. When the negotiation was with countries seeking accession to the GATT, as was the case at Annecy, this was not too great a handicap. For, at least in theory, the United States was able to obtain credit for reductions previously granted on products of export interest to them and often had unused authority covering other products in which they were interested. But where negotiations were with existing contracting parties, as was usually the case in subsequent rounds, most of the available coin that could be used without serious political cost had already been spent. Since no other participant was obliged to negotiate within similar predetermined limits, it is a fair conclusion that this attrition in US authority had much to do with the diminishing results achieved in 1949 and 1950-1951.

Although United States negotiators entered both the 1955-1956 Round and the Dillon Round in 1961-1962 with new powers, this authority did not approach in usefulness that available for the first GATT negotiation. The Trade Agreements Extension Act of 1955 had authorized the President to reduce any tariff by 15 percent of the rate in existence on January 1, 1955, or, alternatively, to reduce a rate to 50 percent ad valorem*—the reductions to be brought into effect in three annual installments. The President was also authorized to employ any unused authority remaining from the act of 1945 in the negotiations for the accession of Japan, which preceded the 1955-1956 Round. But this authority did not extend to the multilateral negotiations that followed.

When the United States entered the Dillon Round, the President again had available new authority, provided by the Trade Agreements Extension Act of 1958, under which he could reduce a duty by 20 percent of its level on July 1, 1958; reduce a rate by two percentage points (for example, from 6 to 4 percent); or re-

---

*The use of "percent" in differing senses is all but unavoidable. In this sentence "15 percent" refers to the allowable reduction in terms of the preexisting level; a 15 percent reduction in a tariff of 20 percent ad valorem would result in a tariff of 17 percent. In certain contexts this could also be referred to as a reduction of "three percentage points." The ad valorem level of the tariff designates its height as a percentage of the unit value of the imported product, whether the duty is expressed in ad valorem, or in "specific" terms.

duce to 50 percent ad valorem any rate that was above that level.[30] Only in the case of tariff rates below 10 percent ad valorem would the power to reduce the rate by two percentage points yield a greater reduction than if the general 20 percent authority were used. Thus, the Extension Act had the rather illogical effect of permitting a reduction of more than 20 percent in rates already so low as to be relatively ineffective. Since it did not permit moving a product from the dutiable to the free list, it would do nothing in the way of eliminating "nuisance tariffs."

In the case of the Dillon Round, there is irrefutable evidence that limits on the President's authority restricted achievement, at least in the negotiation between the United States and the EEC. For, at the beginning of the conference, the EEC had offered to reduce the CXT on industrial products in general by 20 percent if others would do likewise. For most products, the maximum reduction the President could offer was 20 percent. But, as a practical matter, much of this authority could not be used because of the safeguards the Congress had erected against tariff reductions that might injure a domestic industry.

While the drastic reductions in negotiating power help account for the shallowness of tariff reductions achieved in negotiations after 1947, the principal cause of the meager trade coverage of reductions, especially in the Fourth and Fifth Rounds, was the complex of limitations that were placed on the President's ability to use the maximum authority nominally available to him.

The Escape Clause

In the 1942 agreement with Mexico, the United States had obtained a general clause to permit it to withdraw or modify a tariff concession that resulted in serious injury to a domestic industry. In 1945, when Congress was considering the administration's request for a new grant of negotiating authority, it obtained from President Roosevelt a commitment to include a similar clause in any future agreement. No formal machinery was established for dealing with complaints from domestic industries at that time. But in 1947, in order to forestall a move by protectionists in Congress to require a detailed report by the Tariff Commission on the entire Trade Agreements program before the Geneva negotiations could be held, the President issued an executive order that established a formal procedure for handling escape clause cases. Under the order, the Tariff Commission was given a central role in the investigation of complaints, but the decision remained with the President.

When the text of the GATT was drawn up, the US negotiators obtained the inclusion of Article XIX, which closely followed the language in the US-Mexican Agreement and permitted the unilateral withdrawal of a concession if it resulted in increased imports that caused or threatened serious injury to a domestic industry. In the Trade Agreements Extension Act of 1951, however, Congress insisted on including detailed criteria and procedures governing the administration of the escape clause. As incorporated in the act, these provided, *inter alia,* that the Tariff Commission "upon request of the President, upon resolution of either House of Congress, upon resolution of either the Senate Finance Committee or the House Committee on Ways and Means, upon application of any interested party, or upon its own motion" must promptly investigate claims of possible injury, report its findings, and make its recommendation to the President. The commission was also required to send copies of the report to the two congressional committees. If the President failed to follow the recommendation of the commission, he was required to report to the congressional committees his reasons for failing to do so. In the case of perishable agricultural commodities, the Secretary of Agriculture was given powers and responsibilities analogous to those of the Tariff Commission.[31]

In 1955 these escape clause provisions were made even more restrictive. President Eisenhower's administration supported the 1951 provisions and then yielded to demands for still more crippling requirements.[32] The result was the passage of an act that made it difficult for the Tariff Commission to avoid recommending invocation of the escape clause in any case where an industry, defined to include "subdivisions" of industries with diversified production, should be suffering from reduced earnings for whatever cause at a time when imports were increasing.[33] The act of 1955 did not stop with economic injury, but provided an alternative course that a domestic industry might pursue in seeking to insulate itself from competition: to persuade the Director of the Office of Defense Mobilization, and the President, that imports were threatening to impair national security and should be restricted.

The Extension Act of 1958, under which the Dillon Round was subsequently negotiated, again reinforced the escape clause provisions both by increasing the amount by which the President could raise a rate of duty and by providing that the Congress, through passage of a concurrent resolution receiving a two-thirds vote in each house, could override the President if he should disapprove a recommendation of the Tariff Commission.

The effect that the escape clause alone may have had on the administration's use of the authority nominally delegated to it is difficult to appraise. No president is anxious to grant a concession that he is likely to have to withdraw later, especially since under the GATT the contracting parties adversely affected have the right to retaliate unless adequate compensation is paid. On the other hand, the knowledge that a tariff concession was not irrevocable may have resulted in the administration's taking some chances that would otherwise have seemed imprudent. There is no room for uncertainty, however, as to the effect of another limitation placed by Congress on presidental discretion — the so-called "peril point" provision.

Peril Points

Congress, unwilling to rely on presidential self-restraint, restored to the act of 1951 a provision that had been added in 1948 but repealed in 1949. This required in effect that, before any negotiation, the Tariff Commission set, for each rate to be negotiated, a point below which the duty might not be reduced without causing or threatening serious injury to domestic industry. If the President should reduce a rate below this "peril point" he was required to report his action and his reasons to Congress.[34] Though it left the final decision to the President and though superficially it seemed a logical extension of the escape clause concept, this requirement was, in fact, much more restrictive, as it was clearly intended to be. The Tariff Commission was not authorized to weigh the advantages of a tariff reduction against the degree of risk involved. Nor did it have any responsibility for the success of the negotiations. Since the commission was given the impossible task of estimating the effect of a tariff reduction before the fact, understandable caution dictated that it insure itself against unexpected developments by giving predominant weight to the possibility of future injury, however remote.[35]

The peril point provisions remained in the Extension Acts of 1955 and 1958 and were in force during both the Fourth and Fifth GATT Rounds. In the first of these, the President in no case reduced a rate below the points established by the Tariff Commission. But the Dillon Round, where a reduction in the level of the new tariff of the European Economic Community was the most important prize to be achieved, came close to a breakdown because of the inability of US negotiators to respond favorably to the 20 percent linear offer of the EEC. An agreement of sorts was salvaged only by President Eisenhower's decision to "breach" the peril points on products involving some $76 million of US imports.[36]

A few points stand out in this brief survey of earlier tariff negotiating experience. As will be seen, some of them were very much in the minds of the Kennedy administration when it prepared for a new round of negotiations.

In prewar agreements the system of negotiating item by item had worked surprisingly well, even under the handicap of bilateral negotiations, so long as the tariffs of most of the negotiators were high enough to provide a comfortable cushion against competition. But the results achieved in these early agreements were promoted by a recognition on the part of the US negotiators that the high starting levels of the Smoot-Hawley Tariff called for deeper tariff cuts than those made by their negotiating partners. If this recognition had been explicit, it might well have influenced the accepted meaning of "reciprocity," and this in turn could have changed the course of the Kennedy Round.

In the immediate postwar period the traditional negotiating techniques were again able to accomplish impressive results. The circumstances at that time were peculiarly favorable, and the US administration was in a strategic position. Its political influence was reinforced by the compulsion of most other countries to sell more goods to the dollar area and by the knowledge on their part that their balance of payments difficulties would enable them to pay for US concessions in promissory notes.

Returns from subsequent negotiations diminished sharply, however. This cannot be attributed exclusively to the declining usefulness of the item-by-item method of negotiation. For the reduction in usable authority given the President would in itself have precluded US tariff cuts approaching those achieved in 1947. And this limitation, in turn, would inevitably have affected the extent to which others were willing to cut their own tariffs. Basically, however, both the limitations on presidential authority and the item-by-item negotiating technique were manifestations of deeply rooted attitudes, in the United States and elsewhere, toward the value of tariff protection. Before this relationship can be explored further, it is necessary to look more closely at the role played by the concept of reciprocity, which has governed all negotiations since 1934.

2

Reciprocity

There is no definition of reciprocity in the Trade Agreements Act of 1934 or in succeeding legislation; nor does the GATT itself contain a definition. These were fortunate omissions. For, a precise meaning, especially if it had been expressed mathematically, might have precluded much of the progress in tariff reduction that has been achieved since 1934. So long as tariff concessions resulted from negotiations in which the only requirement was that each side accept the result, each negotiator remained free to apply his own system of weighing the results. Without this flexibility it is hard to see how a balance could ever have been struck.

If the concept of reciprocity was fortunately blurred in its outlines, it nevertheless did contain a hard kernel of common agreement: each partner wanted to increase his exports in return for any increase in imports likely to result from his own tariff concessions. Usually, though there were exceptions, the aim of the negotiator was even more precise: to see that the expected increase in his country's exports should at least equal any likely increment in its imports. Harry Hawkins, a former State Department official who participated in early negotiations under the Trade Agreements Act, has written that a strict application of the policy of reciprocal tariff reductions meant negotiating "with a view to producing a dollar's worth of increased exports for every dollar's worth of increased imports."[1] In more recent studies as well, equality of trade increments is assumed to be the universal objective of tariff negotiators, an assumption that was certainly implicit in the procedures followed in every tariff negotiation under the GATT before the Kennedy Round.[2] Each started with the exchange of data on the trade coverage of requests and offers; on this statistical base were built arguments over the "quality" of the proposed concessions, that is, over the increments of trade likely to result from each.

The Problem of Low-Tariff Countries

Reciprocity in this sense has had one paramount claim to validity: those governments that have had valuable tariff concessions to offer have been in a position to enforce it. It has not always been accepted as equitable, however. Thus, within three years of the founding of the GATT, the low-tariff countries of Europe, led by the Benelux Union and the Scandinavian countries, made clear their dissatisfaction with negotiating techniques and objectives which, they contended, favored those participants whose high tariffs gave them greater bargaining power. Their sense of injustice was sharpened by the progressive dismantlement of quantitative trade restrictions in Europe under the aegis of the Organization for European Economic Cooperation (OEEC),[3] a process that focused attention on disparities of tariff levels on the European Continent and resulted in a proposal by the "Low-Tariff Club" in the OEEC that GATT consider the "European tariff problem."[4] This was sidetracked, however, when the French delegate, M. Pflimlin, in September 1951, proposed to the Sixth Session of the GATT a formula for a 30 percent average tariff reduction by all GATT contracting parties.[5] The "French Plan" was later amended by the French delegation and further refined by a GATT working party in October 1953.

The revised plan would have produced only a modest narrowing of tariff-level disparities in percentage terms.[6] But it would have bypassed the problem of differences in bargaining power. It left to each country the determination of how the reduction in its own tariff was to be achieved, as long as the rates in each major sector of import trade were cut by an average of 30 percent. Rates above an agreed maximum would have been reduced to that level, and very low rates would have been excused from any reduction. After much study and debate, this scheme was frustrated by opposition from the United Kingdom and by limitations on the American President's authority to reduce tariffs—a restraint reinforced by his commitment to Congress to use even this limited authority on a selective basis.[7]

Nothing came of these proposals. But, since the completion of the text of the Havana Charter[8] in 1947, the Contracting Parties have conducted tariff negotiations under a rule that was designed to strengthen the hands of the low-tariff countries: "The binding against increase of low duties or of duty-free treatment shall in principle be recognized as a concession equivalent in value to the substantial reduction of high duties."

The omission of any standards of measurement to apply to this rule is perhaps an indication that it was not expected to be effective except where it was simply a statement of fact. There are, of course, cases in which the binding of a low tariff is a valuable bargaining counter. Where there is any likelihood that a rate may in fact be increased, with a restrictive effect on imports, binding it against increase often does have substantial value to some other participant. But where there is no such likelihood, an offer to bind an existing low rate is usually greeted with polite indifference. It is in fact very doubtful that the existence of the low-tariff rule has brought results substantially different from those that would have been achieved through bargaining power alone.

The Problem of Measurement

When a negotiator invokes his right to reciprocity, he is speaking a language that both he and his fellow bargainers understand. Yet his meaning cannot be expressed with mathematical precision. Even after the bargain has been struck and has had time to make itself felt, it is usually not possible to determine exactly what the negotiators thought they were obtaining. To measure the trade value attributed by a negotiator to a concession granted or received would require a knowledge, among other things, of his assumptions concerning relevant elasticities in supply and demand and, when an existing rate is to be bound, of his assumptions concerning the likelihood that it would be increased. Such assumptions may not have been explicit even in his own calculations. Nor, in view of the many extraneous factors that always arise to produce unforeseeable results, can the reciprocity actually achieved be determined by examining later trade flows.

Calculated Departures from Reciprocity

Aided by the inadequacies of the tools available for forecasting the effects of tariff changes, governments have at times been able to depart from the strict reciprocity expected by the public and thus to conclude agreements that would otherwise have been impossible. Nor have such departures always depended on statistical ambiguity. The initial GATT negotiation of 1947 was an instance of open deviation from reciprocity, at least in the short run, it being well understood that concessions granted to the United States by most participants would, at best, have only a delayed effect on US exports.[9] In asking for the legislation that made the negotiations possible, the principal purpose of the Truman administration was to lead the world out of the morass of trade restrictions and controls inherited from the depression and World War II. While testifying in favor of the legislation, William L. Clayton, then Assistant Secretary of State, openly acknowledged this aim.[10] But even with their unassailable reasons for seeking world rehabilitation rather than immediate export advantage, administration witnesses found it necessary to make the point that reciprocity would be automatic and that the dollars earned by the rest of the world would promptly be used to slake an unsatisfied thirst for American goods.[11] Thus, even in the extraordinary circumstances prevailing at the end of the war, it was not possible to overlook the power that the concept of reciprocity exerted on the public and legislative mind.

The Arguments for Tariff Protection

No matter how much weight is given to influences that may have led governments at times to accept less compensation in tariff negotiations than would be suggested by a dollar-for-dollar interpretation of reciprocity, their consistent obeisance to the concept confirms that it is at least a political reality with which they must reckon. They cannot ignore the pervasive belief that, when a country grants a tariff concession, it incurs a cost that must be compensated. What reasons are there, however, for believing that government policy makers also think that the reduction of a tariff (or the sacrifice of freedom to increase it) constitutes a cost to the community? Since most governmental policy makers are reasonably sophisticated, this is much the same as asking whether there are economic arguments for tariffs that have any validity at all.

There are common arguments in favor of tariffs that relate to the economy as a whole. In examining them first, the use of tariffs to transfer real income from one group of the population to another can temporarily be ignored. Some of the more naïve arguments used to justify protecting domestic producers against import competition may be discarded without close attention. Perhaps the prize should be awarded to the US Tariff Acts of 1922 and 1930, which aimed at a "flexible tariff" that would be just sufficient to offset differences between foreign and domestic costs of production.[12] Accomplishment of this goal, if it were possible, would eliminate all foreign trade. Related to this fallacy is one that has proved more durable: the conviction that tariffs are necessary to "prevent the importation of low wage rates" from abroad. It is unlikely that this belief, which in its primitive form, ignores the causal relationship between high productivity and high wages, has influenced government policy makers in recent years any more that the "flexible tariff" concept of 1922 and 1930.[13]

There are, however, more respectable reasons for concluding that a tariff can be beneficial to the country imposing it. But these apply only in limited cases and usually under circumstances that are short lived. A classic case, of course, is that of the revenue tariff. In a country where the immature state of administration makes other forms of taxation impracticable, a tariff may be the only means of raising revenue. But a revenue tariff is an anachronism among the highly developed countries for whom reciprocity in tariff bargaining is relevant. The same may be said of the "infant industry" argument. There are undoubtedly cases where it will pay a developing country to impose a tariff in order to help a new industry surmount the extra costs and uncertainties it must encounter during its formative period. But, as Haberler has pointed out, in a developed country with an organized capital market there is no need for the government to substitute its judgment for that of private investors.[14] In the United States, the electronics and color television industries had no trouble finding the capital to permit them to survive their growing pains.

The Terms of Trade

The "terms of trade" argument for tariffs also has academic respectability. And, unlike the "infant industry" argument, it applies to the major, industrialized, trading nations, at least in theory. No modern economist questions that a tariff imposed by an important trading country will, if others take no counteraction, usually result in reducing the price that the country—as distinguished from its consumers—pays for its imports. The foreign producer pays some part of the tariff and, *up to a certain tariff level,* the loss to the economy of the importing country resulting from the relatively inefficient use of its resources can be more than offset by the reduction in import costs.[15] But even if this "optimum tariff level" could be determined in concrete cases, the theory fails to provide a useful guide to tariff policy, if only because other countries cannot be expected to remain passive while one country improves its terms of trade at their expense. And, even if the certainty of retaliation could be ignored, no country with global interests, like the United States, could rationally adopt a policy aimed at enhancing its own prosperity by deliberately dragging down that of other countries.

"Second Best" Uses of Tariffs

On a more or less equal footing with the "terms of trade" argument for tariffs is the "theory of the second best."[16] Applied to international trade, it provides justification in economic welfare terms for the imposition of a tariff at a certain level for a particular product if the tariffs of the same country on other products cannot be altered, and if the tariff levels of trading partners remain fixed.[17] Governments have, in fact, been influenced, consciously or unconsciously, in fixing the tariff level for a product by the levels of the tariffs of their trading partners and the levels of their own tariffs on other products. But there is no evidence that they have made tariff policy with the theory of the "second best" explicitly in mind. Even if they have been aware of the theory, it has provided them with no yardstick for determining the tariff levels that would best promote the overall welfare.

"Balance of Payments" Uses of Tariffs

The influence of balance of payments considerations on tariff policy has been limited and generally negative; they have probably prevented tariff reductions, but have rarely led to increases in statutory tariff rates. Many influences have militated against the use of increased tariffs to deal with a payments deficit. If an increase were prolonged, the effect on the general level of costs in the economy could easily offset the initial trade effect and worsen the balance. Furthermore, if temporary restriction of imports is needed to halt a drain on a country's gold and foreign exchange reserves, the use of quantitative restrictions, permitted by the GATT in these circumstances, or of temporary surcharges have generally been preferred.[18] In the early postwar years the preference for the use of quotas was decisive because the many countries then suffering deficits had fully operative systems of import licensing and because widespread inconvertibility required a precision in the use of discriminatory controls that tariffs could not provide. Now that postwar quantitative restrictions have largely been dismantled, a tendency among countries having balance of payments difficulties to resist further tariff reduction may develop. But the erection or maintenance of tariffs as insurance against possible future payments problems has not as yet played a noticeable part in shaping tariff policies.

Reciprocity and Political Factors

Transfer of Income

Up to this point we have considered the economic effects of tariffs upon the economy regarded as a whole. But the welfare of an economy is not a simple aggregate of the incomes accruing to its component parts. No government can be concerned only with total income and ignore its distribution. Seen in this light, many government tariff decisions that would otherwise seem irrational emerge as being at least understandable.

Any transfer of income that can be effected by tariffs could in theory be accomplished more directly, without incurring the same

risk of reduced efficiency. Where, for example, all political parties agree that it is desirable to improve the lot of unemployed
coalminers, it would probably be less costly to the economy to
pay them a subsidy until they can find other employment than to
stimulate demand for coal by restricting imports of petroleum.
But it does not necessarily follow that it is irrational for a government to take the latter course if voting consumers prefer a hidden
tax on their consumption to an open tax on their income. In these
circumstances the better solution may be considered politically
unavailable.

It is also simple political wisdom to favor those groups in the
population that wield political power, at the expense of politically
weaker groups. And where no acceptable social objective would
be furthered by a more candid transfer of real income, the use of
the tariff is a rational choice. In such cases alternative methods of
effecting the transfer of income are likely to be too obvious and
too much in conflict with accepted standards of equity to please
even the segments of the population to be favored.[19]

It is easy to find examples of this use of the tariff in the United
States. In the logrolling that went into the constitution of the
Smoot-Hawley Tariff of 1930, Congress tried to benefit most special interest groups in the economy, though it succeeded only in
harming all of them. More recent "escape clause" actions in
which various presidents have raised the tariffs on bicycles, spring
clothespins, watches, carpets, and glass have been more successful in the selective use of tariffs to transfer income.

If there are political reasons for governments to impose tariffs
for the benefit of favored groups, there are even stronger reasons
for the reluctance to make tariff reductions that would withdraw
from these groups privileged positions they already enjoy. And
these reasons are especially persuasive when the groups concerned
are producers no longer able to compete at world market prices.
These are the "sensitive" industries whose products have been
excluded from tariff negotiations in the past and that appeared on
"exceptions lists" in the Kennedy Round.

There can be little doubt that the desire to favor particular
groups of producers in the economy has influenced governments
in deciding whether particular tariffs should be reduced. But,
again, there is no reason to believe that these considerations have

determined their attitude toward the reduction of the general level of tariffs or toward reciprocity in tariff negotiations.

Other Political Motivations for Seeking Reciprocity

There is, of course, no reason to rule out the possibility that governments may be motivated in tariff bargaining by political considerations that are less rational than those discussed above. They may, for example, respond to what they believe is a pervasive prejudice of the electorate against imports. Or, even if there is no reason to believe that the population considers imports per se to be evil or unpatriotic, they may act on the assumption that it will disapprove of any increase in imports that is not directly compensated by an equal increase in exports.[20] But such explanations do not fit very closely with the trend of public opinion in the United States since the end of World War II. In fact, they ignore the change that has taken place in the average American's view of the role of the United States in the world—a change that has not been overlooked by professional protectionists. Current fashions in semantics are revealing. No lobbyist for higher tariffs or import quotas in the first half of the 1960's cared to be labeled "protectionist." Yet, as Bauer, Pool, and Dexter have pointed out, when the Smoot-Hawley Act was being considered, "the prototype of the argument for lowering a particular tariff began in effect thus: 'Of course I favor protectionism, but.' "[21] A similar shift can be seen in the labels under which lobbyists do business. An association which operated from 1885 to the 1950's under the artless title of "The American Tariff League" found it expedient in the 1950's to change its name to "Trade Relations Council." Washington's most single-minded spokesman for industries seeking protection, O. R. Strackbein, operates under the noncommittal title of "President of the Nation-wide Committee of Industry, Agriculture and Labor on Import-Export Policy." Even recent American administrations have found it desirable to avoid the unpleasant words "restriction" or "protection" to characterize their occasional concessions to business pressures; in official pronouncements, for example, the framework within which petroleum imports are curtailed is almost invariably referred to as the "Oil Import Program."

Advocates of protection for particular domestic industries are not hard to find, but in the present decade the evidence does not point to the existence of protectionism as a dominant ideology that would account for the attitude of governments toward reciprocity. To the extent that protectionism in this sense does persist, it would be reasonable to expect that its force would be greater in some countries than in others. But, in tariff negotiations, the United States has been as insistent upon reciprocity as France or Japan. The unanimity with which governments have behaved as if increased imports represented an economic cost cannot be explained in terms of mercantilism. Nor is it necessary to do so. For there is one motivation that is common to all countries that have engaged, or expect to engage, in future tariff negotiations: the urge to retain bargaining power for that purpose.

Preservation of Bargaining Power

In an environment in which negotiation has become firmly entrenched as the method usually employed for altering tariff rates, it is rare to find a government prepared to forego future bargaining power by a unilateral reduction of tariffs, even where to do so would give its citizens an immediate increase in real income. Thus, in the GATT debates in the early 1950's, when low-tariff countries asked for special consideration in the bargaining process, they were preoccupied less with their inability to obtain a balance of advantage from the negotiations immediately in prospect than with a fear that reductions equivalent to those of higher-tariff countries would strip them of the bargaining power needed in future rounds.[22] The same worry strongly influenced the European Economic Community during the Kennedy Round.

The US Congress, too, has been concerned with the preservation of bargaining power. The earliest congressional delegation of tariff-making authority was in the Tariff Act of 1890, in which the President was authorized to increase tariffs against the products of individual countries in order to provide a weapon that could be used to obtain improved treatment for US exports. Much more recently, in Section 252 of the Trade Expansion Act of 1962, the Congress provided that: "the President shall . . . to the extent he deems necessary and appropriate, impose duties or other import restrictions on the products of any foreign country or instrumentality establishing or maintaining [unjustifiable] foreign import restrictions against U.S. agricultural products, when he deems such duties and other import restrictions necessary and appropriate to prevent the establishment or *obtain the removal* of such foreign import restrictions."[23] Admittedly, this provision was aimed at a limited range of trade barriers especially irksome to Congress, and not at customs tariffs. But it serves as a recent illustration of the natural tendency of governments and legislators to attach value to import restrictions for their potential advantage as negotiating counters.

In the few postwar instances in which governments have reduced tariff rates without compensation, they have usually sought to keep as much as possible of the bargaining power associated with previous, higher rates. In some cases, the reductions have been characterized as "temporary," and the previous rates carefully preserved in a showcase labeled "statutory tariff." Rarely, if ever, has the reduced rate been consolidated in the country's GATT schedule until the maximum compensation could be extracted in a subsequent negotiation.

A number of sound economists have also suggested that the tenacity with which government officials cling to their bargaining counters in tariff negotiations is a reflection less of the considered policies of their governments than of their own zeal for negotiation and their desire to enhance their own reputations as practitioners of the art. As Professor Taussig put it: "The negotiators are tempted to try to get the better of each other, to make a show of doing a smart thing."[24] This does help to account for the intensity of the bargaining that takes place. But it cannot be held responsible for the persistence of "reciprocity" as the objective of the negotiations.

The desire of governments to cling to all possible bargaining power is sufficient explanation for the reluctance of negotiators to yield more in the way of concessions than is required in order to obtain valuable concessions from their negotiating partners. Tariffs that have no intrinsic economic value for the country that maintains them have acquired value because of the insistence of other countries on reciprocity in the bargaining process. And this opens up the real possibility that the US Trade Agreements program, in spite of its creditable accomplishments, has itself generated forces that limit its future usefulness. It has created a market for bargaining power, and, precisely because of its earlier success in reducing tariffs, it may have inflated the values governments attach to the tariffs that remain.

Once it is recognized that governments attach value to tariffs for the bargaining power they represent, there is no need to assume that the levels of existing tariffs reflect their judgment of the margin of protection required for maximum collective satisfaction. Tariff levels may be maintained in spite of the fact that a lower level would raise the country's real income.

The urge to hold on to existing tariffs for their future bargaining power is even consistent with an interest in the economic welfare of other countries. The major negotiating powers all have interests beyond their borders. The United States, for example, has reasons for seeking the most efficient use of resources and the maximization of real income throughout most of the world. In these circumstances, the husbanding and efficient use of bargaining power can be viewed not as a means of obtaining national advantage but as an international duty. Each responsible government may believe that its own contribution to global welfare will be enhanced if, in exchange for its own tariff reductions, it exacts the largest possible reduction in the trade barriers of friendly countries.

Summary

No single explanation will cover all the circumstances that cause governments to resist reductions in their tariffs. Efforts to favor special domestic interests, concern with the distribution of real income, temporary balance of payments considerations, even the vestigial influence of long-dead schools of economic thought—all play their part. But all of these domestic concerns together will not explain the persistence of tariff bargaining on the part of countries that could profit from unilateral tariff reductions.

It is here suggested that the existence of tariff bargaining is in itself a sufficient reason for the insistence on reciprocity; anticipation of a future need for negotiating power provides incentive enough for hard present bargaining. Thus, the cost a government incurs when it reduces or binds a tariff may be measured less by any possible disadvantages from increased imports than by the value it believes a negotiating partner would place on that action. Once this simple, and observable, fact is recognized, it becomes less difficult to understand how a number of governments intent on the reduction of tariffs for their mutual benefit can be diverted from that purpose into a contest in which each seems as much concerned with denying benefits to its partners as with obtaining benefits for itself.

3

Nondiscrimination, 1947-1967

Opposition to discrimination in international trade has been the central theme of American commercial policy almost from the beginning of the nation. Washington proclaimed it in his Farewell Address. John Quincy Adams publicly explained that American deviations from this basic principle were "essentially defensive and counteracting to similar regulations . . . operating against us."[1] During the latter half of the nineteenth century the United States officially pursued a policy of conditional most favored nation treatment for bargaining. But agreements negotiated under this policy were "negotiated primarily for the purpose of eliminating discrimination against U.S. exports by European countries rather than for the purpose of obtaining or granting preferential treatment."[2]

Even during the depression of the 1930's, when nondiscriminatory trading in the world had been largely replaced by bilateral agreements, Cordell Hull persuaded Franklin Roosevelt to reject a discriminatory agreement that had been negotiated with Germany for the disposal of US cotton.[3] And, in the 1930's and early 1940's, one of the principal American targets was "to end the British Commonwealth system of preferential trade, which was firmly established and extended in the Ottawa Agreements of

1932."[4] To further this design, the United States, in the Mutual Aid Agreement of 1942, obtained the agreement of the United Kingdom that one of the objectives of the lend-lease settlement was to be the "elimination of all forms of discriminatory treatment in international commerce." Even before the end of the war, in preparing its proposals for an international trade organization, the United States included as a central objective the elimination of tariff preferences and the nondiscriminatory application of other regulations of trade.[5]

By the beginning of the Kennedy Round, however, the form of the discrimination to be combated and the kind of weapons available for use against it had radically changed, both because of the decreasing importance of colonial preferential tariff systems and because of the increase in new forms of regional discrimination that had come to be accepted as consistent with other US foreign policy objectives.

Although the existence of discrimination in international trade was not a subject for negotiation in the Kennedy Round, fears of the effects of the new discrimination inherent in the European Common Market provided the negotiations with their initial impetus and helped dictate their course. To help understand its influence, we must trace the role of "discrimination" in US commercial policy, beginning with an effort to define the term.

Some Definitions

Any definition of discrimination that can be applied to the real world of trade necessarily involves arbitrary elements. First, if we accept the convention—itself arbitrary—of excluding from the term differential treatment in favor of domestic producers, which can be identified by the word "protection," the definition of discrimination that would then fit most neatly into the fabric of international trade theory would be: any official action that has the effect of diverting the pattern of international trade from that which would have resulted had all foreign suppliers received equal treatment. Such a definition may have conceptual meaning, but it has, unfortunately, little practical value. In this sense, discrimination could only be avoided under total free trade. Any protection of domestic producers must inevitably result not simply in reducing imports but in influencing their distribution among different supplying countries. There is no practical way to equalize the amount of protection granted to different products. Even if all tariffs were set at the same ad valorem level, their restrictive effect would differ widely from one product to another.

To be of practical use in international discourse, therefore, the definition of discrimination must be narrowed to include only differential treatment of the same product when imported from different countries or, to use the language of the GATT, differential treatment of "like products." This definition, too, involves arbitrary judgments, and it cannot be applied with precision. The Contracting Parties have, for example, tacitly accepted as "nondiscriminatory" differential tariff rates on different grades or "value brackets" of such products as chinaware. But it is not clear that they would be equally tolerant if a red wine produced in California from Pinot Noir grapes were charged a tariff rate higher or lower than that levied on a Romanée Conti from the same variety of grape grown in the Côte d'Or region of Burgundy and bottled on the vintner's premises. Yet, to a connoisseur, these are hardly "like products." In spite of its deficiencies, GATT usage will ordinarily be followed here. When it is not, the exception will be noted.

A few words also about the term "Most Favored Nation," which can be quite puzzling. As the words would imply, its original meaning depended on the existence of discrimination; the country that obtained the right to MFN treatment, usually in a bilateral treaty, was assured that no other country would be treated more favorably. This is still the formal meaning. But, as the exchange of MFN commitments has spread, the term has become almost synonymous with nondiscrimination. Thus, it is customary to refer to a tariff being applied "on an MFN basis" as if it were applied without discrimination to all imports. But, when a country maintains a two-column tariff (the lower tariff being charged on imports from countries receiving preferences), the higher, and less favorable, rate is known as the "MFN rate." This Alice in Wonderland inversion of meaning is, of course, the natural result of the fact that the MFN obligation incorporated in international treaties and agreements, including the GATT, has normally been subject to exceptions in favor of existing systems of tariff preferences.

Finally, as almost universally used today and as it will be used throughout this discussion, MFN means unconditional most favored nation treatment. The conditional form of the MFN clause has little present importance, though it did play a significant role in the earlier history of US trade relations.

Tariff Discrimination by the United States

The MFN Clause

The general use of the unconditional MFN clause by the United States in its commercial treaties goes back only to 1923.[6] Beginning with the first American commercial treaty with France in 1778, the United States usually accorded only conditional MFN treatment, which entitled treaty partners to receive the benefit of the most favorable treatment granted to a third party only upon payment of compensation equivalent to any that had been paid by the third party. Thus, although the United States usually applied a single-column tariff to goods from all sources,[7] it explicitly reserved the right to discriminate against its treaty partners if that condition were not met. The partners were governed by the same clause in their obligations to the United States, though in their treaties with others they normally accorded unconditional MFN treatment.

In 1923 the US government announced a new policy of including the unconditional MFN clause in future commercial treaties. During the following decade twenty-nine treaties or executive agreements with the unconditional clause were concluded.[8] But most of the United States' major trading partners proved reluctant to exchange unconditional MFN agreements with a country possessing a high, albeit nondiscriminatory tariff, especially since that tariff was nonnegotiable.[9] An opportunity to meet those objections came with the Trade Agreements Act of 1934. The exchange of unconditional MFN commitments that resulted helped lay the groundwork for later MFN multilateralization under the GATT. These contractual commitments to MFN were, of course, subject to the usual exception for established systems of tariff preferences, as among the members of the British Commonwealth and the members of the French Union, as well as the one between the United States and Cuba.

Nontariff Discrimination

During the depression of the thirties, the discriminatory effect of preferential tariff systems was overshadowed by the widespread use of discriminatory quantitative restrictions. Under the impetus of balance of payments difficulties, or simply as the result of efforts to preserve established export markets in the face of declining demand, most of the countries of the world beyond the dollar area became enmeshed in a variety of bilateral payments and clearing agreements that had as their effect, if not as their object, a tendency toward the bilateral equalization of payments between participants. This could be accomplished, of course, only by discrimination. The result of this bilateralism was a drastic reduction in the volume of world trade and the distortion of its content and flow.

During World War II normal trading relations were interrupted. In the early postwar period the acute balance of payments difficulties and currency inconvertibility of most countries, including the former belligerents in Europe, led to a new complex of largely discriminatory financial and trade controls. One of the principal purposes behind the creation of the International Monetary Fund (IMF) and the International Bank for Reconstruction and Development (IBRD), and behind the negotiations that led to the creation of the GATT, was to generate conditions under which multilateralism and nondiscrimination could be restored to international economic relations.

The General Agreement on Tariffs and Trade

In an earlier chapter, the GATT was discussed primarily as a platform for the multilateral negotiation of tariff concessions, but it performs other equally important functions without which the exchange of commitments concerning tariffs would have little meaning. It provides both a body of agreed rules to govern trading relations among the contracting parties and a framework for the administration of those rules and for reconciling conflicts of interest in the international trade field.

A very few basic obligations support the entire GATT structure. Perhaps the most fundamental one, on which many of the more detailed rules rest, is the commitment of contracting parties to accord MFN treatment to each other. This obligation extends not only to customs duties but to other charges, rules, or formalities in connection with importation or exportation.[10] Some articles specify the manner in which the obligation is to be interpreted and applied in specific cases such as the use of quantitative restrictions (when they are permitted) and the operation of state trading monopolies. Almost as basic as the obligation of nondiscrimination is the general prohibition against the use of quantitative restrictions.[11] One of the important reasons for this rule was the drafters' desire to eradicate a practice that had been a powerful aid to the growth of discrimination and bilateralism.

Given the kind of trading world the prospective contracting parties faced in 1947, these basic commitments inevitably were subject to exceptions. Thus, the applicability of the most favored nation obligation to tariffs was qualified by the traditional exception for existing preferential systems; this exception was severely limited, however, by a provision that, even within a recognized preferential system, no new preference could be created nor any preferential margin increased.

Two other exceptions to the basic rules were the most widely used during the first ten years of GATT: the permission to use quantitative restrictions for balance of payments reasons and the accompanying exception that permitted discriminatory application of the restrictions where the country concerned was entitled under IMF rules to discriminate in its exchange controls.[12] So long as important currencies were inconvertible and each deficit country needed to conserve its hard currency reserves, this exception simply confirmed a practice that was almost universal in 1947 and that persisted through most of the following decade. In later years, however, the incidence of discriminatory quantitative restrictions and of preferential tariff systems declined. Another exception to the rule of most favored nation treatment, which permitted customs unions and free-trade areas, has, on the other hand, gained dramatically in importance.

Regional Integration

GATT treatment of customs unions (and free-trade areas) is in sharp contrast to that accorded preferential systems. While new

preferences are prohibited,[13] Article XXIV of GATT explicitly permits the association of two, or more, contracting parties for the
purpose of eliminating trade barriers between them without extending the same treatment to other contracting parties. In the
original US proposals for the ITO Charter, this exception had
been limited to customs unions, that is, to areas involving both
free trade among the partners and an external tariff identical for
all of them. This exception was broadened during the negotiation
of the GATT rules in two respects, both of which were to prove
very significant: the inclusion of "a free-trade area," in which
each partner remains free to follow an autonomous tariff policy
toward outside countries, and an "interim agreement," involving
the gradual completion of a customs union or free-trade area in
accordance with a firm schedule.[14] At the time, the negotiators
did not anticipate that these additional exceptions would have
sufficient appeal for any group of major trading nations to provide a serious loophole in the basic requirement of nondiscrimination.

More than one student has been intrigued by the reasons why
the founders of the GATT, while condemning the exchange of
partial preferences, gave their blessing to total discrimination. The
favorite explanation relates to global economic welfare. Clair
Wilcox, a key American participant in the negotiations, presented
the following defense: "A customs union creates a wider trading
area, removes obstacles to competition, makes possible a more
economic allocation of resources, and thus operates to increase
production and raise planes of living. A preferential system, on
the other hand, retains internal barriers, obstructs economy in
production, and restrains the growth of income and demand. It
is set up for the purpose of conferring a privilege on producers
within the system and imposing a handicap on external competitors. A customs union is conducive to the expansion of trade on
a basis of multilateralism and non-discrimination, a pereferential
system is not."[15]

Both Article XXIV and Professor Wilcox's rationale were written
before the publication of a series of pioneering theoretical studies
of the economic effects of customs unions.[16] In essence, these
analyses point out that a customs union (or free-trade area) can

create new trade, which would otherwise not have occurred, between partners to the union; it can also displace trade that formerly took place between either partner and a third country. Professor Viner argued that at least in the short run, before any secondary effects of economic integration could be felt, the "trade creation" resulting from the union would involve an increase in total welfare through an improved allocation of resources, and the "trade diversion" would produce a deterioration as compared with the existing pattern. He concluded that, where the trade creating role was predominant, the union as a whole would benefit, but, in the short run at least, the outside world would lose. While succeeding literature has qualified these conclusions, it has not detracted from Viner's basic point that both influences will normally be present and that, in order to determine the balance of advantage for the members of the union and for the world as a whole, each customs union would have to be considered on its merits.

It should be emphasized that Viner's conclusions and most subsequent theoretical explorations of the problem were based on static analysis and dealt only with short-term effects. The theory that emerges does not, therefore, either support or refute the belief that has been implicit, and sometimes explicit, in American support of economic integration in Europe and elsewhere—namely, that the dynamic, or long-term, effects will be favorable not only for trade within the union but for the trade of third countries. The economic growth induced by freer competition within the union will, it is believed, raise the level of demand for the imports of third countries and reduce the costs of goods exported to them by members of the union.

One student contends that this official American faith ignores the other side of the equation: "If market expansion within the union is to lead to long-run gains, why should not market contraction outside the union lead to over-all losses for the world in the long run? . . . Similarly, if a union enhances capital formation and growth within the union, why should not trade diversion outside the union damage investment opportunities and hence capital formation and growth outside the union?"[17] It is true that countries outside the union have no assurance of long-term benefits from the creation of trade that can be expected inside the union, but they will certainly lose in the short run from whatever trade diversion results from its formation.

The body of theory that developed from Viner's study was not available to the drafters of the GATT. It has been argued, however, that they drafted Article XXIV with the purpose of minimizing the probability of trade diversion outweighing trade creation in global terms. For example, by requiring the elimination of substantially all barriers to trade within the union they ruled out the possibility that preferences would be established only for those products in which one partner or another could count on replacing the trade of third parties.[18] The desirability of outlawing a selective exchange of preferences in order to prevent a preferential area from being predominantly trade diverting also underlined Clair Wilcox's rationale for the GATT provisions governing customs unions. Insistence on virtually complete free trade within a union, if it was to have the benefit of the GATT exception, was surely aimed at preventing a selective exchange of preferences in the guise of a customs union.*

It should be noted, parenthetically, that a partial customs union or free-trade area involving a limited number of products will not necessarily involve more trade diversion than a complete one. It is unlikely, for example, that the inclusion of agricultural products in the European free trade area would have made it more favorable to the trading interests of third countries. To take a more extreme example, the European Coal and Steel Community, while clearly not falling within the provisions of Article XXIV,

---

*Working with simplified models it is possible to conclude that as barriers within an area approach zero, while barriers against the outside world remain fixed, the increments of trade creation will tend to diminish but that no such diminution will take place in the increments of trade diversion. This in turn suggests that there is a stage in the formation of a union beyond which a further reduction of internal barriers will result in a decrease in welfare, that is, that the optimum result will be achieved from a partial union. It does not, however, justify the conclusion that the distinction made in the GATT rules between a preferential trading area and a customs union is "irrational." (See H. G. Johnson. *Money, Trade and Economic Growth* [Cambridge, Mass.: Harvard University Press, 1962], pp. 45 and 46.) Preferential areas do not typically comply with the assumption implicit in the theorem, namely that of a uniform percentage margin of preference for all products. In a preferential area the members more typically limit the exchange of preferences to those products in which trade diversion is most likely to outweigh trade creation.

could not possibly have involved as great a short-term risk to the trading interests of third countries as did the creation of the EEC.

But this is not to argue against the soundness of the GATT rule. If an exception had been permitted for the exchange of duty-free treatment in selected products, the attempt to prevent agreements aimed solely at trade diversion would have been seriously prejudiced. It is true that nonmembers will receive little if any short-term benefits from greater efficiency within the union. If the dynamic effects are ignored, they may have more to lose from a complete than from an incomplete customs union between other countries. This fact might seem to suggest that the original contracting parties, in insisting on completeness, were more concerned with aggregate world welfare than with their own trading interests. This conclusion does not necessarily follow, however. The United States was prepared to postpone direct trade advantages in favor of speeding the recovery of a world disrupted by war and, more particularly, the economic recovery of Europe, both for reasons of security and to reduce the cost of the Marshall Plan. Other contracting parties had equally compelling reasons for agreeing to the exception and for endorsing its bias in favor of total discrimination even if they did not themselves expect to become parties to any regional arrangement. This was so because an exception for customs unions was traditional in MFN treaties, and there was little reason to believe that a GATT without such an escape could have obtained general acceptance. That being the case, there was merit in making it difficult to resort to the exception by limiting it to cases where the countries concerned were prepared to undertake a drastic realignment of their trading relations.

Trade Discrimination under the GATT

When the GATT was founded, every country discriminated to some degree in its international trading relations. Existing preferential tariff regimes sanctioned by the GATT exception included countries and territories that in 1947 conducted at least 60 percent of total world trade. Discriminatory quantitative restrictions, justified on balance of payments grounds, were even more widespread and were used by countries accounting for some 78 percent of world imports. These percentages were, however, in no way indicative of the proportion of world trade that was affected, either favorably or unfavorably, by discriminatory treatment. For example, those countries involved in preferential areas, except the British Commonwealth, conducted a very small part of their total trade with their preferential partners, and not all of that trade was subject to tariff preference. Even in such a relatively complete preferential area as the British Commonwealth, some imports were unaffected by preferences because imports from third countries encountered no competition from exporters within the Commonwealth.

The scope of discriminatory quantitative restrictions in 1947 was considerably greater than that of tariff preferences if we look only at the number of countries involved and the number of products to which those restrictions nominally applied. But such a count would be misleading. The persistence of a heavy United States positive trade balance during most of the postwar decade reflected the fact that many products demanded by the rest of the world were obtainable only from the dollar area. When these goods were considered essential, the licensing of dollar imports was discriminatory in form but not in effect. On the other hand, most countries maintaining quantitative restrictions also discriminated as between imports from different soft currency areas as the result of bilateral payments agreements. Thus, to determine with any precision the volume of trade benefiting from preferential treatment is extremely difficult.[19].

The Attrition of Preferential Tariff Systems under the GATT

In the fifteen years following the formation of the GATT the importance of both tariff preferences and discriminatory quantitative restrictions in world trade declined greatly. In the case of tariff preferences this can be attributed largely, though not exclusively, to the reduction of MFN duties in GATT tariff negotiations, reinforced by the rule prohibiting the introduction of new preferences. In the field of quantitative restrictions, nondiscriminatory liberalization was made possible by the restoration of convertibility to the currencies of the major trading countries, achieved under the combined impetus provided by the European Payments Union (EPU) and the IMF. The influence of the latter in eliminating discriminatory exchange controls was paralleled by the GATT rule limiting the discriminatory use of quantitative restrictions. Has the direction of change since 1947 established a clear trend either toward or away from the nondiscriminatory trading world that was one of the stated objectives of American policy after the war?[20]

In 1947, by far the largest of the preferential tariff systems in terms of the volume of trade conducted among members was that of the British Commonwealth. In addition to the United Kingdom and some thirty dependent territories, it involved Canada, India, Australia, New Zealand, the Union of South Africa, Ireland, Southern Rhodesia, and a number of smaller independent members. While the area of Commonwealth preferences was not identical with that of the so-called sterling area, a rough measure of the effect of the declining incidence of Commonwealth preferences can be obtained by observing the trend of trade within the latter. In 1953, about 45 percent of total United Kingdom imports originated in the sterling area; by 1961, this ratio had fallen to 34 percent. In the same period the share of the rest of the sterling area in United Kingdom exports fell from about 47 to 37 percent.[21]

Some part of this decline can almost certainly be attributed to reductions in margins of preference resulting from GATT negotiations. According to Gardner Patterson, the average ad valorem margin of preference on those goods that received preferential treatment when imported into the United Kingdom fell from 17–20 percent in 1937 to 11–13 percent in 1949, and to 9 percent in 1957.[22] More recently, the formation of the European Free Trade Association (EFTA), while not affecting the margin between MFN rates and the preferential rates granted to Commonwealth countries, further reduced the value of United Kingdom preferences to the outside Commonwealth insofar as EFTA members compete with it for British imports.

Preferences maintained by the colonial powers of continental Europe at the end of the war were subjected to similar attrition during the GATT tariff negotiations from 1947 to 1960. But the creation of the European Economic Community, instead of diluting these preferences, led to an expansion of their territorial application. Under the Treaty of Rome, each of the six member states agreed to grant duty-free entry to the products of the overseas territories of each of its partners. Each of the overseas territories, in turn, was required to grant to each of the six the same treatment that it granted to the products of the metropolitan territory to which it was attached.[23] Later, after the African territories had become independent, they signed a Convention of Association with the Community in order to preserve this preferential treatment.[24] The same convention, the Yaoundé Convention, however, also substantially reduced the Community's common tariff on a number of tropical products of particular interest to certain other underdeveloped countries, thus reducing the margins of preference.[25] This amelioration was not sufficient to calm the fears of the new countries in Africa outside the area of EEC preference; a number of them expressed an interest in negotiating with the Community in order to extend to their products the preferences accorded to their favored African competitors. In July 1965 the Community reached an agreement with Nigeria providing it preferences on many of its exports to the EEC, but explicitly withholding from this treatment certain products (cocoa beans, palm oil, peanut oil, and plywood) that were key exports of the African signatories of the Yaoundé Convention.[26] In 1968 an agreement was concluded with the East African Community (Kenya, Uganda, and Tanzania) providing for a temporary exchange of preferences between it and the European communities. Ratification of this agreement was not completed before September 1969, when it was replaced by a new association agreement.[27]

The extension of preferences by the entire EEC to the African territories of some of its members was not considered by the Community to be in contravention of the GATT rule against new preferences. Instead, it was presented to the Contracting Parties as a "free-trade area" between the Community on the one hand and those territories on the other.[28] This characterization was difficult to sustain in face of the fact that, under the Association Agreement, protective or revenue tariffs were permitted on a substantial part of the imports into the African territories from the six, and no provision was made for freeing trade among those territories. If the Contracting Parties had faced up to the issue, they would almost certainly have held that the arrangement failed to comply with the

requirements of Article XXIV and contravened the "no new preference" rule. However, probably motivated by the belief that, in a
direct confrontation over a policy which France considered vital,
either the EEC or the GATT would suffer irreparable damage, the
United States supported the Community in avoiding a definitive
GATT finding. In any event, the arrangement was allowed to stand
without interference from the Contracting Parties.

Other than the British Commonwealth system and the preferences between the continental European countries and their African territories, the remaining preferences of any importance in
1947 were those between the United States on the one hand and
Cuba and the Philippines on the other. American preferences in
favor of Cuba were also diluted by successive reductions in MFN
tariffs in GATT negotiations and were totally suspended as a result
of the rupture in US-Cuban relations after the advent of the Castro
regime. In 1962 the United States also declared an embargo on
most trade with that country, and the 1962 Tariff Classification Act
whipped the dead horse by suspending MFN treatment for imports
from Cuba. The preferences granted the Philippines were already
being dismantled at the time of the 1947 tariff negotiation; the
1946 US-Philippine Trade Agreement provided for the gradual
elimination of preferences in both directions, with their final
elimination to be achieved in 1974.

Quantitative Restrictions under GATT

In spite of the definition of discrimination with which this chapter
began, it is difficult to deal with quantitative restrictions without
taking into consideration the incidental and unintentional discriminatory effects of their use even where they are formally nondiscriminatory. In Article XIII, the Contracting Parties made an effort to establish standards for applying quantitative restrictions
without discrimination. A country applying import restrictions was
required to aim at "a distribution of trade ... approaching as closely as possible the shares which the various contracting parties
might be expected to obtain" in the absence of any restriction.
Where quotas were allocated among supplying countries, they
were to be determined either in consultation with the substantial
suppliers or based on the shares in a previous period, "due account

being taken of any special factors" that might have affected the pattern of trade.

These rules were probably adequate to prevent intentional discrimination and thus discouraged the exchange of reciprocal favors between countries, but they could hardly ensure the same distribution of trade that would have taken place in the absence of quantitative restrictions. "There is no such thing as a non-discriminatory quota, but only a quota which may be *more* discriminatory than another."[29] The dismantling of quantitative restrictions, even where not formally discriminatory, has contributed to the restoration of the trading patterns that could be expected to result if the only impediments to trade were nondiscriminatory tariffs. This point having been made, the rest of our discussion will be devoted largely to developments in the field of quantitative restrictions that are discriminatory—in form as well as effect.

In 1947 the only contracting parties not using quantitative restrictions to conserve foreign exchange were the United States, Cuba, and Belgium. All of the other twenty discriminated against imports from the dollar area, as did virtually all non-GATT countries except those in the Western Hemisphere whose currencies were tied to the dollar. Even among soft currency countries, discrimination was widespread, virtually every country outside the dollar area conducting some part of its trade under bilateral payments agreements designed to create or maintain "an approximate bilateral balance in their current trade."[30] Mikesell has described some 50 agreements involving the United Kingdom and 360 agreements outside the sterling area.[31] While these agreements were in force, nondiscrimination, even as between soft currency countries, was impossible.

The history of the gradual liquidation of quantitative restrictions maintained for balance of payments reasons, and the somewhat more rapid disappearance of formal discrimination against imports from the dollar area, cannot be recounted here.[32] By 1963, discriminatory quantitative restrictions had almost entirely disappeared. But the transition to this state had been slow. Both the GATT and the IMF had been more or less continuously involved in efforts to speed the laggards and to consolidate the progress that had been painfully gained. GATT, for example, held annual, and often spirited, "consultations" with the countries that still invoked the right to use quantitative restrictions.[33] In October 1949, after the general move toward the convertibility of European currencies in the late 1950's had removed the monetary basis for discrimination, the Board of Executive Directors of the IMF called for its elimination as quickly as possible.[34] The board recognized, however, that a reasonable amount of time would have to be allowed for the complete elimination of discrimination. After that declaration, formal discrimination as between different Western currency areas was rapidly eliminated by all industrial countries.[35]

The OEEC Code of Liberalization: Seeds of Common Market and EFTA

The roots of the two great European areas of free trade go back to the formation of the European Payments Union in 1949 and to the companion code of intra-European quota dismantlement under the aegis of the Organization for European Economic Cooperation. The EPU was established to eliminate bilateral balancing of accounts by permitting the multilateral clearance of debits and credits in intra-European transactions. Since this arrangement contributed toward the effectiveness of the Marshall Plan, it was supported by the United States, even though one of its immediate effects was to broaden the area of discrimination against dollar imports.[36] In order to accomplish the purposes of the EPU, it proved necessary to remove the intra-European trade barriers that had grown up hand in hand with bilateral payments agreements. From this need grew the OEEC Code of Trade Liberalization, adopted in August 1950.[37]

The essence of the OEEC Code was the establishment of progressively increasing percentages of imports to be liberalized, that is, freed of quantitative limitation when originating within the OEEC area. While the resulting liberalization decreased the incidence of discrimination by the Western European countries against each other, it intensified the discrimination practiced not only against the dollar area but against soft currency countries outside Western Europe.

It will be recalled that Belgium was one of the few countries that did not in 1947 maintain quantitative restrictions for balance of payments reasons. It was also the only country of Western Europe that did not discriminate against dollar imports. One result of the formation of the EPU, however, was the inauguration of discriminatory quantitative restrictions by Belgium. Heavy and persistent Belgian credit balances within the EPU had threatened the breakdown of the clearance system. In order to reduce those balances and to make a greater contribution to the hard currency reserves of the EPU, Belgium undertook to restrict her imports from the dollar area. The needs of the regional system were given precedence over the rules of the GATT. The United States lodged a formal objection in the GATT but was not able to prevail over the large and influential membership of the OEEC. In any event, a respectable body of opinion then held that this departure from the GATT rules would actually hasten the restoration of the general convertibility that was one of the principal GATT objectives.[38]

In the early days of the OEEC Liberalization Code, emphasis was placed on increasing the percentage of liberalization within the area; little attention was paid to relaxing restrictions against imports from the outside as the balances of the EPU countries with nonmembers improved. In fact, there were early indications that the continental European countries looked forward without enthusiasm to the day when they would no longer have the right to discriminate. In 1954, for example, at a meeting of the Contracting Parties to the GATT, Benelux proposed an amendment to the General Agreement to the effect that "the rule of non-discrimination should not be applicable to contracting parties which endeavor, by means of freely concluded agreements, to reach a closer integration of their economies."[39] The European Coal and Steel Community (ECSC) had been formed in 1952, and the Western European Union had very recently been thrown together following the rejection of the European Defense Community by the French Parliament. The main concern of Benelux seems to have been fear that after convertibility any OEEC member in balance of payments difficulties would, if not allowed to discriminate, be forced to restrict its imports from within the OEEC area.[40] The Benelux proposal was supported by other Europeans, notably France, but opposed by the United States and Canada, with some support from the United Kingdom.[41] While this effort to introduce regional considerations into the GATT criteria governing the use of discriminatory restrictions failed at the time, it was significant as evidence of a growing sentiment within Europe for regional discrimination unrelated to the exigencies of international payments.

By 1956, considerable liberalization had been achieved by OEEC members; most had by then liberalized more than 90 percent of their intra-area trade.[42] Though not members, the United States and Canada, as articulate observers, had protested against the intensification of discrimination against dollar imports and sought to persuade the organization to undertake a program for the liberalization of dollar trade as well. Fairly rapid strides were being made in this field by 1956. Between November 1955 and August 1956, for example, Austria increased its percentage of liberalized dollar trade from 8 to 40; Denmark, from 38 to 55; Germany, from 68 to 92; and Italy, from 24 to 40. France, which had lagged in both intra-area and extra-area liberalization, finally removed quantitative restrictions during the same period on some 250 products originating in Canada and the United States.[43] By the time the OEEC Liberalization Code was formally brought to a close in 1960, the major European currencies had been made convertible. Even in 1960, however, eight developed countries continued to invoke the balance of payments provisions of the GATT to justify the maintenance of certain nominally nondiscriminatory quantitative restrictions.[44] In addition, many underdeveloped countries continued to maintain discriminatory restrictions, which they justified on balance of payments grounds.[45]

Protective Discrimination

It can be stated as a general proposition that the purpose of discriminatory quantitative restrictions has not been the protection of domestic industry.[46] The one conspicuous exception to this generalization is the maintenance of discrimination against Japan by many contracting parties.

In August 1955, after negotiating with as many of the contracting parties as were willing to participate, Japan obtained admission to the GATT. But this did not entitle Japan to nondiscriminatory treatment from the entire membership and, of the thirty-three contracting parties at the time of Japanese accession, fourteen declined to apply the GATT in their relations with the new member. This denial of contractual benefits to a new contracting party was made possible by Article XXXV of the GATT, which stipulates that the provisions of the agreement will not apply to relations between two contracting parties if they have not entered into tariff negotiations with each other and if, at the time of the accession of one of them, either does not consent to such application. This provision had been included in the GATT in order to permit participation by countries whose political relations with each other were strained. But its invocation by countries that accounted for about 40 percent of Japan's exports to the contracting parties was motivated primarily by commercial considerations.[47]

The period of the late 1950's and early 1960's was one of rapid increase in the membership of GATT, largely through the accession of newly independent countries. Most of these countries invoked Article XXXV against Japan when they acceded. Some of them probably acted out of genuine fear of Japanese competition with the domestic industries they hoped to establish. Others, more or less automatically, followed the practice of the former metropole which had sponsored their membership in the club. While there is no evidence that the sponsoring governments influenced them to take this action, it is not hard to see that the refusal of a former colony to grant MFN treatment to Japan might prove helpful to a country hoping to maintain its privileged position in a traditional market. Also, some of the newly independent contracting parties withheld GATT treatment from Japan because of the bargaining power they believed this would give them in future economic relations with that country.[48]

Eventually Japan entered into bilateral discussions with the United Kingdom and those continental Europeans invoking Article XXXV and, by the mid-1960's, succeeded in establishing formal GATT relations with all the major contracting parties. The price it paid was potentially heavy: separate bilateral agreements in which Japan agreed to the restriction of imports of Japanese goods, necessarily on a discriminatory basis, if Japanese exports of a product should threaten "market disruption" in the recipient country. The agreement with the United Kingdom also included a list of "sensitive" items, on some of which the United Kingdom was permitted to continue to restrict Japanese goods while Japan agreed to impose "voluntary" export controls on others. Thus, in the Japanese case, the revocation of Article XXXV has not resulted in a significant narrowing of the geographic scope of potential discrimination. And, in December 1968, some thirty small contracting parties still continued to withhold GATT commitments toward Japan.

Formal discrimination against imports from Japan, however, has not been the only device that has been used by GATT contracting parties to ensure themselves against the full impact of Japanese competition. Japan itself was partly responsible in the early 1960's for the introduction of a number of informal agreements with the United States, under which Japan agreed to limit exports of specified products to the US market in order to forestall the threat of still more stringent import restrictions.[49] By the mid-1960's, some twenty countries had reached similar agreements with Japan, and the United Kingdom had extended the same technique to arrangements concerning textile imports from India, Pakistan, and Hong Kong.[50]

The most important case of trade restriction by "voluntary agreement" is the Long-Term Cotton Textile Arrangement (LTA) of October 1, 1962.[51] This agreement will be dealt with in a later chapter, but it would be misleading to omit it from a survey of trade discrimination. While the import quotas permitted by the agreement itself are ostensibly nondiscriminatory, the threat of quota imposition under cover of the agreement has been effective in obtaining adoption by the exporting countries of "voluntary" export quotas, the size of which is at least in part a function of the respective bargaining power and the political influence of the parties. Thus, the enormous volume of world trade in cotton textiles has been effectively removed from the scope of the GATT prohibitions against both quantitative restrictions and discrimination.

Customs Unions and Free Trade Areas

The first major new departure from nondiscrimination after the GATT came into force was not the formation of a customs union or free-trade area, as contemplated by Article XXIV of that agreement, but the creation of regional free trade in a major industrial sector. The Treaty creating the European Coal and Steel Community was signed by France, West Germany, Italy, Belgium, the Netherlands, and Luxembourg in April 1952 and went into effect in July 1952.[52] It provided for the gradual establishment of free trade in coal, iron, and steel among the signatories and the ultimate adoption of common tariff rates by them against imports from nonmembers. Although it clearly fell far short of meeting the GATT criteria for a customs union, it was welcomed by the United States and others as a step in the direction of European economic integration. The GATT Contracting Parties granted the members the necessary waiver to permit them to implement the agreement, subject to annual consultations in which the Community was to report on progress and afford other contracting parties an opportunity to raise any problems that might be created for their trade.[53]

Much later, in January 1965, the United States and Canada made use of the precedent of the ECSC in arriving at a preferential agreement in the automotive sector. The US-Canadian Automotive Agreement established free entry into the United States of automobiles and parts produced in Canada.[54] In applying for a waiver from its GATT obligations, the United States representative argued that 90 percent of Canadian production was owned by US automobile firms, that free entry would simply permit the completion of the virtually total integration that already existed in the sector, and that there was not likely to be any effect on the trade of third countries.

The arrangement, at least on the Canadian side, did not go as far in the direction of sectoral free trade as had the ECSC. Free entry of automobiles and automobile parts into Canada was limited to imports by established automotive manufacturers and conditioned upon their maintaining both the level of their domestic production and the same ratio of domestic production to sales as in a stated base period. On the other hand, the Canadian undertaking was nominally nondiscriminatory and was applicable to imports from all sources, though the manufacturers in a position to take advantage of it were overwhelmingly affiliates of American companies. The Contracting Parties, perhaps influenced by the fact that they had little chance of reversing an agreement already signed and implemented, granted the necessary waiver to the United States on December 20, 1965.[55]

In spite of such aberrations as those involved in the LTA, the ECSC, and the US-Canadian Automotive Agreement, the trend among GATT countries from the 1940's to the mid-1960's was clearly away from discrimination effected through preferential areas or through quantitative restrictions. While the effects of this change were at least partly obscured by a phenomenal rise in customs unions, free-trade areas, and looser associations created in the name of economic integration, it would be misleading to suggest that the two trends canceled each other.

The trade effects of customs unions and free-trade areas are bound to differ from the systems they are replacing. If they comply strictly with the GATT definition of completed unions they must result in some trade creation, and as they continue to proliferate they must reduce the average level of protection in the world and increase the total volume of trade, however much they may divert it from its most economical course.

While there are many distinctions between a completed customs union or free-trade area and other forms of discrimination, the dividing line is not so clear during the transitional stage. Furthermore, in some cases that stage may prove permanent since some preferential areas that have been justified as transitional arrangements are likely never to achieve their ostensible goal of trade integration.

By the end of 1968 there were two virtually completed customs unions in existence, one major free-trade area and a host of other regional associations—all created since the GATT.[56] By far the most important of these was the European Economic Community. On March 25, 1957, the same six countries that had formed the ECSC in the early 1950's signed the Treaty Establishing the European Economic Community (Treaty of Rome).[57] The treaty called for the elimination of all industrial tariffs on trade among the members, the alignment of industrial tariffs imposed on imports from third countries, and the adoption of a common agricultural policy —all to be completed in accordance with a predetermined schedule over a period of twelve years. The timetable was later accelerated. By January 1968 the elimination of industrial duties and the adoption of a common external tariff had been achieved, and a common policy had been adopted for most major agricultural products. In July 1967 a further step toward the economic integration of the six countries was taken when the respective executives of the EEC, the ECSC, and Euratom were merged into a single body.[58]

The European Free Trade Association was created later than the

EEC but reached its more limited goal even more rapidly. In January 1960, at Stockholm, the United Kingdom, Denmark, Norway, Sweden, Austria, and Portugal signed the Convention Establishing a European Free Trade Association (Stockholm Convention).[59] The treaty calls for internal free trade in products other than those of agriculture and fisheries but does not involve the adoption of a common external tariff. The goal of internal free trade for industrial products was achieved on December 31, 1966. The United Kingdom continues to grant preferential treatment to members of the Commonwealth, but Britain's EFTA partners apply their MFN duties to the other Commonwealth countries.

The only remaining regional arrangements that have come close to achieving total free trade are the Central American Common Market and the Caribbean Free Trade Association (CARIFTA). Beginning in the late 1950's a number of tentative free trade combinations were initiated in Central America with relatively small success. But in 1961, Nicaragua, El Salvador, Costa Rica, Guatemala, and Honduras signed the General Treaty of Central American Economic Integration, which has resulted in the establishment of a common external tariff and of free trade in nearly all the goods traded within the area.[60] CARIFTA, a smaller, though relatively complete, free trade area in the Caribbean, has achieved free trade in most products exchanged by a number of Caribbean countries.[61]

The popularity of regional arrangements, inspired by the successful negotiation of the Treaty of Rome, has spread rapidly, particularly among less developed countries. But by the beginning of 1969 most of them had scarcely progressed beyond the scattered exchange of preferences in a few products. In Latin America, an earlier agreement to achieve a free-trade area among eleven countries of South America and Mexico was superseded in April 1967 when all the countries of South and Central America agreed to form a Latin American Common Market within fifteen years, though with no agreed plan or schedule for reaching that result.

In Africa and the Near East a number of incomplete "free trade areas" or "customs unions" have been agreed to but not reinforced by a firm plan or schedule. These include the West African Customs Union, the Equatorial African Customs Union, and agreements to form a customs union among the Maghreb states and among the members of the Arab League.

The only African integration movement that has yet shown much promise of becoming a complete customs union is the East African Common Market, formed by the states of Kenya, Tanzania, and Uganda.[62] Aided by the large measure of integration that existed when the predecessor territories were British colonies, the union at its peak had achieved a common external tariff, internal free trade except for some agricultural products, and a common currency. But in 1963, signs of disintegration began to appear, and by 1967 internal tariffs had been erected on a substantial portion of intraunion trade, the common currency had been replaced by national currencies, and steps had been taken away from the harmonization of fiscal policy and labor mobilization. Present prospects seem to be either that disintegration will continue or that the union will stabilize as a more or less free-trade area.

Even this listing omits a number of lesser agreements, in some cases overlapping those named above, that have been concluded in the name of regional economic integration. If all of the so-called customs unions and free-trade areas that have been agreed upon, at least in principle, since the mid-1950's should eventually achieve free trade among their members, the volume of international trade affected could have revolutionary consequences. In practice, however, the GATT requirement that substantially all trade between the partners to a union be freed has lost much of its force. The manner in which the Contracting Parties dealt with the Treaty of Rome establishing the EEC ensured that the limitations of Article XXIV would no longer be taken at face value. When that treaty was submitted to the Contracting Parties, it contained two features which could reasonably have been found deficient in terms of the GATT definition of a customs union. The first, the absence of detail concerning the "common agricultural policy" which remained still to be negotiated within the EEC, was hardly alluded to in GATT discussions. But the second feature, the provision dealing with the association of the overseas territories, did give rise to vigorous debate.[63] As has already been pointed out, the Contracting Parties finally left the question of conformity to GATT in the air. Thus, by tacit but reluctant consent, both the EEC and the association agreements were given de facto recognition as if they conformed to the provisions of Article XXIV.[64]

When in 1959 the Stockholm Convention establishing the EFTA was submitted to the Contracting Parties, the total omission of agricultural products aroused little serious criticism. And, although certain clearly discriminatory bilateral agreements affecting agricultural trade among the EFTA partners were attacked, the solution that had been adopted in the case of the EEC—to defer judgment—was repeated. When the association agreement of EFTA with Finland was examined, a more serious issue of conformity with the GATT arose because of a parallel agreement between Finland and the Soviet Union under which Finland was required to extend to Russia the same duty-free treatment accorded to its EFTA associates. Since there was no program for a similar extension to the exports of non-EFTA contracting parties, this provision was strongly criticized, but the political desirability of tying Finland as closely as possible to Western Europe apparently outweighed the arguments for preserving the integrity of the GATT rules.[65]

When the Contracting Parties examined the association agreement between the EEC and Greece in 1962,[66] these precedents again prevailed. In this case, the Contracting Parties were probably also influenced by the knowledge that the principal purpose of the agreement was to mitigate some of the damage to Greek trade that could be expected from the preferences that had been created within the Common Market. When, later, a somewhat similar agreement was negotiated between the Community and Turkey, a stiffer attitude by the Contracting Parties would have had explosive political implications; once again, the Contracting Parties avoided reaching a definite judgment.[67]

The industrialized countries in the GATT have long been reluctant to oppose any action taken by underdeveloped countries which the latter believed to be needed for their economic development. Nowhere has this been more apparent than in the passivity with which the Contracting Parties have received notifications by African and Latin American countries of the formation of "customs unions" and "free trade areas" that ignore the GATT criteria. No serious objection has been raised to these arrangements, although, as in the case of the two European areas, the Contracting Parties review them from time to time in order to follow their progress, if any, toward internal free trade.

The Direction of Change

If the extent of discrimination practiced in international trade is gauged solely by the volume of commerce favorably (or unfavorably) affected, it is difficult to say in what direction the incidence of discrimination has changed since the end of World War II. A statistical approach would bring little enlightenment. At the outset it would encounter the question of how to deal with nominal, as opposed to effective, discrimination. How, for example, should one treat the trade of countries which invoked Article XXXV of the GATT against Japan but actually admitted Japanese goods without tariff discrimination? How would one treat countries that maintained licensing systems for the purpose of restricting dollar imports, but admitted many of those imports freely because the required goods were not available elsewhere?

If measurement of the extent of discrimination in any quantitative sense is impracticable, one observation seems justified concerning the means by which discrimination instituted in the 1950's and 1960's has been accomplished. New preferences, whether or not sanctioned by the GATT exception for economic integration, had, at least until 1970, been for the most part accomplished by a reduction of tariffs rather than increased protection against third countries. In terms of their effect on the average level of protection, they can be said to have furthered one of the objectives of the GATT. But the question of what effect the proliferation of preferential arrangements may have had on the future integrity of the GATT as a multilateral contract is a more serious matter and one that will be examined later.

The Momentum of Large Customs Unions

The drive toward regional integration was the most significant commercial policy development of the decade of the 1960's. Any appraisal of the long-term effects of this drive will have to take into account and evaluate the tendency for large customs unions, such as the EEC, to attract new members.

It is not difficult to see some reasons for such a tendency. Third countries which, as a result of the formation of a union, are discriminated against in their former markets have an incentive to obtain admission to the union. At the same time, as the union grows in size, its members may find it progressively easier to face the increased competition involved in the continuous and accelerated expansion of a great customs union. Thus, it is at least a possibility that what started as regional integration could eventually become universal and bring an end to trade discrimination.

By the end of the 1960's, however, it was too soon to find confirmation of such a future in the observable tendency of the European Community to expand its membership. The desire of outsiders to obtain admission, though not necessarily to accept at once the full responsibilities of membership, has been clear in the case of Greece, Turkey, Spain, Austria, Israel, and a number of African countries not included among the original associates. But it is much less clear that such encouragement as the Community has given to many of these applicants has been based on economic considerations. If this encouragement is political, it can as easily result in a proliferation of preferential agreements as true economic integration. Nor is there assurance that the Community will be as receptive to additional applicants.

The renewed efforts of the United Kingdom and other EFTA countries to join the European Community also fail to point clearly the direction of future developments. Their economic motivation is clear and helps to illustrate the attractive force of a customs union as large as the Common Market. But the encouragement they received in 1969 and 1970 after the repeated rebuffs administered earlier by France may have been more the result of political than of economic motives. If politics should continue to prevail, the desire of prospective new members to belong to a larger unit may well lead to the creation of two or more rival communities. In that case, instead of universal free trade and nondiscrimination, the world may be moving simultaneously toward the elimination of discrimination within great "regions" and the growth of discrimination between them.

4

The Problems of Agricultural Trade

Present international agricultural trade problems have deep roots in the farming origins of every industralized country. They are influenced by the social, political, and aesthetic values that all mature countries attach to the survival of the family farm and of a rural society. For this study it is essential to examine the modern development of the restrictive complex that has so far frustrated all efforts to fit the agriculture of the Temperate Zone into a system of competitive trading relations among industrialized countries.

Agricultural Policies during the Depression and World War II

During World War I, agricultural production in North America and Europe was stimulated by high prices. In the postwar deflation, prices dropped sharply. Farmers demanded government intervention. During the 1920's this generally took the form of increased tariff protection. In net importing countries tariffs were a reasonably effective device for transferring real income from the relatively prosperous industrial sector to agricultural producers. The United States also tried higher tariffs. But higher tariffs could do little to compensate American farmers for the loss of their export markets. As Zaglits has pointed out, the failure of US trade statistics at that time to distinguish between agricultural imports competing with American production and noncompetitive imports, such as tropical products, obscured the fact that the United States was a heavy net exporter of the kinds of agricultural goods produced in this country.[1] Ignorance of this fact contributed to demands for protection. President Harding, in asking Congress for emergency tariff legislation in 1921, said: "Today American agriculture is menaced . . . through the influx of foreign farm products, because we offer, essentially unprotected, the best market in the world."[2] The increase in agricultural duties that followed, combined with a substantial increase in US tariffs on industrial products, contributed to the inability of European countries to maintain their former imports of American foodstuffs.

One lasting product of the collapse of farm prices in the 1920's was the popularization of the concept of a "parity price" for domestic agricultural products. On two occasions the United States Congress passed bills under which domestic prices would have been fixed at a level estimated to give the farmer a "fair exchange value" for his product in the United States, it being assumed that surplus production induced by these prices could be exported at world market prices. These bills were vetoed by the President, but the parity concept survived and played an important part in domestic agricultural policy during the 1930's.

Agricultural prices recovered only moderately during the latter half of the 1920's and then, in 1929, both prices and exports joined in the general headlong decline. The high protection afforded by the Smoot-Hawley Tariff of 1930 was, of course, powerless to restore either domestic or foreign demand. It simply reinforced the trend toward higher protection by those countries that had hitherto provided the American farmer with his principal export outlets.

The development of systematic agricultural price supports in the United States did not begin until 1933, when, somewhat paradoxically, the Roosevelt administration was also preparing plans and legislation for the Trade Agreements program. But a frequently unappreciated fact is that the wave of governmental intervention in agricultural prices and production began not in the United States but in Europe.[3] It may be well, therefore, to begin a summary of the developments of the 1930's with a survey of the early European experiments with contrivances for divorcing agriculture from the discipline of the marketplace.[4]

European Agriculture in the 1930's

One European innovation was the licensing of agricultural imports. In the 1930's this was often associated with the introduction of exchange controls. It is, therefore, not always easy to determine whether the dominant motivation for licensing was conservation of foreign exchange or the redistribution of domestic income in favor of farm producers. The former was most likely in Eastern Europe, where intervention in international payments began early in the depression.[5] By the end of 1931 exchange controls were in force in Austria, Bulgaria, Czechoslovakia, Estonia, Hungary, Latvia, Yugoslavia, and Turkey. In Western Europe, however, governmental intervention was more clearly designed to serve the purpose of supporting farm income. Actually, this support put increasing strains on the economies of the countries that pursued it and, according to Svennilson, did nothing to improve the efficiency of agricultural production. "From a productivity point of view the protection of agriculture . . . suffered from a double weakness . . . It was never able to restore the prosperity of the farmer to a level which would have given a stimulus to rapid modernization. On the other hand, it prevented — by maintaining income derived from less efficient production — an increase in productivity."[6]

Nevertheless, as Lamartine Yates has shown in his studies of six Western European countries, in each country the shift from tariff protection to more direct forms of price or income support began in 1930 or even earlier. Long before the close of the decade, each had developed systems, differing from commodity to commodity, that not only transferred real income to farmers from the rest of the economy but insulated producers, to a greater or lesser degree, against outside price competition.

Denmark supported wheat and barley prices with a sliding scale tariff and required that millers use specified proportions of domestic wheat and rye in the production of flour. The prices of sugar and homegrown sugar beets were fixed, and sugar imports were placed under quota limitations. Butter exports began to suffer severely from an increased duty in Germany and from intensified competition by Australia and New Zealand. In response, the Danish government in 1934 established a two-price system under which losses on export sales at competitive prices were compensated by an arbitrarily high price for butter consumed domestically. This system, in turn, required high tariff protection against imports of the raw materials used in the production of margarine. A similar system was adopted to permit the continued export of beef, and the resultant high domestic price was protected against imports through the operations of the Exchange Control Board.

In the *Netherlands* there was less emphasis on the maintenance of export markets; the measures adopted during the 1930's were primarily directed toward maintaining the prices of agricultural products for home consumption. However, a two-price system for butter was introduced, enforced by a tax on domestic consumption and a subsidy on exports. Wheat growers were guaranteed a price that was more than twice the world price, but were allowed to produce wheat on only one-third of their acreage. A Wheat Commission was empowered to monopolize purchases and resales to millers. The latter, in turn, were subjected to mixing regulations. Production of fodder cereals was subsidized and protected against outside competition by an official import monopoly.

Until the depression the Netherlands had been a net exporter of potatoes, and the decline of exports in the 1930's threatened a reduction of prices disastrous to growers. Prices were sustained by direct subsidies, by compulsory reduction of acreage, and by the establishment of minimum prices in the home market and a subsidy for exports. As early as 1931, sugar beet prices were supported by subsidies to beet sugar factories and by acreage limitations.

Since *Belgium* was a net importer of most farm products, it was able to rely largely on tariffs and quotas to protect farm income. However, wheat growers received additional support in the form of a guaranteed minimum price, and millers were required to increase the proportion of domestic wheat used in making bread flour. Producers of cheese and dried milk were subsidized, and imports of dairy products subjected to licensing. Of some historical interest is the fact that Luxembourg, Belgium's customs union partner, agreed to restrict shipments of dairy products to Belgium,[7] perhaps the earliest case of the use of "voluntary" export controls to protect producers in an importing country.

France introduced a "far reaching quota system" in 1931.[8] But import quotas were supplemented by more direct intervention. Millers were permitted to use only domestic wheat in bread flour. Wheat acreage was limited, and exports subsidized. Through the regulatory operations of the Wheat Office producer prices were fixed, small producers received the benefit of a differential price, and producer taxes were used to pay for denaturing wheat to be withheld from human consumption and to defray the cost of export bounties. Domestic offerings of sugar were limited by manufacturing quotas. In the case of dairy products, the conventional devices of import quotas and export subsidies were supplemented by price-fixing agreements between producers and wholesalers, with government sanction.

In *Switzerland,* intervention in support of domestic agriculture antedated the decade of the 1930's. In 1929, the Swiss government created a wheat monopoly to purchase wheat from producers at support prices and to make all sales to millers. Its losses were paid from the public (Confederation) treasury. In 1932, import quotas on feeding stuffs were reinforced by the creation of an official monopoly with power to control trade in and utilization of feed. It even determined the amount of concentrated feed that cultivators were allowed to give their animals. Growers of barley, oats, and maize were paid direct subsidies from the proceeds of an additional tax on imports. Deficiency payments were introduced to support milk producers. Prices of cattle, pigs, and eggs were supported by various devices, including production quotas for pigs and a requirement that egg importers buy any domestic production unable to find a market.

Germany, during the 1930's, more than matched the other countries of Western Europe in the support and regulation of agricultural production, imports, and prices. For balance of payments reasons in the early 1930's, and in preparation for a war economy later in the decade, Germany drastically curtailed imports by the use of trading monopolies, sliding scale duties, and mixing requirements. For some products, control over imports was supplemented by acreage quotas and, for others, by the establishment of maximum as well as minimum prices.

One result of the widespread interference with agricultural prices in Western Europe was to bring about wide divergences in market prices prevailing at the same time in different markets. From 1936 through 1938, in the six continental countries discussed above, the minimum variation between the price in the cheapest market and that in the highest market ranged from 22 percent for barley and oats to 100 percent for wheat.[9] The longer these price differences were maintained, the harder, of course, was bound to be the restoration of anything approaching competitive trade. But the full effect of ten years of agricultural autarchy in Western Europe and its implications for the future were obscured first by world wide depression, then by preparations for war, and finally by the war itself and its aftermath. In spite of the postwar efforts of the victorious nations to untangle the web that had been woven, only meager results had been achieved by the beginning of the Kennedy Round — nearly twenty years later.

US Agricultural Policy, 1933-1941

As has been pointed out, during the 1920's efforts to support farm prices and incomes in the United States were confined to the imposition of increased tariffs. The climax of this foredoomed experiment was reached in the unprecedentedly high rates of the Tariff Act of 1930. By 1933 the continued deterioration of domestic farm prices had created social and economic problems that could not be ignored, and the new Roosevelt administration plunged into more direct forms of governmental intervention that differed in detail but not in spirit from those that had already become common in Europe. The United States then set a course for agriculture that pointed in almost the opposite direction from the initiative it was simultaneously taking to encourage competitive world trade under the authority of the Trade Agreements Act.[10] Once chosen, it could not easily be reversed.

As John Leddy has pointed out, the first effort to solve the problem of farm surpluses might have achieved its purpose without serious conflict with the administration's trade program.[11] The Agricultural Adjustment Act (AAA) of 1933 provided for the payment of "parity prices," in the case of specified "basic" commodities, to farmers on that part of their production required for domestic consumption, on the condition that they cooperate by reduction of their acreage.[12] This subsidy was to be financed from the proceeds of a tax charged on the processing of both domestic and imported products. Since it was to be paid directly to the farmer and did not affect export prices it would not have required non-tariff restrictions against imports or subsidies on exports. In 1936, however, the Supreme Court held the combination of processing tax and subsidy to be unconstitutional.[13] A description of the various devices then developed to restrict acreage and maintain agricultural prices would lead us too far from our topic, but the measures used for preventing increased imports from frustrating domestic price maintenance do require attention.

It is obvious that an effort to support domestic prices at higher than competitive world prices can succeed only if the forces of competition both within the home market and between it and world markets can be prevented from operating normally. If the necessity of subsidizing exports is to be avoided, additional production stimulated by high prices must be restrained, except in cases where domestic demand is comfortably above domestic production. In the United States restraint was first accomplished by limiting the benefits of the higher prices to farmers who voluntarily shifted production out of surplus crops[14] and later by the establishment of mandatory acreage allotments for the "basic" crops of corn, wheat, cotton, rice, tobacco, and peanuts. The tendency for supported prices to attract imports must also be curtailed. Import limitations were authorized by an amendment (Section 22) of the AAA in 1935, which actually went much further than needed to offset this tendency. If the President found, after a report from the Tariff Commission, that imports were interfering with AAA programs, he was authorized to impose quotas and to restrict imports to as little as 50 percent of their level in a base period. Section 32, added to the act at the same time, authorized the use of 30 percent of all customs revenues for certain purposes including the subsidization of agricultural exports.[15]

The original purposes of Sections 22 and 32 were not protective. In other words, they were not designed "to take markets away from other countries."[16] American agriculture as a whole was not inefficient, and even under conditions of free competition it could have retained its share of both the domestic and foreign markets. But free competition did not exist abroad and was out of the question within the United States if the smaller and weaker farm units were not to be sacrificed. The purpose of the act was to maintain farm income at home and regain foreign markets that had been lost as a result of increased protection and governmental support. What it accomplished, however, was to help ·freeze the pattern of agricultural policies in other countries and to make changes more difficult later.

Before World War II, Sections 22 and 32 of the AAA were little used; imports in the "basic" commodities were minimal, and domestic droughts in 1934 and 1936 eliminated the surplus problem during much of the period. But on two occasions the establishment of Commodity Credit Corporation (CCC) loan rates, and, consequently, the US price level, at above world prices did lead to the introduction of both import restrictions and export subsidies. In 1939 American cotton exports fell sharply, and the Department of Agriculture instituted export subsidies in July of that year. The effect was to reduce world market prices to the point where it would have paid to ship cotton to the United States. To forestall this, the first import quotas under Section 22 were instituted. On the other hand, the rate for the wheat loans in 1938-1939 was set at so high a level as to threaten a further reduction in US wheat exports. To forestall this, an export subsidy was instituted. The outbreak of war and the closing of European markets led to a curtailment of exports in spite of the subsidy, but the spread between the supported US price and the Canadian price neared the point at which it would have been profitable for Americans to import Canadian wheat or flour in spite of the US tariff of forty-two cents a bushel. Import quotas were imposed to prevent this from occurring.

The export subsidies for cotton and wheat had more serious repercussions on the foreign relations of the United States than did the related import quotas.[17] This country had not been an important market for other countries in wheat or in the restricted types of cotton. But the potential loss to other exporters of their markets in third countries as a result of US export subsidies was a serious threat. Countries exporting any of the products eligible for this treatment under Section 32 were naturally apprehensive over signs that export subsidies had become a feature of US policy.

If the establishment of domestic prices at above world levels had been the only way to relieve the hardships of farmers during the depression, it might have been justified. But it made almost indispensable the introduction of export subsidies to avoid the loss of existing markets, and of quotas to prevent imports from frustrating the domestic program.

Agriculture in Prewar Trade Agreements

It will be remembered that, while the United States was experimenting with direct intervention on behalf of domestic agricultural prices, it was also engaged in the negotiation of bilateral trade agreements aimed at the reciprocal reduction of tariffs. It was essential to all parties that these agreements contain provisions to prevent the nullification of tariff concessions by the use of other forms of import restriction. But the clash between this need and the provisions of Section 22 had to be resolved. As might be expected, it was resolved in favor of the latter. Thus, to the standard clause in trade agreements prohibiting import quotas on items that had been made the subject of tariff concessions was added an exception for import quotas imposed in connection with governmental measures operating to regulate or control the "production, market supply, quality or price" of the like domestic product.[18]

It may seem surprising that the United States was able to obtain acceptance by others of an exception tailored so closely to accord with its particular form of agricultural supports. In fact, this agreement might have been more difficult to obtain if its effect had been to jeopardize any important tariff concession. But, as the United States did not grant tariff reductions in prewar agreements on any of the "basic products" on which import quotas were likely to be imposed,[19] the exception had little practical effect.

Effects of the War

During World War II, all the countries of Europe, including the United Kingdom, introduced direct governmental management of agricultural production and distribution. Even neutral Sweden and Switzerland intensified governmental intervention in agriculture in an effort to increase domestic production and replace the imports that could no longer be obtained.

The United States also stepped up its price supports and controls during the war. In 1941, in the "Steagal Amendment" to the Commodity Credit Corporation Appropriation Act, Congress broadened the scope of price support legislation by making supports mandatory for a number of nonbasic commodities, including dairy products, and authorized the Secretary of Agriculture to provide support for other products, at his discretion.[20] In 1942 it raised mandatory price supports for the basic products to 92.5 percent of parity and for the Steagal commodities to 90 percent.[21] And in the Surplus Property Act of 1944 it increased the borrowing power of the CCC and authorized it to sell from its stocks for export at below domestic prices.[22]

In Europe, at the end of the war, a new incentive for restricting imports was added to the desire to protect domestic producers: the necessity of conserving scarce foreign exchange. Thus, when the rules of the GATT were negotiated in 1947 and 1948, both the United States and the industrial countries of Western Europe had in effect extensive machinery for supporting their domestic agricultural production and limiting imports by one device or another.

The "United States Exception"

Reconciling GATT rules with the methods used by the United States for the support of its agricultural producers was more difficult than the similar problem had been in prewar bilateral agreements. The application of the GATT prohibition against the use of quantitative restrictions was broader and encompassed not only items on which tariff concessions had been granted but trade in general. Thus the GATT rules, unless qualified, would have prevented the kind of action Congress had contemplated in Section 22, even if no tariff concession were granted on the product concerned.

Given this background, the United States delegation at the GATT negotiation could not have pressed for a general prohibition against import quotas without insisting on an exception that would permit their use to prevent imports from frustrating the purposes of domestic production or marketing controls. On the other hand, too broad an exception could have rendered the GATT valueless as an aid to American agricultural exports. The dilemma was resolved by an exception that permitted a contracting party to restrict the imports of an agricultural product where necessary to the enforcement of measures "which operate . . . to restrict" the production or marketing of the like domestic product (Article XI, 2 [c]).

It was clear to all that this exception had been drawn to meet the American case, for the United States was the only major agricultural producer making widespread use of direct price supports combined with domestic acreage or marketing limitations. Again, it may seem surprising that the exception was accepted by others in this form, but it would have been difficult to argue against the logic of limiting it to cases in which domestic production was restricted. Furthermore, other agricultural exporting countries, such as Canada and Australia, must have welcomed this limitation since it imposed contractual limits to the use of Section 22 which that legislation did not, itself, contain. As for the European negotiators at Geneva, they were primarily concerned with efforts to obtain the greatest possible freedom to use quantitative restrictions for balance of payments reasons, and they were probably relieved to learn that the United States was also unable to accept an unqualified prohibition against the use of import quotas.

The "Protocol of Provisional Application" and the US Agricultural Waiver

Most contracting parties would have had to obtain some changes in domestic legislation in order to accept all the GATT obligations. If the ITO Charter had been submitted to the Senate as a treaty and so accepted, its status in domestic law would have been unequivocal.[23] Other countries would presumably have obtained the legislative sanction required by their own constitutional systems at the time that their parliaments consented to ratification. Pending ratification of the charter, however, the signatories to the GATT brought the latter instrument into force by acceptance of a "Protocol of Provisional Application," under which each government committed itself to carry out the obligations of Parts I and III of the agreement, and the obligations of Part II to the fullest extent not inconsistent with existing legislation. Because the charter was never ratified, all the contracting parties continue to apply the agreement subject to that qualification. The result has been to permit the continued use of those protective systems that were required by legislation on their books on January 1, 1948.[24]

The problem of making the GATT rules fit the system of American price supports did not end with the agricultural exception in Article XI. Beginning in 1948, members of Congress repeatedly chided the executive branch for being too backward in its use of Section 22, and Congress amended the law on several occasions to make it increasingly difficult for the President to limit the use of import quotas to cases in which domestic production was curtailed, as required by the GATT provision. But the escape provided by the Protocol of Provisional Application would not have permitted the United States to ignore the limits of the GATT exception, since the language of Section 22 at the time of signature of the protocol left to the discretion of the President the decision whether or not to impose quotas.

In 1951, the Congress, unimpeded by the international obligation contained in the GATT, passed an amendment to the Defense Production Act that virtually required the Secretary of Agriculture to impose restrictions on imports of a number of products, including dairy products, for which no domestic production controls existed or were feasible.[25] The action the administration subsequently felt required to take in accord with this legislation was clearly contrary to its GATT commitments. The violation was not overlooked by the agricultural exporting members of the GATT. In the fall of 1951, the Contracting Parties held that injured parties were entitled to seek compensation from the United States. In 1952 they authorized the Netherlands to restrict its imports of American wheat flour in compensation for US quotas against some types of cheese produced primarily in that country.

In 1951 Congress also amended Section 22 of the AAA to require the President to carry out its provisions regardless of any international agreement.[26] Beginning in 1953, the executive branch began applying Section 22 more nearly in accordance with the wishes of agricultural senators and congressmen. When the GATT was subjected to general review and amendment in 1955, the United States sought to regularize its quota system and requested a waiver, which the Contracting Parties granted.[27] Once again, US negotiators were assisted by the preoccupation of other countries with their own balance of payments restrictions. For, as their international balances reached or approached the point where they no longer required the use of import restrictions, many countries found that the protection afforded by quotas was difficult to dispense with. In the published record of the review session, the reproduction of the US waiver is followed immediately by a decision of the Contracting Parties specifying the circumstances under which the obligations of Article XI would be temporarily waived on behalf of countries no longer in balance of payments difficulties in order to allow them more time in which to dismantle these "hard core" restrictions.[28]

The GATT Record

Although international trade in Temperature Zone agricultural products has greatly increased since 1947, it is difficult to appraise the extent to which this can be credited to the application of GATT rules and to GATT tariff concessions. Much of it must have been the natural consequence of general liberalization in international trade and payments, some of which would have taken place in any event.

While many tariff bindings and some tariff reductions on agricultural products have been granted by the United States and other countries, an examination of those that affected more than negligible volumes of trade shows that they usually consisted of concessions by temperate countries on tropical and subtropical products; by tropical countries on Temperate Zone products; on products of use to farmers in the importing country, such as seeds and breeding animals; on partially processed specialties of the exporting country; and on seasonal fruits and vegetables, limited to a time of year in which the domestic product is not available.

There were important exceptions, however. For example, in order to save the 1947 Geneva negotiations from threatened breakdown, the United States granted valuable reductions in its duties on raw wool. At Geneva, and again at Torquay in 1950-1951, the United States reduced duties moderately on certain cheese specialties of Italy, Canada, and the Netherlands. For its part, in pre-Kennedy Round negotiations the United States obtained valuable tariff concessions on canned fruits and "variety meats" and tariff bindings on industrial tallow and tobacco. Free bindings for cotton, soybeans as well as soybean oil, cake, and meal, and duty bindings for canned fruits and vegetables granted by certain member states of the EEC in earlier negotiations were assumed by the Community as a whole in the "Article XXIV:6 negotiations" of 1960-1962.

Any evaluation of the concessions that have been exchanged in GATT negotiations on agricultural products is complicated by the widespread resort to nontariff barriers. In 1948 the panel of experts appointed by the Contracting Parties to review the impact of impediments to world commodity trade identified a long list of measures that were used by contracting parties to discourage imports, encourage exports, or stimulate home production of Temperate Zone agricultural products.[29] In addition to import duties the measures the panel identified as restricting trade included: import quotas or embargoes, the operation of state trading organizations, multiple exchange rates, mixing ratios, and agreements with foreign exporters to limit their exports. They did not attempt to measure the economic impact of these nontariff barriers, but they concluded that "agricultural protectionism in the highly industrialized countries is now a major factor restricting the world trade in such products."[30]

The panel's findings — the so-called Haberler Report[31] — led to a number of procedural decisions by the Contracting Parties aimed at making the GATT rules more effective for agricultural products. The most important was the inauguration of regular "consultations" with the principal importing countries concerning measures employed by them for the protection of their domestic agriculture. In spite of the pressures thus brought to bear, however, the dismantlement of quantitative restrictions enforced against agricultural imports continued to lag well behind the liberalization of industrial imports. When, in 1965, the GATT secretariat collected and tabulated data from contracting parties on the measures they still used to affect agricultural trade, all of the twenty-one industrialized, non-Communist countries that responded admitted to restricting trade in one or more agricultural products by devices other than tariffs. All of them made some use of quantitative restrictions; ten operated trading monopolies; four (counting the EEC as a unit) imposed variable levies on some imports; at least four, including the United States, supported prices of some products at predetermined levels; and one, Great Britain, made wide use of deficiency payments.

A Longer Perspective

In the light of frequent demonstrations that industrialized countries were not prepared to subject their farm producers to international competition, it has sometimes been suggested that the Contracting Parties should abandon any attempt to enforce the GATT in the agricultural sector. If the support of farm incomes by means of fixed agricultural prices is to be considered a permanent feature of national agricultural policies, this would be realistic advice, at least with respect to those basic products for which price supports are technically feasible. The assumption that price supports are here to stay is easy to understand. Most inhabitants of developed countries have become accustomed to societies in which farmers demand supported prices and have the political power to enforce their demands.

Is this really a stable situation that is likely to endure or is it more likely to prove transitory in the longer sweep of history? In attempting to answer this question, differences of detail between countries and temporary deviations due to wars, depressions, and the creation of new economic boundaries may be ignored. Then it becomes possible to see some degree of inevitability in a model built somewhat along the following lines: The early stages of industrialization bring increased income not only to the townsman but to the rural population. As urban incomes rise, per capita consumption of food increases. The introduction of new manufacturing techniques expands the demand for agricultural raw materials, while the migration of labor to the factories ensures fuller employment and higher incomes to those remaining on the farms. The distribution of income within the agricultural sector, however, does not undergo any important change.

Sooner or later some changes begin to be felt that cause the incomes of one group — the smaller and less efficient farmers — to move against the trend of increasing prosperity, as measured by the growth of real income for the rest of the population. As urban incomes continue to increase, the income elasticity of demand for food declines, and food prices cease to respond to still further increases in incomes. The share of agriculture in the national income begins to decline. And at the same time the distribution of that share changes. The farmers who combine necessary personal qualifications with access to capital and adequate land are able to apply the new technology to their production. Their unit costs fall more rapidly than those of small farmers, whose per capita incomes then decline rapidly in relation to those of the urban population.

If economic forces were allowed to play themselves out, the small farmer would leave the land for the city, and a new equilibrium would be established with only "efficient" farmers surviving and prices continuing to reflect progressively lower agricultural costs. But, typically, there is a protracted period in which economic forces are not allowed to establish a new equilibrium. At the outset of industrialization, small farmers are necessarily the majority group in the population and wield dominant political power. This power is extended, even after the rural population has been reduced to a minority, by a tendency for the democratic processes to move slowly in response to geographic or occupational shifts in the population. The state responds to this political power and intervenes to prevent farm prices from falling. As a result, the tendency for surplus farm labor to move into industry is held back. This in turn delays the rise in farm productivity, and the spread between competitive prices for farm products and supported prices creates surpluses that require further state intervention.

While these changes are taking place, the decline in agriculture's share of the total wealth created by the economy paradoxically enables the small farmer to exploit his political power more effectively, for it makes feasible a deliberate transfer of income to him from the rest of the economy—a transfer that would not have been possible when the major source of wealth was the output of family farms. The small farmer's new minority position has another positive effect on his political power. As a minority he has a real or imagined need to organize in order to protect himself against exploitation by the rising power of the cities. And organization is made possible by the class solidarity that arises out of his new position. To the disproportionate political power he is able to exert through his own efforts is added the support of large farmers, who also profit from high agricultural prices, and of the manufacturing and service industries that are tributary to agriculture.

The stage of supported farm prices can last a long time, but it does not rest on a foundation that can endure permanently. For one thing, while supported prices can retard the shift of population from rural to urban areas, that movement continues, and, with it, rural voting power declines. At the same time, the continued trend toward larger, industrialized farm units increases the share of agricultural income received by those who do not need special help from the consumer or the taxpayer. It is not too difficult to believe that, as this process continues, the point will be reached when the declining political power of the farmer will no longer be able to impose on the urban population a method of income transfer that provides unnecessary windfalls to wealthy industrialized farm units.[32]

The time may eventually come when the now highly industrialized country can adopt agricultural policies determined by considerations of the general welfare rather than the political power of the farmers. The decision may, even then, be made to provide a level of income to high-cost farmers that is not justified by considerations of optimum utilization of the economy's resources. But this can then be accomplished by direct assistance, in the form of income supports that will not burden the consumer with artificially high prices. The understandable preference of the farmer for receiving his support in the form of high prices will not forever be backed by sufficient political power to enforce his will.

Recent Trends in Industrialized Countries

Does this idealized model of the historic progression of societies from rural to urban economies bear any resemblance to reality? A brief survey of the present trends of agricultural policy in the Western industrialized countries provides some cases that seem to support the affirmative and others that either call its validity into question or that may be explained as further instances of temporary, if prolonged, interruptions in the trend.

Take the case of Great Britain. In spite of frequent reversals of policy caused by wars, depressions, and political realignments, Great Britain has for many years conformed more closely than other industrial countries to a pattern of agricultural policy that could be expected of a mature industrialized society. In general, the support of agricultural incomes has been made a charge on the taxpayer rather than on the consumer. While the method of deficiency payments used results, in effect, in the farmer receiving a higher price for his product than competitive world prices, these payments have been limited to "standard quantities" and have thus provided less stimulus to increased high-cost production than direct price supports would have. They have also reduced the need for extraordinary measures to control imports. After convertibility was restored to the pound in the late 1950's, the only trade restriction used to supplement these supports was a moderate duty on imports from outside the preferential area. Since 1962, however, the system has been modified by the enactment of legislation to permit the government to enforce minimum import prices for grains by means of "equalization fees." The purpose of this change was to limit the burden on the exchequer and to pave the way for transition to the Common Market system in the event of British accession to the EEC. The use of import fees has, however, been subject to bilateral agreements negotiated with exporting countries. In these agreements the United Kingdom undertook to reduce incentives to domestic producers if the share of imports in the British market should decline, but this undertaking has not been fully carried out.[33]

The future of these policies is obscured by uncertainty as to whether Great Britain will succeed in obtaining membership in the Common Market. If not, it is unlikely that Britain will incur the liability of stimulating further uneconomic agricultural production by the support of noncompetitive prices. But if accession to the Community should occur while the present agricultural policies of the six prevail, Great Britain will probably have to accept increased costs to its consumers and industry in order to obtain access to European markets for industrial products.

The United States entered on the road toward an industrial society much later than Great Britain. And because much of its land is well suited to mechanized farming, the end of the road is bound to look quite different from the British model. With the aid of research supported by the government and massive private investment, the larger part of American agriculture has been brought to a position where it can compete under free-trade conditions with the most efficient producers abroad. The less competitive sectors such as sugar and dairy products still require government aid at present levels of production, as do most small farmers. But as more producers either leave their farms or receive progressively more of their income from the industrial and service sectors of the economy it is possible, setting politics aside, to visualize a future in which American agriculture will consist almost entirely of large units capable of profitable operation at competitive world prices.

It is risky to look for signs of a trend in the developments of only a few years. But we may be justified in attaching more than transitory significance to certain changes that have taken place in American agricultural policy during the 1960's. For, even if these policies should be reversed for a time, as is always possible, the fact that it has been politically possible to adopt them even temporarily increases the likelihood that any reversal will itself be temporary.

What happened was that the reappearance of food deficits in the world during the 1960's, and the resultant reduction of stored surpluses in the United States, helped greatly "to reestablish the market place as the primary factor in farm pricing."[34] Although the trend toward the ascendancy of market price was limited largely to grains and cotton, in these two products the changes were significant. In the years 1963-1965 the Commodity Credit Corporation purchased only 4 percent of the US wheat crop, as compared with an average purchase of 27 percent from 1953 through 1960, though farmers received substantial additional payments through domestic marketing certificates. Corn purchases, which amounted to from 8 to 16 percent of the crop in those earlier years fell to 1 percent. In December 1966, John A. Schnittger, Undersecretary of Agriculture, predicted that exports of corn and cotton would require no subsidy in the following year; grain sorghum, little or none; and wheat, but twenty to twenty-five cents per bushel—"far below former levels."[35] Six months later Gale Johnson wrote that the market had been permitted to function in the distribution of corn and cotton but that in 1966-1967 substantial export subsidies were paid on wheat "even though the market price of wheat was significantly above the loan rate or support price."[36]

These steps away from noncompetitive price maintenance were facilitated both by changes in world supply and demand and by changes in the character of US support legislation. In the case of feed grains, wheat, and cotton, loan rates were reduced to world market levels or lower, and producer payments were used to supplement farm income. Financial incentives were provided for the diversion of acreage from those crops still in surplus, such as short-staple cotton.[37] In August 1968 President Johnson signed an act[38] which drastically revised the price support and acreage allotment program for extra-long-staple cotton and substituted direct payments to producers in place of price support.

Even if there are no future setbacks in this trend toward a market economy, it has so far bypassed some important American crops. Dairy supports have continued to be supplemented by import quotas and export subsidies, and the support level for industrial milk was raised in response to a decline in production in 1966-1967. Whether the American dairy industry will eventually be able to compete in world markets without assistance or in the United States market without high protection remains uncertain.

Poultry meat represents a different kind of exception to the trend away from intervention. American exports had for some time been competitive and were expanding rapidly without the aid of subsidies until, in 1962, the EEC adopted a variable levy system that virtually closed Community markets to outside imports. Denmark, which had shared the important German import market with the United States, tried for a while to regain its position in that market by pricing poultry for export at below its domestic price. When this was frustrated by a corresponding increase in the Community levy, its low-priced exports were diverted to Switzerland and replaced Swiss imports from the United States. The American response, in 1966, was to begin to subsidize exports to Switzerland. Domestic prices in the United States continue to be determined by market forces. When domestic demand catches up with the production that has been made surplus by the direct and indirect effects of the EEC policy, there may be no further reason to continue the subsidy.

The likelihood of permanently achieving a market economy for agriculture is enhanced by the diminishing manpower devoted to agricultural production. In the United States, for example, annual man-hours spent in agricultural production declined from 1949 to 1964, by nearly one-half, and labor costs fell from 15.5 percent to 9 percent of production costs.[39] However, a substantial part of this decrease has taken place in such capital-intensive crops as grains and soybeans. If the full potentialities of the agricultural sector for independent viability are to be realized, the present movement away from small family farms and from labor-intensive to capital-intensive crops will have to be carried considerably further. Furthermore, because of the tendency of agricultural production to overcompensate for price changes, it may not be possible, or even desirable, to leave all crop prices entirely free to fluctuate with changes in supply and demand. Typically, in deciding what and how much to plant, the farmer tends to respond to the supply-and-demand conditions of the previous crop year rather than to those that will prevail when his product next comes to the market. The dissemination of information about plantings and forecasts of market conditions can at best mitigate but not prevent the resulting tendency of farm production, when regulated solely by a free market, to produce alternating surpluses and shortages. A price stabilization program designed to cushion the impact on both the producers and consumers may be necessary, perhaps through stocking and destocking by governments.

If it should prove possible to dispense with the use of price supports designed to maintain domestic prices permanently above a world equilibrium level, market forces could play a more decisive role in agriculture. And negotiations designed to liberalize international trade would have a better chance of succeeding.

In contrast to the United States, the countries of Western Europe have not, on the whole, traveled far along the road toward unsupported prices, partly because the continental system of land inheritance delayed by decades the introduction of industrialized farming methods and the movement of farm labor from the land. Denmark and the Netherlands are exceptions; during the 1950's, until the formation of the European Common Market, both achieved something closely approaching free trade in agricultural products. Since the end of World War II, however, the technological revolution in agriculture has also made rapid progress elsewhere in Western Europe. In France, for example, wheat yields per acre increased by nearly 50 percent from 1950 to 1960. Given a chance to work itself out, this technological revolution may contribute to the movement of labor from the land and eventually lead to a lower level of protection against outside competition.

It now appears that the Common Market may have to be put in a class with wars and depressions as an interruption in the natural evolution of the agricultural sector in industrialized economies. In effect, the Common Market added two new factors to the still formidable political power of the small farmer: exposure of the less efficient farmers to new competition from within the Community intensified the demand for protection against imports from third countries; at the same time, European Community member states with the lowest agricultural costs, such as France in the case of wheat and Italy in the case of fruits and vegetables, had a strong incentive for demanding higher protective walls around the Common Market. Before and during the Kennedy Round the demands for agricultural autarchy by both the lowest cost and the highest cost countries of the Community appeared to be overriding.

Nor had the EFTA countries other than the United Kingdom shown much tendency toward freeing agricultural trade or toward the substitution of income support for the maintenance of producer prices; Switzerland, although the largest per capita importer of agricultural products, relied heavily on price supports and on the quantitative limitation of imports. Sweden and Norway protected virtually all their agricultural production by nontariff barriers. Austria made extensive use of quantitative restrictions and subsidies. The agricultural populations in both Sweden and Switzerland are, however, declining, and if this trend continues those countries should have an increased incentive to move away from price supports toward a system of income support more compatible with the restoration of price competition in international trade.

GATT and the Common Agricultural Policy

The Treaty of Rome, while laying down specific rules for the establishment of the customs union in industrial products and some agricultural products, provided little more than procedural guidance for the construction of a common market in most of agriculture. For such basic products as meat, dairy products, vegetables, cereals, fats, sugar, wine and tobacco,[40] the treaty established alternative objectives for a Common Agricultural Policy (CAP) in such broad and general terms as "common rules concerning competition," the "compulsory coordination of national market organizations" or "a European market organization," but left the details to be worked out by the commission with the approval of the Council of Ministers.[41]

In 1962 and 1963, as the EEC began to develop the details of the CAP for specific farm products, much of the attention of the GATT Contracting Parties was directed to a debate over the evolving policies of the Community as they affected agricultural import prospects. Feelings ran high, in part because the other GATT countries were conscious of their inability to influence materially the trend toward agricultural autarchy that appeared to be developing in the Common Market. Spokesmen for the Community, emboldened by the unqualified support the six had received from the United States in earlier GATT discussions of the Treaty of Rome, presented the CAP as a *fait accompli,* not subject to change. Their defense of the regulations had a plausible legal basis: for the multitude of restrictions that had previously affected agricultural production and trade in the member states, they said, there was to be substituted a comprehensive device—the variable levy—which was not ruled out by any provision of the GATT.[42] Furthermore, a legal impediment to the use of variable levies had been removed during the 1960-1962 negotiations, when the Community had denounced the fixed tariff bindings previously granted by member states in the case of products for which a variable levy was anticipated.[43]

The details of the variable levy system differ according to the economic characteristics of the farm products involved. But the concept is basically the same for all. In contrast to the fixed margin of protection afforded by a tariff, the variable levy is based on a predetermined price to be received by producers. This price is enforced by the establishment of a corresponding minimum price below which the product is not permitted to enter without payment of a supplementary levy. Then an import levy is imposed equal to the difference between the minimum import price and the lowest price at which the product is offered for importation. If the offering price falls, the reduction is compensated by an increase in the levy. For some products, the internal producer price is further protected against errors in calculation, or delayed adjustment, by a governmental guarantee to purchase the product from producers at an "intervention price," which is only marginally below the support price. Finally, in order to permit disposal abroad of the surpluses that high price supports induce, provision is made for automatic "refunds" to exporters, normally equal to the amount of the levy on imports.

In short, Community producers are insulated from the effect of any price competition with the outside world.[44] If, because of the general trend toward increased agricultural productivity, production costs decline both within the Community and abroad, the Community producer can lower his price in order to increase his share of the Community market. A comparable decrease in the offering prices of foreigners will not help them, for it will be fully offset by an increase in the levy. The variable levy system, with differences in detail from product to product, has been adopted for grains, livestock, dairy products, sugar, poultry, and eggs. Some elements of the system have also been introduced for certain fruits and vegetables.

In some respects, the variable levy system is reminiscent of the US system of price support that occupied the early attention of the drafters of the GATT. Although its methods differ substantially from the American system, the objective is the same: the maintenance of a domestic price unrelated to the world price and defended by import restrictions and export subsidies. But Article XI of the GATT provides that imports may not be restricted unless domestic production or marketing are also curtailed. If the United States had not later had to provide for its own departures from this criterion—by the "U.S. waiver"—it would have been in a position to insist, though not necessarily with success, that the EEC similarly limit the damage that variable levies are permitted to do to imports.

The Common Agricultural Policy, or at least the variable levy, poses a much more difficult problem for the tariff negotiator than the US system of price support. It is true that the existence of Section 22, and the GATT waiver to permit its use, presents the threat that US tariff concessions on many agricultural products may be impaired by the imposition of quantitative restrictions. But impairment can be identified and compensated for under the provisions of the GATT. Under the variable levy system, on the other hand, the level of protection cannot be bound without abandonment of the system itself. If any limit were to be imposed on its effectiveness without destroying its purpose, it would be the level of the price that is guaranteed to domestic producers that would have to be bound. As the Kennedy Round demonstrated, the Community has been unwilling to contemplate such a binding except in the context of an agreement under which world prices and producer prices in other countries were also fixed.

If the Common Agricultural Policy in something like its present form is assumed to be a permanent feature of the Common Market, the barrier to further liberalization of trade in agricultural products is a formidable one. There are reasons to doubt, however, that it can survive for long without fundamental revision. The absolute support of agricultural prices without relation to world prices will impose costs on the economy as a whole that are likely to prove unacceptable, especially to those member states that are net importers of agricultural products in intracommunity trade. These costs are already proving to be particularly difficult to overlook when they take the form of export subsidies paid out of a common fund to which all member states contribute.[45]

In 1968, Commissioner Sicco Mansholt made a number of far-reaching proposals[46] for reducing the cost of the CAP in general, and for eliminating the most uneconomic producing units. No action had been taken on these proposals by early 1970, but they promised, even before new strains brought on by the French franc devaluation in August 1969, to provide the Community with fuel for future internal crises. While it seems certain that progress toward a less costly system will be slow, the forces working for lower costs are likely to triumph. The dependence of the Common Market countries on international trade, and on the export of industrial goods, is too great to permit them to ignore the impact of an autarkical agricultural policy on their overall price structure.

The Trend of Agricultural Protectionism

There is no satisfactory means of measuring the amount of international trade that is prevented by the existence of nontariff barriers. Because such barriers are most frequent and widespread in agriculture, it is especially difficult to determine whether, on balance, agriculture has shared in the trend toward freer trade that has taken place in industrial materials and manufactured goods since the end of World War II. Even if there has been such a sharing, it is evident that the liberation of trade in agricultural products has lagged far behind that in other sectors. The postwar dismantlement of quantitative restrictions, which reached its climax in the late

1950's, was concentrated largely in industrial goods. With the exception of Japan no major industrial country continues to impose import quotas on these goods. But many of these countries have retained a hard core of restrictions on certain agricultural imports. The most important movement away from the use of agricultural quotas has been their dismantlement by the member states of the EEC. But this was accompanied by the introduction of the Common Agricultural Policy, including variable levies.

Tariffs do, however, play an important role in world agricultural trade. The concentration of quantitative restrictions, state trading, and variable levies tends to be in such basic products as grains, meats, dairy products, and tree crops, on which large masses of farmers depend. Other products, individually less important but representing a significant total, are traded freely, with imports limited only by customs duties. Even among products subject to quotas and other nontariff barriers, the tariff frequently constitutes the effective protection.

In spite of a widespread belief to the contrary, agricultural products have been included in postwar tariff negotiations. But the reductions achieved have been substantially less on the average than those in other sectors. Thus, when the Kennedy Round was launched, the tariffs that had survived previous tariff negotiations were far from negligible.[47] From the point of view of the agricultural exporting countries, therefore, a major objective of the new negotiations was to obtain a substantial reduction in tariffs against agricultural products even if the simultaneous dismantlement of nontariff barriers should prove to be impossible.

5

Nontariff Barriers

When the GATT Contracting Parties decided to launch the Kennedy Round, they decreed that it should deal with nontariff barriers as well as tariffs.[1] But they failed to say what they meant by the term. Neither the GATT, nor any other convention, establishes precise limits to its application. If taken literally and in its broadest sense, "nontariff barrier" would include even those geographic features that, within historic times, have impeded trade: the Atlantic Ocean before Columbus, or the Alps before the building of the Simplon and Saint Gotthard Tunnels. But students and practitioners of commercial policy have not customarily included in the term phenomena over which governments have no control. Some writers have however included in the term: regional differences in consumer preferences and private cartel arrangements; quasi-environmental barriers, such as the absence of international uniformity in electrical safety standards; and barriers resulting incidentally from governmental actions unrelated to foreign trade, such as the administration of health regulations and patent laws.[2] If these impediments are to be treated as nontariff barriers, then one of the more important environmental phenomena to which attention should also be drawn is that of bureaucratic zeal. Who is more familiar than a customs official with the maze of regulations created by governments to ensure that duties are fully paid, statistics collected, and the health, safety, and morals of the citizenry protected? Why should he not conclude that his government's intent was to reduce trade to a minimum and, accordingly, do his patriotic bit toward that end?

To bring the discussion down to more concrete terms, nontariff barriers may usually be distinguished from customs duties by the fact that the nontariff barriers usually have, or once had, a rationale independent of trade. Their total abandonment would rarely be feasible. Sanitary regulations and safety standards are essential to a modern society. Importers complain that customs formalities are unduly burdensome and discourage trade. But customs officials must classify imports in order to determine the applicable rate of duty, and where a tariff is expressed in ad valorem terms the value for customs purposes must be established. So long as the regulations and administrative practices designed to achieve these purposes are not carried beyond the point of genuine need, they cannot usefully be classified as nontariff barriers even if they have the incidental effect of impeding international trade. And, since what is necessary in one country may be excessive in another, the problem of formulating international rules to limit the use of nontariff barriers involves complications that do not exist in the case of tariffs.

In deciding that nontariff barriers were to be included in the Kennedy Round negotiations, the Contracting Parties had in mind only measures taken by governments or removable by government action without the sacrifice of essential nonprotective objectives. Even these limitations leave so large a field that the following summary will have to be limited to those barriers that have been under international discussion or negotiation since the end of World War II.

Of the twenty-three articles in the General Agreement devoted to good conduct in trading relations, fourteen prohibit or regulate the use of specified nontariff measures that can restrict imports. If universally applied, the existing rules would have gone far toward protecting the results of the tariff negotiations. But the Protocol of Provisional Application permitted each Contracting Party to continue practices required by legislation existing on a specified base date.[3] To give some of the original rules their intended force was one of the reasons for subjecting nontariff barriers to negotiation. But this was not by any means the only one. There were sound reasons for including in the Kennedy Round a complex of trade practices that had entered only peripherally into previous bargaining sessions. The depth of the tariff reductions contemplated increased the potential importance of existing practices and the temptation to introduce new ones. At the outset of the Kennedy Round, it was hoped that some of the more restrictive devices used by individual contracting parties for which the protocol provided a legal escape, as well as practices not mentioned in the GATT, would succumb to the negotiating process.[4]

Paratariff Barriers

In GATT discussions and elsewhere, the term "nontariff barrier" is customarily applied not only to measures entirely unrelated to customs duties but also to those whose incidence is felt through their effect on the amount of duty collected. At times, however, a useful distinction has been made between the former, called "nontariff" and the latter, called "paratariff" barriers. Paratariff barriers, such as arbitrary standards of valuation or classification for customs purposes, are qualitatively different from other nontariff barriers in that they can restrict only where there is a duty. Furthermore, any reduction in the applicable rate of duty must have the effect of reducing the additional protection afforded by the standard of valuation, however arbitrary.[5]

On the question of tariff classification, the rules of the GATT are virtually silent, though one provision does obligate contracting parties to publish relevant judicial decisions and administrative rulings so that traders may take them into account.[6] With respect to valuation, however, the provisions of the agreement are much more explicit. The key requirement (Article VII, 2[a]) is that the dutiable value "should be based on the actual value of the imported merchandise . . . or like merchandise, and should not be based on the value of merchandise of national origin or on arbitrary or fictitious values."[7] But the Protocol of Provisional Application permitted contracting parties to retain standards of valuation already required by their laws. As a result, while the GATT has probably prevented the adoption of more restrictive standards of valuation, it has had little effect on those already in existence.

Even where the GATT members are convinced that their valuation practices conform with the GATT criteria, individual variations create uncertainties for international traders. As the GATT Technical Working Party charged with a comparative study of valuation procedures and standards applied by contracting parties pointed out in 1955, the variations in practice, even among countries nominally using the same standards for determining dutiable value, are numerous.[8] Although the United States was the only contracting party which admitted that it sometimes applied "arbitrary or fictitious values," other reported practices could also have justified that description. In Canada, for example, customs officials were authorized, on goods purchased for reduced prices at the end of the season, to assess duty on the basis of average prices during the previous six months. In France, pharmaceuticals were assessed on the basis of retail price rather than on their wholesale value. Nevertheless, presumably because its customs law has been constructed piecemeal over the years, the United States surpassed all major trading countries in the bewildering variety of its valuation practices.[9] Even in the 1960's, after two simplifying changes in US law applying to most products, US valuation practices are more complex and prove more confusing for the importer than those of most other countries. In 1961, for example, the Treasury Department reported that about 87 percent of US customs invoices were appraised on a basis similar to that used by countries adhering to the "Brussels Definition" of valuation.[10] But, of the remainder, some were valued at a calculated export (FOB) equivalent of the wholesale price of the import when sold in the United States ("United States Value"),[11] others at a valuation estimated from whatever information could be obtained on cost of production in the exporting country,[12] and still others at the price at which similar goods are offered by US producers.

American Selling Price

By far the most notorious of US valuation practices is that of assessing some duties on an "American Selling Price" (ASP) basis, a "paratariff" barrier that was to become a key issue in the Kennedy Round. Unlike "United States Value," ASP does not bear even a tenuous relationship to the true export value of the merchandise, being based on the domestic price of competing merchandise produced in the United States. It is, however, applied only to a relatively small segment of US imports: benzenoid chemicals, rubber footwear, canned clams, and low-value knitted woolen gloves.

ASP protects domestic production on two different levels. First, in almost all cases use of ASP results in a higher tariff than would have been the case had the nominal tariff rate been assessed on export value. According to a US Tariff Commission study, tariffs collected on ASP items in 1966 ranged up to 172 percent of their export value.[13] Kelly has estimated that, on the average, the use of ASP approximately doubles the duties that would otherwise be collected.[14] But, since any ad valorem duty becomes meaningful only in connection with the standard of valuation used and since ASP has been in effect for the products to which it now applies throughout the life of the GATT, these high duties do not exceed the levels the United States has bound against increases in GATT negotiations.

A similar generalization applies to the valuation practices of other countries. The EEC and EFTA countries base their calculations of ad valorem tariffs on the imported (CIF) value of the merchandise, thus including freight and insurance costs in the valuation base, whereas the normal United States basis for valuation is the value of the merchandise when shipped from the exporting country (FOB), that is, without freight and insurance costs. If, however, the GATT should be accepted definitively and the Protocol of Provisional Application should disappear, the provisions of Article VII, 2(a) quoted above, would require that the United States alter the ASP and "United States Value" bases of valuation, whereas the European system of valuing imports at their CIF prices would probably still conform to GATT requirements.

The second inhibiting effect of ASP is, simply, uncertainty. This uncertainty is of two kinds. Whether a benzenoid chemical or a shipment of rubber footwear will be subject to ASP valuation depends on whether there is a competitive domestic product. Its customs status, especially in chemicals, is subject to rapid change since the industry is constantly experimenting with the commercial production of new products or variants of old ones. A domestic producer can thus affect that status by beginning the manufacture and sale of a product not previously produced domestically. What is perhaps even more galling to foreign exporters is the fact that American producers, when they set their selling prices, also determine the level of the duty. Uncertainty as to whether a particular import will be subject to ASP valuation and as to the level of that valuation can present a serious obstacle to trade even when the foreign product is sufficiently low in price to be profitably sold after payment of a duty based on ASP.[15]

Administrative Impediments

Articles IX and X of the GATT are devoted to the establishment of some simple guidelines designed both to minimize customs fees and formalities and to reduce the likelihood of unnecessarily onerous marking requirements for imported goods. But, by the nature of the problem, the GATT provisions themselves can do little more than exert moral pressures in this field and provide a basis for complaint in flagrant cases. On a number of occasions the Contracting Parties have attempted to increase the effectiveness of these provisions by supplementary undertakings. In 1952 they adopted a Code of Standard Practices concerning documentary requirements[16] and recommended the total abolition of consular invoices and fees that "represent an indirect protection to domestic products or a taxation of imports or exports for fiscal purposes."[17] The latter effort met with modest success; a number of contracting parties subsequently abolished all consular formalities,[18] and by 1957 only a handful of governments, all in less developed countries, still required consular invoices for most imports. In 1956, the Contracting Parties examined a number of proposals concerning certificates, and marks, of origin, made to them by the International Chamber of Commerce. Some were adopted in the form of recommendations to governments.[19] Reinforced by the influence of the International Chamber of Commerce, they have had the effect of gradually wearing away some of the more onerous customs formalities and administrative practices.

Safety and Health Restrictions

Article XX of the GATT exempts from the general rules of the agreement measures "necessary to protect human, animal or plant life or health." These measures must not however be so applied as to result in "arbitrary or unjustified discrimination" or in "a disguised restriction on international trade."

Naturally enough, such regulations have given rise to dissatisfaction, especially those in the field of health. US restrictions on the importation of certain meats from Argentina, because of hoof-and-mouth disease in some sections of that country, have been most vigorously criticized. For its part, the United States objected when France excluded imports of American poultry on the ground that hormones fed to American chickens might have a deleterious effect on the fertility of Frenchmen. The United States also objected when British health authorities refused to permit the importation of American lemons treated externally with a preservative they thought might injure the health of consumers.

Safety standards unrelated to health have less freqently given rise to charges of unreasonable restriction of trade. During the Kennedy Round, however, there was considerable criticism of the requirement, imposed by several states and local communities in the United States, that boilers and pressure vessels be stamped with the seal of the American Society of Mechanical Engineers, a seal that is not issued to manufacturers outside the United States and Canada. Some foreign complaints also arose when US safety standards, initiated in 1967, were applied to European automobiles. While these standards do not involve overt discrimination between domestic and imported vehicles, European manufacturers have declared some of them to be unnecessary and impracticable when applied to smaller cars. Furthermore, they feel an American manufacturer can more easily afford the added cost of these innovations since his major competitors are subject to the same requirement.

Internal Taxes

The GATT rule concerning the application of internal taxes to imported goods is simple in concept. Briefly stated it is that no internal tax or charge should be levied on an imported product that is not levied equally against the like domestic product. In other words, except for import duties, imported products are entitled to "national treatment" in the imposition of taxes.[20]

Charges of clear-cut violations of this rule have been rare. In fact, the only case that formally engaged the Contracting Parties was Brazil's imposition in 1948 of a number of internal taxes distinguishing between like products of domestic and foreign origin.[21] In this case, there was little disagreement that the Brazilian taxes contravened the agreement, and the item was removed from the agenda of the Contracting Parties only after the taxes in question had been repealed in 1956.[22]

More difficult problems involving internal taxes have arisen in instances not covered by the GATT rule or where the interpretation or equity of the rule was in dispute. Thus, the US assessments on imported spirits as well as European road taxes and border tax adjustments all figured prominently in the Kennedy Round.

US "Wine Gallon" Assessment

Though it does not formally distinguish between domestic and foreign production, the US system of assessing the excise tax on distilled spirits does in practice place the latter at a disadvantage. This is so because such spirits, when imported at less than 100 proof, are nevertheless taxed as if they were 100 proof, a rule that would also apply to domestic products if they were less than 100 proof when withdrawn from bond. The spirits may be withdrawn at the higher proof and then diluted to a lower proof before bottling, however, so the domestic bottler does not have to pay the full tax on weaker spirits. On the other hand, if imported spirits are to be sold at lower than 100 proof, the importer's choice is either to import in bulk and bottle in the United States or to pay a tax on the water that was added when the spirits were bottled abroad.[23] Since foreign spirits such as Scotch whisky or French cognac are customarily bottled at less than 100 proof and are more saleable in the US if bottled in Britain and France, respectively, a nominally nondiscriminatory tax in fact bears more heavily on the foreign than on the domestic product.

European Road Taxes

Another example of taxes that were protective in effect before the Kennedy Round (and still are) is the imposition by a number of European countries of differential automobile road use taxes. These taxes are designed to fall more heavily on the larger, more expensive, or higher-powered cars. If this goal had been accomplished by an evenly graduated tax based on any one of these criteria or a combination of them, the heavier tax burden borne by the type of car produced in the United States could have been considered an unavoidable by-product of the American manu-facturer's preference for automotive bulk. But, in some cases, the progression in tax rate was anything but gradual. The French tax, for example, which was based on "fiscal horsepower," was graduated fairly evenly up to sixteen horsepower and then was abruptly multiplied more than five times; the highest tax paid by any standard French automobile was 150 francs, while most American cars attracted a tax of 1,000 francs.[24] When expressed as a percentage of value, the inequality of treatment appears even greater. Kelly cites a case in which the tax per unit of value was more than sixteen times greater for an American car than for a European one.[25]

Austria levied a similar road tax. Based on cylinder capacity, the rate jumped from 816 schillings for 2,500 cubic centimeters to 3,600 schillings in the bracket from 2,500 to 3,000 cubic centi-meters. The Mercedes 220SE coupé paid a road tax of about $31 a year; the Chevrolet Belair, $208. Belgian and Italian taxes were graduated more evenly, but they, too, imposed much heavier levies on American types of cars than European types, even when the latter were more expensive.

Border Tax Adjustments

During and after the Kennedy Round a hitherto modest flurry of American business and governmental protest over the "border taxes" of European countries grew into a minor storm. Because the subject has attracted so much attention, it deserves fuller treatment than do most other nontariff barriers. Involved were the imposition of internal taxes on imported products and the re-mission of such taxes when the similar but domestically produced product was exported. (The term "border tax adjustments" is used to cover both these related practices since they almost in-variably occur together.)

The use of border tax adjustments is nearly universal. The US excise tax on whisky is, for example, imposed on the imported product as well as on the domestic, but American whisky is excused from the tax when it is exported. The disadvantage to which American trade is reputedly subjected because of border tax adjustments arises out of the fact that US opportunities for such adjustments are much more limited than are those of major competing countries. Every continental Western European country, for example, imposes a "turnover tax" or manufacturers' sales tax, in one form or another, on the value of most domestic production. The United States, on the other hand, has relied much more heavily on a corporate income tax. Under GATT rules, border tax adjustments are not permitted as compensation for income taxes, usually referred to as "direct" taxes, but are permitted for taxes on products, referred to as "indirect" taxes.

The GATT does not use the terms "direct" and "indirect" in relation to taxes. But it does authorize the imposition of any internal tax on an imported product, provided it is "applied, directly or indirectly, to like domestic *products*."[26] It also specifies that exemption of an exported product from taxes borne by the like product when destined for domestic consumption, or the remission of such taxes, is not a subsidy.[27] In view of the key role played by the word "product," neither of these provisions could reasonably be interpreted to cover taxes on income derived from production.

The storm occasioned by these provisions and their application originated in the observation of American businessmen that foreign countries engaged in a practice the United States was not in a position to emulate. But academic and government economists have developed a rationale that has supported and intensified the businessman's reaction. The theoretical case made with increasing frequency during and after the Kennedy Round may be stated in somewhat oversimplified terms as follows:

1. The GATT rules are based on the classical theory that indirect taxes are always fully "shifted forward" into the price of the product and that direct taxes are always shifted backward, that is, are absorbed by the producer in the form of lower returns.[28]

2. The intention of the GATT rules, and their effect if the assumptions on which they are based were correct, would be to neutralize the effect of internal taxes on international trade. But most modern economists today agree that an indirect tax may in part be shifted backward — the amount of backward shifting de-

pending upon the degree of imperfection in the market and on the price elasticities of supply and demand. Similarly, they tend to agree that some forward shifting of direct taxes is likely to take place, though there are wide differences of emphasis, and some economists suggest full forward shifting while others suggest full backward shifting.[29]

3. Because their underlying assumptions are wrong, the GATT rules do not ensure that the border tax adjustments they permit, or prohibit, will result in neutralizing the effect of internal taxes on international trade. Therefore, the rules should be changed.

This line of reasoning contains the questionable premise that the GATT rules were based solely on the classical theory of tax shifting. In fact, in their formulation they simply reflected the universal practice of governments. And that practice can easily be explained by practical and political considerations. When they imposed a tax on a domestic product, governments did not want to place their domestic producers at a disadvantage vis-à-vis their competititors, either in their own or in export markets. To make sure that such a disadvantage did not exist, they had no choice but to apply the domestic tax to imported products and to exempt the domestic product from the tax when exported. It made no difference whether they were aware that the classical theory of tax shifting was imperfect. If their object was to be sure that the domestic producer was not placed at a disadvantage, total compensation was necessary so long as it was impossible to determine that part of a tax on a product was not shifted into its price. From the viewpoint of the domestic producer the case was also simple. Any part of the domestic tax on his product that was not charged against the competing imported product was bound to put him at a disadvantage of some kind — a competitive disadvantage if the tax were shifted forward into his own price, or a reduction in his profits if, as a result of the exemption of the competing import, he found it necessary to absorb part of the tax.

But why were the architects of the GATT not equally interested in neutralizing the adverse competitive effects of income taxes? Here, it is likely that the classical theory of tax shifting did play some part. But even if governments had been skeptical of the full validity of the theory, practical considerations would have discouraged the effort to draw up a GATT rule permitting a contracting party to offset a direct tax at the border. If such an effort had been made, the first problem would have been: what level of tax? A compensatory tax on imports would of necessity have to be charged on a product; it could not be assessed on the income of a foreign producer. It would be necessary, therefore, to assess a tax against imports equivalent to the tax paid by the competing domestic producer on income attributable to his sale of the product concerned. But there would be as many levels of income tax per unit of output as producers, the producer at the margin perhaps making no profit and paying no income tax. If the problem of allocating the tax among several products sold by one producer were added to this problem, there would seem to be reason enough why governments, or the drafters of the GATT, did not attempt to provide for border tax adjustments to compensate for the direct taxation of business enterprises.

It may be noted, parenthetically, that the practical considerations arguing against attempts to determine the amount of income tax borne by a product are consistent with the classical theory that, under conditions of competition, income taxes are not shifted forward. This is not to say that the level of corporate and other income taxes in a country will not affect the overall price level and therefore indirectly affect the prices charged by the producer who pays an income tax. But that is quite different from concluding that a relationship can be established between the price of a particular product and the rate of income tax paid by its producers.

Changes in Border Tax Adjustments

If consideration of border tax adjustments is carried only this far, it seems possible to conclude that, while the GATT solution does not ensure that all adjustments will be "trade neutral," it does provide the only basis likely to be both politically generally acceptable and workable in practice. Alternative rules are unlikely to approximate trade neutrality as closely until techniques are devised for measuring the precise amount of tax shifting in the case of each tax and each product. So long as no important changes occurred in the level of border tax adjustments, these considerations would be enough to account for the fact that the GATT rules aroused no controversy during the first fifteen years of

their application. But their general acceptance was reinforced by a tacit recognition that any trade distortion the institution of a border tax adjustment might initially cause would eventually tend to be offset or overshadowed by changes in other factors affecting the competitive position, such as changes in relative wages and prices and in exchange rates. Thus, if there has been no recent increase in the level of taxes, the argument that border tax adjustments give a competitive advantage to the country using them becomes increasingly difficult to sustain.[30]

One reason why border tax adjustments came to the fore during the Kennedy Round was that changes in European internal taxes and in the level of the related border tax adjustments were impending, the EEC having at the time of the Kennedy Round launched a program to eliminate the differences among the internal tax systems of member states.[31] Although all the EEC countries except France were scheduled to change their systems of taxation, the impending German changes attracted most attention not only because they were to come first but because of the large German balance of payments surplus.

The German changeover involved an increase in its border tax adjustments stemming from two separable causes: a change in its domestic system of taxation and an increase in the average level of tax. The effect of the change of system was a shift, on the average, from undercompensation at the border to full compensation. Before changing its system in the interest of Community tax harmonization, Germany had for many years imposed the "cascade" form of turnover tax on business transactions. Each time a product changed hands, even though it was destined for further processing or manufacture, a tax was imposed at a uniform rate based on the value of the product at the time of transfer. Under this system the cumulative tax borne by the final product depended on the number of times there had been a change of ownership, from the raw material to the final product. A border tax could not be based on the total amount of tax charged on the domestic product at various stages, as, depending upon their degree of vertical integration, that amount would differ among producers. Germany therefore assessed border taxes that were estimated to be not more than the average tax paid on the domestic product. In fact the border taxes so determined were generally agreed to have been well below the average domestic tax; both border taxes and export rebates undercompensated for the domestic turnover tax.

But under the French tax on "value-added" (TVA), which served as the model for the EEC, there is no reason for undercompensation. The tax imposed on each transaction is calculated on the basis not of the total value of the product when it changes hands but on the value that has been added by the seller since his purchase of the raw materials or components going into its production. Under this system the cumulative tax on the final product is always a known percentage of its total value, and the amount of tax to be charged at the border can be determined precisely.

Under the tax harmonization program of the Community, Germany was required not only to change its system of tax collection but to raise the level of its domestic tax rate above the previous average level and to compensate fully at the border for this new level. Because of the previous undercompensation, the result was an increase in border collections greater than the increase in internal taxes. Although the first change along these lines did not take place until January 1968, it was known to be in prospect through much of the Kennedy Round and was one of the points at issue between the delegations of the Community and the United States.

State Trading

Several interrelated provisions in the GATT deal with those practices of state monopolies that result in import restrictions and in discrimination among sources of imports.[32] Except for state monopolies created to produce revenues, their use by contracting parties with market economies has been largely limited to trade in agricultural products, where the protective effect has tended to be obscured by the use of many other nontariff barriers. Nevertheless, the opportunities that state trading offers for the erection of more or less invisible nontariff barriers remain. And the temptation to exploit those opportunities may well have been increased by the substantial reduction of tariffs in the Kennedy Round.

As the term is used in the GATT, state trading exists where a government agency exports or imports for resale. But the term also covers cases in which an autonomous, or quasi-autonomous, enterprise receives from the government the exclusive power to import or export a product. Such agencies are, of course, as old as international trade itself. The earliest examples were probably monopolies established for the purpose of raising revenue through the sale of such essential products as salt. Later, more modern necessities such as matches, and near-necessities such as tobacco and alcoholic beverages, became favorite vehicles. It must be obvious that, in the absence of special rules to govern its trading decisions, such monopoly could frustrate the intent of many GATT commitments without involving its government in overt violations. It can discriminate between foreign sellers solely on the basis of source. It can charge a markup on the resale of imports higher than the markup charged on the comparable domestic product, with the same effect as a protective tariff. It can also, by the simple act of limiting its own foreign purchases, restrict the quantity of merchandise that is imported.

With theoretical success but little practical results, GATT drafters tried to devise rules that would subject the decisions of governments implemented through state trading monopolies to the same kind of limitations that applied to the laws and decrees through which governments influence private trade. Discrimination, for example, was outlawed by the requirement that such a monopoly should choose among foreign sources "solely in accordance with commercial considerations."[33] Price protection was proscribed by the rule that the markup charged on resale of an imported product must not exceed the country's tariff rate on the product, if bound in its GATT schedule.[34] And, finally, actions equivalent to the quantitative restriction of imports were outlawed by the requirement that the monopoly "import and offer for sale . . . quantities of the product . . . sufficient to satisfy the full domestic demand."[35] Both the limitation on the resale markup and the requirement that domestic demand be met were waived in the event that some other form of treatment was specified in the GATT tariff schedule of the country concerned.

Except for instances in which special arrangements were negotiated and included in the schedule of a contracting party, there has been no case in which the state trading provisions of the agreement have been invoked or in which any contracting party has complained of their violation by another. In 1947, as a concession to the United States, France in its GATT tariff schedule recorded an undertaking to limit the resale markup on imported wheat. In 1949, Italy granted a similar concession on wheat and rye. France also agreed in the 1947 negotiations to a minimum annual purchase commitment for leaf tobacco and cigarettes.

In the case of a larger number of state monopolies, operated for revenue purposes, no effort appears to have been made to apply the GATT provisions. France has state monopolies for the import of petroleum and coal; Germany, for alcoholic beverages; Italy, for cigarette paper and lighters. The operations of the French coal monopoly and the Italian cigarette monopoly clearly have protective effects.

Contracting parties have not, however, demanded compliance with the GATT state trading provisions in these instances, almost certainly because of the difficulty of obtaining accurate information concerning the details and results of monopoly operations. But it is rather curious that available GATT records show no case in which a contracting party has demanded that a country maintaining an import monopoly reveal its resale markup for imported goods in order to determine whether it exceeds any tariff binding in its GATT schedule.

Twenty years after the founding of the GATT, the devices formulated by the Contracting Parties to prevent state trading from frustrating other commercial policy commitments have yet to prove their worth. It is interesting, nevertheless, that there was no noticeable increase in the use of state monopolies during a period when tariff protection was being lowered and quantitative restrictions progressively dismantled. There is no evidence to show whether this resulted in any way from the GATT rules or entirely from political inhibitions in capitalist societies against state incursions into fields already occupied by private trade.

The drafters of the Treaty of Rome also struggled with the question of state monopolies. They evidently recognized the danger that state trading could negate the objective of free trade among the member states. But the treaty does little more than empower the commission to make proposals for the "adjustment" of existing monopolies and, where a member state maintaining a monopoly has failed to make such adjustments, to authorize other members to apply "safeguard" measures.[36]

Both the GATT and the EEC deal with systems in which most trade is conducted by the private sector. Within their respective spheres, they aim at giving the forces of the marketplace maximum opportunity to do their work on behalf of the most efficient allocation of resources. Perhaps further experimentation will prove that state trading can be fitted into these systems. If not, both the GATT and the EEC may be forced to outlaw state monopolies — a formidable task. If this proves impossible, members of these systems may have to negotiate directly with the state monopolies of other members without too much regard for liberal trading principles in order to wrest from them some other assurances against the abuse of their monopoly power.

East-West Trade

The drafters of the GATT were aware that the rules governing state trading by capitalist countries do not provide an adequate basis for regulating the commercial policies of Communist countries or for bringing about a measure of equality between the obligations of countries on either side of the hyphen in "East-West trade."

The necessity of dealing with the problem did not arise in the initial GATT, as there were no Communist countries among the original Contracting Parties. In 1948, however, one of the original signatories, Czechoslovakia, fell into the Communist orbit and adopted a totally planned economy. This could have raised the issue of how the trading system of such a country could be reconciled with GATT rules. But, in fact, the problem was never directly faced. In 1951, at the request of the United States, the Contracting Parties authorized the United States and Czechoslovakia to suspend the application of all GATT obligations between them on political grounds.[37] In the ensuing years, contractual relations between Czechoslovakia and all other contracting parties have nominally remained in force, but there is ample evidence that they have not been taken literally by either side. Thus, though all "Western" contracting parties have been involved in many complaint actions against each other, there has been no case since 1951 of a complaint procedure involving Czechoslovakia, either as plaintiff or respondent.

The case of Yugoslavia is quite different. For some time Yugoslavia has been building a competitive trading system within a planned economy. In November 1959 the Contracting Parties acted favorably on a Yugoslav request for a form of association with the GATT short of full membership. But it was clear that Yugoslavia was not yet "in a position to assume all the obligations involved in accession to the General Agreement." While continuing to move toward such a position, it agreed to apply the provisions of the GATT to its trading relations with contracting parties "to the extent compatible with its current economic system." For their part, the Contracting Parties agreed to take the objectives of the agreement as the basis for their own trading relations with Yugoslavia and to grant it treatment comparable to that Yugoslavia might extend to them.[38] In December 1961 Yugoslavia reported to the Contracting Parties that it had made further progress toward the development of a competitive trading system and that on March 9, 1961, it had adopted a new provisional tariff applicable to all commercial imports, which it was prepared to subject to negotiation in the GATT.[39]

When the Kennedy Round was projected, Yugoslavia was accepted as a participant in the negotiations in order to provide a basis for its full accession to the GATT. This recognition of Yugoslavia's ability to carry out the obligations of the agreement was based upon the development of a trading system that differed substantially from that prevailing in the USSR and other East European countries. It represented no exception to the Contracting Parties' general recognition that the trading systems of the other Communist countries were incompatible with the obligations of the GATT.

The one remaining effort at reconciling the GATT rules with the trading systems of totally planned economies was Poland's negotiation to obtain full accession to the GATT. As will be seen in a later chapter, this negotiation was quite different from the Yugoslavian. It broke new ground that may set a precedent for the future accession of other Communist countries.

Government Procurement

Where a government purchases for its own use (and not for resale, as in the case of state trading), the GATT explicitly exempts it from the usual rules requiring national treatment in the application of internal regulations[40] and from the requirement of non-discrimination among foreign suppliers.[41] There is no economic justification for these exemptions. If participating countries want to obtain the economies associated with an optimum allocation of resources, there is as much advantage in competition for public as for private purchases. Furthermore, so long as countries differ in the role of the public sector, the effect on trading patterns will vary from country to country. These exemptions were dictated at the time by what seemed to be political necessity; it was not thought that any government would agree to forego the right to grant some priority to domestic suppliers when public funds were expended. Both during and since the Kennedy Round, however, it has been apparent that the total exemption of government procurement from any international disicipline is a source of dissension among contracting parties and that it tends to weaken government resolve to live up to the spirit as well as the letter of the GATT obligations that relate to private trade.

Since 1962 a working party of the Organization for European Cooperation and Development (OECD) has been studying the practices of member governments in the fields of public procurement and the award of government contracts. An interim report in August 1965 revealed that comparatively few countries would admit that their official purchasing agents were required to give preference to domestic suppliers.[42] Many, however, reported that the governmental departments concerned were given discretion to decide whether the purchase of foreign goods was in the national interest; nearly all admitted the absence of any rule that foreign firms be invited to submit bids. Some did require that tenders be advertised in the case of certain categories of procurement, but usually with exceptions. In many countries, a patriotic procurement officer would seem to have even more chance than a customs official to strike a blow in favor of domestic producers at the cost of the taxpayer.

The "Buy American" Act

The distinguishing features of the US system of preferences for domestic producers in the award of government purchase contracts are that such preference is required by law[43] and that the legal requirement is implemented by an executive order specifying the margin of preference to be granted when the prices of a domestic and a foreign purchase are compared.[44] The United States is the only contracting party to the GATT to enact such obviously protective legislation. Few other governments have provided officials with explicit, numerical bench marks for determining when a purchase from foreign sources should be judged in the public interest.

Intercountry comparisons of the degree of protection for domestic suppliers of government purchases are complicated by the fact that a number of countries claiming not to give priority to domestic suppliers have no established procedure for insuring that qualified foreign suppliers are given an opportunity to submit bids. The guidelines in the executive order cited above have the merit at least of reducing the uncertainty faced by foreign suppliers. The executive order adopted in 1954 established as a general rule a 6 percent price margin in favor of domestic production and one of 12 percent in the case of goods produced in depressed areas or by small businesses. But, it also authorized the heads of government departments to exceed those margins if they decided that it was in the national interest to do so. Making use of this exception on the grounds that it was required as an aid to the US balance of payments, the Secretary of Defense instructed purchasing officials in the Defense Department to apply a 50 percent margin to purchases of materials to be used within the United States and, with certain exceptions, to "offshore purchases" as well. This decision came shortly before the passage of the Trade Expansion Act and the commencement of active preparations for the Kennedy Round. As will be seen later, "Buy American" became one of the first nontariff barriers to which the negotiators addressed themselves.

Antidumping Duties

Next to ASP, the nontariff barrier receiving the greatest attention during the Kennedy Round was that resulting from the administration of antidumping laws.

"Dumping," as the term is used in the GATT and in international agreements in general, is simply a special case of "differential pricing." Goods are said to be "dumped" in a foreign market if they are offered for sale at a price lower than that at which they are sold in the home market or in a third market. Except in the unreal world of perfect competition, it is often profitable for a business enterprise to sell its product at different prices in different markets. An enterprise that enjoys a monopoly in a market where the price elasticity of demand is low may be able to maximize its profits by a permanent policy of selling at above average cost in that market and below average cost in another where that elasticity is relatively high. Even firms that do not enjoy a complete monopoly in any market may find it worthwhile in selected markets to sell at below both marginal and average cost if goods that have already been produced would not otherwise be sold.

Most economists who have studied dumping agree that, except where it has the effect of stifling competition and is later succeeded by high monopoly prices, the country "victimized" by dumping is really its beneficiary.[45] Obviously, the receipt of dumped goods is likely to improve its international terms of trade. But the effect on a competing domestic firm can be destructive, and it is understandable that governments which insist on protecting individual domestic industries by means of tariffs will insist on the right to take counteraction against dumped exports that compete with domestic production.

The GATT endorses what was already a common governmental practice and permits contracting parties to impose "antidumping duties" against dumped imports equal to the margin of dumping, but only if they cause or threaten injury to a domestic industry or materially retard the establishment of such an industry. In Article VI of the GATT, dumped imports are defined as articles introduced into the commerce of an importing country at less than the comparable price charged for the like product in the exporting country or, in the absence of a domestic price with which the import price can be compared, if sold at less than the highest comparable price charged in a third country or at less than the cost of production. Finally, the GATT provides that, in making these price comparisons, due allowance be made for "differences in conditions of sale, differences in taxation, and other differences affecting price comparability."[46]

These rules, of course, open up endless opportunities for conflicting interpretations. How serious does injury need to be before it is considered "material"? Is a reduction in profits to be considered "injury"? If so, how should the blame be assigned among various possible causes? Is it legitimate to compare an end-of-season sale for export with a domestic sale at the height of the season? Can losses incurred by an individual firm be considered injury to the "domestic industry"? How inclusive is the term "industry" intended to be? Can export prices of one seller be compared with domestic sales by another in the country of export in order to determine whether differential pricing has occurred? If goods are offered at the market price prevailing in the importing country, should this be taken as proof that domestic producers have not been injured? These are only a few of the opportunities for disagreement, some of which might be resolved by a more detailed international code of antidumping practices and some of which could only be resolved by some procedure for international adjudication or arbitration.

But the most serious issues that have arisen in recent years over dumping and antidumping are related not so much to the actual imposition of antidumping duties as to the restrictive effect of administrative procedures pursued by an importing country in deciding whether or not to take antidumping action. Before the Kennedy Round the United States was the target of more complaints on this score than all the other contracting parties combined. This did not necessarily mean that US antidumping policy was more restrictive than that of other major trading countries. It could conceivably have meant that business firms in other countries engaged in export dumping more frequently than American firms: this hypothesis would not be inconsistent with the frequency of monopolies and cartels in some countries. It could also have stemmed, in part, from the fact that, during much of the postwar period, most countries except the United States and Canada resorted to the use of quantitative restrictions for balance of payments reasons and thus were able to counter dumping without the use of antidumping duties.

The most likely reason that the United States was the most frequent object of complaints in this field was the complex of cumbersome and time-consuming procedures imposed by American antidumping regulations until the end of the Kennedy Round. In fact, it would seem that foreign exporters actually suffered from the care exercised by the US Treasury and Tariff Commission to collect and weigh all the relevant facts before a finding of injurious dumping was reached.[47]

Foreign countries complained of the US practice of withholding customs "appraisement" of the imported goods until the case was finally settled. In many cases that settlement did not come for a year or more after importation. While the importer could obtain release of the imported goods by posting a bond, he could not know what the eventual "duty paid" cost would be.

Paradoxically, the fact that the majority of antidumping cases in the United States had been resolved in favor of the importer simply added to the complaints of foreign countries since it tended to support their charge that American procedures were put into motion before there was even a prima facie finding that injurious dumping had taken place. This impression was strengthened by the procedure followed under US regulations in existence before and during the Kennedy Round. The most controversial of these was the practice of conducting two independent investigations in each case: one to determine whether the import involved sales "at less than fair value" and one to determine whether imports involving such sales were injurious to a domestic industry. The second investigation was begun by the US Tariff Commission only after the first had been completed by the Treasury Department. As a result, months often elapsed after the withholding of appraisement before any attention was given to the question of injury, and more months passed before a final decision was reached. This problem became the central theme in the negotiation of an Antidumping Code in the Kennedy Round.

Between the end of World War II and the Kennedy Round, most other countries were much more sparing in the initiation of antidumping action than was the United States,[48] but American exporters have often complained that their trade was being harassed by unreasonable antidumping action by Canada. Under a law that was in effect before the GATT, and which was therefore exempted by the Protocol of Provisional Application, Canada assessed antidumping duties on products offered at below a "fair value," determined in advance, and it did not, as called for by the GATT provisions, require a finding of injury before assessing an antidumping duty.

Although American exporters had not encountered similar difficulties in Europe in recent years, there was, nevertheless, increasing concern during the Kennedy Round lest the possibilities for impeding imports through antidumping action might be increasingly exploited as tariffs were reduced. This fear was based, in part, on the belief that the GATT definition of dumping was broad enough to include pricing practices commonly followed by American exporters. Some degree of differential pricing between markets is fairly normal business practice in firms enjoying a measure of oligopoly. While these price differences are generally too small to justify significant antidumping duties, they could serve as a basis for harassment of normal trade. Before the Kennedy Round, the legally prescribed procedures of most European countries were typically less detailed than those of the United States and left more latitude for administrative discretion. While this tended to make for more expeditious handling, it also deprived the affected importer of some of the safeguards provided by US laws and regulations, such as an assured hearing and access to information submitted against him.

As the Kennedy Round opened, therefore, antidumping presented a promising field for fruitful negotiation — a field in which all parties stood to gain from the development of a code of uniform behavior by governments. Under such a code, it appeared possible that the practices of the US could be streamlined so as to reduce the uncertainties and delays experienced by foreign traders, and the procedures of other governments, particularly those of Western Europe and Canada, could be revised to safeguard exporters of other countries against future uncertainties.

Differential Application of Domestic Regulations

Many domestic laws or regulations that are essential for the protection of health, public security, safety, or industrial property rights have a nontariff barrier effect, usually unintentional, that arises out of the different conditions under which domestic and imported products are introduced into the market. Inspection at the border provides a more effective means of enforcement than usually exists within a country's territorial limits. This fact has, quite understandably, been exploited by governments. If one American firm infringes the trademark of another, the owner of the trademark must seek redress in the courts.. But US law places on the customs inspector the responsibility of denying entry to any foreign product that infringes a domestic copyright. If food produced in the United States fails to meet the standards imposed by domestic regulation, the violator may or may not be prosecuted. But, if an attempt is made to import substandard food, it can be confiscated at the border.

Often a genuine effort is made to equalize the treatment of domestic and imported goods, but complete equality is difficult to achieve. Officials of the US Department of Agriculture certify meat-packing plants abroad that meet US federal standards, but they can do so only when they are satisfied that the standards of the foreign country are sufficiently high and are fully enforced. The approach to equality in the enforcement of health and safety standards may yield, in time, to effort and to the establishment of mutual confidence among governments. In other cases, such as the US "Wine Gallon Assessment," the protective effect of the law is an anomaly that could easily be removed by legislative action.

Restrictive Business Practices

There are some areas of incidental trade barriers that arise simply out of government inaction. In one of these, that of private restrictive business practices, the United States is less subject to criticism than most other governments The American antitrust laws not only protect domestic producers against conspiracy in restraint of trade, but give the foreign exporter similar protection in the US market. But, in countries which do not share the American prejudice against cartels, American exporters can be effectively precluded from the market by agreements between a private monopoly and the available wholesale and retail outlets.

Disparate Standards

The inaction of governments is responsible for an even more elusive category of nontariff barrier. Through tradition and domestic laws, wide variations in standards of industrial measurement and design have developed. Anyone who has attempted to use an American electric shaver in Europe knows that it must be equipped with a built-in transformer to convert 220 volt or 180 volt current to 120 volts and a set of adapter plugs to fit the bewildering variety of wall outlets to be found in Great Britain and on the Continent. When and if uniform standards for electrical goods, for screw threads, and for the measurement of weights and distances should be adopted by all countries, the problem of selling in foreign markets will involve much less costly preparation and risk.

This summary of some of the more important nontariff barriers is far from complete. But it is probably sufficient to explain both why the Kennedy Round negotiators could not ignore the field and why any progress they might have made was bound to leave most of the field unplowed.

6

Trade of Less Developed Countries

Preparations for the Kennedy Round coincided with a developing crisis in economic relations between the developing and the developed parts of the world. The rising sense of frustration felt by the less developed countries in the pace of their progress found expression in mounting complaints against the wealthier countries and demands for positive action by them to narrow the gap in living standards between industrialized and unindustrialized countries.

These demands extended well beyond the realm of trade policy, covering, as they did, direct financial aid, supported commodity prices, stabilization of export proceeds, shipping policies, and loans at low interest rates. These issues were considered by a United Nations conference convened in Geneva from March 23 to June 16, 1964.[1] But the issues directly related to trade had been explored before. They had occupied much of the attention of the Contracting Parties for nearly ten years, a period that culminated in detailed consideration during the meeting of the GATT ministers in May 1964.

The GATT and Developing Countries

The original text of the General Agreement gave no explicit recognition to the special export problems of less developed countries. It will be remembered that, as an agreement intended to bridge the time until the International Trade Organization should come into being, the GATT was patterned in large part on the prewar bilateral trade agreements of the United States. It did, however, contain some important extensions of the traditional rules, extensions that reflected both postwar conditions and the special preoccupations of the founders. Among these, the less developed countries did obtain some recognition of their special needs in Article XVIII.[2] But that article contains no evidence that attention was devoted to a problem that has in recent years occupied the spotlight — the need to provide special stimuli for the exports of less developed countries.

Article XVIII did not single out less developed countries alone as its beneficiaries. The special facilities accorded to a contracting party in the interest of its economic development were paralleled by identical facilities for use by any contracting party engaged in postwar reconstruction. Such facilities were thus legally available not only to Brazil and Burma but also to France and the United Kingdom. Still under the influence of the tradition of reciprocal trade agreements, the drafters went to some lengths to avoid making any formal distinction between different classes of members. Article XVIII was, therefore, concerned exclusively with the circumstances that would justify a country — presumably underdeveloped or unreconstructed — in imposing import barriers not otherwise permitted under the agreement. In facilitating the use of measures to prevent imports from interfering with development plans, it reflected the prevailing fear, in Europe as well as in Asia and Latin America, of unrestrained competition with the United States.

When, a few months after the close of the Geneva conference, fifty-six countries met to agree on a charter for the ITO, this mistrust of competition persisted, especially among the greatly enlarged contingent of less developed countries. Now representing a majority of thirty-two, these countries insisted on, and obtained, many changes in the Geneva draft of the charter. But instead of using their influence to make it more difficult for developed countries to evade their commitments, they threw their weight in general with those developed countries that wished to weaken those commitments. Their opposition extended even to the most favored nation (MFN) clause, on which most of the benefits they could hope to derive from the GATT necessarily depended: "The most violent controversies at the conference and the most protracted ones were those evoked by issues raised in the name of economic development . . . The underdeveloped countries attacked the Geneva draft at several points. They challenged the commitment to negotiate for the reduction of tariffs. They objected to a provision which enabled parties to the GATT to determine whether this commitment had been fulfilled. They sought freedom to set up new preferential systems, impose import quotas, and employ other restrictive devices without prior approval. And they proposed that a semi-autonomous economic development committee be established within the trade organization for the purpose of facilitating these escapes."[3]

Tariff Negotiations

Given the GATT emphasis on the negotiation of reciprocal benefits, it is not difficult to understand why the less developed countries were skeptical of their ability to obtain worthwhile benefits from the GATT and why they concentrated their efforts on preserving the maximum freedom of action to protect their domestic markets against import competition. That such misgivings have persisted throughout most of the two ensuing decades requires explanation, however. In 1965 a spokesman for one of the largest of the less developed contracting parties, looking back over the record until then, said: "The developing countries of course had had no bargaining power, politically or economically. The rule of reciprocity has required them to give a matching concession, but clearly they were not in a position to give any. While over the last fifteen years, tariffs on industrial products of interest to industrial nations have been gradually brought down, those on products of interest to developing countries have remained at a high level."[4]

No one has made an empirical study of the extent to which the developed GATT countries have held their less developed partners to the principle of reciprocity in tariff negotiations. The sheer volume of labor that would be involved in a statistical analysis of the thousands of tariff concessions granted in the five GATT negotiating conferences before the Kennedy Round is sufficient to discourage the most ambitious student. But there are conceptual difficulties as well. A less developed country is the principal supplier of only a relatively small number of products, but in many cases one or more such countries have been substantial beneficiaries of tariff reductions negotiated between two developed countries. What weight should be given to these indirect concessions? Statistics will not show whether they entered into the tariff bargaining or were crumbs dropped accidentally from the table of the rich. Consider another problem. In the early GATT negotiations, especially, many less developed countries, now independent, were represented by the governments of their respective metropoles. The tariff concessions obtained on their behalf may have been extracted in exchange for concessions in the tariff of the colony or in exchange for a concession by the metropole itself. What sort of allowance should be made in the negotiating balance sheet for this sort of reciprocity? Most difficult to deal with is the fact that the perceived value of a tariff concession at the time it is negotiated involves judgments as to its probable effect on trade that are not subject to statistical measurement.

There are sufficient facts concerning one important negotiation, however, to make it possible to test the generalization that less developed countries did not receive significant benefits from the pre-Kennedy Round negotiations. In 1949 the US Tariff Commission published an analysis of the results of US tariff negotiations showing, for all "principal" dutiable articles (those imported into the United States in amounts of $500,000 or more in 1939), the tariff concessions granted by the United States both at Geneva in 1947 and in previous bilateral negotiations, together with the value of imports from the leading suppliers to the United States market.[5] If we designate as "less developed country items" all those articles of which a less developed country was the principal supplier to the United States or on which a tariff concession was negotiated directly with a less developed country, we find the following results. Of the 246 principal articles in the United States Tariff Classification (omitting preferential rates applied only to Cuba), 53 were of special interest to less developed countries. Of these, tariffs on 21 items, or 40 percent, were reduced at Geneva, and the tariffs on 14 items, or 26 percent of the total, were reduced by the full 50 percent permitted by the law.

Some of these reductions might be discounted on the grounds that they were of principal benefit to American processors of the raw material involved, such as manganese ore, bauxite, raw wool (of a type principally supplied by Uruguay), and zinc ores, though imports of a number of these directly competed with the output of domestic producers. But tariff reductions were also granted on processed products and simple manufactures, such as mica films and splittings, zinc metal, shelled Brazil nuts, burlaps, and jute bags. Geneva concessions included not only tariff reductions but the binding of reductions that had been granted to one or more countries in previous bilateral tariff negotiations. If these are included in the tally, 65 percent of the less developed country items were subjects of concessions.

Unfortunately, data concerning the results of later negotiations are not available in sufficient detail to permit a similar analysis of concessions on products of particular interest to less developed countries. But it is possible to trace the effects of those negotiations on the same products discussed above — those that were clearly of special interest to less developed countries in 1947. Of these 53 items, by 1966 the tariffs on 3 had been removed entirely, and those on 2 others had been temporarily suspended. The 1966 rates (ad valorem equivalents in the case of five items involving compound rates) represented reductions to below the 1948 level in 23 cases, of which 7 were reductions of more than 50 percent. The tariffs on 3 items had been increased by termination of an earlier bilateral trade agreement. It should be noted that some of the tariff changes included above resulted from the reclassification of the United States tariff and not from negotiations.

Even had they been more complete, these cuts would not of course have refuted the contention that the less developed countries lack tariff bargaining power. Given their poverty of bargaining power, however, the fact that substantial direct concessions were obtained suggests that concessions, at least by the United States, were granted to them without the requirement of strict reciprocity. This impression is strengthened by an analysis of the rather scanty facts available concerning the concessions they granted. The Tariff Commission study cited above reveals that less developed countries granted tariff concessions to the United States in 1947 on products of which their imports from that country were less than $14 million.[6] A precisely comparable figure for the other side of the bargain is not available. But, excluding products of which total US imports were less than $500,000, US concessions on products of which a less developed country was the principal supplier, together with concessions negotiated directly with a less developed country, involved more than $45 million of imports from those countries.[7]

Dispensations from the GATT Rules

The escape hatch in the GATT for "economic reconstruction and development" was never used by a developed country. Nor, with one notable exception, was it extensively used by less developed countries. The exception took place in 1949, when, following the procedures of Article XVIII, Ceylon applied for and was granted "releases" permitting it to impose quota limitations for specified periods on imports of a long list of simple manufactures under the provisions of its Industrial Products Act.[8] In response to further applications, these releases were later extended and supplemented to cover other products. In no case was a request by Ceylon denied by the Contracting Parties, though the representatives of that country obtained little pleasure from the laborious sessions in which successive working parties struggled to satisfy themselves that the criteria of Article XVIII had been met. Cuba, India, and Haiti also had recourse to the provisions of the original Article XVIII, though on a much less extensive scale than Ceylon. In 1949, in a single decision of the Contracting Parties, Cuba was granted the right to continue to restrict imports of certain cordage fibers, and India was permitted to maintain restrictions on the importation of grinding wheels.[9] In the same year Haiti was granted the right to continue to limit imports of tobacco and tobacco products by means of a state monopoly.[10] But the Haitian release was later judged by the Contracting Parties to have been unnecessary, on the ground that the restriction was required to enforce a domestic mixing regulation that was sanctioned by the GATT. The United Kingdom, too, applied for a release on behalf of its territory, Northern Rhodesia, but withdrew the application after encountering opposition on the ground that injury would accrue to the trade of another less developed territory, the Belgian Congo.[11]

In 1956 Article XVIII was amended to increase the ease with which it could be used for economic development and to eliminate the possibility of its application to postwar reconstruction. In addition to a new section that provided more lenient standards for the periodic "consultations" with less developed countries resorting to quantitative import restrictions for balance of payments reasons, the amended article liberalized the conditions under which protective measures might be imposed for purposes of economic development. But the only less developed countries to take advantage of this new dispensation were Ceylon and Cuba; moreover, these countries invoked the amended article only for the purpose of renewing or enlarging the coverage of measures that had previously been authorized by the Contracting Parties. And when, as has frequently been the case, a less developed country has found it expedient to apply an import restriction other than the quantitative limitations permitted for a country in balance of payments difficulties, it has usually proved not too difficult to obtain a waiver of its obligation by the required two-thirds of the Contracting Parties. Neither developed nor less developed countries have hesitated to seek waivers when needed, though requests by the former have often encountered stiff resistance. Of the 39 successful requests for waivers from 1949 to 1963, including extensions of earlier waivers, 24 involved dispensations granted directly or indirectly for the benefit of less developed countries. Most of the waivers granted directly to less developed countries were designed to permit the use of surcharges on imports for balance of payments reasons or the temporary increase of bound duties, pending renegotiation. The indirect waivers were in all cases granted to a developed country to permit the continued use of tariff preferences for the benefit of formerly dependent territories or territories for which it had assumed special responsibilities.

The Program for the Expansion of Trade

As early as 1954, and repeatedly in the next few years, annual progress reports prepared by the GATT secretariat had underlined the widening gap between the trade expansion of developed and less developed countries. In 1958, the Haberler Report, which confirmed the findings of the GATT secretariat, marked a turning point in GATT history.[12] This report did not find any general tendency toward discrimination against the exports of less developed countries per se, but it did identify many factors, including trade barriers and unfavorable price trends, that impeded the growth of the earnings of those countries from the export of foodstuffs and industrial raw materials, and it provided the impetus for a wide-ranging search for novel methods of improving those earnings. The first fruit of the Haberler Report was the decision of the Contracting Parties in November 1958 to launch a program directed toward an expansion of international trade and, *inter alia,* toward "maintaining and expanding the export earnings of the less developed countries."[13]

The GATT program that was launched by this report included: analysis of the development plans of individual countries in order to help channel development efforts into products for which export prospects were favorable; establishment of a trade information and advisory service; and technical assistance in market development and export trade promotion. Most important of all, the Contracting Parties also initiated a program, pursued with moderate success, that was aimed at the unilateral reduction, by developed GATT countries, of their barriers to the importation of products of less developed countries, with special emphasis on tropical products.

The Haberler Report thus introduced a radical change in the status of the less developed members of the GATT. The benefits they were to derive from their participation were no longer assumed to depend on what they were able to offer in return. Their wealthier partners had tacitly abandoned the expectation of reciprocity in favor of a sense of unilateral obligation. But such results as followed in the ensuing period of mutual exhortation and voluntary action by developed countries served only to increase the expectations of the poor countries and to give rise to demands that voluntary action be replaced by the assumption of contractual commitments.

Beginning with the GATT ministerial meeting in the fall of 1961, the Contracting Parties were occupied with the effort to reach agreement on a new set of GATT provisions that would formalize and institutionalize the movement to expand the exports of the less developed members. This movement reached a climax in

1964 when the Contracting Parties wrote into the agreement a new section (Part IV), which entered into force in 1966.

The new Part IV of the GATT was essentially a qualified, and at some points emasculated, version of a set of provisions submitted by the less developed contracting parties themselves to the drafting committee,[14] which preceded the November 1964 meeting of the Contracting Parties. Among these were demands that the developed countries bind themselves not to increase any barrier to the import of products of particular interest to less developed countries. Instead, they should "take immediate steps" for the reduction and elimination of such barriers; take similar action concerning internal taxes that impeded consumption of those products; eliminate differentials between low tariffs on raw materials and higher tariffs on processed products; "take full account of the need" to improve the prices of products exported by less developed countries in relation to the prices of products imported by them; give priority in tariff negotiations to reducing tariffs on products of interest to the less developed countries without reciprocal action on their part; grant less developed countries tariff preferences on imports of manufactured products; and stabilize the prices of primary products "at remunerative levels" through international commodity arrangements.

As the agreed text emerged, most, though not all, of these proposals survived, but in qualified form. Developed countries committed themselves not to increase existing import barriers or internal taxes affecting imports from less developed countries "except when compelling reasons" necessitated such action. They also agreed to "accord high priority" to reducing these barriers and tariff differentials between raw materials and processed goods. They agreed to procedures calling for reports, complaints, and confrontation of individual contracting parties in order to make these commitments as effective as possible.[15] They also accepted as a contractual commitment the pledge they had made earlier, in a ministerial resolution, whereby they would not expect reciprocity from less developed countries in tariff negotiations.[16]

Preferences

One of the more insistent demands that remained unsatisfied was that the developed Contracting Parties grant preferential tariff treatment to imports from less developed countries. This issue not only separated the developed from the less developed countries; it also created divisions within both camps. Most of the former, with a few exceptions, including the United States, declared that they agreed with the idea of preferences "in principle." But the majority held widely differing views as to the conditions under which preferences should be granted. Although the less developed countries presented a united front in their demands for preferences, a fundamental conflict of interest among them persisted in private. The African countries enjoying preferential access to EEC markets were aware that they would probably lose exports if the preferences they enjoyed were extended to all less developed countries. More generally, there was a divergence of outlook among less developed countries, depending upon their relative size and on the stage they had already reached in the development of manufacturing industries. The least industrialized among them saw little likelihood that they would gain from generalized preferences under which they would have to compete on equal terms with, for example, India or Brazil.

The failure of the less developed countries to obtain the agreement of the developed countries in 1964 did not end their campaign for preferences. It did, however, ensure that the rules under which the Kennedy Round was to be negotiated would still require the generalization of tariff concessions to all contracting parties.

Effective Tariff Rates

It was noted above that, when Part IV of the GATT was negotiated, one of the demands made by the less developed countries was that the developed contracting parties reduce the "differentials" between their tariffs on raw materials and processed goods. More explicitly, they asked that the tariff structures of developed countries be realigned so as to remove an artificial obstacle to the initial processing of raw materials in the exporting countries. And in back of this demand lay a doctrine that had already received some attention under the GATT program of action: namely, that the tariff pattern typical of most developed countries — low tariff rates on raw materials and progressively higher rates at later stages of processing — can result in "effective tariff rates" on processed products that are higher, sometimes a great deal higher, than the protection suggested by nominal tariff rates.[17]

To take the simplest example of the effect of tariff differentials, assume that a raw material not produced in the country of import is admitted free of duty and that the same material, after a simple stage of processing, bears a nominal duty of 20 percent ad valorem. Then, the entire amount of that duty serves as protection to the domestic processing industry. If the value added by processing is half the value of the processed product, the "effective rate" of tariff protection to the domestic processing industry will be 40 percent. If the value added is only one-fifth of the product value, the effective rate will be 100 percent.

The tariff rate on the product of the processing of a raw material imported free of duty is a special and simple case of a more general formula for determining the influence of tariff structure on the effective rate of protection afforded by a nominal tariff rate. For a difference between the nominal rate and the effective rate to exist, it is not necessary that material inputs be admitted free of duty. If the duty on imported inputs is lower than the nominal rate of duty on the final product, the latter, when applied against the value added in processing, will yield a higher effective rate of protection to the processing industry than that indicated by the nominal rate.

In 1968, the secretariat of the GATT produced a study of the tariff structures of certain industrialized countries to serve as a basis for estimates of the "effective incidence" of duties on various copper products.[18] This study is relevant to the export problems of less developed countries because they provide a substantial part of world exports of copper ore, concentrates and mattes (59 percent in 1965), unrefined copper (91.3 percent), and refined copper (48.5 percent).[19] On the basis of the tariff rates that will be in force after the full Kennedy Round reductions have taken effect, the secretariat found that copper in its simple forms, through refined metal, will enter the EEC, the United Kingdom, and the United States either free of duty or at very low rates. In the same countries, the rates for such simple forms of processed copper as bars, rods, and wire range from an ad valorem equivalent of 7 to 13 percent. The secretariat found, however, that effective rates of protection for the domestic production of wire, to take a representative example, were 40 percent in the EEC and the United Kingdom and 37.5 percent in the United States.

Several students have attempted to estimate effective tariff rates for a broad range of manufactured products. Because published input-output data are rarely available at the level of individual tariff items, the results necessarily involve excessive aggregation, which limits their usefulness for some purposes. Nevertheless, the results do confirm the conclusion that was to be expected: that effective rates of protection for domestic processing and manufacturing are in most cases substantially higher than the corresponding nominal tariff rates.

In 1965, Bela Balassa estimated effective tariff rates of the United States, the United Kingdom, the EEC, and Japan in 1962 for a list of 36 product groups, covering the entire manufacturing sector except for food processing. The input-output coefficients for this study were based on the manufacturing pattern in Belgium and the Netherlands. The selections from Balassa's findings, given in Table 2, are incomplete but illustrative.

Table 2.   Estimated effective rates of protection for selected product groups in four developed countries, 1962 (percent).

Product	US	UK	EEC	Japan
Thread and yarn	31.8	27.9	3.6	1.4
Textile fabrics	50.6	42.2	44.4	48.8
Hosiery	48.7	49.7	41.3	60.8
Leather	25.7	34.3	18.3	59.0
Ingots and other primary steel forms	106.7	98.9	28.9	58.9
Bicycles and motorcycles	26.1	39.2	39.7	45.0

Source: Bela A. Balassa, "Tariff Protection in Industrial Countries: An Evaluation," *Journal of Political Economy*, LXXIII (Dec. 1965), Table I.

In 1966, Giorgio Basevi calculated effective rates for the United States, at the four-digit level of the Standard Industrial Trade Classification (SITC), by using the input-output data of the Census of

Manufactures for 1954 and 1958. Some samples of his findings for 1958 are given in Table 3.

Table 3.   Comparison of nominal and effective tariff rates in the United States for selected products, 1968 (percent).

SIC	Industry title	Nominal rate	Effective rate
2031	Canned seafood	13.6	28.4–33.5
2071	Confectionary products	16.5	25.6–30.8
2824	Synthetic rubber	10.0	15.7–20.2
3151-3152	Leather gloves and mittens	35.3	73.0–75.9
3333	Primary zinc	6.6	6.8– 8.3

Source: Giorgio Basevi, "The U. S. Tariff Structure: Estimates of Effective Rates of Protection of U. S. Industries and Industrial Labor," *Review of Economics and Statistics*, XLVIII (May 1966), pp. 147-160.

The concept of effective tariff rates is of much broader significance than simply its application to the trade of less developed countries. But the subject has come to be associated with that trade because a number of students have maintained not only that effective tariff protection against imports from less developed countries tends to be higher than nominal protection but that effective rates in general bear more heavily on imports from those countries than from developed countries.[20]

This conclusion has been based in part on Balassa's findings that effective tariff rates tend to be higher on consumer goods than on other categories of manufactures[21] and on the assumption, probably correct, that less developed countries are more likely to have a comparative advantage in the production of consumer goods than in other manufactures. But developed countries are the dominant exporters of the largest number of consumer goods. They would be the principal beneficiaries of an elimination of tariff differentials on an MFN basis.

The category in which the lowest effective rates occur is, of course, that of raw materials, in which the less developed countries as a whole have the greatest comparative advantage. Among the remaining categories, Balassa found the second lowest average effective rates to be in products involving an early stage of processing, including a number of products that are typical exports of less developed countries. The evidence supplied by these averages would seem to be at best inconclusive.

Johnson has also applied effective tariff rates estimated by Balassa and Basevi to two lists of products "of special interest to less developed countries."[22] Some very high effective rates are revealed. But here, too, the evidence does not seem to justify the conclusion. Because less developed countries are presently important exporters of comparatively few manufacturers, recourse has been had to lists of products in which those countries themselves, in the GATT and in the UNCTAD, have expressed a particular export interest. But these lists include many products of which developed countries are the dominant suppliers. One list, for example, includes metal manufactures, nonelectrical machinery, precision instruments, synthetic materials, and chemical products.

These considerations not only call into question the frequently expressed belief that the typical tariff structures of developed countries are peculiarly unfavorable to the exports of less developed countries; they also suggest that the benefit of the elimination of tariff differentials, even on the products in which those countries have expressed a special interest, may well accrue to developed more than to developing countries.

Potential Benefits to Less Developed Countries

The importance of the effective tariff rate concept to the trade prospects of less developed countries is its demonstration that protection against many of the exports of those countries, and against the exports of developed countries as well, is higher than is suggested by nominal tariff rates alone. But efforts to apply it as a more precise guide to policy formulation suffer not only from insufficiency in the data available but also from certain serious limitations in the general applicability of the formula that is universally used.

1. Neither nominal nor effective tariff rates tell the whole story of the obstacles that imports face in penetrating the market in competition with domestic production. The domestic producer may be, and in fact usually is, favored by lower transportation costs, proximity to his customers, consumer preferences, and so forth. Furthermore, the total restrictiveness of any tariff rate, nominal or effective, will depend on the elasticities of supply and demand

in the importing and exporting countries. Therefore a direct comparison cannot be made either of rates on different products in the same country or of rates on the same products in different countries. At best, the "effective tariff rate" can be said to measure the extent to which the domestic producer can be less efficient than would have been the case in the absence of the tariff and still compete in the domestic market against imports. For this purpose, however, an effective rate, where the necessary data are obtainable for application of the formula, does provide a more meaningful approximation to reality than the nominal rate.

2. The formula that is universally used in the calculation of effective tariff rates involves the assumption that the ratios between different material inputs and between them and the output remain constant even if tariffs are changed. This assumption, the validity of which will vary from case to case, decreases the likelihood that effective rates can be determined with the precision that would be needed if, for example, an effort were made to reduce effective rates to a predetermined level.

3. The formula assumes that the cost of each material input to the domestic producer is equal to its world price plus the rate of tariff on it. This relationship commonly does not exist. Often the material input will be available at the world price or even below it, regardless of tariff. One of the important inputs in steel manufacture is coking coal. The United States is an exporter, not an importer, of coking coal. If the United States were to impose a substantial duty on it, the formula would show a very much lower effective rate for steel ingots than the 106 percent estimated by Balassa, but the competitive position of a potential exporter of steel ingots to the United States would not be affected by the change. The imposition of a tariff on coking coal would represent surplus protection for a product that is not affected by import competition at any tariff level. This qualification in the application of the formula is required wherever the material inputs are subject to surplus protection. In that case, part or all of the tariff on those inputs is irrelevant to the measurement of the effective protection afforded to domestic processing or manufacture.

The extent to which the reduction of tariff protection, whether achieved by the elimination of tariff differentials or simply by a reduction in tariffs, could assist the exports of a less developed country will in part depend upon the availability to it of the necessary material and nonmaterial inputs. Again using steel as an example, if a less developed country has cheap iron ore but no coking coal and if the cost of importing the latter is prohibitive, a decrease in the effective rate for steel in foreign markets will not affect the composition of its exports.

The technological advantages of vertical integration in a developed country can also stand in the way of the practical benefits a less developed country could obtain from the reduction of effective tariff rates. An industry will sometimes find that the savings due to carrying a raw material through the various stages of processing and manufacture domestically more than offset any savings that might be made by importing a material in an advanced state of processing or semimanufacture.

With all these qualifications, however, there seems little doubt that some less developed countries would obtain substantial benefits if the tariff structures of industrialized countries were to be revamped so as to eliminate those artificial obstacles that now tend to make it more profitable for the former to export their indigenous raw materials than to export them in processed or manufactured form. The cases in which these benefits are most likely to accrue, at least in the short run, are those with which this discussion began: namely, those where the raw material inputs are presently exported in raw form by less developed countries to developed countries. In these cases the exporting country has proved that it can produce the needed raw materials at a price no higher than the world price. And, since processors or manufacturers in the importing country are currently purchasing the same material at no less than the world price plus the tariff, the formula for determining effective protection is most likely to be valid. If, in addition, the processing does not require sophisticated skills or a highly developed infrastructure, and if the cost advantages involved in shipping the product in processed form are not offset by the technological advantages of vertical integration in the importing country, the likelihood that the less developed country can increase its foreign earnings over those yielded by its present trade pattern seems to be good indeed.

One final factor must be taken into account in an appraisal of the benefits that could be derived from a restructuring of the tariffs of industrialized countries. Other things being equal, the cases in which the largest spread exists between nominal and effective rates, and therefore where the most dramatic reductions in the latter are possible, are those in which the potential increases in export earnings of the less developed countries are the smallest. For these are the cases in which the value added by processing is smallest in relation to the total value of the end product.

These considerations tend to confirm a conclusion that emerges from almost any examination of the problems faced by the less developed countries in expanding their exports: the difficulties are both formidable and varied. Some of the obstacles are the result, often accidental, of the trade policies of developed countries. Others can be removed only by fundamental changes in capital flows and in the domestic economic, social, and political structures of the less developed countries themselves. No single approach will succeed, but neither should any promising avenue be abandoned simply because it alone is inadequate.

Part Two: The Climate

7

The United States and the EEC:
The Trade Expansion Act of 1962

In one way or another, all of the developments that combined, in mid-1961, to create an unprecedented demand in the United States for new initiatives in the trade field involved the rapidly changing scene in Western Europe. During the first three years of its existence the European Common Market had achieved spectacular successes, which coincided with economic frustrations in the United States. While the members of the new economic bloc in Europe had accumulated gold and foreign exchange, the United States had been steadily losing gold and increasing its liquid liabilities to foreigners. At the same time, the remarkable acceleration of economic growth and investment in Europe contrasted sharply with relative stagnation at home.

Unaccustomed to a passive role in world economic events, Americans were nearly all united on one theme: something should be done. If, it was thought, the growing market in Europe could be made more accessible to outside competition, the disappointing performance of American exports could be corrected. But this would require a vigorous initiative on the part of the United States, since what information there was about the evolving external policies of the Community was not encouraging. Then, at the end of

July 1961, Prime Minister Macmillan announced in the House of Commons that Her Majesty's government would seek membership in the Common Market. This step promised to intensify both the dangers and the opportunities inherent in the resurgence of Europe.[1]

The adverse trend in the United States' balance of international payments had begun long before 1961, though it had attracted little public attention. But complacency had been shattered by the quickening loss of gold—the depletion of the hoard in Fort Knox that had for a generation been, for Americans, a symbol of their invulnerability. In the three years preceding John F. Kennedy's election (1958-1960), the United States had lost $4.7 billion in gold, or almost three times as much as in the previous seven years.[2] This was not an auspicious climate in which to begin an administration. It must have been clear to the new President that his most ambitious plans for exercising American leadership in the world would have to be weighed against their potential effect on the US balance of payments.

The contrast with the position of the EEC added to Washington's concern. The treaty creating the Community had gone into effect in January 1958. In the next three years the six, collectively, increased their reserves by over $6.5 billion.[3] During this time, the member states exerted a strong attraction for foreign capital and outstripped the US rate of economic growth by more than two to one, as measured by Gross National Product.

It almost seemed that the European Economic Community had skipped the stage of infancy and begun life as a healthy adolescent, threatening to outgrow its elders before it came of age.[4] It is true that some of the essential features of maturity were still missing, such as a common agricultural policy without which not even a customs union, much less a full economic union, could be achieved. But in mid-1961 there was little serious doubt, at least in Washington, that the members would succeed in reaching the compromise necessary to bring agriculture within the Community framework. The apparent confidence of the member states in their ability to complete their integration had been demonstrated in December 1960 when they had, six months ahead of schedule, unanimously agreed to make a further reduction of 10 percent in their remaining tariffs on imports from within the Community. At the same time they had agreed to a further acceleration that would bring the elimination of internal tariffs to the halfway point by July 1962—a full two and a half years ahead of the timetable specified in the Treaty of Rome.[5] There were, therefore, persuasive reasons to believe that the Community had acquired a momentum that would surmount any remaining obstacles.

If the state of the American domestic economy had been more encouraging, the sight of the Common Market soaring into orbit could only have been interpreted as proof of the success of American policy. The creation of a Europe able to stand on its own feet had been the purpose of the Marshall Plan. The same goal, together with the desire to tie Germany to its Western neighbors, had led the United States to shield the Community, during its infancy, from any breeze that might retard its growth. Washington had opposed the efforts of European outsiders to broaden the area of the Community, for fear that its progress toward full integration would suffer.[6] And, when some members of the GATT had questioned the conformity of the Treaty of Rome to the provisions of the General Agreement, the American delegation had given its support to the Community's refusal to submit to the procedures proposed.[7]

The Kennedy administration continued to lend sympathetic support to the EEC, but it is apparent from later developments that the speed with which the six were developing their muscles had aroused anxiety lest this newly emerging force the United States had helped to create might weaken the Western alliance as a whole. This was a likely outcome should the six fail to pursue the liberal trade policy toward the outside world that had been proclaimed in their treaty[8] and promised by their spokesmen.[9]

By early 1961 any doubt as to where the US interest lay had been resolved by the gold loss and the apparently irreversible progress of the Common Market. In his balance of payments message of February 6, President Kennedy therefore stressed the need to increase American exports and to lower the trade barriers maintained by others. He also promised to use the tariff negotiations then being conducted in the GATT to obtain "the fullest possible measure of tariff reduction by foreign countries."[10]

Some unpalatable facts emerged during those negotiations, and they were to play a significant part in the policy decisions of the first few months of the new administration. For one, the negotiating tactics of the Community, which was, for the first time, represented by the European Commission, had dispelled any hope that the commission would prove more "outward looking" than the individual member states from which it had received its mandate. Related to this lesson was the even more important one that the bargaining authority with which the US delegation was equipped (a maximum tariff reduction of 20 percent, further curtailed by "peril points") was woefully inadequate to the task of opening up the Community's markets.[11]

It will be recalled that, for the United States, the double goal of the 1960-1961 round of negotiations was to obtain tariff bindings from the Community equal in value to the former bindings of the member states and, in addition, to achieve a substantial reduction in the Common External Tariff. It had originally been intended that negotiations concerning the first of these objectives would be concluded before talks on the second began, but this proved to be impossible. The United States was unable to reach agreement with the Community concerning compensation for the tariff bindings withdrawn by the six until it had also concluded the second phase, known as the Dillon Round.

The most serious problem that arose in the first phase—the "XXIV: 6 Negotiations"—involved agricultural imports. The six had not yet agreed among themselves on the Common Agricultural Policy (CAP) foreseen for the more basic products such as grains, meats, and dairy items. They declined, therefore, to bind any tariff rates on about one-third of their agricultural imports from the United States, thereby keeping their hands free to pursue whatevery future policy they might decide to adopt. Thus, in early 1961 the US administration had solid reason to suspect that some unpleasant surprises lay ahead, especially for American agricultural exports. President Kennedy expressed this concern to Walter Hallstein, president of the European Economic Commission, when they met in Washington in May, four months after the President's balance of payments message. While the details of their interview were not made public, the communiqué issued at the close of the meeting confirmed in diplomatic language the impression that

Kennedy had referred to the problems that would be raised for the United States and the alliance by a protectionist policy on the part of the Community.[12]

This was the stage onto which Great Britain stepped as a new actor at the end of July. There were other actors in the wings. The smaller EFTA countries had been even more concerned than Great Britain over the commercial division of Europe; British accession was expected to be followed promptly by the accession of Denmark and Norway and by some form of association for the EFTA neutrals.[13] Thus, the prospect was not simply for a community enlarged by one but for a single market in most of Western Europe. Washington could hardly have been surprised at the British move. The subject must have been discussed when Undersecretary Ball visited London in March 1961 and again in the following month when Prime Minister Macmillan met with President Kennedy in Palm Beach.[14] At any rate, when the news was out, the American administration gave emphatic support to British accession.

Clearly, an expansion of the European Community carried some economic risks for the United States. An enlarged Community meant a greater area of preferential treatment, to the disadvantage of US exports, at least in the short run. But there were potential economic advantages as well. When the United Kingdom took its seat in the council of the Community, there was a good chance that it would cast its weight on the side of a liberal trading policy. It was generally accepted that Germany and the Netherlands favored maximum trade with the outside world. They also had shown themselves most anxious to welcome the United Kingdom as a partner. The three together, it was thought, would wield decisive power in Community deliberations. And if a genuinely liberal approach to external trade were adopted, the resulting reductions in the level of protection against outsiders might more than offset the additional trade preferences to be created between Britain and its EEC partners.

The political reasons for welcoming the British initiative were, however, probably decisive. The smaller members of EFTA had tried to forestall what they feared would be a serious division of Europe by proposing some form of tariff accommodation between EFTA and the EEC. The United States, which had greeted the creation of EFTA "with a coolness that for a time verged on hostility,"[15] supported the successful efforts of the EEC commission to block this move. At the time, the American intervention was attributed to concern over the effect of increased discrimination on the US balance of payments.[16] This concern would also have provided a reason for opposing an enlargement of the Common Market by accession. But accession would have avoided features which had turned Washington policymakers against both EFTA and proposals for incorporating EEC within a Europe-wide free-trade area. Because EFTA had been created as a reaction to the formation of the Common Market, it was regarded, not entirely rationally, as a threat to the successful integration of the six. A similar lack of confidence in the survival power of the EEC was presumably responsible for part of the opposition to bridge building between the EEC and EFTA, though that hostility was compounded by fears lest a union that included the neutrals would threaten the survival of NATO. To policymakers already disposed to support a common market, enlargement of the EEC seemed to avoid these causes for concern and to have the added advantage of bringing about the end of EFTA. Finally, American support for accession could have erased the resentment which had, at least in Great Britain, Denmark, and Norway, resulted from active American opposition to their "bridge building" efforts.[17]

It was true that the accession of the United Kingdom, Denmark, and Norway to the Common Market would leave the neutrals, Sweden, Switzerland, and Austria, further out in the cold than before. This had its potential dangers. Even though they could not contribute directly to the alliance, it was undesirable to leave them as prey to seduction by Eastern Europe. But, if the Kennedy administration weighed this risk, it evidently felt that the danger would be reduced by a successful Kennedy Round and that it was not so serious as to offset the advantages of British entry into the Community.

Although abortive, the British application for membership served one purpose that did produce lasting results. It provided an ideal background for the President's request for new powers in the trade field. Without this new element, it would have been difficult for President Kennedy to inject into his request to Congress the necessary sense of urgency, at least while the outcome of the Dillon Round was uncertain. With the prospect of a greatly enlarged

Community, however, the administration could present a compelling argument for asking for power to take new and more heroic measures before it was too late.

The Campaign for New Trade Legislation

The inadequacy of existing negotiating powers to cope with the situation developing in Europe had been clear to the new administration even before it had taken office. Shortly before his inauguration John Kennedy had received a detailed plan for dealing with the problem. It had been prepared by a quasi-official task force hastily organized under George Ball, who was to become his Undersecretary of State for Economic Affairs. Reporting much later in the *New York Times,* Felix Belair provided a description of this report that accurately forecast many of the features in the administration bill presented to Congress in January 1962.[18] Significantly, however, Belair's account did not include certain provisions which, in the administration bill, were most closely linked with the prospects for an enlarged European community.[19] These features were apparently added later, in light of the British bid for accession.

A little more than two months after Macmillan's announcement of the British decision, an intensive and skillfully managed campaign was launched, culminating in the passage of the Trade Expansion Act of 1962.[20] The opening gun was fired not from the White House but from the other end of Pennsylvania Avenue. On October 6, 1961, after returning from a tour of Europe, Representative Hale Boggs, a supporter of the administration, told the press that a simple extension of the existing trade agreements legislation, due to expire in June 1962, would be "grossly ineffective in dealing with the common economic front of Western Europe."[21]

On November 1, two more balloons were launched in circumstances that ensured front-page treatment. Speaking before the forty-eighth meeting of the National Foreign Trade Council, George Ball emphasized the need for new negotiating authority "sufficiently broad in scope to meet the opportunity and challenge of the European Economic Community." Nor was increased authority enough. The President should have the right to negotiate in ways that departed radically from "the traditional form . . . We can no longer afford to limit our negotiations to trading on an item-by-item basis."[22]

On the same day, the press carried news of a report by Christian A. Herter, Secretary of State under President Eisenhower, and Will Clayton, who had been President Truman's Undersecretary of State for Economic Affairs. In their report, the two former statesmen formulated a creed that was to be heard repeatedly in the ensuing crusade. "We believe that the United States must *form a partnership* with the European Common Market and take the leadership in expanding a free world economic community."[23]

On November 8, the major offensive began with a news conference by President Kennedy. Having outlined the need for action in the tariff field, he added: "My judgment is that the time to begin is now . . . One third of our trade generally is in Western Europe, and if the United States should be denied that market we will either find a flight of capital from this country to construct factories within that wall, or we will find ourselves in serious economic trouble." Again, "the people of this country must realize that the Common Market is going to present us with major economic challenges and, I hope, opportunities." Finally, he made it clear that he had no intention of waiting for the conclusion of the Dillon Round before coming to Congress for new and more powerful bargaining weapons; he would present his request in January 1962.[24]

The terms in which the choices open to the United States were presented in these preliminary sallies created some confusion as to what was meant by "partnership" and whether it implied more than friendly competition. In an address to the National Association of Manufacturers on December 6, President Kennedy made an effort to clarify his administration's intent. New authority was requested because: "a trade policy adequate to deal with a large number of small states is no longer adequate. The EEC cannot bargain effectively on an item by item basis. I am not proposing, nor is it either necessary or desirable, that we join the Common Market, alter our concepts of political sovereignty, establish a 'rich man's' trading community, abandon our traditional most-favored-nation policy, create an Atlantic free trade area, or impair in any way our close economic ties with Canada, Japan and the rest of the free world."[25] Not until the following month did the administration reveal just how it proposed to avoid the more damaging consequences of an exclusive free-trade block within Europe without departing from these engagements. But in his speech on December 6 the President gave more content to what had up to then been envisaged as quite a modest partnership: "What I am proposing is a joint step on both sides of the Atlantic, aimed at benefiting not only the exporters of the countries concerned but the economies of the free world. Led by the two great common markets of the Atlantic, trade barriers in all the industrial nations must be brought down."

Traditionally, in tariff matters the legislative machinery begins to turn with hearings before the Ways and Means Committee of the House of Representatives. Formal congressional examination of the bill that was to become the Trade Expansion Act followed the normal pattern. But more than a month before the administrations proposals had been submitted to the Congress, Representative Boggs and the influential subcommittee he headed were already playing a role in the campaign of education and persuasion.[26] The subcommittee opened its public hearings on December 4, 1961, with statements by Governor Herter and Mr. Clayton. It then heard a succession of witnesses, almost all favorable to the general approach of the Kennedy administration, though there were substantial differences in emphasis and some disagreements over detail. Chairman Boggs was able to bring out a rounded picture of the views of those who favored vigorous action in the trade field. But he also obtained the pungent opposition testimony of Mr. O. R. Strackbein who, as president of the Nation-wide Committee of Industry, Agriculture and Labor on Import-Export Policy, was presumably able to represent all interests opposed to tariff negotiations.[27]

The Administration Bill

The hearings before the Ways and Means Committee were based on a draft bill submitted by President Kennedy, together with an explanatory letter dated January 25, 1962.[28] The features of the bill most relevant to the key issues that arose during the hearings and in the Kennedy Round itself can be briefly summarized as follows:[29]

Summary of HR 9900

A. Delegation of negotiating authority to the president:
  1. General authority:
     a. To reduce existing tariffs by 50 percent from existing levels, reductions to be staged over five years;
     b. To reduce to zero existing tariffs of 5 percent or less, ad valorem equivalent.
  2. Authority tied to an agreement with the EEC:
     In an agreement with the EEC: (a) to reduce to zero the duty on any category of articles in which the United States and EEC (including new members, if any) together supplied 80 percent of world trade; (b) to reduce to zero the tariff on any agricultural commodity or product if this would tend to maintain or expand US exports of the same commodity or product; (c) to reduce to zero the tariff on any tropical product not produced in significant quantity in the US, if the EEC should take comparable action on a nondiscriminatory basis.
B. Limitations
  In addition to the normal provision for public notice and public hearings before negotiations, a stipulation that the president should reserve from negotiation products subject to current escape clause or "national security" actions.
C. Adjustment assistance
  Elaborate provisions for assisting industries or workers injured by increased imports resulting from tariff reductions.
D. Extraordinary assistance
  The counterpart of the traditional escape clause, providing for withdrawal of tariff concessions (that is, restoration of tariffs to higher levels) resulting in increased imports which cause or threaten serious injury. Frivolous utilization of this provision was discouraged both by a tightening of the definition of injury and the requirement of a prior finding that adjustment assistance would be inadequate to redress the injury.

It will be noted that these legislative proposals omitted a peril point procedure. President Kennedy also attempted to free himself from negotiating precedents established in previous rounds. In his message to Congress, he said: "It would be our intention to employ a variety of techniques in exercising this authority, including

negotiations on broad categories or sub-categories of products."
And "the traditional technique of trading one brick at a time off
our respective tariff walls will not suffice to assure American farm
and factory exports the kind of access to the European market
which they must have . . . We must talk instead of trading whole
layers at a time . . . as the Europeans have been doing in reducing
their internal tariffs, permitting the forces of competition to set
new trade patterns."[30] The old limitation to item-by-item bargaining was dead, so far as the legislative record was concerned. If it
should also prove possible to drive its ghost irrevocably from the
negotiating table, a new era in international commercial relations
could be said to have begun.

The request for authority to reduce certain tariffs without limitation went far beyond any previous authorization to reduce a
rate by more than 50 percent.[31] In favorable circumstances, the
sweeping delegations of power under the so-called "dominant
supplier" (or 80 percent) clause and that dealing with tropical and
agricultural products, could mean the total elimination of tariffs
over a significant range of US imports. The draft also reflected the
importance the administration attached to reaching an agreement
with the EEC, as each of these unique powers was contingent on
joint action with the Community. In the case of the provisions on
tropical and Temperate Zone agricultural products, the Community's cooperation could certainly not be taken for granted. The
kind of action required of the EEC in the case of the dominant supplier authority was not specified. But in the context of the rest of
the bill and the emphasis placed by administration witnesses on
"reciprocity," the Congress probably assumed that this authority
would not be used except where the Community should also agree
to reduce a tariff by more than 50 percent. Even in 1962, however,
there were good reasons to question whether the six would be
able to agree among themselves on tariff reductions of that depth
affecting an appreciable number of products.

What, then, was the rationale for the dominant supplier provision? The fact that 80 percent of world trade was conducted by the
United States and the EEC, taken together, did not, of course, ensure that the two areas would be equally competitive for the products in question. Since there was nothing in the formula to require
that both areas be on a net export basis, it seems clear that the pro-

vision was not designed primarily to avoid "injurious" competition with domestic producers. The only plausible rationale for the 80 percent provision was that it would have permitted deeper tariff cuts by the United States for the benefit of the EEC than the administration was prepared to make for the benefit of other negotiators; the percentage limitation would have ensured that unrequited benefits to third countries would be minimized. In fact, the provision was strongly reminiscent of efforts in the OEEC two years earlier to draw up a list of European commodities on which the EEC and EFTA could reduce tariffs without undue benefit to third countries entitled to most favorite nation treatment.[32] If used to the maximum, and reciprocated by the EEC, the authority could have resulted in a quasi free-trade area, limited in commodity coverage, without departure from MFN obligations. There was no public evidence at the time that such a result was desired by the policy makers of the Community. But the dominant supplier provision probably did serve one purpose: to bring to the support of the legislation many Americans who felt that the United States should share in some manner in the success of the Common Market without any real departure from its established policies.

The Congressional Hearings

The Ways and Means Committee began its hearings on the administration's bill on March 12, 1962. Whatever else the hearings may have accomplished, they made a significant contribution to the employment of printers and papermakers, for the published record ran to 4,233 pages. Some aspects of the proceedings before both the Boggs subcommittee and the Ways and Means Committee itself are worth recalling for the light they cast on the objectives of the administration and the attitudes of other participants, public and congressional.

The theme that appeared most frequently in the testimony of nongovernmental witnesses was the threat represented by a system of tariff preferences from the benefits of which American exports were to be excluded.[33] On the other hand, a number of witnesses welcomed the European economic explosion; they felt that it reminded the United States of its traditional faith in the therapeutic value of competition. One witness who appeared before the Boggs subcommittee called this "the most important single lesson from European experience."[34] This view also found expression in the report of the subcommittee: "Europe, through the Common Market, is rediscovering the benefits of a very old economic principle, namely, that rising productivity and increasing economic opportunities stem from an increasing specialization or division of labor — and from a wide area of competition to stimu· late the energies . . . of free enterprise."[35]

It had been a long time since the faithful had been presented with so convincing a miracle. A group of industrialized countries had undertaken the total elimination of tariff protection against each other's trade. And what had followed? A growth rate twice our own and an impressive increase in reserves. True, the relationship of cause and effect was not so simple. The upsurge in European economic growth had begun before the Community was formed. And other forces contributing to growth detracted from the clinical value of the European experience.[36] But the argument was persuasive enough to worry those who opposed the bill on protectionist grounds. One congressman saw this clearly and did his best to show that the glittering vision on the horizon was only a mirage: "I am amazed that all the testimony we have had before us has been with reference to the great economic and political strength of the European Common Market. I think that it is a false premise. I do not think it is a strong economic and political unit. It is my belief that in two years it will dissolve of its own weight. What are these agreements going to mean to Italy when the Fanfani government changes to a Communist government, which it will in the next twelve months? What is it going to do to Germany when it makes a deal with Russia . . . That will leave nothing but a heartbeat in France. When that man's heart quits beating, that country will go into the Communist orbit."[37]

But not all the opponents of the bill discounted the power of the Community. When Representative Keogh taxed Mr. Strackbein with merely updating the doom "that you predicted might have been reached 3 years ago, or 5 years ago, or 7 years ago," the president of the Nation-wide Committee of Industry, Agriculture, and Labor on Import-Export Policy joined the ranks of the admirers of European integration. "We have been able to bask in this country in great comfort because we had the know-how, we had the ingenuity, we had the great mass market. Now that day is gone. Europe is establishing a mass market. Those people . . . have bought our system and they are in full cry."[38]

Third Countries

Relations with the rest of the world were not completely over-looked in the hearings. They were treated as important, but at a far lower level of excitement and urgency. The Report of the Boggs subcommittee, for example, after discussing the pressing problem of trade with the EEC under the general rubric of "Trade Policy," introduced the discussion of the rest of the free world with the words, "Relations with Third Countries."[39] It is true that the President's message,[40] and much of the testimony of the government's star witnesses, made it clear that one of the important, though subordinate, purposes behind the administration's request for new authority was to permit the participation of other friendly countries in the fruits of the proposed tariff negotiations. Japan and the less developed countries were especially singled out as worthy beneficiaries. Canada sometimes received favorable mention.[41] But even here, much of the contribution of the negotiations to the trade of these "third" countries was to consist of their improved access to the market of the Community, brought about at least in part by a judicious use of the President's new power to bargain with the EEC. The "partnership" was to be between the US and Europe, but it was to benefit the world as a whole.

Agriculture

The problems of agriculture played a prominent part in the Ways and Means Committee hearings. Even more than in the case of industrial trade, European protectionism provided the principal theme. By the time the hearings opened, the general lines of the Community's Common Agricultural Policy had been revealed and they were not reassuring. At its marathon meeting from December 29, 1961, to January 14, 1962, the EEC council had surmounted its, up to that time, greatest crisis and had agreed on the framework of that policy, including the use of the variable levy.[42] That action led many witnesses and congressmen to demand that satisfactory access to Europe's agricultural markets be made a *sine qua non* for any commercial disarmament between the two great trading powers. During the hearings, all three of the national associations of agricultural producers supported the legislation in general, but both the Farm Bureau Federation and the Grange asked for amendments designed to deny benefits to the EEC should it unduly restrict agricultural imports.[43]

The spokesmen for particular agricultural interests were more blunt. Presaging the "chicken war" that was to erupt over a year later, the spokesman for the poultry industry saw in the Common Agricultural Policy "grossly unfair treatment." While supporting the bill, he asked that the President's bargaining kit be strengthened "by adding the same kind of tools and authorities which are threatened to be used against us" so that variable import levies would not be used against US agriculture "without effective counteraction being taken."[44]

The administration showed its own concern. The Secretary of Agriculture said, "we must try to make certain that any swap with them [the EEC] includes assurances that reasonable terms of access will be provided for our agricultural products."[45] And Mr. Ball assured the committee that the act was designed "to maintain the position of US farm products in the enormously important Western European market."[46] Spokesmen for the administration avoided too many commitments, including any commitment that agriculture would necessarily be treated in the same manner as industry. But some public witnesses were more explicit in predicting that if any dent were to be made in agricultural protection, techniques different from those applied to industrial products would have to be used. One witness foresaw some of the most difficult negotiating problems, if not their outcome, when he suggested that a coordination of national policies would be needed, not only at the level of international trade "but including domestic levels and patterns of production and marketing."[47]

Reciprocity

The diversity of view expressed or implied as to the meaning of "reciprocity" was as great as that which was later to develop in the Kennedy Round itself. There was, however, almost no dissent from one demand — namely, that reciprocity must be obtained. President Kennedy, in his speech to the American Association of Manufacturers, had said that he did not propose a unilateral reduction of trade barriers. In the hearings, most of the witnesses and congressmen who touched on the question of balancing concessions emphasized the necessity for obtaining reciprocity, especially from the EEC. An exception, however, was generally made for less developed countries. There appeared to be at least tacit agreement among all those who favored negotiations of any kind that the backward and newly emerging countries should receive substantial benefits but that they could not be expected to grant equivalent concessions in return.[48]

With this exception on behalf of the less developed countries, it is interesting to note that no witness, even from among those who considered that the reduction of American tariffs would have a directly beneficial effect on the American economy, contemplated the possibility of a grant of authority to the President to cut American tariffs in the absence of comparable action by others. In the years that had intervened since 1934, the concept of tariff reduction by bargaining had become so deeply entrenched that no witness mentioned the possibility of any other approach.

There was little effort by administration or other witnesses to define what they meant by reciprocity, but their concepts of an acceptable bargain were far from identical. Many witnesses, including some administration spokesmen and a number of independent experts, appear to have taken it for granted that "linear" tariff negotiations would necessarily involve equal percentage cuts by the participants, and they were satisfied, without further analysis, that this would produce a bargain fair to the United States and acceptable to the other participants. Some who started from the same premise, however, welcomed the linear approach because they believed it would increase American exports more than imports. The reasons varied. Believing that the EEC tariff was on the whole higher than that of the US, some concluded that equal percentage reductions would mean deeper absolute cuts in the former than the latter.[49]

Secretary of the Treasury Douglas Dillon arrived by a different route at the conclusion that the US trade balance would benefit from equal linear tariff reductions. Pointing out that the US had a positive balance in its trade with the EEC, he reasoned: "If tariffs on our exports and imports are reduced to a comparable extent, the neutral assumption would be that exports and imports would rise by the same percentage. As a result, the American trade surplus would become larger." He went on, however, to express his own belief that competitive conditions would for some time be such as to give the United States a greater advantage than was suggested by this simple mathematical demonstration.[50]

Rather curiously, no witness explicitly expressed a more cogent reason for believing that the United States could expect to achieve a net trade advantage from equal percentage tariff reductions, though this alone could explain the urgency with which new initiatives in the tariff field were being pressed. A reduction of the external tariff of the Community would not only reduce the level of protection afforded to domestic producers within each member state; it would also forestall a part of the preferential advantage the exporters of each member state were due to receive in the markets of other member states at the expense of outsiders. If we can assume that, in the absence of a customs union among the six, the United States would have been willing to trade equal percentage tariff cuts with each of the constituent states, the added advantage to be derived from reducing the margins of preference within such a union would make the bargain more than worthwhile. Jacob Viner made a related but different point during the hearings when he said that the US was entitled to receive more than equality from the negotiations because the creation of a Common Market had placed American exporters at a competitive disadvantage going beyond that which resulted from tariff protection by each member state. This, of course, amounts to an assertion that outside countries could expect compensation for the formation of a customs union even though it conformed to the criteria of the GATT. Whether or not the United States had a legal right to such compensation has never been established; it did, however, clearly lack the bargaining power with which to extract it. But the disadvantage Professor Viner had in mind would at least be mitigated by any reduction in the Common External Tariff of the Community.

A number of witnesses who talked about reciprocity believed that the United States should demand more than equality from its trading partners for a different reason: in order to obtain payment for what was believed to be short payment received in past negotiations or to offset the use by European countries of nontariff barriers, such as quantitative restrictions, which had nullified some earlier tariff concessions.[51]

One industry spokesman, who had been a public adviser to the American delegation to the Dillon Round, objected to equal percentage cuts on still different grounds: "this proposal made by the Common Market in the current GATT negotiations made for untold difficulties. The same percentage cuts on high tariffs as on low tariffs did not bring about the desired position of equitable reciprocity." In place of linear cuts, he proposed the adoption by the members of GATT of a maximum or ceiling tariff for all products — to which any higher rates would promptly be reduced — and a timetable for the progressive lowering of this ceiling until, by 1970, it should reach 5 percent ad valorem.[52]

This last proposal bore a family resemblance to a less systematic divergence from equal cuts espoused by many witnesses, namely, equalization, or "harmonization," of US and EEC tariff rates on the same products. Witnesses who advocated the elimination of rate disparities ran the gamut from those who simply proposed it as a desirable objective, to be achieved through the normal bargaining process,[53] to those who believed that the tariff of the EEC was generally much higher than that of the United States and that the United States had a right to expect unilateral reductions on the part of the EEC to eliminate this inequity. A popular comparison was between the 22 percent EEC tariff on automobiles and the US rate of 6.5 percent.[54] Similar disparities between US and EEC tariff rates on aluminum, photographic equipment, and shoes were invoked as evidence that a fair balance could be achieved only by unilateral European action to reduce or eliminate the unfortunate imbalance that had been allowed to develop through the complaisance or incompetence of American representatives in past negotiations.[55]

There is no way to be sure whether those American businessmen who believed in achieving reciprocity through equalization of tariff rates would have maintained their faith in that position had they realized that, in more cases than not, the shoe was on the other foot. Undersecretary Ball provided the committee with a list of products, including such important items as watches and woolen textiles, on which the US tariff was from twice to several times as high as that of the EEC.[56] But this testimony came too late in the hearings to influence many witnesses. It is likely that enlightenment came, if at all, a year later, when in May 1963, the United States was to react indignantly to the Community's proposal that the tariff bargain include the unrequited reduction of tariff disparities.

Consciously or unconsciously, concepts of reciprocity were adjusted either to harmonize with the proposed new form of tariff negotiations or with the objective of reducing the deficit in the American balance of payments. One of the more explicit expressions of the latter appeared in the following editorial submitted for the record during the Ways and Means Committee hearings: "Our negotiators will certainly be instructed to win more than they grant. If the program does not result in a greater dollar increase of our exports than our imports the whole program will be a failure, as the Administration obviously knows."[57] The congressional hearings must have made interesting reading for the Community's negotiators.

The Linear Approach

The formation of the Common Market did more than underline the need for new tariff initiatives. It gave impetus to the conviction of experts that tariff liberalization by formula was not only essential but practicable. As far back as 1958, Raymond Vernon, who was later to be a member of President-elect Kennedy's task force, had suggested the negotiation of agreements in which the participants would undertake to reach "some average goal in trade-barrier reduction, such as an overall average reduction of some stated percentage . . . As a practical matter, this is the most promising technique of tariff negotiation now at hand. And it is an approach that meshes well with the plans of the European Economic Community for the creation of a common external tariff applicable to the products of outside nations."[58]

When the administration proposed abandonment of the traditional item-by-item negotiation, it could not have foreseen the exact shape of the negotiating rules subsequently agreed upon in the GATT. A possibility that was considered likely at the time of the hearings followed the lines of Vernon's suggestion: an equal, av-

erage reduction in tariff levels, leaving each participant free to determine how this average was to be arrived at in its own case. A variation of this approach would have consisted of the application of the same technique within broad groups of products.[59]

Administration witnesses avoided a commitment to any one negotiating technique, but it appears either that their individual estimates of the techniques likely to be decided upon in the GATT were not identical or that the administration's views were modified during the course of the hearings. During the Boggs committee hearings, Undersecretary Ball had said that "this type of negotiation amounts to proposing uniform concessions of a certain percentage on much broader commodity groupings. It may mean negotiations on anything a country produces; it may mean negotiations on all industrial items defined in a particular manner."[60] During the Ways and Means Committee hearings, however, Secretary Dillon seemed to expect an equal percentage cut "across the board."[61] In the form in which the act was passed, no negotiating technique was favored; for the first time the President obtained complete freedom of action as to the techniques to be used. Except for the overriding but ambiguous pledge to obtain reciprocity, the legislative record freed him from the bonds of tradition and left him with maximum room to maneuver.

Whatever the differences of view concerning the kind of linear tariff reduction that might be desirable or feasible, there was virtual unanimity among witnesses that a radical departure from the item-by-item approach was essential. Many witnesses in the hearings believed that the very nature of the Community's institutions precluded their agreeing among themselves on an item-by-item list of offers or concessions.[62] As will be shown later, this argument had a substantial element of truth, and the failure of the negotiating plan to take it fully into account contributed toward some of the problems of the Kennedy Round. Many witnesses, however, rested their case on a simpler argument; they believed that Community spokesmen themselves had stipulated across-the-board tariff reductions as the only method they were willing to contemplate.[63]

In fact, before the House hearings were well under way, the European commission had formally stated not only that a linear negotiation was their strong preference but also, by implication, that it meant to them equal linear cuts: "It is a matter of special satisfaction that the President should have decided to ask Congress for fresh powers to enable him to negotiate tariff reductions on the across-the-board principle followed by the EEC. If the President obtains these powers, the proposed tariff negotiations between the Contracting Parties of the GATT should be able to advance more rapidly and effectively."[64]

The 20 percent across-the-board offer of the Community in the Dillon Round[65] had also been interpreted as confirmation of its determination to cut tariffs more deeply if others would join in a linear reduction.

As later became clear, the 20 percent "linear" offer by the EEC was shaky evidence upon which to base a conclusion that the Community was ready to employ the equal linear method in a negotiation for another and deeper cut in tariffs. Their offer had in fact not been fully "linear," but had involved substantial exceptions. More importantly, it was not a proposal to reduce the level already decided upon for the common external tariff, on which member states were committed to align their own tariffs, but rather an offer to bind a reduction already decided upon as a compromise among the six for internal reasons. But, whatever the limitations on the Community's will to carry this process further, the proponents of the linear approach were right in their belief that the difficulty the six would have in deciding on individual tariff offers would multiply the obstacles to a fruitful tariff negotiation under any form of item-by-item bargaining.

Other Issues

While the main debate in the congressional hearings naturally centered on the proposed delegation of powers to the President, a number of subordinate issues attracted their share of attention and generated their own heat. In any detailed history of the hearings, some of these topics would be entitled to fuller treatment than can be given here. Our purpose will be served, however, by the briefest reference to some of them.

Most favored nation treatment — There was almost no serious dissent from the administration's position that the closer rapprochement with Europe should be accomplished within the framework of the most favored nation clause; that is, without abandoning the traditional US policy of applying identical tariff rates to imports from all friendly countries. The only divergence that had important support was the proposal of many witnesses and some members of Congress that the President be authorized to discriminate against countries which denied US exports reasonable access to their markets.

Nontariff barriers – Related to the desire to equip the President with retaliatory weapons were complaints, registered by both supporters and opponents of the legislation, against quantitative restrictions or other "nontariff barriers" maintained by others, especially by member states of the European Community. As will be seen, the intense interest in these barriers found some reflection in the act as it finally emerged.

Adjustment assistance — No one topic excited more discussion than the novel provisions of the bill concerning assistance to business firms or labor groups injured by import competition. Supporters of the legislation saw in them a means of breaking away from the strictly negative escape clause and peril point procedures that had, over the years, diluted the bargaining power of American negotiators and belied American claims to commercial liberalism. For the same reason, opponents of the bill greeted adjustment assistance with suspicion and hostility. They attacked it as an invasion by government of the domain of free enterprise. To support an industry by protecting it from foreign competition was in the American tradition. To help it by more direct means was alien and intolerable: "The total abdication of Congressional controls and restraints . . . removes the last crutch [sic] of this and other fisheries and abandon us to the mercies of an influx of imports which sound the death knell of a vital . . . industry. The energy and individualism of those Americans who have developed a substantial domestic industry, under our American system of free enterprise, now faces the surrender of Congressional protection . . . H.R. 9900 says to him, 'after you are ruined, prove it, and some government bureau will retrain you.' What will they make of this rugged and independent man? Keep taking from America the spirit of these entrepreneurs and you move into a stifled, state-dominated society closer to the Russian model than that to which we are entitled by our heritage."[66]

The Senate Hearings

The hearings held by the Senate Finance Committee[67] three months after the close of the Ways and Means Committee marathon brought out little that was new. During the interval, some developments had cast doubt on one of the premises underlying the administration's legislative proposals. Public statements by both Chancellor Konrad Adenauer and President Charles de Gaulle had been interpreted as opposing British entry into the Common Market. Late in July, for example, a correspondent of the *New York Herald Tribune* wired from Brussels that the betting odds on British accession had been "reduced to 50-50."[68] The administration did not, however, consider it necessary to alter its approach. George Ball, recently returned from a trip to Europe, believed that the negotiations between Britain and the Community had already achieved a wide measure of agreement and that solutions could be found to the problems that remained.[69]

Senator Paul Douglas was less sanguine and referred to the "grave doubt" that Great Britain would accede to the Common Market. To him, this doubt suggested that the dominant supplier authority in the act, as then written, could easily become a dead letter. He pointed out that he and Representative Henry S. Reuss had been studying the problem and had learned that, if Britain were not included in the Common Market, the only item on the original list of products[70] that would still meet the 80 percent test was aircraft. They therefore proposed an amendment to preserve the dominant supplier authority, no matter what the outcome of the British effort, by permitting the trade of EFTA countries to be counted in arriving at the 80 percent mark, whether or not they should become EEC members. During the hearings, he asked Ball's endorsement of this change.

Ball opposed the Douglas proposal because he felt that it would be difficult to use the authority in a negotiation with several countries, as opposed to a single entity such as the EEC; any change in the legislation at so late a date could be interpreted as interference in the UK-EEC negotiations, or at least as an indication that the US had written off their chances of success; and opponents (presumably British) of accession could use the change to argue that there was an alternative presented to Britain that had not been available before.

The first of Ball's reasons could be interpreted to mean that the intention of the administration was to use the 80 percent authority only in cases where the EEC was prepared to take action comparable to that of the United States. The argument which may have had the most substance was the second; such a change might have implied a US judgment concerning the outcome of the negotiations. Senator Douglas, however, took particular issue with this point and suggested that the 80 percent provision in the administration bill had itself been designed to influence the prospects for British entry. But, whatever may have been its decisive reason, the administration did not change its position, and the dominant supplier authority remained in the bill without change.

The Act as Passed

After some difference between the two houses of Congress had been compromised in conference, the Congress passed the Trade Expansion Act of 1962 in a form that, in substance, granted virtually all the powers President Kennedy had requested.[72] Some of the amendments adopted strengthened the President's hand. Some imposed minor restraints. None were crippling.

The amendment which most affected the governmental negotiating machinery was the provision, concurred in by the President,[73] that required the appointment, with the advice and consent of the Senate, of a Special Representative for Trade Negotiations. The special representative was to take charge of the negotiations and chair the interagency organization that was to advise the President on the execution of the act. This change, while presumably giving some satisfaction to members of Congress who believed, or professed to believe, that the Department of State had misused its position as a coordinator and negotiator, took no authority away from the President. President Kennedy later demonstrated that the provision need not have a protectionist effect by appointing to the new post Christian Herter, who had supported the purposes of the bill from the outset and who had the courage to resist any efforts of special interest groups to divert him from achieving them. A less drastic change in the staffing pattern for negotiations, also specified in the act, was the requirement that the President include in each US negotiating delegation two members, of different political parties, from each house of Congress.

There were two respects in which the act did curtail authority that the original bill would have conferred on the President. The administration's draft had included a provision requiring that the President "reserve" from negotiations products that were currently the subject of presidential action under the escape clause provisions or national security provisions, either of the existing law or of the new act. To this limitation the Congress added a requirement that the President similarly reserve articles on which a majority of the Tariff Commission had previously found that imports were causing injury or threat of injury to a domestic industry and subsequently found that economic conditions in the industry had not substantially improved.[74]

The only other significant change that curtailed the President's authority was the restoration of the prohibition that had been included in all trade agreement legislation since 1951; it denied most favored nation treatment to countries "dominated or controlled by international Communism."[75] For most Communist countries this would merely have frozen the existing situation, but the legislative history made it unmistakable that the President would be required, after a decent interval, to introduce discrimination against Poland and Yugoslavia, with whom he was attempting to work out satisfactory trading relations.[76] The administration opposed this provsion, but did not obtain its removal from the act until December 1963.

Another amendment served to give vent to congressional frustration over the Common Market's variable levies on agricultural imports and the maintenance by foreign countries of nontariff barriers against American products. This amendment instructed the President to refrain from negotiating tariff reductions in order to obtain the removal of any "unjustifiable" restriction that impaired the value of tariff commitments received by the United States and authorized him to adopt discriminatory measures against a country or *instrumentality*[77] maintaining such restrictions penalizing American agricultural exports. It also authorized him *inter alia* to withdraw or withhold the benefit of trade agreement concessions in retaliation for nontariff barriers under certain circumstances. And it made clear the intent of Congress by referring in this connection to "variable import fees," which were at the heart of the Common Agricultural Policy already adopted by the European Economic Community.[78] However, since these provisions were made subject to the President's discretion, they cannot be counted among the changes that curtailed the authority he had requested.

Epilogue — The Elusive Partnership

Among all the arguments, slogans, and facts that the Kennedy administration relied upon to persuade the Congress to enact the Trade Expansion Act, the keystone was the need to maintain — or, alternatively, to create — a unique relationship with Western Europe. The terms "Atlantic partnership" and "special relationship" were prominent in much of the testimony in the Boggs Committee hearings.[79] They were still being used more than six months later in the Senate hearings.[80] It is not surprising that they led at least some members of Congress to assume that the administration had in mind an agreement with the European Community in which "third countries" would be assigned a less favored nation position. This interpretation was explicit in certain comments and puzzled questions by committee members.[81] And the pains to which spokesmen for the administration were put to explain what "partnership" did not mean, beginning with President Kennedy's speech to the National Association of Manufacturers,[82] suggests that the misunderstanding was widespread. That it was a misunderstanding, there can be no doubt. Nothing in any administration statement supports a departure from nondiscriminatory treatment of all friendly countries, in spite of the ambiguous connotations of the terms "partnership" and "special relationship." Nor would the administration bill, itself, have permitted such departure.

Under the circumstances, it may seem unnecessary to pursue further the question of what was not meant by "partnership," but it may be worthwhile to look more closely at the record to determine what kind of relationship with the EEC was actually visualized and what, if anything, passage of the act would do to facilitate it. Here, a reading of the hearings suggests that the role anticipated for the new legislation was less to provide a bridge across the Atlantic than to remove a barrier to closer consultation and cooperation with Europe, possibly in the OECD in Paris. What the act might have been designed to achieve in facilitating this cooperation was: first, to close the widening schism within Europe and between the two continents; second, to provide the United States with power to match that of the EEC in a concerted movement to free world trade for the benefit of all. It must also have been assumed, on the basis of the declarations of the Community spokesmen, that the six were ready, when the United States should be in a similar position, to join in such a drive.

8

The International Campaign:
From Harmony to "Chicken War"

While the Kennedy administration was occupied at home with its campaign to obtain unprecedented authority from Congress, it was also busy preparing the international stage for a new departure in tariff negotiations. Early meetings with its prospective negotiating partners were encouraging.

Preliminary Activity

Meeting of GATT Ministers, November 1961

The campaign for new trade legislation was, it will be recalled, launched in the fall of 1961. Some months earlier the Kennedy administration had begun laying the international foundations for utilization of the authority it was to request of Congress. At the May 1961 session of the GATT, the US delegation had proposed, and the Contracting Parties agreed, that the session scheduled for November of that year should be attended by ministers who would consider new approaches to trade expansion. This proposal was advanced and accepted on the grounds that the results of the Dillon Round, still in progress, would be wholly inadequate to meet the new situation created by the success of the Common Market.

By the time the GATT ministers met in Geneva that fall, the need for action had been underlined by the British negotiations for Common Market membership, but some of the elements needed for decisive action were still absent. Encumbered by the impotence of the American negotiators and the determination of the Community to keep its hands free to construct its common agricultural policy, the Dillon Round continued to drag on. The President of the United States had not yet made his legislative proposals to Congress. The ministers, however, made their contribution to the campaign for new legislation by adding an international voice to the rising chorus in favor of a new form of negotiation. They agreed that the traditional GATT techniques were "no longer adequate" to meet the changing conditions of world trade and that new devices, "in particular some form of linear tariff reductions," were required. They expressed "great concern" about the "degree and extent of agricultural protectionism and about widespread resort to non-tariff devices" impeding trade in agricultural products. To make a start toward the solution of the problem of farm products, they called for the formation of a group to study the possibility of bringing into a more ordered relationship the world-wide complex of tariffs, quotas, price supports, and subsidies that governed international trade in wheat. In this way, and in their decision to look later at the possibility of similar groups for other basic crops, they set in motion some of the machinery that was to function later as part of the Kennedy Round.[1]

The seeming harmony of the ministers' report correctly reflected the atmosphere of common purpose that prevailed among the highly industrialized members of the GATT. But, beneath its diplomatic language one could read the serious reservations of two other groups of countries: both the less developed countries and certain more advanced countries dependent on exports of agricultural or other primary materials contested the view that they could obtain a fair balance of advantage from participation in a linear reduction of tariffs. The less developed countries were especially motivated by fear of the import competition they would encounter if they were to join in a general razing of tariff walls. The primary exporters were both reluctant to expose their inefficient industries to more competition in their home markets and doubtful that tariff cuts by others, even if applied to all their exports, would greatly help their exports in the face of the nontariff barriers that weighed with special force on trade in agricultural products.[2] Canada, too, expressed reservations about its ability to participate in negotiations on a linear basis, primarily on the ground that its common border with the United States would make Canadian industries particularly vulnerable to drastic tariff reductions.

While the less developed countries failed to obtain the explicit guarantees they would have liked, they did achieve their biggest gain up to that time when the GATT ministers recognized that "a more flexible attitude should be taken with respect to the degree of reciprocity to be expected" from them.[3] They were less successful in their efforts to obtain general agreement to a draft declaration identical at many points with the joint proposals of the less developed countries that, three years later, were to form the basis for the new Part IV of the GATT.[4] These countries did, however, obtain acceptance of the declaration "as a basis for future work" and an undertaking that it would be observed "to the fullest extent possible." Although they obtained no assurance that they would receive the sweeping advantages they sought in the negotiations, the ministers' acceptance of the declaration did provide them with a set of standards around which they could rally in later meetings.

The more advanced raw material exporting countries—notably Australia, New Zealand, and South Africa—were, together with Canada, content at this stage simply to record their view that a linear tariff reduction would not give them "reciprocity." But, in spite of their dissent and the rising thunder from the side of the emerging nations, the meeting of the GATT ministers seemed to reveal a sufficient unity of purpose, at least among the industrialized countries surrounding the North Atlantic, to justify the Kennedy administration in its pursuit of new authority.

Declaration of the EEC Council, February 1962

Further support for President Kennedy's initiative came a few weeks later from the source that mattered the most—the European Economic Community. On February 6, 1962, the Council of Ministers of the EEC adopted a declaration concerning the President's legislative message to Congress which was obviously intended for foreign ears. On February 22 it was read to the Council of Representatives of the GATT by the commission's representative.[5]

The satisfaction Americans derived from the declaration hardly resulted from its tone. Within the limits of diplomatic nicety, the language was clearly critical. Thus the EEC council, "having taken cognizance of the statement by the [US] President . . . on 25 January 1962 . . . *and having been informed of the status of the [Dillon Round of] tariff negotiations taking place at Geneva,"* expressed the hope "that further progress will be made in the reduction of customs duties."[6] American representatives had no trouble understanding the meaning. It was merely a formal translation of the reproaches they had heard in private; if the US administration were not hamstrung by the constitutional separation of powers and by the niggardly grant of authority from Congress, it could match the 20 percent across-the-board tariff reduction offered by the Community, and the Dillon Round could take a worthwhile step in the direction of that sweeping liberalization of world trade that the Community ardently desired.

What was welcome in the EEC council's declaration was its almost explicit promise that, if the President could obtain the powers he was requesting, the Community would join in a linear negotiation and would match whatever the US could offer: "[The council] notes that . . . the CONTRACTING PARTIES . . . at their nineteenth session declared themselves in favor of new tariff negotiating techniques . . . [and] expresses the firm conviction that . . . the essential requirements for the effectiveness of any further multilateral endeavour undertaken in the future in the tariff field *is that all the parties concerned should have equivalent powers from the legal point of view."*[7] This official confirmation of the position that had been earlier taken informally by Common Market spokesmen helps to account for the confident statements of administration witnesses during the hearings that the Community was only willing to negotiate on a linear basis and that it had insisted that the United States equip itself for such an approach.

Formal Preparations Begin

During the spring and summer of 1962, further international preparations for the Kennedy Round were suspended, but passage of the Trade Expansion Act in the early fall led to a new surge of activity. In the autumn of 1962, the executive secretary of the GATT toured GATT capitals to test the temperature and found it favorable.[8] In October, a GATT working party was appointed to develop the details of a new negotiating plan.[9]

At the twentieth session of the GATT, in November 1962, the United States administration, armed with its new authority, proposed that, early in 1963, the Contracting Parties be convened again, at ministerial level, to make plans for a negotiating conference in 1964 and to provide directives necessary "to ensure the successful mounting and conclusion of a broad movement for the further liberalization of tariffs and trade."[10] Canada, perhaps in order to correct any false impressions created by its claim to special status in a linear negotiation, was a joint sponsor of the proposal.

The Contracting Parties accepted the US-Canadian initiative and selected May 16, 1963, as the date for a meeting at which GATT ministers would make final arrangements for the negotiations. They also appointed a Tariff Negotiations Working Party to prepare proposals for the conduct of the negotiations. This decision virtually ensured that negotiations would take place and that they would use new techniques. But there was a wide gap between the judgment of ministers that some form of linear approach should be considered and agreement on the precise techniques to be employed and negotiating rules to be followed. The issues outlined by the executive secretary for the working party to explore[11] may be reduced to the following:

1.   Should there be a uniform percentage reduction — which appeared to be the meaning attached to "linear" by the GATT ministers—or some other formula, such as equal average cuts by sectors? In either case, was there any further role for the concept of "reciprocity" that had governed all previous negotiations?

2.   Should the staging requirements of the Trade Expansion Act (cuts to be spread over five years) be applied by all participants or be taken as the outside time limit for giving effect to tariff reductions? Also, would the willingness of the United States to reduce certain rates by more than 50 percent be matched by others?

3.   On the assumption that cuts would be equilinear, should the inevitable exceptions[12] be limited by compiling a "common list" of exceptions to be used by all, or by the negotiation of individual lists?

4. Were any special rules needed in the case of agricultural products?[13]

5. What rules should apply to countries claiming that special difficulties would prevent their applying the linear approach to their own tariffs?

6. How much — or little — contribution would be expected from the less developed countries if they were to be considered participants?

7. Should countries be permitted to exclude an item from reductions when the "principal supplier" of the product was not a participant, without invoking an "exception"?

The first meeting of the working party, held in mid-December 1962, settled none of these questions, but it did avoid head-on collisions, especially among the highly industrialized countries. With the usual reservations from the less developed countries and "special problem" countries, it based its deliberations on the assumption that the negotiations would involve equal linear cuts across the board. Some of the prospective "linear" participants, including the United States, however, made it clear that they would have difficulty in applying the basic rule to products whose principal suppliers did not participate. This, of course, agitated the countries that had declined to participate on a linear basis and opened up a new field for disagreement—the definition of "participant."

It was disappointing, at least to the United States delegation, that the goal of a 50 percent linear reduction was accepted by the working party only as a basis for further discussion and not as a firm recommendation to the GATT ministers. And there was a foretaste of future troubles in the working party's failure to reach agreement that the percentage reduction should be the same for all linear participants, though at this stage deviation from that uniformity was proposed only by Switzerland and Sweden, two low-tariff countries

On a more nearly unanimous note, the working party tentatively rejected the notion of a common list of products to be excepted from the linear reduction because such a list would result in more exceptions by all participants than were required by any one of them. Its rejection was undoubtedly in the interest of maximum results, but the technique chosen in its stead was not necessarily the one best calculated to minimize exceptions. The US delegation had suggested that the exceptions lists of all participants be limited to a uniform maximum percentage of their total imports, and had tentatively proposed 10 percent as this maximum. That figure would have been large enough both to cover the mandatory withholdings required by the new US legislation and to leave a generous margin for other especially "sensitive" products. But it would also have been small enough to permit a very respectable result from the industrial negotiations. If tariffs on the 90 percent of trade not excepted were reduced by 50 percent, the overall average reduction on dutiable products would have been 45 percent. However, the US suggestion received little support in the working party; it leaned toward the submission by each participant of a list of "minimum" exceptions, which would then be subject to negotiation. There is, of course, no way of knowing on what percentage of permissible exceptions agreement might have been reached if the US suggestion had been accepted. Its negotiation would have been time consuming and difficult. But it might have proved less difficult than the negotiation of individual exceptions lists and would have avoided a practice that was destined to plague the negotiations and probably to diminish their results: the "padding" of exceptions lists for bargaining purposes.

The working party also managed to skirt the potentially divisive question of the scope of the forthcoming linear negotiations. The agricultural exporters, including the United States, reiterated their watch cry: that the negotiations must provide market access for agricultural products comparable wtih that anticipated for industrial products. But the differences between those exporters and the EEC, while vaguely discernible beneath the surface, did not break through until the working party's next meeting.

On the whole, this first attempt to convert the apparent harmony of the GATT ministers into a set of operating rules was moderately encouraging, but the questions left undecided provided ample material for future disagreements.

Storm Clouds

While comparative harmony dominated the multilateral preparations for the next assault on trade barriers, the Contracting Parties were concerned, as always, with the operation of their existing contract. Disputes over interpretation and compliance are part of the normal business of the GATT; in fact, they are the best evidence that its provisions are being taken seriously by the member governments. Normally, confrontations between plaintiff and respondent occupy the stage briefly and usually with due regard for decorum and the traditions of diplomacy. During the period of preparation for the Kennedy Round, however, several issues involving the principal actors in the forthcoming negotiations broke through the customary barriers of reticence and achieved a level of public attention not normally accorded to international differences over commercial policy. The behavior of the actors may or may not have been caused by the heightened tension that precedes a major battle, but these skirmishes did have their effect on the future attitudes of participants in the Kennedy Round.

"Carpets and Glass"

In March of 1962, for example, while the Congress was in the early stages of its consideration of the Trade Expansion Act, President Kennedy signed an executive order substantially increasing import duties, until then bound under the GATT, on certain types of wool carpets and glass.[14] A storm arose immediately. Before it had subsided, diplomatic notes had been exchanged and less diplomatic statements made to the press; the Belgian Parliament had passed a unanimous resolution calling on the American President to renounce his action; the American ambassador had flown home for consultation, and EEC commissioners had made ominous forecasts of the effect on the Kennedy Round.

President Kennedy's action was, of course, not without precedent. Nor was its legality under domestic law or international contract seriously challenged. Domestically his action rested on the "escape clause" in the Trade Agreements Extension Act. Internationally, his right to withdraw a tariff binding from the US schedule agreed to under the GATT rested on the provisions of Article XIX of that instrument. Article XIX, however, also contains provisions designed to protect other contracting parties against capricious use of the GATT escape clause and against impairment of the balance achieved in previous negotiations. It requires consultation with affected contracting parties, normally before action is taken. If those consultations do not result in agreement, it also authorizes

the affected parties to suspend the application of equivalent benefits to the trade of the country utilizing the escape clause.

Article XIX had been used before by the United States on several
occasions. And, while its invocation has never been popular in
other countries, it had rarely aroused such a violent reaction.[15] If
we discount the possibility that protectionist elements in Europe
may have welcomed an excuse for approaching the Kennedy
Round with caution, the explanation for the unprecedented outcry
appears to lie in a combination of unfortunate coincidence and de-
plorable timing. The coincidence lay in the fact that the decisions
affecting both carpets and glass struck a potentially heavy blow at
the exports of the same two countries, Belgium and Japan. But the
pill was somewhat sweetened for Japan by the fact that, in the
same decision, the President had rejected two other recommendations of the US Tariff Commission, both of which would have
meant a serious loss to that country.[16] No similar consolation tempered Belgium's reaction, which was reinforced by the fraternal
indignation of its partners in the Community and of the EEC commission.

The timing of the President's proclamation was even more unfortunate. It came when the Community was being asked to join
in a partnership that would lead the world toward freer trade. Still
worse, it followed by only twelve days the signature of a new
agreement between the US and the EEC signaling the conclusion
of their "Dillon Round" negotiations. This fact was dramatized by
the monthly *Bulletin* of the EEC; the April issue carried an optimistic appreciation of the US-EEC agreement by Commissioner Jean
Rey, followed by a retraction branding the "escape clause" action
as "a poor prelude to the proposed negotiations with us on future
trade relations."

It was public knowledge that the two reports of the US Tariff
Commission, on which the President's decision was based, had
been in his hands for many months.[17] This made it difficult to com-
bat the widely held belief that the United States had intentionally
delayed action until it could conclude the Dillon Round negotiations on as favorable terms as possible. It also brought into question the existence of an emergency sufficiently pressing to justify
the President in making his decision before consulting the coun-

tries most affected. The atmosphere was so charged with suspicion and distrust that the United States was also believed by some to have granted, in the Dillon Round settlement, new concessions on the very products affected a few days later by the escape clause action. This was not true, but it was an understandable deduction from the open indignation of European official spokesmen.

Although the Tariff Commission's recommendations had been arrived at by unanimous vote in the case of carpets and by a 4 to 0 vote in the case of glass, with one abstention, there was public skepticism in the United States as to the merits of its conclusion that imports were responsible for the troubles of the domestic producers. A *New York Times* editorial suggested that the President had yielded to domestic pressure in order to obtain the support of the industries concerned and of certain members of Congress for the Trade Expansion Act.[18] President Kennedy may have contributed to the general atmosphere of suspicion when he publicly defended his action largely on the grounds that the US was experiencing difficulties with its balance of payments while Belgium was not.[19] These grounds, of course, were irrelevant to the legal basis for invoking the GATT "escape clause."

The errors of judgment were not all on one side of the Atlantic. The violence of the European reaction and the rigid position into which it necessarily froze the Community led to a denouement that helped no one and compounded the damage to all. Edwin L. Dale, Jr., wired the *New York Times* from Brussels about "reactions of anger and suspicion . . . among key officials of the Common Market," and quoted "a high French official" as saying: "The decision shows once again that when a European industry successfully breaks into the American market, it is always threatened with a tariff increase after the fact. It makes us wonder what will be the advantage to us of negotiating for the sweeping new tariff reduction your President has prepared."[20]

The Council of Ministers of the EEC demanded that the United States enter into consultations with them, as required by the GATT, and said that the action of the US president had not been "in the spirit of the recent talks or the coming talks."[21] The official *Bulletin* of the EEC undiplomatically threatened "retaliatory measures" in lieu of the more conciliatory "compensatory withdrawals" favored in the GATT vocabulary.[22] Meanwhile the Japanese, who had as much to lose as the EEC, more politely claimed that heavy losses would be incurred on orders already in production and requested a delay in execution to the end of August.[23] This request was not granted, but on March 30 President Kennedy did extend the effective date from April 18 to June 12, to allow time for consultations in GATT.[24]

The GATT consultations between the United States and the EEC were doomed to fail. For while the US representative indicated that he was authorized to negotiate for compensatory tariff concessions of comparable value, the EEC negotiators were interested only in obtaining a reversal, or at least a substantial modification, of the President's proclamation. When their effort to extract from the United States a compromise offer along these lines failed, the EEC council voted to suspend the application to US trade of certain tariff bindings negotiated with the United States in the Dillon Round.[25]

That ended the consultations. To the evident surprise of the Community's representative, the United States was unwilling to continue the discussions in the face of the retaliation already announced though not yet put into effect. The EEC may thus be credited with the final miscalculation in the series of mistakes that characterized the unpleasantness. In a complete misreading of the style of the Kennedy administration, they had apparently thought that a decision to retaliate would dislodge the United States from what they interpreted to be a bargaining position. When President Kennedy was asked at a news conference a few days later whether he was going to reconsider his executive order, he said simply, "No, it's going to stand."[26]

There is no way of knowing whether, by reacting more circumspectly to the President's decision, the Community could have obtained its modification. It does not seem at all likely that this result could have been achieved in the consultations even if the EEC council had not brought them to an end by its abortive power play. It is certain, however, that the Common Market could have obtained some other concessions of positive value, and it is equally certain that different tactics by the Community would have lessened the rising tension in the atmosphere surrounding preparations for the Kennedy Round. But to say this is not to excuse the

US administration for a decision which, even with the benefit of more imaginative execution than it actually received, was bound to make the principal objective more difficult to achieve.

Gallic Veto, Number One

The controversy over carpets and glass was the first of a string of developments that demonstrated the fragility of the special Atlantic relationship that had been successfully invoked by the Kennedy Administration in obtaining passage of the Trade Expansion Act. The next, and most dangerous, crack in the Atlantic bridge developed at its European anchor, but its effects spread to the entire structure, drastically altering the relationships among the parts. On January 14, 1963, after fifteen months of negotiation, General de Gaulle brought to an end the British quest for membership in the Common Market.[27] When the French President decreed that the British were not yet ready to be Europeans, he influenced not only the composition of the Common Market but all Atlantic relations, including the patterns of cooperation and influence among the six themselves and the position of the EEC in the Kennedy Round negotiations.

The most direct effect of the veto on the trade negotiations was, of course, that the United Kingdom would have to participate as an independent negotiator, with its own tariff on the table, and not as a member of the Community. Looked at in isolation, and ignoring the political repercussions that were set in train, this was not necessarily damaging to the Kennedy Round. It is true that, as Senator Douglas had predicted, the dominant supplier authority in the Trade Expansion Act was virtually extinguished as a result,[28] but, as has already been suggested, it is problematical whether the authority to reduce tariffs to zero on an "Atlantic list" of products would have been usable in practice.[29] Nor is it at all certain that the addition of the United Kingdom to the Community members whose agreement would have to be obtained would have made the task easier. While outside the six, Britain had a powerful incentive to cooperate in obtaining deep tariff cuts: namely, the necessity to reduce the growing EEC preferences that threatened to impede its exports to the six. But once inside the Common Market, its immediate interests would have been radically changed. The Common External Tariff would have become its own tariff, and any zeal it might have had toward trade liberalism would eventually have been tempered by the need to give British producers time to accustom themselves to unrestrained competition from the Continent before taking on the rest of the world.

In this narrow context, therefore, there was no certainty that the veto was harmful to prospects for the trade negotiations. The same cannot be said of its indirect effects. One of these, though probably not the most important, was to bring into the open De Gaulle's distrust of the "Anglo-Saxons," which had its echo in an increased wariness among American and British negotiators toward any Community initiatives believed to have been dictated by France. It will be recalled that the De Gaulle veto closely followed on the meeting of Prime Minister Macmillan with President Kennedy in Nassau, and on the resultant Polaris missile agreement which had aroused the general's ire.[30] But, while De Gaulle's veto may have influenced subsequent relationships by revealing his attitude toward Atlantic partnership, his antagonism would presumably have found some other vehicle for expression if the UK negotiations had not been available for that purpose.

The veto had a more significant effect on the course of the Kennedy Round through the changes it wrought in the locus of power within the Community and in the ability of the six to reach decisions. Although the currents it set in motion were far from straight, and even reversed their direction more than once, they appeared always to be out of phase with the trade negotiations in Geneva. The first reaction of the other five to the veto was a burst of resentment that "stultified the development of the Community"[31] and delayed decisions needed for progress in the Kennedy Round. This phase, however, was brief. The overriding concern of the others with the survival of the Community itself led them to suppress their anger and to find ways of meeting subsequent French demands in order to avoid further vetoes that could lead to its dissolution. Thus, by late 1964, it was possible to look back on a period of at least superficial solidarity and to say: "The fact that the Six did not break up in 1963 makes it almost impossible for them to break apart over any lesser issue."[32] This judgment was confirmed when, in June 1965, De Gaulle's boycott of the Council of Ministers again put dissension in top position and again paralyzed the Community's ability to conduct its external relations for over seven months, but did not lead to dissolution of the Community.[33]

The effect of these periods of paralysis on the trade negotiations is obvious. But the influence of the veto on those negotiations during the intervening periods of solidarity will justify further attention when we examine the next phase of the preparatory work in Geneva. Meanwhile, one fact should be noted here. Community decisions from March 1963 to June 1965 were dominated by France. This seeming paradox is not difficult to understand. There can be little doubt that, as the other five drew back from the brink of destruction, they resolved not to come close again unless forced to do so in order to save the Common Market. And since France had established itself as the only member prepared to risk dissolution, it followed that it was General de Gaulle who had to be satisfied.

This may well have been the result De Gaulle had in mind in choosing as the method for exercising his veto that best designed to humiliate not only Great Britain but his Common Market partners. There were many rocks on which the UK negotiations could have been allowed to founder, with some inconspicuous aid from France. But, by choosing a method that demonstrated his willingness to risk dissolution of the Community he made certain that France would be able to exercise an effective veto in the future over Community decisions, even after the date when, under the Treaty of Rome, they were to be reached by qualified majority voting.

Thus, after the briefest of periods in early 1963, the EEC council again became an operating institution, capable of establing policies and giving negotiating instructions to the commission—provided France agreed with them.

The "Chicken War"

The dispute between the United States and the Common Market over the Community's barriers against imports of poultry covered too long a period to fit neatly into the plan of the present chapter. From the preliminary skirmishes in 1962 to the anticlimax in January 1964, the "Chicken War" encompassed both the initial period of harmony in the Kennedy Round preparations and the first phase of sharp contention over the negotiating rules. Some of the heat generated by frozen chickens, therefore, may have been merely a reflection of the rising temperature in the negotiations. Nevertheless, as a foretaste of broader disagreements that arose later, the poultry controversy must be included in the catalogue of external factors influencing the bargaining in Geneva.

From the beginning, public awareness of the issue was heightened, but understanding was clouded, by the tendency of the subject to turn the soberest journalists into wags. Presumably because of the low intellectual attainments of barnyard fowl, or because of their unprepossessing physique when plucked, there was something incongruous about their occupying the diplomatic spotlight. Whatever the reason, the "Chicken War" proved irresistible to cartoonists, and those who composed headlines lost no opportunity for puns based on the vernacular verb "to chicken" or the adjective "foul."

There is no way to determine whether this hilarity on the part of the press led the Community to take the issue more lightly than would otherwise have been the case. But it had no such effect on the US Congress or the Kennedy administration. In their view, what was involved was the almost certain loss of a profitable US export market. During the four years ending in 1961, the American poultry industry had built up its exports fivefold to $68 million annually, about three-quarters of the total being taken by West Germany.[34] Then, as a result of the adoption of a Common Agricultural Policy for poultry, German import charges rose from less than 5 cents a pound in July 1962 to 13.5 cents in July 1963.[35] This story is fully told by the US Department of Agriculture.[36] For the present purpose, it is sufficient to outline the legal basis of the EEC action and the ensuing controversy over the rights held by the United States under the GATT. When, in the Article XXIV: 6 negotiations, the Community withdrew the tariff bindings previously granted by the six member states, it established new bindings of the CXT for most products, but not for a list of agricultural items which were candidates for the imposition of a variable levy.[37] Poultry was one of these. The best the United States negotiators had been able to obtain was recognition by the EEC that the United States retained for these products unsatisfied "negotiating rights."[38]

The increase in levies resulting from adoption of a Common Agricultural Policy for poultry in July 1962 was followed almost immediately by a drastic decline in German imports from the United States. In August US exports, which had reached 33 million pounds in June, fell to 11 million pounds, virtually all of the decrease being attributed to a reduction in sales to West Germany.[39] Neither the United States nor the EEC acted promptly to initiate the negotiations foreseen in the March agreement, but activity at the domestic and diplomatic levels intensified without tangible result. In November, Secretary of Agriculture Freeman talked with EEC Commissioner Mansholt in Brussels and followed his apparently unsatisfactory interview with a saber rattling statement to the press.[40] Committees of both houses of Congress held hearings that provided farm groups and legislators an opportunity to exhort the administration to take more aggressive action. Further formal discussions between US officials and the European commission in Brussels brought no relief, though they inspired the commission to propose to the EEC council a slight reduction in the levy on US chickens and an increase in the levy applied to imports from certain other sources suspected of dumping.[41] The Council of Ministers rejected this proposal and instead decreed an additional small increase in the levy on poultry from all sources.[42]

The council's decision to increase rather than reduce the levy against US chickens brought a prompt response from Washington. Governor Herter issued a statement to the press deploring the decision and announcing that the United States would invoke its rights of negotiation under the bilateral agreement. The first objective would be to obtain improved access to the EEC market. Failing that, the United States would insist on "balancing compensation" from the EEC.[43] The ensuing negotiations, which began in Geneva on June 25, brought no result except an offer by the EEC commission to recommend to the council a reduction of about 10 percent in the levy. On August 6, Governor Herter announced officially that, having failed to obtain a satisfactory offer, the United States was making arrangements for the compensatory withdrawal of concessions covering about $46 million of EEC exports to the United States.[44]

It was now the turn of the EEC to be indignant. On the day of Governor Herter's announcement, Commissioner Rey officially deplored the US decision and said it would "not help the atmosphere" at the forthcoming Kennedy Round negotiations. He also expressed surprise at the figure of $46 million, which "greatly exceeded U.S. negotiating rights."[45]

The "Chicken War" then moved into its final phase—that of contention over the value, in terms of trade volume, to be attributed to the negotiating rights reserved to the United States under the bilateral agreement with the Common Market. In contrast to the US figure of $46 million, the Community set the amount at $13 million, but conceded that a case might be made for $19 million.[46] It is not difficult to understand the obstinacy with which each side clung to its original estimates. Both saw the dispute as involving much more than the few million dollars of trade immediately at issue. More important than the disagreement over the economics of the poultry trade was the question of how to interpret the negotiating rights the United States had retained on all of the agricultural products covered by the variable levy system.

The adversaries were agreed on two fundamental facts: first, that the United States was entitled, both under the GATT rules[47] and in equity, to compensation for the withdrawal by the EEC of the valuable binding of the German tariff and that, in the absence of an acceptable offer from the EEC, it had the right to withdraw from its own GATT schedule concessions of comparable value to the EEC; and, second, that the amount of these withdrawals, as measured by EEC exports to the United States, should not exceed the value of potential exports from the United States to Germany during a period that would reflect the retained US negotiating rights.[48]

In spite of this measure of agreement, at least two essential factors in the equation were in dispute and were bound to remain so unless resolved by a referee. The first of these arose out of the ambiguity of the language of the bilateral agreement of March 1962, which referred to "the negotiating rights held under the General Agreement . . . as of September 1, 1960." The EEC contended that these rights, which existed at the outset of the "XXIV: 6 negotiations," should be measured by the volume of trade in 1958, as that had generally been used as the "reference year" during those negotiations, though they conceded that trade in 1959 had been used in some cases. The United States argued that trade in the year 1960 was the relevant base. Since the volume of US chicken exports to Germany totaled 4.9 million pounds in 1958, 37.7 million pounds in 1959, and 63.6 million pounds in 1960,[49] the selection of the reference year was cardinal.

The second issue was equally incapable of objective solution. In each of the three years referred to above, Germany had maintained discriminatory quantitative restrictions on the importation of chickens. Under pressure in the GATT, these were removed in April 1961. Both sides agreed that the proper basis for measuring the trade coverage of the withdrawn concessions was the trade level that would have been attained in the reference year (whatever it might be) in the absence of quantitative restrictions. But this agreement opened the door to new labyrinths of uncertainty. American spokesmen focused on the fact that German imports from the United States had doubled in the twelve months after Germany lifted its quantitative restrictions. A similar doubling of the imports in 1960 would have yielded a total of $46 million in that year. The EEC, on the other hand, asserted that a removal of the restrictions would have resulted at the most in only a 50 percent increase above actual imports. Applying this increment to the higher of the two reference years that had been used in the "XXIV: 6 negotiations," they arrived at a maximum constructed trade value of $19 million.[50]

Any chance that differences of this magnitude might be reconciled by negotiation was virtually eliminated by the fact that each side had staked its claim in public;[51] a movement toward the position of the other side sufficient to permit a compromise agreement would probably have involved unacceptable political costs. In fact, however, the question was not made a matter for negotiation. The United States stood on its unilateral right to determine the withdrawals from its own schedule of GATT bindings, but there was open speculation that if it should proceed on the basis of $46 million, the Common Market would itself make further counterwithdrawals to which the United States might in turn have found it necessary to respond.[52]

It did indeed appear that the world's two greatest trading entities were on a collision course. Yet it must have been obvious that, while a unilateral change of compass was unthinkable for either, the consequences of the impending shock were also unacceptable to both. Having failed to obtain relief from the increased levy, the United States had nothing to gain from the proposed withdrawals except avoidance of the potential loss involved in accepting the EEC evaluation of American negotiating rights. A conceivable course might have been to maintain its position "in principle" but, in the interest of the Kennedy Round, to refrain from pressing it to the point of action. But this would have released a storm of protest from US farm interests[53] and might well have been so misinterpreted in Europe as to lead to still more serious consequences in the future. Similar considerations would undoubtedly have deterred the Community from making a move toward accommodation to the American position. Furthermore, any conciliatory voices in Europe would have had to contend with the rule of unanimity in the Community and the carry-over of bad feeling from the carpets and glass case.

The collision was avoided in the only possible way—by adjudication, or, more accurately, by a procedure resembling arbitration. In choosing this course, the combatants made GATT history. For, while the Contracting Parties had on various occasions used expert panels to deal with matters on which they were required by the agreement to reach a judgment, no dispute over GATT rights or obligations had ever before been voluntarily submitted by the disputants for GATT determination. When the United States proposed this course to the Community in September 1963, the commission hesitated at first to accept it. The hesitation to accept any compromise proposed by the other side was a natural enough reaction. But the commission specifically objected to the American proviso that the decision of the proposed panel should be binding on both parties. Both this US stipulation and the commission's resistance to it illustrate the level of mutual distrust that had been reached. For, in practice, the panel's finding was virtually certain to settle the issue, even though not formally binding on the parties. The Common Market could not legally have taken retaliatory action against US withdrawals that they considered excessive without approval by the Contracting Parties,[54] and there was virtually no chance that the Contracting Parties would approve retaliation against a level of US withdrawals that an impartial panel, constituted by the Contracting Parties themselves, had found to be reasonable. Thus, both the US stipulation and the EEC objection to it were pointless.

Fortunately, the United States dropped its proviso, and the EEC Council of Ministers approved the proposal on October 15, 1963.[55] Agreement was quickly reached between the parties on the form of a joint request to the executive secretary of the GATT, and, on

November 21, the GATT Council of Representatives established an expert panel[56] with the following terms of reference: "To render an advisory opinion to the two parties concerned in order to determine: 'On the basis of the definition of poultry provided in paragraph 02.02 of the Common Customs Tariff of the European Economic Community, and on the basis of the rules of and practices under the GATT, the value (expressed in United States dollars) to be ascribed, as of 1 September 1960, in the context of the unbindings concerning this product, to the United States exports of poultry to the Federal Republic of Germany'."[57] For practical purposes ,the appointment of the panel represented the end of the "Chicken War." The unconvincing arguments submitted by both sides in their briefs[58] and the somewhat questionable reasoning of the panel itself in its choice of the right reference period would provide material for an interesting monograph, but are not sufficiently pertinent to the Kennedy Round to warrant treatment here. As was almost inevitable, both parties promptly accepted the panel's finding of $26 million.[59]

The anticlimactic phase of the drama was concluded in January 1964, when President Johnson signed an order raising US duties on four products of primary interest to the EEC: high-priced brandy (affecting French cognac almost exclusively), trucks (primarily affecting Volkswagen), and dextrine and starch (of interest primarily to the Netherlands). The selection of these products in itself established another precedent in the GATT and in the external relations of the six. Although the dispute had been over entry to the German market, the United States correctly judged that its quarrel was with the Common Market as a whole. Thus, it was under no obligation to limit its withdrawals to products of primary interest to Germany. On the other hand, instead of adhering entirely to this logic, it selected products for withdrawal that would affect the three Common Market countries most directly concerned: Germany, plus the two countries that had the most to gain from the exclusion of American chickens.

These withdrawals were hardly popular with the affected countries, but they occasioned no such storm in the European press as had earlier episodes in the conflict. The submission to the GATT panel had at least served the purpose of damping public interest. The press no longer saw the "Chicken War" as a prelude to bloodier hostilities, and this in itself helped end the shooting.

Although the earlier warfare left some scars, it is difficult to appraise its effect on the Kennedy Round. The tragic death of President Kennedy in November 1963 and the spontaneous wave of sympathy in Europe temporarily overcame some of the European resentments that had been aroused. But the controversy had brought to the surface some fundamental conflicts of interest that could not be so easily buried and that would continue to dominate the broader negotiations in the field of agricultural products.

Part Three: Sparring over the Rules

9

The Negotiating Rules

A year and half elapsed between the tentative decision, made by the Contracting Parties in November 1962, to hold a new round of trade negotiations and the date when the Kennedy Round was officially opened. It was another six months before negotiations, in the traditional meaning of the term, could be said to have begun. The reason for this unprecedented period of gestation was, of course, the fact that for the first time the problem of reaching agreement on a rule for automatic tariff reductions had been injected into the preparatory phase.

In all GATT tariff conferences before the Kennedy Round, the preliminary decisions required of the Contracting Parties had been simple and procedural. But this new factor insured that the conference rules would be as tightly negotiated as the ultimate concessions themselves. In fact, had they been possible, totally automatic tariff reductions would have shifted the entire bargaining process forward to the opening phase of the conference. The rules would no longer have been procedural; they would have determined the shape and content of the final agreement. The "negotiating conference" would then have been reduced to the dull task of verifying and recording results.

There was, of course, no prospect that the Kennedy Round would achieve total automatism. The legal requirement that the United States administration withhold certain products from the negotiations, the certainty that others would also require lists of exceptions, and the inadequacies of any formula as an approach to agricultural protection, made it inevitable that an automatic plan would have to be supplemented by bargaining over individual products. Compared with earlier negotiations, the Kennedy Round did not succeed in avoiding, or even in shortening, the period devoted to product bargaining. What made the new negotiations unique was that the bargaining period was preceded by a preparatory phase in itself as long as any previous negotiating Round.

It would simplify this presentation had there been a single date on which the first phase was concluded and the next begun. In a strictly ceremonial sense, there was such a date. When a meeting of GATT ministers was convened in May 1963 to confirm the earlier decision of the Contracting Parties, it established a date one year later for the end of the preparatory phase and the opening of negotiations. If all had gone well, by May 1964, with the rules for automatic reductions settled, preparatory work in national capitals and at EEC headquarters would have been concluded, and participants would have been ready to begin negotiating over those residual problems that had not been solved by formula. In fact, when the ministers met for the formal opening, they were able to do little more than take note of the stage that had been reached by the committees and working parties.

Six months after the formal opening, negotiations on individual tariffs began, but only for tariffs on industrial products. Other sectors of the negotiation — those concerning agricultural tariffs, nontariff barriers, and the participation of less developed countries — did not begin until after even greater delays. Each had its own date for the completion of the bargaining over rules and the start of the bargaining over specific products.

Linear Reductions

The effort to translate into specific rules the agreement reached in principle to seek across-the-board tariff reductions turned up more problems than had been anticipated. Though they had been held below the surface as long as possible, some problems had been apparent from the beginning: whether the linear approach would encompass all sectors or be limited to industrial products; whether the standard reduction under the linear rule should be the 50 percent permitted in the general authority of the Trade Expansion Act or some lesser percentage; and how exceptions should be determined and limited. All of these provided ample room for disagreement.

But the most significant and far-reaching of the issues that developed — reciprocity — had previously caused no visible disagreement. All prospective "linear" participants in the Kennedy Round had at least this much in common: while they favored, or were at least prepared to accept, the procedural implications of linear tariff reductions, they would not trust them to produce the kind of reciprocity they had sought in past negotiations and still continued to seek. In a note to the Working Party on Procedures for Tariff Reductions, the executive secretary of the GATT displayed some uncertainty as to the role reciprocity would play in a linear negotiation.[1]

The first meeting of this working party, in December 1962, revealed no dissent from the consensus, as reported by the secretariat, that "the linear approach must lead to a departure from the rigid balance-of-benefits theory that had governed the negotiations under the item-by-item approach" but "the participating countries would, nevertheless, expect a general 'across-the-board' balance between concessions granted and received."[2]

When the GATT ministers met in May of the following year, they not only accepted this view, but specified the way in which the goal of reciprocity should be reconciled with linear reductions: "in the trade negotiations it shall be open to each country to request additional trade concessions or to modify its own offers . . . to obtain a balance of advantages between it and the other participating countries."[3]

Clearly, by the time the prenegotiating phase was officially opened, any thought of substituting a concept of automatic mutual benefit for a balance of concessions had been discarded. Since it seemed generally accepted that the results of the linear reductions would in the end be subjected to some process of adjustment for the sake of reciprocity, it might have been expected that this acceptance would have made agreement easier as to the nature of the linear reduction. In fact, it did not prevent a prolonged and sometimes bitter debate over the nature of the procedures and standards to be used.

Tariff Disparities

It had been clear from the beginning that the traditionally low-tariff countries of Europe were unconvinced that equal across-the-board tariff reductions would be as beneficial to them as to countries whose tariff reductions would start from a higher level. But it was the EEC which, during the prenegotiations, emerged as the most vigorous opponent of equal percentage cuts. While there had been earlier hints, this opposition first crystallized at a meeting of the working party on April 22, 1963, when the Community's representative presented as an "informal suggestion" a formula for automatic but unequal cuts.

The origin of this proposal cannot be stated with certainty. According to one version, the proposal had originally been suggested on a personal basis by a German official in the Community's "Article 111 Committee," but had been quickly adopted by France. When others in the committee refused to make it an instruction to the commission, it was agreed that the commission be authorized to "float" the idea informally in the GATT working party in order to obtain the reactions of others. Its implications for the success of the Kennedy Round may not have been fully understood by its authors. But even though presented as a "suggestion," the proposal created the first major storm of the Kennedy Round. Some of the bitterness of the ensuing debates remained even after the suggestion had been abandoned in favor of a quite different method of dealing with tariff disparities.

"Ecrêtement"

The first Community formula for unequal tariff cuts became universally, though not very appropriately, known as "écrête-ment," meaning "leveling of the peaks." In fact, if adopted, the suggestion would have resulted in a smooth progression of tariff reductions, approaching 50 percent in the case of very high rates and reaching zero at the lower end of the scale. Target rates were to be established: 10 percent ad valorem for manufactures, 5 percent for semimanufactures, and zero for raw materials. Then each existing tariff was to be reduced halfway to the target. Table 4 will illustrate how the scheme would have worked in the case of manufactured products.

Table 4. Hypothetical results of the EEC's *écrêtement* formula (differences in absolute and percentage reductions at selected starting tariff levels).

Starting rate (ad valorem)	Percentage points above target	Reduction, in percentage points[a]	Reduction, as a percentage of starting rate
50	40	20	40
30	20	10	33.3
15	5	2½	16.6
10	0	0	0

[a]One-half of amount in second column.

The commission fought almost as hard to obtain acceptance of its suggestion as it would have if it had been a formal proposal. Based on the premise that the tariffs of other major participants (the US and UK) were substantially higher than the Common External Tariff (CXT) of the Community, its representatives argued that a uniform percentage reduction in all three tariffs would produce an unbalanced result. This premise was probably closer to the truth than that of the witnesses who reached the opposite conclusion in the Ways and Means Committee hearings. But the commission was on still firmer ground when it maintained that tariffs of the United States and the United Kingdom had many more very high rates than the Common External Tariff of the Community. These high tariffs, it argued, would be protective even after being cut in half, whereas the community's moderate tariffs would have been reduced to impotence. The claim that such a result would be inequitable was based almost exclusively on the argument that it would leave the six without bargaining power for obtaining the future reduction of those American and British tariffs that would remain at highly protective levels even after having been cut in half.

The Embattled Tariff Averages

Much of the debate set off by the *écrêtement* proposal concerned the relative height of the tariffs of the United States and the Community. It was bound to be inconclusive both because of the inherent difficulty of measuring the protective incidence of individual tariffs and because of the impossibility of arriving at meaningful tariff averages. In its simplest terms, the problem of measuring protective incidence centers about the wide differences between products in their price elasticities of supply and demand.[4] The problem of averaging is equally difficult. A simple arithmetical average of tariff rates overlooks, of course, the vast differences in the commercial importance of different items. On the other hand, as has long been recognized by students of the subject, the weighting of each tariff by the country's import trade in that item understates the importance of high rates that seriously inhibit trade. A prohibitively high tariff would, of course, receive no weight in such an average.

During the debate over *écrêtement*, important sections of the European press asserted that the US tariff was much higher than the Common External Tariff of the Community. US spokesmen were equally firm in contending that the average level of the US and EEC tariffs was about the same. In fact, neither claim could be proven. A number of more or less contemporaneous calculations found the average levels of the CXT and the US tariff to be within less than five percentage points of each other. But which was found to be higher and which lower depended on whether agricultural tariffs were included or not and on whether the average used was unweighted or weighted, as well as on the method used for weighting.

Whatever the merits of the argument about tariff averages, one fact was not in dispute: the US tariff contained a much larger number of high rates than did the common tariff of the EEC. According to a study submitted by the United States Delegation to the Tariff Reductions Working Party, the unweighted distribution of US and EEC tariffs was:

| | Percent of tariff items | |
Ad valorem incidence	US	EEC
0– 9.9	38	28
10–19.9	30	58
20–29.9	14	13
30 and over	18	1
	100	100

In brief, there was a much higher concentration of community tariff rates in the "moderate" range, while the dispersion of the US tariff on both sides of the moderate range was much greater.

Tariff Concentration versus Tariff Dispersion

The concentration of EEC tariffs within a middle range was, of course, the consequence of the manner in which the CXT had been established: most rates had been determined by a simple arithmetical average of the rates in force in the member states.[5] Both unusually high and unusually low rates of member states were moderated in the process. The Community argued that, whatever the averages might show, this concentrated tariff structure would place them at a disadvantage if all rates were reduced by an equal percentage. In its most primitive form, the argument consisted of the assertion, impossible to prove, that moderate rates, when cut in half, would no longer be protective; whereas, the protective effect of the many high rates in the US tariff would survive a 50 percent cut. The United States attempted to counter this argument by the equally debatable contention that halving a high rate of duty could have more effect on trade than the same percentage cut in a low or moderate rate.

A somewhat more sophisticated argument occasionally used by Community spokesmen was based on the theory, expounded by Bertrand,[6] that, *ceteris paribus,* the greater the dispersion of a country's tariffs from their mean, the higher the average effective rate of protection. Since the dispersion of the rates in the CXT was clearly less than that of the United States, the relevance of this argument to the debate was obvious. The applicability of Bertrand's argument to a comparison between the US and EEC tariffs has, however, been challenged by Cooper.[7]

Like most debates of this kind, the position taken by various protagonists was determined not by theory but by their perception of their national interests. The *écrêtement* formula proposed by the EEC would have required the Community to make very few tariff reductions of more than 25 percent. All of its major negotiating partners — the United States, the United Kingdom, and Japan — would have contributed many more reductions approaching a full 50 percent cut. Their adverse reaction to the Community's proposal was not surprising. While opposing the EEC formula, Japan, however, advanced its own suggested sliding scale for tariff reductions. Under this, only those tariffs that were 44 percent ad valorem or above would be reduced by a full 50 percent. Those below 44 percent would be reduced by varying amounts, depending on their starting height, with rates of below 10 percent being reduced by only one-fifth.

The European countries that had in the past argued that low-tariff countries were at a disadvantage in item-by-item negotiations naturally displayed some sympathy for the concept of differential tariff cuts but could find little reason for supporting the proposal of the Community. They had much more to gain from a deep reduction in the tariffs of others, especially the common tariff of the EEC, than in maintaining the existing levels of their own rates. What was decisive, however, in depriving the Community of support and in isolating it from all the other negotiators was the fact that its formula would, from the outset, have doomed the Kennedy Round to results almost as meager as those of the Dillon Round. The US delegation calculated that, under the EEC formula, the average of the CXT would be reduced by only 10 percent and that of the US tariff by only 12 percent — results that cast doubt on whether the proposal was seriously meant or only put forward for bargaining purposes. The impression that the proposal was not serious is borne out not only by what is known of the circumstances in which the commission was authorized to bring it to the GATT working party, but by one of the arguments used in its favor by the Community spokesman — namely, that under the *écrêtement* formula the EEC would forego the right to except any tariff from automatic reduction if others would do the same. Since it was public knowledge that US legislation made some exceptions mandatory, it was clear that the Community's challenge would not be accepted.

The May 1963 Ministerial Meeting

In late May 1963, the Contracting Parties met at the ministerial level in an effort to resolve the many differences that had emerged over the rules for the Kennedy Round. One of their most pressing tasks was to find a solution to the problem of tariff disparities. The chairman of the conference was Hans Schaffner, Federal Counselor of Switzerland. Christian A. Herter, who had been appointed by President Kennedy as his Special Representative for Trade Negotiations, led the delegation for the United States. The European Economic Community was represented by Commissioner Jean Rey. The United Kingdom was represented by Frederick Errol, President of the Board of Trade. The two most influential member states of the EEC, France and the Federal Republic of Germany, sent, respectively, Giscard d'Estaing, Minister of Finance, and Ludwig Erhard, Minister for Economy.

Among the governmental representatives, the position of Erhard was a pivotal one. West Germany as a nation and Erhard as an individual were as interested as the United States in a major liberalization of trade, at least in industrial products. And Germany, while more limited than France in its freedom of action, occupied a position of political and economic importance in the Community that gave it powerful leverage if it was prepared to use it. In April Germany had used this leverage to obtain agreement in the EEC council to a program for the synchronization of future steps toward the completion of common economic policies within the Community.[8] This decision made further progress in the development of a Common Agricultural Policy and the Association of African States — major demands of France — dependent on progress in other fields, including positive participation in the Kennedy Round. At the May 1963 ministerial meeting, Erhard was in a position to invoke this agreement in his dealings with D'Estaing.

The treatment of "tariff disparities," though not necessarily more important than other areas of disagreement faced by the ministers, was the most contentious. This was the issue over which the ministerial meeting appeared, at various points, close to total collapse. Both the European and the American press sensed this possibility. Calculated press leaks and delegation press conferences became standard tools of negotiation. Headlines used the vocabulary of conflict. The words "clash," "crunch," and "dead-

192 Sparring over the Rules

lock" were frequent. The *Observer* of May 18 led its story with "the SIX against Herter." The *Journal de Genève*[9] used the lead "le dessein de Gaulle s'oppose au dessein de Kennedy." A correspondent of the *Christian Science Monitor* wrote "a French spokesman has remarked that this is the crucial meeting of the United States with the realities of a new economic situation in which Europe has again at least equal power."[10]

The issue over tariff disparities no longer pivoted about the *écrêtement* proposal. Early in the ministerial meeting, EEC spokesmen made it clear that they would not insist on *écrêtement* for bringing disparate tariff rates closer together. The United States also moved a bit from its earlier position and agreed that there might be cases in which a disparity would justify departure from percentage equality in tariff reductions. But desertion of their former positions still left the two major protagonists far apart. The United States, with substantial support from others, insisted that the basic rule should be equal linear cuts. Any deviations would require clear evidence that a disparity between the respective rates on the same product was such that equal cuts could not achieve reciprocity. The EEC, however, demanded that disparities be dealt with by some formula that would be automatic and not subordinated to qualitative appraisal.

That was where the disagreement remained until the ministers achieved the semblance of a truce by a judicious mixture of those two most valuable instruments of diplomacy: postponement and ambiguity.

The Ministerial Compromise of 1963

Although the compromise was generally credited to Erhard, the executive secretary had played a leading role; it was precariously reached in two postmidnight sessions among the main protagonists. The ministers decided that "in those cases where there are significant disparities in tariff levels, the tariff reductions will be based upon special rules of general and automatic application."[11] This language, standing alone, would have been too flagrant a postponement of the issue. For its force hinged on the meaning of "significant." Was significance to be measured by an arithmetical comparison of tariff levels or by economic criteria? The fact that the ministers also agreed to instruct the Trade Negotiations Committee to propose criteria was, of course, no solution. That committee would have to be given guidance or the whole debate would have had to be renewed from the beginning. But it was typical of the temper of the meeting, and of the resistance by each side to any formulation proposed by the other, that the answer, though negotiated in advance, had to be attributed to a ruling by the chairman and not incorporated in the text of the resolution attributed to the ministers themselves. Thus, appended to the document recording that resolution was the following quotation from the chairman: "the Chairman understands that . . . 'significant' means 'meaningful in trade terms,' and that this is acceptable . . . the purpose of the special rules mentioned . . . is among other things to reduce such disparities and this is acceptable."

The American negotiators had gained their principal point. No mathematical formula could be substituted for economic criteria in determining whether a disparity was "meaningful in trade terms." Therefore, the automatic application of the rules referred to in the body of the resolution could only refer to the manner of dealing with those disparities that survived the process of identification and not to that process itself.

After the ministerial meeting, the battle shifted to the Trade Negotiations Committee, where it continued with undiminished spirit for most of another year. But the ministers' decision had made it possible to divide the debate into two parts: the first, and much the easier, was over the formula for the identification of those disparities large enough to be worth considering; the second was based on reaching agreement on criteria that could be used for eliminating, from among these prima facie disparities, those that did not meet the test of economic significance.

The "30:10" Formula

The first proposal made by the Community to the Trade Negotiations Committee for the prima facie identification of significant disparities was to include all cases in which the higher tariff of the pair being compared was 30 percent more ad valorem, and there was a difference of at least 10 percentage points between it and the lower tariff. Initially, this proposal would have required a comparison of all tariffs of each linear participant with those of all others, but before long the EEC sought to increase its acceptability by suggesting that it be limited to a comparison of the tariffs of certain "key participants": the United States, EEC, and the United Kingdom. In thus focusing its fire on the allegedly higher tariffs of the United States and the United Kingdom and ignoring the many high tariff rates of others, especially Japan, the architects of the disparity formula may have hoped to drive a wedge between the "Anglo-Saxons" and the rest. But this modification failed to gain the adherence of either Japan or the smaller EFTA countries. For they stood to lose as much as others if, as a result of disparities between the CXT and the tariffs of the United States and the United Kingdom, the EEC should be excused from deep tariff reductions on hundreds of tariff positions.

In a paper submitted to the working party, the UK delegation analyzed the effects of the EEC proposal. Considering only a comparison between EEC and US rates, it found that 557 subheadings in the CXT of the Community would qualify as prima facie disparities under the "30:10" formula. But, it argued, the Community's rationale for raising the issue had been to avoid the loss of bargaining power that might occur if it and the United States were to reduce these tariffs by the same percentage. This rationale was inapplicable in the many cases in which the Community was not a substantial importer from the United States. The British delegation was able to identify only some 190 products in which at least 20 percent of the EEC imports came from the United States and also amounted to as much as $50,000. For the rest, it pointed out the bizarre situation that would follow if the EEC and third countries should maintain relatively high duties against each other for no better reason than the existence of a still higher US tariff, even though the United States might not be a material exporter of the goods in question. The conclusion, of course, was that any automatic formula could be ludicrous, and its cumulative effect severely restrictive, unless each case was subjected to careful screening based on an examination of the actual effects that could be expected to follow from an equal reduction of disparate tariffs.

Switzerland carried the British analysis further and illustrated the potential impact of the Community's formula on innocent bystanders. The Swiss representative claimed that, of the 190 potential disparity cases in which the United States was an important supplier to the Community, in 27 cases the *principal* supplier of the product was the United Kingdom and in 20 cases, Switzerland. Swiss exports to the Community endangered by the proposed disparity formula amounted to $176 million annually.

"Double Ecart" Formula

Of course, some of the limiting effects of the "30:10" formula, especially the adverse impact on the interests of third countries such as Switzerland, could be ameliorated if the list of prima facie disparities that emerged were to be subjected to a rigorous examination to determine their economic significance. The effort to find agreement on criteria that could be more or less automatically applied in such an examination soon claimed the principal attention of the negotiators.

But before the debate over economic criteria could be carried far, the Community withdrew its "30:10" proposal and replaced it by a new formula. Under this so-called *"double écart"*[12] test, the 30 percent minimum to be applied to the higher rate was replaced by a ratio of 2:1 between the rates being compared. To qualify as a prima facie disparity, the higher rate had to be at least twice the lower, and the spread between them at least 10 ad valorem percentage points. In the case of semiprocessed goods, however, the latter requirement would not have to be met.

There is no evidence that the Community's new formula was intended as a concession either to other "key" countries or to third countries whose interests were threatened. It is true that, for cases in which the higher rate was 30 percent or above, the new formula would have identified somewhat fewer disparities than the earlier formula. But in cases where the higher rate was below 30 percent many prima facie disparities would have been identified that would have been eliminated from consideration under the "30:10" formula. Even rates as low as 10 percent might qualify as "high," and in the case of semiprocessed goods there was no lower limit.

In an effort to appraise the effects of the new and older formulas suggested by the Community, a fact-finding group was established. Considering only the disparity claims that could be made by one of the three major negotiators against another, it concluded that the *double écart* formula would permit the invocation of disparities in many more cases than would the "30:10" formula. It also concluded that under *double écart* the EEC would appear to be able to invoke prima facie disparities for about half the headings in the industrial sector of the Common External Tariff.[13]

Whatever may have been the reason for this new proposal by the community, the Trade Negotiations Committee recorded that most of the other participants preferred a "cutoff," that is, a standard rate below which no tariff would be considered "high" for purposes of identifying a disparity.[14] However, the committee allowed the Community's new proposal to lie on the table while they turned their attention to the more important question of the qualitative criteria to be used in reducing to manageable size the number of "meaningful" cases to be identified from among the formidable number of prima facie disparities revealed by either formula.

The Qualitative Criteria

The formulation of criteria to be used in determining whether a disparity was actually "meaningful in trade terms" was bound to be difficult, since most of the participants disputed whether there was any economic reason for taking disparities into account. However, accepting the rationale on which the Community had placed the greatest stress — namely, the loss of future bargaining power that would be suffered by the lower-tariff country if disparate tariffs were reduced equally — they vied with each other in proposing criteria to be used in reducing the list of disparities to workable proportions. If all of these criteria had been accepted, a disparity would have been automatically excluded from special treatment where any one of the following circumstances existed:

1. the low-rate country imported little or none of the product concerned;

2. the high-rate country imported substantial quantities of the product in spite of its higher tariff;

3. the low-rate country had no domestic production;

4. the high-rate country was not the principal supplier to the low-rate country;

5. a "third country" participant was a major supplier to the low-rate country.

The Community, more anxious than the others to reach agreement on a disparity formula, went part way toward meeting the general demand that the list of prima facie disparities be narrowed by some qualitative criteria. In its counterproposals, however, it accepted only the less important of the criteria proposed by the others. A disparity would be eliminated from consideration where there were no imports, or only negligible imports, into the low-rate country, provided this condition did not result from the maintenance of quantitative import restrictions by the low-rate country; or, where the low-rate country was not a producer of the product and had no short-term plans to undertake production.

In addition, the Community indicated that it would be prepared to discuss with third countries whose trade prospects were threatened by the invocation of a disparity the possibility of limiting the adverse effects on them. A similar offer to consult was also proffered to a high-rate country in those cases where it imported substantial amounts of the product from the Community at existing tariff levels.

These counterproposals were generally attacked as inadequate. The qualification regarding quantitative restrictions would "reward" the low-rate country for the maintenance of a form of trade restriction outlawed by the GATT. The offer to consult affected third countries did little to reassure them, as there was no way of knowing in advance what reciprocal concessions might be demanded of them as the price of obtaining the linear reduction of tariffs on products of special interest to them. And to the "key countries," the same offer raised the specter of special bilateral deals which might damage their interests or the Kennedy Round as a whole. The United States, supported by Japan, Norway, Sweden, Switzerland and the United Kingdom, also vigorously opposed the offer to consult with the high-rate country where its imports of the product were already substantial and demanded that this criterion be automatically applied, taking into consideration imports from any source and not simply those from the low-tariff country.

The only EEC offer that was accepted as meeting one of the demands of the majority, though even this somewhat warily, was the offer to exclude products which the community neither produced nor had any present intention of producing. So far as the mathematical formula for identifying prima facie disparities was concerned, opposition to the community's proposal concerning semiprocessed products — that only the relative height of the two tariffs be considered and the requirement of a 10 percent ad valorem spread not apply — continued unabated. The effect of this proposal would have been to make disparity treatment possible even in cases where the spread was absurdly small, as, for example, between rates of 3 and 1.5 percent.

Treatment of Disparate Rates

Throughout most of the debate over the identification of disparities, it had generally been assumed that when a disparity had been accepted as "meaningful in trade terms" the treatment originally proposed by the Community would be applied: namely, that the lower rate need only be reduced by half the standard reduction, this is, by 25 percent if the linear reduction should be 50 percent.[15] Nor were the majority, which remained unconvinced of the underlying logic behind any special treatment of disparities, greatly concerned by the fact that so simple a formula might have ludicrous results. For example, it was at least theoretically possible that the rates of the three key countries on the same product could be such that two of them could claim a disparity vis-à-vis the highest rate country and each would then have the right to reduce its tariff by only 25 percent even though one of the two might have had a right to claim a disparity against the other. Even if its basic premise were accepted, the plan lacked internal logic. To forestall criticism on these grounds, the EEC submitted a proposal for a sliding scale of duty reductions in which the depth of cut by the low-rate country would depend upon the ad valorem level of its existing rate; the reduction of the lower rate would range from 15 percent, for rates already below 6 percent ad valorem, to 35 percent for rates between 25 percent and 30 percent ad valorem. This proposal was not a reversion to *écrêtement*. For the suggested deviations from the 50 percent, linear reduction would have applied only where the existence of a disparity, in comparison with the rate of another key country, had been established.

The Community's sliding-scale formula added one more element of disagreement to be carried forward to the opening of the Kennedy Round. While the majority conceded that this formula might be revised so as to be workable, it was criticized both on the ground that it did not itself fully avoid anomalies[16] and that it would result in an even lower average tariff reduction than the rough-and-ready 50-25 percent formula. But any accurate calculation of the overall results depended on what rules were agreed for identifying disparities, and the debate was suspended.

The Ministerial Meeting of 1964

In May 1964, the Trade Negotiations Committee met at ministerial level for the formal opening of the Kennedy Round in an atmosphere that was far from cheerful. Since May of the previous year it had cleared up a number of minor differences over the negotiating plan, but no progress had been made in the two most important areas: agriculture, which will be discussed in another chapter, and the form that linear tariff cuts should take. In the latter area, tariff disparities were at the heart of continued and total disagreement.

The prospects of reaching agreement on the disparity issue looked as remote as a year earlier, unless a way could be found to move the debate from the plane of abstraction and principle to one of concrete negotiation. This course was suggested by the executive secretary: "agreement has not yet been reached on those important elements in the negotiating plan, and I would cite in particular the question of tariff disparities and the rules regarding agriculture. This is disappointing and it would be foolish to pretend otherwise. However, we have found that in the course of trying to elaborate negotiating rules we have inevitably been led into some of the basic issues which need to be resolved in the negotiations themselves."[17]

The principal protagonists were so deeply dug into their respective positions that retreat by either side would have involved an unacceptable loss of face. The only possible solution was to bypass the abstract issue of disparities and leave it to be fought out later if necessary in the negotiations that were to take place over the exceptions lists. The Committee agreed to this procedure, with both sides reserving their positions concerning disparities. It is true that they also agreed to cooperate in a continued effort to resolve their differences. But the Committee decided that exceptions lists should be tabled on September 10, 1964, that these exceptions should be held to a bare minimum, that they should be limited to cases that were necessitated by reasons of "overriding national interest," and that they should be subject to "confrontation and justification."[18] This decision effectively precluded any chance, probably nonexistent in any case, that there would ever be agreement on automatic rules governing the handling of tariff disparities. If the issue remained alive at all, it could only arise on a case-by-case basis in the negotiation of the exceptions lists and the search for reciprocity to which all participants continued to give their allegiance.

The Community had fought hard for a general rule. It had been outnumbered. And, while not admitting defeat, it had demonstrated its interest in the negotiations by bowing to the majority. The true negotiations would not begin for another six months, but by May 6, when the committee reached its decision, it was clear that there would be a Kennedy Round, at least so far as the tariffs on industrial products were concerned.

Other Rules for Linear Reductions

The disparity issue, though by far the most difficult problem encountered in drawing up the linear rules, was not the only one. When the Trade Negotiations Committee met in May 1964 it was able to solve some issues that had been contested from the start, but more often it used the same technique as in the case of disparities and left the issue to be fought out in the negotiations that were to follow. The procedural compromise that was arrived at for dealing with the depth of the linear cut accomplished its purpose of bypassing an issue that was more formal than real. But the other issues discussed below were only temporarily shelved and persisted as problems through much of the Kennedy Round.

Depth of Linear Cut. One of the curiosities of the May decisions was that they did not succeed in elevating the 50 percent target for linear cuts to a firm undertaking. If there had actually been much doubt about it, the decision to table exceptions lists would have been meaningless. Nevertheless, the EEC continued to withhold its formal approval, presumably in the hope of increasing the credibility of its reservation concerning disparities. The formula adopted was that "exceptions lists will be tabled on the basis of the hypothesis of a 50 percent linear reduction."[19] This could only mean that the failure to list a product as an exception would be the equivalent of an offer to cut the tariff in half. But, as will be seen later, it did not preclude offers of less than 50 percent on particular products so long as they were made explicit either at the time of tabling exceptions or in the subsequent bargaining for reciprocity.

Base Dates. If linear reductions were to be made, it would have been logical that they should be made from the rates in force on a single date applicable to all. Such a date should also, logically, have been late enough to include the results of the Dillon Round but early enough to prevent participants from raising their unbound rates before the base date for bargaining purposes. As so often proved to be the case, however, not all participants were prepared to accept the logic of the linear approach. The difficulty arose in the case of rates not already bound and rates on which bindings had been granted at higher rates than were actually in force. Within both these groups there were cases in which a country had "temporarily" reduced or suspended a duty. To such a country it seemed logical that its tariff reductions should be based on its permanent or statutory rate. Similar reasoning influenced countries that in previous negotiations had reserved the right to raise a rate to a specified level but had not yet exercised that right.

Both the EEC and Sweden argued against the use of actual rates in those cases. In fact, the issue had no great importance except in one case, that of the tariff rates of the European Coal and Steel Community. Although this problem remained to add to later negotiating problems, the committee again decided, probably wisely, that it could not be solved in the abstract and that "it would be left to each participating country to propose the basis for its own cuts."[20] If its proposal were not acceptable to others, that would be one more issue to be resolved in the negotiations.

US Exclusions and the Problem of Petroleum

From the beginning of the discussion of the linear rules, the United States took pains to avoid the need for including petroleum in the calculation of its total exceptions. The administration was precluded, by Section 225(a) of the Trade Expansion Act, from offering a tariff concession on petroleum or on those petroleum products subject to import quotas imposed for "national security" reasons. Venezuela, the largest supplier, was neither a GATT Contracting Party nor a participant in the Kennedy Round. Canada also was an interested supplier but, as a contiguous neighbor, received favored quota treatment. In any event, as a nonlinear participant, Canada was not in a position to influence the rules that would apply to exceptions lists. The United States, therefore, was emboldened to propose that a country might exclude from its linear cuts products principally supplied by nonparticipants without inscribing these products in its exceptions list.

Although the proposed rule could not have any practical effect on the negotiated results, this effort at window dressing by the United States received little support. But, like other issues, it never became the subject of a formal decision. When exceptions lists were finally tabled, the United States adopted the rule it had proposed; others did not. About the only result was to remove from the area of discussion, at least on the part of the United States, a sector involving very substantial trade but one in which the height of the US tariff was not of serious interest to its negotiating partners.

Scope of the Linear Negotiation

By far the most important question raised by the linear approach was whether it should apply to all tariffs, subject to exceptions, or only to the tariffs on industrial products. But a discussion of this issue primarily involves the position of agriculture in the negotiations.

10

Agriculture

Before the ministerial meeting in 1963, the full extent of the differences concerning the part of agriculture in the negotiations had not come to the surface. The EEC had been unable to resolve its internal differences over the form and timing of its Common Agricultural Policy; accordingly, its spokesmen, while not inhibited from opposing the proposals of the agricultural exporters, were not in a position to advance counterproposals.[1]

The initial position of the principal agricultural exporters, such as the United States, Canada, Australia, and New Zealand, was at best visionary: agricultural tariffs should, like industrial tariffs, be subjected to across-the-board reductions of 50 percent. The executive secretary had earlier taken a more realistic position when, in his suggestions to the working party, he had drawn a distinction between those agricultural products that were protected only by tariffs and those in which other forms of protection or support were dominant. The exporters had some logic on their side when they argued that the elimination of nontariff barriers should supplement, but could not be a substitute for the reduction of agricultural tariffs. But, as the later debates showed, this position ignored the interrelationship between the nontariff measures maintained by exporting countries and the protective policies of importers.

To the large agricultural importers, determined to preserve at least a part of their indigenous farm production, the case for linear tariff reductions was not persuasive. The United Kingdom and Japan were not prepared to cut agricultural tariffs as a whole by the 50 percent projected for industrial tariffs. The EEC had more complex reasons for vigorous opposition to the inclusion of agriculture in any linear assault on tariffs, whatever the depth of cut. The six saw in the proposal to reduce and bind all agricultural tariffs a threat to the use of the variable levy system, and, therefore, an attempt to undo the results of the "Article XXIV: 6 negotiations" in which the Community had withdrawn the bindings granted earlier by member states on products for which a Common Agricultural Policy was projected.

Since the original position of the exporters was clearly an impossible one, they tacitly abandoned it fairly early in the discussions of the committee, at least for those agricultural tariffs which the EEC had not re-bound in the "XXIV: 6 negotiations" settlement. In its place the United States, with the support of other exporters, proposed, first, that those agricultural tariffs which the EEC had not explicitly reserved from the "XXIV: 6 negotiations" should be subject to the linear tariff reduction; and, second, that negotiations on the reserved items should be postponed until the EEC had formulated its regulations. But, in the meantime, the Community should provide interim assurances that the existing level of imports into the Common Market of those products would not be permitted to decline as a result of the protective measures, often including variable levies, that the member states had adopted pending the formulation of Community regulations and common prices.[2]

The Community's delegation did not, however, permit itself to be trapped by the logic of its position. In spite of its failure to obtain even tentative instructions from the council, it had two good reasons for resisting any effort by the exporters to break the impasse so simply. Probably the less important of these reasons was the knowledge that Italy was dissatisfied with the position accorded to fruits and vegetables in the agricultural plans of the commission and of the other member states. Tariffs on fruits and vegetables had not been unbound in the "Article XXIV: 6 negotiations," but Italy was still trying to persuade its partners that it was entitled to the same impregnable position for its principal agricultural products that France was to receive for cereals and animal products. Until this internal disagreement could be resolved, the Community's negotiators were hardly in a position to prejudge the outcome by accepting so clear a distinction between agricultural products already reserved for the CAP and others.

Probably a more important reason for refusing to accept the position of the exporters was that the commission was in the course of developing an original approach to the agricultural negotiations — an approach that would shift the emphasis away from import protection and focus attention on the entire range of controls and supports affecting agricultural production and trade.

"Montant de Soutien" is Foreshadowed

In late 1962 and early 1963, the commission's embryonic plan for the agricultural negotiations had not yet been revealed, if, indeed, it had already been fully formulated. But in informal conversations representatives of the commission and France made clear their adherence to the philosophy that had been enunciated at the 1961 GATT ministerial meeting by the French representative. In simple terms, this was that world agricultural prices did not reflect the free play of market forces and could not be made to reflect this simply by the removal of barriers to imports. All countries, including the major exporting countries, controlled the prices of the agricultural products with which they were most concerned. Negotiations that addressed themselves only to restrictions by importers would be dealing with but part of the problem affecting international agricultural trade. The solution proposed was to raise world prices to a level that would permit producing countries to maintain production without subsidy and that would commit all countries to defend those prices through both their import and export policies.[3]

Agricultural "Groups"

By the eve of the ministerial meeting the working party had only been able to agree that agriculture as a whole "presented special problems." There were, however, two limited sectors of agricultural trade for which procedures for the negotiations, if not their objectives, had been formulated. In these cases some progress had been possible because the commission and France had together established the direction in which they wished to move. French spokesmen had for some time made it clear that their approach to the solution of problems in agricultural trade was based on the negotiation of commodity agreements that would control competition and subordinate it to what was euphemistically called "organisation du marché."[4] As was to become clear from Commissioner Mansholt's later initiatives, this approach was also embraced by the commission; the Community's delegation made it clear that its demand for a postponement in the adoption of rules for the negotiation of agricultural tariffs did not prevent it from exploring the possibility of comprehensive commodity agreements in key agricultural sectors.

While their objectives bore little resemblance to those of the commission, the major exporting countries welcomed the chance to move the discussions on agriculture from the abstract to the concrete. It was possible that the agreements that gave some satisfaction to the commission's desire to control competition and to limit the use of price supports and subsidies by exporting countries might also provide some assurance of continued access to the markets of countries that were still net importers. In any event, if a start could be made in this direction, it would represent the first breach in the defensive position of the Community. It was comparatively easy for the working party to reach agreement on a recommendation: that two ad hoc groups be established to explore the possibility of arriving at some sort of global "arrangement," in cereals and meats, respectively, possibly to be followed later by similar groups for other agricultural sectors. This was the extent of the progress the working party was able to report to the meeting of ministers in May 1963. It had to report failure to reach agreement on most of the important issues that would have to be resolved before the rest of agriculture could be included in the negotiations: interim assurances by the EEC on CAP items; the manner of dealing with non-CAP items; and the depth of tariff cuts, if any.

The Ministerial Meeting of 1963

The meeting of GATT ministers in May 1963 failed to resolve any of these issues. The Community remained deadlocked over important details of the CAP. Germany was either unable or, because of the weak competitive position of high-cost German farmers, unwilling to press EEC council to provide the commission with a less defensive mandate. The exporters, while maintaining a united front on the necessity for reducing barriers to agricultural trade, were also unable to agree on the details.[5] The principal accomplishment of the meeting was to obtain the formal acknowledgment of the protagonists that they had abandoned some of the more extreme salients of their initial positions. Governor Herter agreed that, for those products in which commodity groups had been formed, the United States would be willing to deal with more than the question of market access. "My government is prepared to negotiate within the context of such agreements its production, price, export and import policies on a reciprocal basis."[6] And the EEC, without commitment as to how it was to be achieved, appeared to agree that "access" was to be one of the objectives of the general negotiating plan. The concluding resolution of the ministers gratefully turned over to the Trade Negotiations Committee the responsibility to "elaborate a trade negotiating plan" and to seek agreement, among other things, on "the rules to govern, and the methods to be employed in, the creation of acceptable conditions of access to world markets for agricultural products in furtherance of a significant development and expansion of world trade in such products." The ministers also decided that: "the Special Group on Cereals and Meats shall convene at early dates to negotiate appropriate arrangements and a Special Group on Dairy Products shall be established."[7]

The task assigned to the Trade Negotiations Committee was formidable. In mid-1963 all progress was still blocked by the refusal of France to agree to grant the Commission any negotiating authority in the field of agricultural products until the common prices of grain in the Community and the date for putting those prices into effect had been agreed upon among the member states.[8] Even if the internal problems of the Community were solved, there was no assurance that France would agree to tariff reductions. In June, the French Minister of Agriculture, M. Pisani, told a group of agricultural journalists at Grignon that negotiations on agriculture should take place not in the GATT but in an ad hoc agricultural conference.[9] However, this potential irritant to US-Community relations passed virtually unnoticed in the atmosphere of suspicion and contention that had already been generated by the "Chicken War," then nearing its climax.[10]

In November 1963, the European commission made an effort to solve the internal and external deadlocks simultaneously. It proposed to the Community's Council of Ministers, and announced to the press, two proposals dealing with agriculture, which came to be known as "Mansholt I" and "Mansholt II."[11] The first of these proposals was only indirectly concerned with the Kennedy Round, though one of its advantages, according to the commission, was that its acceptance by the council would make possible the start of agricultural negotiations in Geneva.[12]

The Mansholt Plans

"Mansholt I" was a proposal to establish common Community prices for cereals promptly and in one step and to make this acceleration politically possible for the member states whose prices would have to be reduced in order to reach the common level. This was to be accomplished by compensating their farmers by direct payments out of Community funds.[13] The claim that acceptance of this proposal by the member states would facilitate negotiations in the Kennedy Round proved to be unduly sanguine. It is true that some settlement of outstanding differences within the Community was a prerequisite to any international negotiation affecting agriculture, but any solution acceptable to all member states of the EEC was sure to erect new obstacles to an agreement between the Community and other countries interested in access to the Common Market.

There can be little question that the commission used the favorable attitude of some of its members toward the Kennedy Round as a spur to obtain their agreement to the first of Commissioner Mansholt's proposals. But the two proposals together contained features designed to appeal not only to those who wanted a successful Kennedy Round but also to those who would be satisfied if, at least in the agricultural field, it came to little.

"Mansholt II"

Although the commission had exposed its GATT negotiating plan to the press in November 1963, it was not considered by the EEC council until December. Together with the instructions to the commission concerning the industrial side of the Kennedy Round negotiations, Mansholt II was the subject of bargaining in the council, which ended only two days before Christmas with a package deal. As has so often been the case with Community deadlocks, Germany yielded to France, both on the internal issue concerning the financing of the Community's agricultural fund and on the mandate for the GATT negotiations.[14] While not all of the commission's proposals survived the council meeting in their original form, the negotiating proposal for agriculture was not changed in any material respect, and it was formally submitted to the Committee on Agriculture of the Kennedy Round in February.[15]

The community's proposal for negotiating on agricultural products consisted of two distinct elements: a method of measuring the margin of protection or support provided by each country to its agricultural producers; and a proposal that a binding of those existing margins take the place of the negotiation of customs duties.

The "Montant de Soutien"

The first of these elements, generally called in English "the margin of support," became better known by its original French formulation, *montant de soutien*. To use the words of the Community's spokesman: "The margin of support for a given agricultural product is equal to the difference between the price of the product on the international market and the remuneration actually obtained by the national producer."[16]

This conceptually simple yardstick, applied to the agricultural price structure of each participating country, was intended to provide a means of cutting through the maze of tariffs and nontariff barriers, price supports, and export subsidies, and to establish a common base from which negotiations could commence. From the point of view of the Community, pressed by the United States and other exporters to put its tariffs and variable levies on the negotiating table, it had the advantage of directing attention to the support mechanisms employed by others, especially the export subsidies and import quotas of the United States. It served to dramatize the Community's thesis that the level of protection required by the EEC was affected by the extent to which other countries produced or exported at prices that were determined by other than free market forces. But as a yardstick that could be applied in actual practice it had serious deficiencies. Its economic validity depended on the existence of a truly competitive world price for purpose of comparison. But existing world prices for the major agricultural products were themselves influenced by the domestic price support and subsidy measures employed by exporting countries and the protective devices employed by importing countries.

To this theoretical weakness in the approach were added the practical difficulties arising out of the wide variety of grades and qualities and differences in the degree of preparation for market that exist for each of the products concerned.

The Negotiating Plan

In spite of these difficulties, the proposal to reduce to a common denominator all governmental measures that influence price and to obtain a rough gauge of the resulting distortion by measuring the difference between world and domestic producer prices had much to recommend it. If the proposal had been to negotiate "margins of support" downward and to bind the result firmly, it is conceivable that it might have been accepted even though it would have involved a radical departure from previous negotiating methods and would have disturbed deeply entrenched domestic policies. But what ensured that Mansholt II would meet with violent opposition from the exporters was that the Community proposed that the *montant de soutien* be used not as a basis for further negotiations but as a substitute for them. Tariff bindings would have been replaced, in effect, by a binding of minimum import prices, which each country would remain free to defend by any level of import protection required for the purpose. The Community's proposal contained the following elements:[17]

1. Each participant would "bind" against increase during a three-year period its margin of support for each product, that margin being defined as the difference between the remuneration actually obtained by the national producer and a "reference price." The reference price was to be either: the price on the international market; or, a price negotiated between the contracting parties concerned "in the event that recorded prices do not seem satisfactory."

2. If actual offering prices at the border should fall below the

"reference price," protection at the frontier could be increased to the extent necessary to maintain the price received by domestic producers from which the original margin was calculated.

3. Unlike bindings resulting from other tariff negotiations, the binding of the *montant de soutien* would be reviewed after three years in order to make "any necessary adjustments."

In the course of the intensive discussions that followed, some of the obscurities in this proposal were elucidated by the commission, but none in such a way as to make it more attractive to the exporting countries, which still hoped that the Kennedy Round would bring a reduction in agricultural protection. The most important clarification was that relating to the possible negotiation of a reference price. Since the Community had suggested that the reference price need not necessarily be the world price, hope was entertained for a while that the protective effect of the system could be limited by negotiation. If the margin between the reference price and the price received by domestic producers were bound and the reference price then negotiated downward, the effect would be to reduce the level of the price support and to limit the stimulation that would be afforded to uneconomic domestic production. In response to questions on this score, however, the commission made it clear that, at least so far as products subject to the Common Agricultural Policy were concerned, it was improbable that the Community "would be able to go further than to bind the situation resulting from the Common Agricultural Policy."[18]

With this further clarification, it became clear that the Community's negotiating plan was not in fact a proposal for negotiating the "margin of support." What was proposed was not a negotiation but the freezing of the status quo. And the status quo to be frozen was not the "margin of support" but rather the level of remuneration to domestic producers. The margin of support was simply another name for the variable levy.

In the debate set off by "Mansholt II," the depth of the philosophic difference between the Community and most other negotiators became clearer than it had been when the Kennedy Round was proposed. Thus, when the US delegation objected to the Community's proposal that the margin of support be altered if world prices should change, the commission replied that exporting countries could avoid any increase in the Community's levy if they discharged their obligations to observe the reference price and to refrain from offering products at lower prices.[19] Since the Community proposed this quasi binding of the *montant de soutien* as the universal method of dealing with agriculture in the Kennedy Round, the US delegation objected that its adoption would extend the variable levy system far beyond those products earmarked for the Community's Common Agricultural Policy, to include even those for which the EEC had bound fixed tariffs in the Dillon Round negotiations. The Community, for its part, accused the United States of rejecting the Mansholt Plan because it was unwilling to include American domestic agricultural policies in the negotiating process.

Some of the heat generated by this debate resulted from the failure of either side to state its proposals with precision. For example, the US delegation, seeing that the variable levy system could not itself be dislodged, attempted to preserve the existing share of US exports in the European market by proposing that the Community permit imports to compete for a stated share of the EEC market. This was interpreted by some Community spokesmen and by most of the European press as American insistence on a "guaranteed share" of the European market. For its part, the Community, influenced by disagreement among its members concerning the ultimate limits of the variable levy system, made no effort to dispel the impression that it was proposing to extend it throughout the agricultural sector.

Deadlines Missed

The meeting of the Trade Negotiations Committee in May 1964, intended to signal the formal opening of the negotiation, was able to do little more in the field of agriculture than confirm its failure to agree on negotiating rules. "In view of the importance of this subject to the success of the negotiations," it added optimistically, "the necessary rules and procedures shall be established at an early date."[20] That was all, except to note that negotiations had been initiated in the cereal and meat groups "with a view to the formulation of general arrangements."[21]

During that spring and summer, efforts continued in the hope of agreeing on a basis for the exchange of agricultural offers that could take place when the industrial exceptions lists were tabled in the following fall. The Community's representatives concentrated on assuring the agricultural exporters that they had misunderstood the purpose and effect of their negotiating proposals. They were pressed for assurances that if their own "offers" were cast in the *montant de soutien* model the reference prices would at least be negotiable. But in August, in reply to questions put by the US delegation, the commission again had to confess its helplessness in light of the Community's own disarray: "It is improbable that, generally speaking, the Community would be able to go further than bind the situation resulting from the Common Agricultural Policy . . . Since the Community's margins of support *are not yet known*[22] any categorical judgment as to the value of the undertakings given by the EEC would be premature."[23]

It was true that by August the EEC did not yet know the Community's level of support for any of the products covered by the Common Agricultural Policy. No progress had been made in reaching agreement on unified Community prices for cereals. Nor were the prospects for early progress bright. Relations between France and Germany were deteriorating and were exacerbated later in the year by General de Gaulle's flirtation with the USSR and Eastern Europe.[24] The Community seemed to be headed for another period of paralysis in which decisions could not be reached.

The most immediate effect on the Kennedy Round of the deepening freeze within the EEC was to rule out any possibility that the Community could table agricultural offers in November 1964, the latest date for the exchange of industrial exceptions lists. Reluctantly, the other negotiators accepted this as a fact and, as has been noted, proceeded with the industrial tabling even though agreement on the agricultural rules was no closer than it had been when the ministers met in May.

The struggle between France and Germany over the level of the unified Community price for cereals was sharpened by the divergence in their attitude toward European political integration and toward Europe's relations with the outside world. To France, Germany's acceptance of US leadership in NATO and its support of President Johnson's proposal for a Multilateral Force (MLF) approached disloyalty. The issue over the common price to be established for grains, however, involved differences that were almost as serious. The Erhard government was unwilling to accept the political cost of a reduction in cereal prices that might endanger its position with German farmers in the Federal elections due to take place in the autumn of 1965. From the viewpoint of France, on the other hand, the ideal Community price was one that would be high enough to support the existing levels of French production but low enough to discourage high-cost German production. Such a level would permit French producers to take a large part of the German market, while any remaining surplus could be disposed of in world markets with the aid of a moderate subsidy. A proposal made by the European commission in October was acceptable to France, but rejected by Germany. Once again a threat by De Gaulle to destroy the Community was wielded effectively,[25] and, in a marathon meeting of the Council of Ministers in December 1964, the German government yielded to France on most of the important points.

For a while, the resulting settlement appeared more auspicious for the Kennedy Round than if the agreed community price for grains had been at a higher level. But a potential offset was the decision in principle obtained by Italy: that fruits and vegetables, which had hitherto been excluded from the CAP and on a number of which the United States had obtained tariff bindings in 1962, would receive "Community preferences" comparable to those given to CAP products. Neither the grains decision nor that concerning fruits and vegetables, however, went into detail. In both cases the definitive arrangements were left for future settlement under an agreed timetable.

Once again, the resolution of internal difficulties in the Community proved to be short lived. But it created enough optimism in Geneva to encourage the executive secretary of GATT in January 1965 to submit his own proposal for negotiating agricultural products in the Kennedy Round.[26] After suggesting procedures for moving from the technical to the negotiating phase in the special groups for cereals and meat and proposing a date for convening the similar group for dairy products, he suggested a procedure for dealing with other agricultural products that was reminiscent of his successful proposal for bypassing the dispute over tariff disparities in the industrial sector. The effort to obtain agreed rules for the agricultural negotiations was dropped. The confrontation between the advocates of "market access" and stabilization of prices was ignored. He proposed simply that each participant should, on April 1, 1965, table "a list of offers on individual products." These offers were to relate to "all relevant elements of agricultural support or protection or to the total effect of these elements" and should be designed to achieve "acceptable conditions of access." Thus the Community obtained an oblique reference to one facet of the *montant de soutien* but not to the variable levy, and the agricultural exporters were given the word "access" but no explicit reference to the reduction of tariffs.

The EEC objected to the executive secretary's proposition, but two months later accepted a slightly revised version, with the date for tabling agricultural offers postponed to September 16, 1965. The revised proposal also provided that the interval before September 16 should be devoted to discussions among the participants which should attempt to "identify the relevant elements of support" to be dealt with in the negotiations.[27] This amendment was, of course, calculated to make the procedure more acceptable to the Community since it at least implied that offers would not be limited to tariffs, but would take into account the domestic policies of the participating countries.

The 1965 Community Crisis

The renewed hope of progress was again overtaken by crisis. In 1964, the conflict had been between France and Germany. In 1965, De Gaulle's even deeper antagonism against the European Commission and President Hallstein touched off a new attack of paralysis. The immediate occasion for the crisis was French dissatisfaction with the EEC council's failure to agree upon the future financing of the Common Agricultural Policy. But later developments suggest that De Gaulle's primary motivation was to force a revision of the majority voting provisions which, under the Treaty, were to be progressively introduced. Majority voting would have weakened France's veto power and have strengthened the role of the commission.[28]

France boycotted most Community meetings from early July 1965 until January 1966, including all meetings of the European council, the only body with authority to decide on Community offers in the Kennedy Round. When it became clear that the boycott would prevent the Community from submitting its agricultural offers on September 16, as agreed, the other Kennedy Round participants were faced with the question of whether to proceed on their own. Most of them, in the interest of restoring some momentum to the negotiations, decided to do so, but tried to minimize any future negotiating advantage this might give the Community by withholding offers on products of particular export interest to the member states. If they also permitted themselves to hope that this action might exert pressure on France to return to the negotiating table, they were disappointed. But their own exchange of offers did permit "technical" discussions to proceed among them. For the major agricultural products, however, meaningful negotiations without the EEC were impossible. Once again, the Community (involuntarily, so far as most of the members were concerned) demonstrated that its assent was essential not only to the achievement of the more ambitious goals of the Kennedy Round but even to a useful agreement among the remaining contracting parties.

The Luxembourg Compromise

During the fall of 1965, it was widely suggested that the negotiations be resumed on a conditional most favored nation basis, leaving the door open to eventual adherence by the EEC.[29] But in January 1966, the Community reached a compromise that restored the hope of negotiators in Geneva that it might still be possible to conclude a useful Kennedy Round based on unconditional MFN. It is true that the terms of the "Luxembourg Compromise" ensured that France would continue to exercise a de facto veto over vital Community decisions. But such a veto would have existed as a practical matter in any event, so long as France was able to persuade its partners that it was prepared to leave the Community if overridden on a question it considered vital. In exchange, Germany had obtained a commitment that, in any settlement later reached on the details of agricultural pricing, a decision would be reached on the agricultural offers to be made by the EEC to its Kennedy Round partners.[30]

Another five months were required before it was possible to convert this agreement into action. But, on July 24, 1966, the European council agreed on enough of the outstanding questions concerning the Common Agricultural Policy to clear the decks for approval, three days later, of the Community's Kennedy Round offers in the agricultural sector. Two and a half years after the official opening of the negotiations, the bargaining over agricultural protection could begin.

Part Four: The Struggle for Reciprocity

11

Industrial Tariffs

There is one notable difference between the emphasis in the negotiations so far chronicled and those in the phase to follow. Before industrial exceptions lists were exchanged or agricultural offers were tabled, the maneuvering had centered around two concerns: the United States and some others had sought to prejudice the rules in favor of a maximum overall liberalization of trade; and, all the participants had sought to ensure that they would receive reciprocity from the application of the rules, with a minimum need for subsequent negotiation. Once the rules had been agreed to or agreement had been reached to proceed without specific guidelines, however, attention shifted to individual products, and each negotiator attempted to extract a maximum of concessions from his negotiating partners with a minimum of concessions on his own part. The search for reciprocity moved from the abstract to the concrete, from the blackboard to the bazaar.

In May 1964 the GATT ministers had agreed to table their exceptions lists in September of that year. The deadline was postponed twice because of the inability of the six to reach agreement among themselves in the agricultural sector and the initial unwillingness of the United States to permit the industrial and agricultural negotiations to get out of phase. When this objection was withdrawn, agreement was reached on a new deadline: November 16 of the same year.

The absence of any agreement on rules to govern disparities introduced a large measure of uncertainty into the meaning of the exceptions that were to be listed, especially the meaning of the list to be submitted by the Community. Would the EEC take disparities into account and except items that would have been eligible for disparity treatment under its proposed formula? If so, would it distinguish between these products and those excepted because of considerations of "overriding national interest"? Or would it keep its freedom of maneuver by explicitly reserving products for future offers? As will be seen, the Community chose the last of these courses.

Uncertainties arising from the lack of a disparity rule were not limited to the meaning of the EEC exceptions. In July, Sweden made it known that it would submit no list of exceptions, and this position was soon adopted by the other Nordic countries and Switzerland. The decision was clearly tactical. It is hardly possible that the low-tariff countries expected that their example would inspire their larger partners to make linear reductions without exception. There could be no doubt that at some point in the negotiation they would announce the massive withdrawal of offers in order to obtain the reciprocity they had always demanded. The low-tariff countries must have believed that their inadequate bargaining power could be enhanced if their more powerful partners were kept in doubt as to their final contribution. Uncertainty concerning the course the EEC would take about disparities and the outcome of the discussions it had undertaken with "third countries" was probably the deciding factor in the adoption of this stratagem. It is significant, though, that such a transparent departure from the spirit and letter of the linear rules met with no criticism from other negotiators. The original linear concept had suffered too much damage for a further departure to arouse indignation.

The Tabling of Exceptions List

On November 16, as scheduled, the representatives of the linear participants and Canada met in the office of the executive secretary and simultaneously exchanged exceptions lists. The participants tabling exceptions were the EEC, the United States, the United Kingdom, Japan, and Finland. The remaining Nordic countries, joined by Switzerland and Austria, confirmed that "subject to obtaining reciprocity from their negotiating partners," they were not tabling exceptions.[1] Canada tabled a list of positive offers, and Czechoslovakia announced its intention of doing the same.

In accordance with an established GATT tradition, the contents of tariff offers — and, therefore, the details of exceptions lists — are confidential. The agreement of each participant to observe such secrecy was at the time reasonably well observed. It was, however, to receive a more severe test when each participant submitting a list was subjected to the procedure of "justification" previously agreed upon.

The Justification Procedure

In the following month, December 1964, the same countries met in order that each might justify its exceptions in accordance with the criteria previously approved. It was a dreary procedure. Whatever purpose could have been served by the confrontation had been accomplished before it took place. Only if the negotiation had been truly "linear" would there have been any chance of obtaining an improvement in exceptions lists on the ground that they did not meet the agreed criteria. As it was, those criteria were simply not consistent with the universal reservation of the right to demand reciprocity. And even if there had not been a general, though tacit, acceptance of this fact, the absence of agreed rules covering many points at issue in the negotiations provided a reason for ignoring the criteria.

The Press Takes a Hand

If the proceedings behind closed doors were languid, the atmosphere in the corridors was lively enough. Excluded from the meeting room, journalists tried to piece together the contents of exceptions lists from such crumbs of information as they could obtain from delegates in the hallways of the Palais des Nations. Sometimes a delegate could be persuaded to talk, especially if challenged with an untruth attributed to one of his negotiating partners. And once a fact or another untruth, so extracted, had appeared in print, the most conscientious delegation was apt to feel that the record had to be set straight by a judicious leak to a favored journal. On the whole, the secrecy rule seems to have been kept well enough to prevent lobbyists and pressure groups from obtaining the sort of detail they needed in order to operate effectively. But it did not prevent a careful newspaper reader from making a shrewd guess as to the basis on which the next stage in the negotiations was about to begin.

Most of the news stories agreed that the list of exceptions submitted by the EEC was especially heavy.[2] It also became widely known that the Community's list included many items designated as "partial exceptions," for which the offered tariff reductions were not specified, and that it also contained an especially high proportion of products of export interest to the Nordic members of EFTA.[3] On the other hand, the EEC had its loyal defenders among the European press. *Le Monde* of February 11, for example, paraphrased in detail the arguments presented by the EEC spokesman in his justification of the Community's list.

One of the most detailed appraisals of the exceptions lists of the EEC and the United States appeared in the *New York Times* of January 20, 1965. According to this account, imports covered by the American list represented about 18 or 19 percent of total dutiable imports of industrial products; the figure given for the Community's list was 40 percent. The latter, however, included the steel items for which the Community had offered a 50 percent reduction from what United States negotiators insisted was a fictitious base rate — evidence that the source of the *Times* story was sympathetic to the US side of the controversy. If these steel items were not considered exceptions, the EEC list was said to represent about 29 percent of dutiable industrial imports. The *New York Times* story, however, did not specify how the products which the EEC had listed as "partial exceptions" were dealt with in these calculations. Nor did it say whether the calculation for the United States included those products which the United States recorded as "exclusions" rather than exceptions because they were principally supplied by countries not participating in the GATT or in the Kennedy Round.[4]

Nevertheless, contemporary leaks to the press did establish one fact of considerable importance: the negotiating phase of the

Kennedy Round was to be inaugurated on the basis of offers generally more liberal, in terms of both trade coverage and depth of cut, than the offers that had launched any previous negotiations. Hard bargaining lay ahead, but the customary process of extracting offers, one by one, from a reluctant partner had been partly circumvented.[5]

The Bilateral Negotiations

After the linear participants had expended a decent quota of time and energy on the justification procedures, the negotiation of industrial tariffs moved to the bilateral stage. With the exception of a few efforts at multilateral negotiations within certain sectors, they remained essentially bilateral until almost the end of the negotiations.

Facts about the bilateral negotiations were more closely guarded than the justification procedures. Even during the largely bilateral phase, however, the effort to achieve multilateral agreement in certain industrial sectors resulted in further leaks.

Negotiation of Industrial Sectors

The sectoral approach had not been part of the tariff negotiating plan originally conceived by the GATT ministers. But the bilateral confrontations that followed the examination of exceptions lists soon revealed important groups of products in which the difficulties were unlikely to be resolved in bilateral bargaining. Each of these sectors had characteristics that set it apart from the others, but most shared the common problem that a major participant had made any worthwhile concessions conditional upon obtaining some specified concession from one or more of its negotiating partners.

Steel. The sector of iron and steel products was affected from the outset by the fact that the major importers were also substantial exporters; none was prepared to open its markets to increased imports unless it could see concrete benefits for its own industry in doing so. The steel sector was also set apart by the special problem of the base rate used for the European Community's offer affecting those products that fell under the jurisdiction of the European Coal and Steel Community.[6] After the establishment of the

EEC in 1961, its members had obtained a waiver from the Contracting Parties to permit the necessary departure from their MFN
obligations.[7] That waiver was based, among other things, on an
assurance by the member states that, under the ECSC, their harmonized tariffs would be less restrictive than the general incidence
of their duties and other import restrictions before its institution.[8]
According to an estimate presented by the Community during the
Kennedy Round, the arithmetical average of those tariffs at the institution of the ECSC had been 14.4 percent. By 1962 that average
had been reduced to 6.7 percent. But it had been temporarily increased to about 9 percent in 1964.[9] The Kennedy Round offer by
the Community was to reduce the rates on all ECSC items to 50
percent of their pre-ECSC levels, and to reduce by something less
than 50 percent most of the remaining steel items, that is, those
not under the jurisdiction of the ECSC.

Not only were other steel exporters unwilling to recognize a 50
percent reduction from pre-ECSC levels as a full linear cut, but
the United Kingdom maintained that it had "paid" for the reduction to the 6.7 percent level when, in 1958, it had agreed with the
ECSC to the mutual reduction of steel tariffs.[10] The United Kingdom conditioned the maintenance of its own linear offer on an
improvement in the Community's offer. To complicate the problem still further, the Community, which had not harmonized the
rates of the member states, insisted that four tariff schedules (those
of Benelux, France, Germany, and Italy) should be negotiated
separately; a common external tariff would only be established at
some later date. The other participants in the steel sector negotiations insisted that common external tariffs should be established
and bound in the Kennedy Round itself.

The offer of the European Community was not the only source
of contention. Although the United States had offered a linear
reduction on all steel items, Japan maintained that the value of
this offer was impaired by the restrictive nature of US antidumping
procedures and conditioned the maintenance of its own linear
offer on a liberalization of those practices.

The United States, whose average steel tariff was already lower
than that of the EEC, would have had a good deal to gain from
an agreement by the steel producing countries to bring their tariff
rates into closer alignment. "Harmonization" would have brought
a substantial reduction in the Community's tariff, while bypassing

the dispute over the appropriate base rate to be used in a linear reduction. Such a reduction by the Community would have paid additional dividends, for it would have met the British argument and permitted reduction of the British rates. Of perhaps greater interest under the conditions prevailing in the mid-1960's, it might have diverted to Europe some of the low-priced Japanese exports that were contributing to the growth of protectionist sentiments in the US steel industry.

Given these complexities, the judgment of the director general* that steel was a prime candidate for sector negotiations was justified, at least in the sense that bilateral negotiations held little hope of achieving anything better than the status quo. However, efforts at negotiation in a multilateral framework failed to break the deadlock over the problem of the base date, and a compromise was not worked out until the closing phase of the Kennedy Round.

Chemicals. The issues in the chemicals sector were less complicated than in steel but in some ways even more difficult.[11] In this case, the United States, rather than the Community, stood at the center of attack. Although the former had offered a full 50 percent reduction in virtually all chemical tariffs, the resultant rates in the case of those benzenoid chemicals that were competitive with US production would still have been subject to the American Selling Price.[12] Both the EEC and the United Kingdom reserved a substantial number of chemical products from their linear offers and made abolition of ASP a condition for any concessions in the chemical sector. At the time there were differing views as to whether Sec. 201 (a) (2) of the Trade Expansion Act would have permitted the President to alter a standard of customs valuation established by law. But there was no room for doubt that the elimination of ASP, combined with a 50 percent reduction in rates, would have exceeded the administration's authority. Even with more attractive offers by other countries than had been proffered, the US delegation would have been unable to meet the demands of the other chemical exporting countries. The resulting deadlock appeared to be insoluble during most of the rest of the Kennedy Round.

For a while, there did appear to be some prospect that the US

*The title of executive secretary was changed to director general on March 23, 1965.

offer of a linear cut would prove sufficiently attractive to bring a compromise. Benzenoid chemicals represented only about 8 percent of the total output of the US chemical industry, and imports of all other chemicals were subject to normal standards of valuation. According to the chairman of the US delegation,[13] out of some eight hundred chemical rates in the US tariff, only seventy-one were inflated by the application of ASP. But ASP had become a symbol of American protectionism not only for European governments but for the European press and public. It would surely have been difficult for those governments to accept even a highly advantageous bargain in the chemical sector if it did not include some assurances concerning the removal of ASP. Thus, ironically, the EEC and the United Kingdom had themselves conferred upon the removal of ASP a bargaining value far out of proportion to the increased trade that could result.

Under the circumstances, the obvious strategy for the US delegation was to extract the maximum offers obtainable in return for removal of ASP and then to ask the Congress to ratify the bargain. But if this strategy had been adopted in so simple a form, the authority Congress had already delegated to the President would not have been used and might have been lost. Presumably with this in mind, the US delegation offered a chemical settlement in two "packages." One agreement would have been concluded as part of the Kennedy Round and would have involved generous reductions in chemical rates by the United States but not the removal of ASP. A separate package, conditional on congressional action, would have been based primarily on the removal of ASP in exchange for further benefits to American exports, both inside and outside the chemical sector.

During most of 1965 and 1966 the EEC and the United Kingdom resisted the "two package" approach and continued to insist on a promise to do away with ASP as a precondition to any chemical negotiations. In late December of 1966, the director general made an effort to break the impasse. In a paper submitted to the chemical sector group, he reviewed the positions of both sides. He expressed understanding of the reluctance of the Europeans to accept the idea of two packages; they naturally wanted to leave the United States no incentive for settling without repealing ASP. Nevertheless he suggested that they could accomplish their purpose by making the "second package" the more attractive to the United States. He therefore recommended that, in an *ad referendum* agreement: The United States would maintain its 50 percent offer on non-ASP items, convert ASP tariffs to non-ASP rates yielding the same ad valorem equivalent, cut the converted rates by 50 percent, and make reductions of more than 50 percent where the resulting rate was still high. The EEC would reduce all chemical tariffs by as close to 50 percent as possible and offer a worthwhile concession to the United States in some important nontariff barrier. The United Kingdom would maintain its 50 percent offer on most chemicals, negotiate a reduction of more than 50 percent on those rates over 33⅓ percent ad valorem, extend its reductions to include plastics, and grant the United States a nontariff barrier concession such as the liberalization of restrictions on the use of imported television programs. Switzerland would grant 50 percent reductions on all chemical tariffs and also grant some nontariff barrier concession.

In the end, the European countries did agree to a dual settlement along the lines of the director general's proposal. Since this was part of the final compromise that made the Kennedy Round agreement possible, the details appear in a later chapter.

Pulp and Paper. The key issue in the paper sector was primarily between the EEC and the Scandinavian countries, the chief source of pulp for the Community's paper industry. The EEC withheld any offers to reduce its paper tariffs until it could obtain assurance of improved access to Scandinavian pulp; its export prices, the EEC contended, were being held at artificially high levels by the Scandinavian countries.[14]

The resultant disagreement between the Community and the Nordic countries affected all negotiations in the paper sector, since the Community argued that its paper industry could not compete with others while it was being denied a source of pulp at competitive prices. It therefore withheld offers even on paper items of primary interest to Canada and the United States. An early transfer of negotiations into a multilateral group proved impracticable because of the Community's insistence on a solution to its pulp supply problem before it would discuss tariff concessions. On the other hand, the EEC-Nordic discussions led to serious concern among the suppliers of paper that they would result in some kind of "special deal" under which Scandinavian paper exporters would receive preferred treatment in the Common Market in exchange for lower pulp cost to EEC importers.[15] In fact, according to Congressman Thomas B. Curtis, such a plan was proposed by a combination of large Community paper producers[16] but, perhaps because of opposition from the United States and Canada, was never consummated.

Until very late in the Kennedy Round, continuing bilateral discussions between the EEC and the Scandinavian producers precluded multilateral negotiations. The United States had an interest in obtaining tariff reductions from the EEC in such capital-intensive products as linerboard. From the United Kingdom it wanted reductions in linerboard and kraft paper in order to reduce the preferential tariff margins enjoyed by Canada and the EFTA countries. But the United Kingdom was not willing to move before the EEC did. In the end, the Community did grant appreciable reductions in items of interest to the United States, and Britain made a moderate reduction in its MFN rate for linerboard. These were, however, results of bilateral negotiations. The multilateral technique cannot be credited with whatever success was achieved in the pulp and paper sector.

Cotton Textiles.   On February 9, 1962, the Contracting Parties principally involved in the import or export of cotton textiles and clothing had drawn up the Long-Term Arrangement Regarding International Trade in Cotton Textiles (LTA),[17] which entered into force on October 1 of that year. The stated objective of the arrangement was the "orderly" expansion of international trade in cotton textiles, but its most important operative articles provided that:

a. If imports from a participating country "should cause or threaten disruption" in the market of another participating country, the latter might ask the exporting country to restrict its shipments.

b. If no agreement on the level of restraint were reached, the importing country might, regardless of the provisions of the GATT, impose quantitative restrictions on imports from the exporting country in those categories of textiles causing the market disruption.

c. Any import quotas so imposed could be no lower than the

level of imports in the year ending three months before the request. Where such quotas were maintained for more than one year they were required to be increased by at least 6 percent each year.[18]

During the first year of the LTA, the United States had invoked its restraint provisions to justify restriction of imports from ten countries, most of them less developed. Canada had restricted imports from six countries; Germany, from one. Those countries imposing import quotas at the time of the arrangement were obliged simply to increase their quotas each year by 5 percent from the levels specified in the arrangement and were not required to invoke "market disruption" to justify their maintenance.

By the opening of the Kennedy Round, the exporting countries had made clear their dissatisfaction with the manner in which the LTA was being administered. They complained that restraint requests by some importing countries, including the United States, had become an automatic reflex to increased imports whether or not "disruption" was actively caused or threatened. The pattern of restraint requests gave substantial support to this charge.

The dissatisfaction of the exporters had reached such a pitch that the major importers had reason to fear that the LTA, in its existing form, would come under heavy attack during the review of the agreement, scheduled for the fall of 1965, and that it would not be renewed when its five-year term expired in October 1967. If the arrangement were not renewed, the importers could continue to restrict imports only at the cost of violating their GATT commitments. With this danger in mind, the United States and the EEC conditioned their Kennedy Round offers in cotton textiles upon renewal of the LTA. With this qualification, United States offers were full linear reductions. Those of the EEC consisted in part of reductions of less than 50 percent. Canada, while not making a similar condition explicit, simply offered to reduce tariffs on many cotton textiles "if other countries do so also." The United Kingdom did not refer to the LTA, but indicated that its offers in the sector, which were limited to "mixed duties" on goods containing cotton and man-made fibers, would be reviewed in light of the outcome of the negotiations in the sector as a whole.

It was clear not only that no significant results could be obtained from the bilateral negotiation of tariff rates in the cotton textile sector but that the key to a successful outcome was the renewal of the LTA. But those countries that were primarily exporters did not seem to have been convinced that they would receive, in the form of higher prices, any substantial part of the reduction in duties that was offered. And, since they could anticipate that any potential increase in their exports due to tariff cuts would be frustrated by quotas, they did not consider a tariff reduction adequate recompense for continuation of the LTA. In fact, if tariff reductions had been the only inducement to the exporters to agree to renewal, it is more than doubtful that they would have agreed to that continuation as, in the end, they did. A more persuasive form of payment was used to accomplish this result when, as permitted by Article IV of the LTA, the United States and other importers negotiated, with individual exporting countries, increased levels of imports of specific products to be admitted under a renewed agreement. These negotiated quotas were above the minimum levels required by the existing agreement.

The strategy of negotiating improved quotas with individual exporting countries, in lieu of a basic change in the long-term arrangement, was successful in obtaining the agreement of the exporting countries to renewal even though the major importing countries failed to apply the full linear tariff cut to cotton textiles. But the details of the tariff settlement arrived at in the Kennedy Round itself belong to the account of the closing phase of the negotiations.

Aluminum. Six industrialized participants — the United States, the EEC, the United Kingdom, Japan, Canada, and Norway — participated in negotiations concerning primary aluminum.[19] Because of the extent to which the major producers of primary aluminum had internationalized their operations, early in the negotiations there appeared to be a fair prospect that a free-trade agreement, at least in unwrought aluminum, could be negotiated. The three largest American aluminum companies, for example, had among them subsidiaries or affiliates producing unwrought aluminum in Australia, Brazil, Greece, Germany, India, the Netherlands, Norway, Spain, Surinam, the United Kingdom, and Venezuela. Aluminium, Ltd. of Canada had producing affiliates in Australia, India, Italy, Norway, and Sweden. The French complex of Pechiney-Ugine had affiliates in Greece, Spain, and the United States. Similarly, most primary producing companies had not only integrated their operations vertically in their own countries, but had acquired outright ownership or stock interest in semifabricating capacity in other producing countries. Thus, the Reynolds Company had semifabricating affiliates in Germany, the Netherlands, Belgium-Luxembourg, Italy, and Japan; Kaiser in Germany, Italy, and Japan; Alcoa in Japan; and Pechiney in Belgium-Luxembourg and the United States.

The international connections of the largest producers did not mean, however, that their interests were identical. While two of the three great American producers had semifabricating capacity in a number of EEC countries, none of them had affiliates in France. All three were represented in Japan, but no Japanese company had major primary or fabricating affiliates anywhere abroad. The United Kingdom, the United States, and the EEC were both large importers and large exporters of aluminum, but the EEC and the United Kingdom were also importers of unwrought and exporters of wrought metal. The large export balance of the United States in wrought aluminum was more than offset by its import balance in unwrought metal. Canada and Norway had heavy exports of unwrought and small imports of wrought metal.

In spite of the unbalanced pattern of trade, the prospects for achieving free entry for unwrought aluminum did not seem bad. In most countries the domestic producers of primary aluminum were either heavy exporters or needed imports, often from their own facilities abroad, to supplement their domestic supplies.

Industries in the largest exporting countries — Canada, Norway, and the United States — seemed quite ready to accept any possible increase in imports that might result from the removal of their tariffs on unwrought aluminum. Canada made a formal offer to eliminate its duty if others would do the same. The United States offered the full linear reduction, which would have resulted in a duty with an ad valorem equivalent of less than 3 percent. Norway, a substantial net exporter, and the United Kingdom, the largest net importer, already admitted unwrought, unalloyed aluminum free of duty. But Japan, a marginal net importer, excepted primary aluminum from its linear offers and undertook to reduce its rate only from 13 percent to 10 percent.

If Japan had been the only exception to a general desire for free trade in unwrought aluminum, the others might still have been able to agree (with US agreement subject to implementation by Congress) to free trade or at least to harmonization of tariffs at around 3 percent. But France's interest coincided neither with that of the other negotiators nor with that of its EEC partners. Although a Pechiney affiliate had substantial semifabricating capacity in the United States and might have welcomed duty-free treatment for unwrought metal in this country, it also had a promising export market in the rest of the EEC. In 1964 the EEC, excluding France, imported some $85 million of unwrought aluminum over exports. France already had an export balance within the EEC and stood to gain a substantial part of the growing markets in Germany and Belgium if competition from third countries could be restrained. French opposition throughout the negotiations frustrated the hope of Canada and Norway, in particular, that aluminum might serve as a demonstration of what could be achieved in sectors in which industrial integration had developed along international lines. In the final settlement, only slight improvements were obtained in the original EEC and Japanese offers.

The Role of the European Community

The pace of both the sector negotiations and bilateral bargaining was largely a function of the fluctuating ability of the commission to obtain new instructions from the Council of Ministers of the Community. Since all tariff decisions required unanimous approval, the structural impediment to decision making in the Community was formidable at any time. But it was compounded during the first half of 1965, since France prevented any movement toward further European integration except in matters of particular interest to France. These evidently did not include progress in the Kennedy Round.[20] The frustrating delays of the first half of the year were followed, as we have noted, by the almost total paralysis resulting from the French boycott of nearly all Community activities, a paralysis that was promptly transmitted to the Kennedy Round and lasted until the "Luxembourg Compromise" in mid-January 1966.[21]

During much of 1965 and some of 1966 the Community's representatives in Geneva were unable to negotiate in any real sense of the word. It is difficult to avoid the impression that many of the "technical discussions" held during that period could have been dispensed with had real negotiations been possible. Their principal function seems to have been to provide governments with a sense of activity and an excuse for the continued presence of their negotiators in Geneva. It is true that, in February 1966, there was again some reason to hope that the major roadblock had been removed and that true negotiations could get under way, provided governmental positions had not become irrevocably frozen by constant repetition. Encouraged by the breaking of the deadlock in the EEC, the director general, in his capacity as chairman of the Trade Negotiations Committee, initiated a series of maneuvers designed to move the negotiations off dead center.

In February 1966, Wyndham White visited the capitals of the principal negotiating countries in the hope of transmitting to governments some of his own sense of urgency and his conviction that a basic change of attitude would be required if industrial bargaining were to get under way and agricultural negotiations were to be opened.

The Appraisal of Offers and "Withdrawal Lists"

In June 1966, the director general took the unusual course — but one that seems to have been justified by the circumstances — of intervening more directly in the negotiating process. Only a year remained before the deadline by which the final agreement would have to be signed, that is, before expiration of the President's negotiating authority under the Trade Expansion Act. But it was then believed that, once an agreement in principle had been reached, three months would be needed to put it into legal form, translate and check the thousands of individual tariff concessions, and prepare the necessary documents for signature. Thus, in about nine months, the participants would have to accomplish far more than they had achieved in the previous three and a half years. In the face of the occupational reluctance of any negotiator to seem more anxious to reach agreement than his opponents, the director general found it desirable to play the role of gadfly and even to propose to the negotiators how they should conduct their bargaining. On June 3, he proposed to the Trade Negotiations Committee that, later in the year, a new kind of confrontation should take place. At that time, the head of each negotiating delegation should communicate to the other delegations his appraisal of the then outstanding offers of all participants and indicate what improvements in those offers he considered indispensable, if his own offers were to be maintained, and which of his own offers he would have to withdraw if his demands were not met. Probably the most important purpose of this proposal was to force the Community to face up to the need for granting more negotiating authority to its commission. It might, it was hoped, do so in anticipation of the proposed "warning" exercise. But, if not, the combined pressure exerted during that exercise might lead to an improvement in the Community's offers at a later date. At a minimum, a multilateral presentation of "withdrawal lists" would precipitate the belated but inevitable submission of a list of exceptions by the Scandinavian and Swiss delegations, so that all negotiators would know what offers they could take seriously in determining their own negotiating positions.

After some initial disagreement over the date, the director general's proposal was accepted and the multilateral confrontation began at the end of November and lasted through the first half of December. In the meantime, the Scandinavian delegations organized themselves to make maximum use of the opportunity offered and decided not only to pool their withdrawal lists but thereafter to negotiate as a unit under the leadership of the Swedish Representative, Ambassador Nils Montan.

The country submissions were, of course, subject to the general rule of secrecy and not divulged in detail to the press. But the totals of the withdrawals that were threatened were a less closely guarded secret, and enough became known to reveal that the EEC was the almost universal target of attack. The Nordic countries promptly took the offensive and presented a list of potential withdrawals; between $700 million and $1 billion of imports from the EEC would be affected, as compared with $80 million from the United States. The United Kingdom also concentrated most of its fire on the EEC, as did Switzerland. All of the threatened withdrawals by Canada were directed against the EEC or Japan. Japan also came in for criticism by the United States both for its inadequate tariff offers and for its continued maintenance of quantitative import restrictions. The relatively temperate assaults on the

United States by the United Kingdom and Japan were concentrated on nontariff barriers: the administration of the antidumping law and the ASP.

Even in this relatively easy and negative kind of bargaining, the institutions of the Community were apparently unable to function efficiently. The EEC submitted neither appraisals of the offers of others nor a withdrawal list of its own, though the Community's representative did announce that he hoped soon to submit a definitive list of disparities that the Community proposed to invoke.

At the end of 1966, it was still too early to say whether the director general's strategy would work. But if there had ever been any doubt within the Community that the other negotiators as a whole considered the positions taken by the EEC to be the principal obstacle to a successful Kennedy Round, that doubt must have been dispelled.

12

Agriculture

On July 24, 1966, after two years of more or less continuous paralysis, the Community placed itself in a position to reach decisions in the field of agriculture when the member states agreed on the Common Market regulations for dairy products, beef, sugar, fruits, and vegetables. The common prices arrived at, however, did not hold much promise for international trade. The Dutch and French considered them too high.[1] According to *Le Monde,* these prices were "much more protectionist" than the proposals that had been made earlier by the commission.[2] The decision did, however, make it possible for the EEC to table its positive offers on agricultural products two weeks later. These offers included some tariff reductions, ranging for the most part between 5 and 20 percent of existing rates. But, the binding of a reference price was all that was proposed for the CAP products and for some others, including those products for which special negotiating groups had been formed.

Following their receipt of the Community's offers on August 5, 1961, the other Kennedy Round participants tabled additional agricultural offers of interest to the Community. But when the agricultural offers as a whole were considered in the Agricultural Committee in mid-September, all the major participants except Japan expressed dissatisfaction with the Community's contribution.

For his part, the EEC spokesman complained of the offers made by the United States on the ground that they were limited to tariff concessions and did not deal with other instruments of US agricultural policy.

At last, the negotiations concerning agriculture in general could get under way. But the fundamental divergence between the objectives of the EEC and those of the agricultural exporters had not been removed. Nor was there much optimism for the future; there was no reason to believe that any member state would risk another Community crisis for the sake of the Kennedy Round.

Bulk Product Groups

More than two years earlier, the participants had exchanged specific proposals that had enabled them to begin "negotiations" in wheat and coarse grains. They had also begun "technical discussions" that gave promise of leading to negotiations on meat and dairy products. These "group" products had already been earmarked by the Community for variable levies, and the exporters had grown used to the idea. Furthermore, under prescribed GATT procedures, the EEC had withdrawn the tariff bindings formerly granted by the member states on these products. Application of variable levies to them did not, therefore, threaten existing contractual rights as did the Community's apparent effort to obtain international sanction for a disregard of its tariff bindings in other agricultural products. That the United States had this distinction very much in mind was shown by its indignant reaction to an EEC suggestion in the fall of 1964 that a group be formed to negotiate a commodity agreement in oilseeds. One of the oilseeds, soybeans, the duty-free status of which the EEC had bound in 1962, constituted the fastest growing and one of the largest of US agricultural exports to the Community.

True, there still seemed to be a possibility that the group negotiations (covering cereals, dairy products, and meat) might provide access assurances of some value, though one influential American farm organization, the Farm Bureau Federation, apparently discounted even this possibility. In September 1966, Charles B. Shuman, president of the federation, wrote to Christian A. Herter urging that the United States withdraw all its offers, both industrial and agricultural, and not resubmit them "until the European Economic Community agrees to present meaningful offers."[3]

In the case of the products for which the Community had adopted variable levies, exporting countries were faced with accepting the commodity agreement approach, or nothing. But that approach also had certain attractions for some. If it should result in a limitation of US wheat subsidies, it could benefit Canada; New Zealand might gain from regulation of the subsidized competition that was limiting its export earnings from meat and dairy products in a number of major markets; and, as mentioned earlier, Australia was in favor of higher wheat prices.

The Cereals Group

While there was little dissent as to the need for a world grains agreement, the written proposals submitted by all participants shortly before the formal opening of the Kennedy Round in May 1964 showed wide divergence of view concerning its objectives.

In its submission to the Cereals Group, the EEC emphasized the need for achieving an "equitable balance" between the interests of exporters and importers, the establishment of "equilibrium" between production and demand, and the stabilization of prices. It proposed that the central feature of the arrangement should be the binding by each participant of its *montant de soutien* ("margin of support").[4]

A group of major exporters (the United States, Canada, Australia, and Argentina) advocated an agreement that would preserve to cereal exporting countries the opportunity to compete "for at least their present share" of the consumption of the importing countries.

The United Kingdom submitted an evenly balanced compromise between the extreme positions of the EEC and the exporters. Japan obviously had no enthusiasm for any international regulation of markets in grains and took the position that if an importing country granted reasonable access to its market it should be free to adopt such domestic policies as it chose.

These conflicting positions were reported by the Cereals Group to the Trade Negotiations Committee just before it met at ministerial level in May 1964.[5] The group was able, however, to record a greater measure of agreement on one facet of the proposed arrangement: the coordination of the "noncommercial disposal of surpluses." Many details, however, of what was later to become one of the principal features of the agreement remained to be worked out, especially the problem of the nature of the contribution to food aid by those participants without surplus production. It was presumably in anticipation of the demands that would be made on it later that Japan in principle objected to the injection of food aid into the Kennedy Round.

These disagreements over the general purpose and structure of a grains agreement provided adequate material to occupy further meetings of the group until the impasse within the EEC over the Community's wheat price effectively prevented further progress. But after harmony was temporarily restored in December 1964, discussions were resumed, and the commission was able to agree the following March to the director general's proposal that the negotiations be resumed the following May "on the basis of specific proposals, including concrete offers by participating governments." This date was met, and negotiations on the basis of definite proposals were at last possible.

The Community's position had not changed. Its "offer" consisted of a proposal that all participants bind their existing "margins of support." The United States, of course, opposed this approach and argued that the freezing of existing differences between the domestic prices of the respective participants was unlikely to achieve the objectives the Community had itself espoused. But before the debate could be carried much further, the French boycott of Community meetings began and was extended to include attendance at meetings of the Cereals Group, effectively preventing further progress until the "Luxembourg Compromise"[6] in January 1966. When negotiations resumed, the participants still had to find agreement on all of the major issues: limitation of domestic subsidies and price supports, competitive access to import markets, an internationally accepted price or range of prices, and a system for coordinating noncommercial disposal of surpluses and the pooling of food aid.

The Self-Sufficiency Ratio

The first sign of a possible breakthrough over the issue of market access for cereals came as the result of a proposal by the commission to the European council that the Community offer to limit its domestic production to an agreed percentage of domestic consumption. France at first opposed this proposal, but later agreed to have the commission explore the question in the Cereals Group. As outlined to the group in July 1966, the idea was welcomed by the exporters but not at the level or in the form proposed. The EEC offer set 90 percent of current consumption as the target for indigenous production, reserving for imports a somewhat lower percentage than had actually entered in recent years. Furthermore, the ratio would have become operative only when the council of the Cereals Agreement determined that a world surplus existed. Finally, the EEC reserved the right to supply, from indigenous production, any increase in Community consumption above existing levels.

At the same time, however, the Community did reveal its acceptance of one request to which the US negotiators attached great importance: the principle of joint responsibility for food aid. On this issue, the interests of France and the United States, as surplus producers of wheat, coincided. Both would be better off if other countries were to share in the cost of food aid, especially if that contribution included payment for surpluses produced in North America and Western Europe.

During the final year of the Kennedy Round, the efforts of the exporters in the Cereals Group were largely concentrated on persuading the Community and the United Kingdom to accept a self-sufficiency ratio that would operate automatically and that would reserve some part of increased domestic consumption for imports. The desired automatism was to be achieved by provisions to require a country that exceeded its ratio to remove the excess from the market, by purchase for the food aid stock if necessary.

As the negotiations proceeded, the position of the United Kingdom, the largest importer of wheat, moved closer to that of the EEC. In 1964, in order to limit the cost of deficiency payments, the United Kingdom had negotiated bilateral agreements with the major countries exporting grain; these provided that Britain's support of domestic production would be curtailed if imports fell below an agreed percentage of domestic production and that "equalization fees" would be charged on imports if world prices fell below a stipulated minimum. These fees resembled the Community's variable levies, but they were made more palatable to exporters by the limitation placed on the level of domestic production to be supported. In the early days of negotiation in the Cereals Group, the exporters often cited the British system as an example of the way in which a variable levy could be made acceptable. But when, during the first year of these bilateral agreements, the share of imports into the United Kingdom in fact fell, the United Kingdom made only a minor reduction in the price guaranteed to domestic farmers and increased the quantities eligible for deficiency payments.[7] And, in the latter stages of the group negotiations, the United Kingdom joined the EEC in resisting the demands of exporters for better assurances of access.

Japan continued to object both to the concept of the self-sufficiency ratio and to the sharing of responsibility for food aid.

Both exporters and importers were divided among themselves as to the desirable maximum and minimum levels for world prices. But this issue did not appear as intractable as the problems of access and at no time threatened the breakdown of the negotiations. Though there was still disagreement at many vital points, by the end of 1966 the possibility of achieving some sort of grains agreement seemed reasonably hopeful.

The Meat and Dairy Product Groups

The groups established to negotiate agreements covering international trade in meat and in dairy products got off to a considerably later start than the Grains Group. Six months before the last possible date for closing the Kennedy Round, they had not proceeded beyond the stage of "technical discussions." Their progress, or lack of progress, for a while paralleled that of the agricultural negotiations in general and was influenced by the same factor — the inability of the Community to reach agreement on its internal policies and prices. But even after that deadlock had been broken and the EEC was able to table its overall agricultural offers, these two groups could not agree on a date for the submission of concrete proposals. Thus, the optimism that had generally been felt at the beginning of 1967 concerning the possibility of reaching an agreement on grains did not extend to the other two bulk products in which the technique of group negotiations had been tried.

Summary

The agricultural products involved in the special groups included most of the products that loomed largest in international trade. But the emphasis that was justifiably placed on the group negotiations should not be allowed to obscure the fact that tariff reductions were negotiated on a significant volume of agricultural trade. In the agreement that was reached in the late spring of 1967, tariff concessions by all participants affected some $870 million of US agricultural exports. And, while comparatively little in the way of concessions was obtained from the EEC on products dealt with in the agricultural groups, the United States did receive from the community tariff reductions, largely of modest depth, on about $238 million of exports to the EEC. At the end of 1966, however, none of these results had crystallized into a final settlement, and several months of hard bargaining still lay ahead.

13

Other Issues

It must be apparent that the Kennedy Round resembled a many-ringed circus with the action in the two central rings — linear reductions and agriculture — overlapping but not synchronized with each other. In the first ring, the exchange of exceptions lists in November 1964 has been taken as the end of the preparatory period. In the second, the comparable period was not reached until September 1966. The dates have in common the fact that they marked the beginning of the period when confrontation over trade barriers affecting particular products could begin.

At the cost of some loss of symmetry, a chronological discussion has been abandoned in the case of the "secondary" rings of the circus:[1] the participation of less developed countries, participation of countries having "special economic structures" and the negotiation of nontariff barriers. The present chapter summarizes the negotiations in each of these areas, from the opening of negotiations and, where this can be done without obscuring the essential elements of the overall settlement, through to their formal conclusion in June 1967.

The Participation of Less Developed Countries

At no time during Kennedy Round planning had there been any serious expectation that the less developed countries would participate on the same basis as most industrialized countries, that is, through linear reductions of their own tariffs. Nor did anyone expect that these poorer countries would be able to match even the "nonlinear" developed countries in tariff reductions. Thus, the ministers, meeting in the spring of 1963, were able fairly easily to agree that "every effort should be made to reduce barriers to exports of less developed countries but the developed countries cannot expect to receive reciprocity" from them.[2]

Defining the contribution to be made by the less developed countries to the Kennedy Round was, however, more difficult. Many spokesmen for these countries argued vigorously that they were not in a position to grant any tariff reductions. They maintained that the contributions of less developed countries to the negotiations would be automatic — that, regardless of the level of their tariffs, they would have no choice but to expend any increased export earnings on increased imports. And from these premises they argued that products exported by the less developed countries had no legitimate place in the exceptions list of any developed country. Most developed countries, however, wanted at least a token contribution by those less developed to the objectives of the negotiations, even if it were to consist only of measures that were desirable, in any event, in the interest of their own economic development plans.

One factor that complicated the discussion was the treatment to be accorded less developed countries not participating in the negotiations. This issue was closely related to a more general question that was still unresolved: Should linear tariff reductions be made in the case of products of interest to participants but principally supplied by nonparticipants? If these products were to be excluded from the linear rule, one had to be able to distinguish a participant from a nonparticipant. This implied that some affirmative action would have to be taken by a country if it wished to be recognized as a participant. The insignia of participation promised to have more than ceremonial significance.

Distinguishing Participants

The question of how a less developed country would obtain the status of a participant first had to be faced in connection with the plan for the distribution of exceptions lists to be tabled by "linear" countries and the arrangements for confrontation and justification of those lists. Among the nonlinear countries, only Canada, which tabled positive offers at the same time, was permitted to participate in the confrontation. For a while, the less developed countries insisted that, as a corollary of the "no reciprocity" rule, they too should be permitted to receive and criticize the exceptions lists of the linear countries. To have acceded fully to this demand would have raised a serious question as to whether other nonlinear countries should have the same privilege. The compromise procedure finally agreed upon was that:

1. Each less developed country had the right to submit to the developed countries as a whole a list of products on which a maximum tariff reduction was considered to be of special importance to its export trade; the linear countries would take these lists into consideration and make every effort to avoid including the products listed in their own exceptions lists.

2. Any one of the less developed countries could establish its status as a participant by notifying the director general of its intention to contribute to the negotiations, with no requirement that the nature of that contribution be detailed at that time.

3. Each linear country would deliver to each of the "participating" less developed countries a list of those items on its exceptions list that were also on the list submitted by that less developed country of items of special interest to it.

4. As soon as possible after the completion of the mutual confrontation and justification meetings among linear countries, those countries would subject themselves to a similar confrontation by the participating less developed countries.

5. Developed countries could then submit to any less developed participant their suggestions as to the nature of the contribution (not necessarily to consist of tariff reductions) that the latter might make to the overall objectives of the Kennedy Round without endangering its own economic development.

6. Following the receipt of these suggestions, each "participating" less developed country would submit to the other participants a statement of the contribution it proposed to make, and bilateral negotiations could then begin.[3]

The Requests of Less Developed Countries

In accordance with the procedures decided upon, twenty-five less developed countries indicated their intention of participating in the negotiations, and a number of them submitted lists of products they hoped would be omitted from the exceptions lists of the linear participants. Among the self-designated participants were several countries which were not universally recognized as less developed and therefore as entitled to special treatment. The developed countries, which had until then generally avoided the issue of where the line should be drawn between "developed" and "less developed," had to decide to which countries they would disclose their selected lists of exceptions. In the absence of an agreed list of less developed countries, each linear country was in a position to make its own determination. The United States at this stage declined to submit its list of exceptions to Israel, Portugal, Spain, or Yugoslavia, all of which claimed less developed status. It also declined to submit its list to Greece and Turkey but, as associates of the EEC, these countries had undertaken to align their tariffs, over time, with the Common External Tariff of the Community and therefore could not be expected to offer independent tariff concessions.

When, in mid-1965, the linear countries met with the less developed countries to justify their exceptions lists, the latter made clear their disappointment at finding in those lists a number of products of importance to their exports. They were not, however, able to compare the treatment they had received with what the linear countries had accorded to each other since they did not have access to the complete lists.

In the case of the US exceptions list, the principal complaints by the less developed countries had to do with products which were either mandatorily reserved from negotiation by the provisions of the Trade Expansion Act, such as lead and zinc, or were excluded because the principal supplier was not a participant in the negotiations. But the US list was also criticized because it included, as total or partial exceptions, wool textiles, some leather footwear, rubber galoshes, and certain handmade articles, which were excepted by administrative decision because of the danger of injury to competing domestic industries.

The Offers of Less Developed Countries

The statements of the less developed countries concerning the contributions they were prepared to make included some offers of modest tariff reductions, but more frequently consisted of statements that their imports would necessarily rise in response to any increase in their export earnings. Among those offering some tariff reductions were Argentina and the United Arab Republic. India indicated that its partial loss of tariff preferences in the United Kingdom as a result of British MFN tariff reductions represented the extent of the sacrifice it could make and that this would leave India with a net loss from the negotiations unless developed countries should improve their offers. One improvement requested by India was that the developed countries grant tariff reductions of more than 50 percent on products of interest to less developed countries. Indonesia offered tariff reductions on cloves and raw jute, both of interest solely to other less developed countries. The majority of the countries that indicated their intention to participate either limited their offers to some liberalization, often unspecified, of nontariff restrictions or made no offers.

Tropical Products

The program for the voluntary and uncompensated elimination of duties and excise taxes on tropical products, initiated by the Contracting Parties in the late 1950's, had met with some success but had not yet achieved its full objective.[4] Special procedures were therefore adopted that were designed to carry the program further in the Kennedy Round.

A joint proposal by the Nordic countries led the Trade Negotiations Committee to create a Tropical Products Group and to decide that each developed country should notify the group of its intention concerning any restrictions it still maintained against imports of tropical products or any taxes still imposed on their internal sale.

The key to maximum progress in this field was the EEC, for the authority vested in the US administration to eliminate tariffs on noncompetitive tropical products was conditioned on comparable action by the European Community. When the EEC unveiled its Kennedy Round intentions for tropical products, its offers included a substantial number of 50 percent reductions. But the largest volume of trade was covered only by bindings of present duties; in no case was there an offer to eliminate the tariff.

The Community explained that it was unable to do more because of its obligation to maintain meaningful preferences for the benefit of its African associates. The attitude of those associates, as expressed in a meeting of the Tropical Products Group, confirmed that the Community was indeed under pressure from them to minimize its concessions to other less developed countries. The existence of British Commonwealth preferences reinforced the conflict of interest between different categories of the less developed countries, though the beneficiaries of those preferences placed less emphasis on preserving them intact than on demanding that they be compensated for their loss.

Results of "Negotiations" by Less Developed Countries

No myth concerning the Kennedy Round has proved more durable than the widely accepted view that the less developed countries received little or no benefits as a result of the negotiations.[5] At the closing meeting of the conference, the participating less developed countries issued a joint statement that made no reference to the positive results they had obtained but catalogued the benefits they had hoped for but had not received: "elimination of duties on products of particular export interest to developing countries, tropical products, commodity agreements, compensation for loss of preferences and removal of nontariff barriers."[6]

At the time this statement was made, little detailed information concerning the results was available. But in the fall of 1967, the GATT secretariat, under the direction of the Committee on Trade and Development, prepared an analysis of the concessions of value to the less developed countries granted by six major industrialized participants. The study covered seven sectors representing 65 percent of the dutiable imports into the six markets from the developing countries.[7] It showed that tariffs on 58 percent of those imports were reduced in the Kennedy Round. About seven-eighths of these reductions were by 20 percent or more and over two-fifths were by 50 percent or more, including those items on which the duty was entirely eliminated.

The results differed greatly, however, in different sectors. Table 5, derived from the GATT study, summarizes these differences. The sector that saw the smallest proportion of reductions of 50 percent or more was that of cotton textiles and clothing, a reflection of the

Table 5. Kennedy Round tariff reductions on imports from less developed countries in important commodity groups (1964 imports into US, EEC, UK, Japan, Sweden, and Switzerland).

Group	No reduction	Reduced less than half	Reduced by half	Reduced more than half	Eliminated
		Kennedy Round action			
		(percent of imports in group)			
Tropical products	50.5	34.5	4.0	4.5	6.0
Processed foods	43.5	13.0	33.5	1.0	9.0
Nonferrous metals and products	37.5	27.0	33.5	0.0	2.0
Cotton yarn and fabrics	22.5	73.5	4.0	0.0	0.0
Clothing[a]	19.0	71.5	7.0	0.0	0.0
Other textiles	12.5	29.0	7.0	0.0	51.5
Leather and manufactures	23.0	22.0	53.0	1.0	1.0

Source: GATT Doc., COM.TD/48/Rev. 1, Nov. 21, 1967.
[a]Information unavailable for 2.5 percent of imports in this group.

apparent willingness of the exporting countries to accept increased quotas into the Common Market as a substitute for deep tariff reductions. The sector involving the greatest shortfall from pre-Kennedy Round expectations was that of tropical products, where tariffs on only 6 percent of dutiable imports into the six major markets were eliminated in spite of the special tropical product authority (Section 213) that had been granted to the US administration in the Trade Expansion Act. Because of the rather narrow definition of tropical products in the act and the limitation of the authority to products not produced in significant quantities domestically, the maximum that could have been accomplished was not great. But some of the available authority was nullified by the failure of the

EEC, under pressure from its African associates, to agree to comparable reductions on its part, a statutory condition to the use by the President of the authority in Section 213 of the act.[8] In spite of this, by using the authority to reduce very low tariffs to zero, the United States did eliminate duties on 15 percent of its tropical product imports.

In contrast with these moderate accomplishments, the record in some sectors was impressive. More than half of the dutiable trade of less developed countries in textiles other than cotton was freed from any tariff restrictions. When the Kennedy Round concessions are in full effect only 21 percent of these noncotton textile imports from the less developed countries into the six markets will encounter any duty.[9] In leather and leather manufactures, tariffs on 55 percent of the dutiable trade were reduced by at least the full linear reduction of 50 percent. This leaves 75 percent of leather imports still subject to duty, but only 20 percent are subject to post-Kennedy Round rates of more than 10 percent ad valorem.[10]

This analysis, of course, does not in any way reveal whether the results obtained by less developed countries were comparable with those obtained by developed countries. The significance of such a comparison would be open to question, in light of the fact that few less developed countries participated actively as negotiators. Nevertheless, the UNCTAD secretariat did attempt it and concluded that the reductions in tariffs faced by exports from the less developed countries were substantially less than in those faced by members of the OECD.[11] The UNCTAD study was based on a sampling technique and divided imports of the EEC, the United States, the United Kingdom, and Japan between those in which less developed countries had expressed a particular interest during the Kennedy Round and those in which they had expressed no interest. Considering manufactured products alone, it found that the average tariff reduction in "products of interest" to less developed countries was 29 percent compared with 38 percent for other products. Taking all imports, manufactured and primary, the percentage reductions were 26 and 36 percent, respectively.

Because of the differences in methodology and presentation, a direct comparison between the GATT and UNCTAD studies cannot be made. Neither, however, supports the common belief that the benefits of Kennedy Round reductions were systematically withheld from less developed countries, whether the emphasis is on products they actually export or on those in which they are believed to have an export potential. There is, of course, no way to estimate the future importance to them of tariff reductions in products in which they have not as yet developed exports. If the less developed countries should succeed in achieving their goal of diversified production, any Kennedy Round tariff reduction could improve their prospects.

Most of the less developed countries that did not participate in the Kennedy Round shared in the benefits of the reductions revealed by these studies since the developed GATT countries extend the benefit of their tariff concessions to virtually all of them whether or not they are GATT Contracting Parties. This was at least partially offset in the case of those countries that lost some part of the margins of preference they had hitherto enjoyed.

Relatively few of the twenty-five less developed countries that achieved recognition as "participants" actually engaged in negotiations. Only nine of them, for example, negotiated with the United States.[12] Of these, Argentina negotiated for admission as a full contracting party, and Chile negotiated to obtain the right to modify previous tariff bindings where this was necessary to permit the adoption of a new and simplified tariff schedule.

Detailed data are not available to determine whether the developed countries in general complied with their promise not to expect reciprocity. There are, however, data from which to compare the concessions granted to less developed countries and received from them by the United States. Direct concessions (concessions granted in response to requests) by the United States to nine active less developed participants covered about $700 million of US imports from them. Their own imports from the United States affected by the concessions they granted in the Kennedy Round came to about $200 million. Almost all of the US concessions consisted of duty reductions of 50 percent or more. On the other hand, all but $20 million of the concessions granted by the less developed countries consisted of the binding of existing tariff rates[13] and only about 3 percent of the tariff reductions were by as much as 50 percent.

Countries With Special Economic or Trade Structures

It will be recalled that Canada, Australia, New Zealand, and South Africa had claimed recognition as countries that could not be expected to make linear tariff reductions. Australia and New Zealand objected that their industries had not developed to a point that would enable them to compete in their domestic markets with low-duty imports and also predicted that any linear tariff reduction adopted was unlikely to affect appreciably the general level of agricultural protection in their principal export markets. South Africa, too, asked to be considered semi-industrialized.

Canada also vigorously denied that mutual linear tariff reductions would result in a balance of advantage to its trade. This denial rested less on the agricultural content of Canada's exports than on the vulnerability of its industries to competition from the United States.

The major industrialized countries, which had in principle already committed themselves to the linear method, were understandably reluctant to excuse such highly developed countries from a similar obligation, not so much from fear of an unbalanced outcome (the right to withdraw items from their initial linear offers to obtain reciprocity was adequate safeguard) but because of the danger it might pose to the depth and scope of the final agreement, already threatened by the dilution of the linear approach.

Fear that the adoption of a special rule for Australia, New Zealand, South Africa, and Canada might curtail the results to be expected from the negotiations was reflected in the May 1963 ministerial meeting, at which the ministers merely referred the problem to the newly formed Trade Negotiations Committee. The committee, however, had little real choice. The most likely alternative to admitting the borderline countries on their own terms would have been to give them most of the benefits, under their MFN rights, with no compensation at all. To this consideration, which was probably decisive, was added the growing realization that the pessimism of the agricultural exporting countries concerning the likelihood of their achieving substantial benefits from the negotiations was well founded. Thus, before the ministers met a year later, in May 1964, to open the negotiations, the Trade Negotiations Committee had been able to reach agreement on procedures that would permit the participation of these four countries in the negotiations.

Canada volunteered to table positive offers simultaneously with the tabling of exceptions lists by the linear countries. These offers were to be subject to the same justification and confrontation procedures as the exceptions lists of others, and Canada would be treated as a full participant when the lists of linear countries were examined.

Australia, New Zealand, and South Africa were to follow the same procedure, provided that the rules governing agriculture were settled soon enough to permit them to assess the benefits they were likely to receive in time to enable them to table offers.

When the date for the tabling of exceptions lists was reached, Canada adhered to the timetable. But agreement on the rules to govern the agricultural negotiations was still far in the future, and the three countries whose offers had been made contingent on that agreement at first invoked their right to postpone their own offers. As has already been seen, the effort to arrive at any rules for agriculture was eventually abandoned in favor of the tabling of selective agricultural offers in September 1965. When it became clear that the Community would not be able to meet that date, adherence to the logic of their earlier position would have required these three "special structure" countries to postpone their offers once more. But, perhaps in an effort to induce the EEC to be more forthcoming in the field of agriculture or perhaps in order to permit them to begin negotiating with the other linear countries, Australia and New Zealand tabled industrial and agricultural offers in September 1965, and South Africa followed in December of the same year.

The negotiations between the "special structure" countries and their linear partners largely followed the traditional pattern of item-by-item negotiations. Because of their almost wholly bilateral character, few details concerning their negotiating sessions are public knowledge. But some of the principal issues can be deduced from the final Kennedy Round results. These countries were not as far out of the mainstream of the multilateral negotiations as their abstention from the linear negotiations might suggest. All of them were, of course, deeply involved in agricultural negotiations in general and in one or more of the special agricultural groups in particular. Canada and Australia were key participants in the grains and meat groups. New Zealand was involved in the latter and pinned much of its Kennedy Round hopes on achievement of a dairy products agreement — hopes that were destined to be disappointed. In the industrial sectors, Canada would also have had an important role to play if it had been possible to reach a sector agreement in aluminum or pulp and paper. The contributions made by the special structure countries to the final results of the Kennedy Round must be judged in light of the extent to which the agricultural groups and industrial sectors of concern to them achieved their purpose.

Nontariff Barriers

At their meeting in May 1963 the GATT ministers decided that the forthcoming trade negotiations should "deal not only with tariffs but also with nontariff barriers."[14] Individual nontariff barriers had occasionally been the object of negotiations in the past, especially where the value of a tariff concession was directly affected. But the Contracting Parties had never before in negotiations given these barriers a status comparable to that of tariffs. The lack of previous experience in this field, however, was not the most difficult problem the negotiators were to face.

As a subject for negotiation, nontariff barriers raised a number of problems that did not exist in the case of tariff negotiations. One was that no single category of nontariff barrier was as universally applied as the tariff. Thus, it was easy for most participants to single out for attack barriers used by others and not by themselves. This, perhaps, was one reason why it was much easier to initiate discussion of nontariff barriers than to engage in negotiations for their removal. But it was not the only reason. Many governmental practices that can have a restrictive effect on trade are also essential to the protection of domestic health, safety, or security; only when they are unnecessarily restrictive are they potential objects of negotiation. And, even in those rare cases where there was no dispute about the existence or the restrictiveness of a barrier, its negotiation suffered from the difficulty of measurement. There is no such common yardstick as the ad valorem equivalent of tariffs to help the negotiators formulate their bids and offers or to provide them with a mathematical basis for defending at home whatever bargain they might strike.

The 1963 GATT ministerial meeting provided comparatively little guidance to the Trade Negotiations Committee when it assigned the committee the task of drawing up rules and methods to be employed in the negotiation of nontariff barriers. Furthermore, in the year that elapsed between that meeting and the formal opening of the negotiations the committee itself was too deeply involved in the controversies over tariff disparities and agriculture to devote much attention to resolving the problem. It did, however, take the first step of trying to identify those barriers that particular participating countries wanted removed or modified by their negotiating partners.

In October 1963, in response to a general invitation by the executive secretary, the United Kingdom, Japan, the United States, and Sweden submitted simple lists of measures they considered should be the subject of negotiations. These initial submissions for the most part refrained from naming the offending country or countries. As summarized by the secretariat, the topics covered were: escape clauses, antidumping policies, state trading, government purchasing policies, customs valuation "including use of arbitrary or excessive values," administrative and technical regulations including marking rules and consular formalities, "residual" quantitative restrictions, discriminatory import restrictions, border tax adjustments, sanitary regulations, restrictive import policies on coal, and the US "Wine Gallon Assessment."[15]

Soon after the Kennedy Round was officially declared open, the negotiation of nontariff barriers began. Each participant was invited to designate in writing those nontariff barriers that it wanted other named participants to modify or eliminate.[16]

Government Procurement

The United Kingdom, the EEC, and Japan complained of US regulations under the "Buy American" law. In return, the United States asked for more open procedures by government procurement agencies of other countries in advertising and awarding contracts.

Arbitrary Valuation of Imports

Many complaints were registered against the American Selling Price and the use of "foreign value" for items in the US "Final List." But Canada, Australia, New Zealand, and South Africa were also cited for practices similar to "foreign value" assessment. Finally, the United States received requests that it abolish its "Wine Gallon Assessment" basis for determining the excise tax and duty on distilled spirits and its "standard of strength" basis for assessing duties on certain dyes.

Administrative and Technical Regulations

The United Kingdom registered a number of complaints against restrictive administrative practices: against the United States for permitting various states to require the seal of the American Society of Mechanical Engineers (ASME) on boilers and pressure vessels, a seal which ASME does not issue to foreign producers; against the requirements enforced by the US Interstate Commerce Commission for seamless gas cylinders, which could be met only by inspection in the United States; against the US law that prohibited the use of foreign-built dredges in American waters; against German standards for electrical equipment, which precluded internationally recognized certification by foreign authorities; and against the French standard for gasoline pumps which, it contended, was so administered as to preclude any imports.

Internal Taxes

Austria, Belgium, France, and Italy were the targets of complaints by the United States that their road-use taxes burdened US makes of automobiles, as compared with the automobiles of other countries, out of proportion to any differences in their size or value.

Quantitative Restrictions

Although many contracting parties continued to maintain some quantitative restrictions not justified under GATT rules, the United States singled out for special consideration measures that impeded import of coal into Belgium, Canada, France, Japan, the Netherlands, Spain, the United Kingdom, and Germany.

Negotiating groups consisting of participants expressing an interest in the barriers concerned were established to attempt to deal with each category. In addition, the United States put the other participants on notice that it might insist upon the establishment of two more groups: one to deal with protection through state trading, and one to reexamine the GATT rules concerning border tax adjustments. In neither case did it follow this up with a formal request, at first because of the difficulty of formulating concrete proposals for dealing with these complex cases and later because the lack of progress achieved in other groups presumably discouraged the initiation of negotiations that had even less prospect for success.

It is obvious that the measures selected for attention in the Kennedy Round fell short of representing a complete roster of nontariff barriers.[17] It would appear that the United Kingdom was more thorough than other participants, with the possible exception of the United States, in canvassing its businessmen for information about the practices of other countries that impeded their exports. But the fact that US practices were more frequently the subject of complaint than those of others was at least in part brought about by the peculiarities of the American constitutional structure. First, the separation of executive from legislative authority in the United States has meant that the details of customs administration and governmental procurement practices, to take two examples, have had to be committed to statute, while in most countries the government officials concerned exercise much wider discretion. In addition, the constitutional rights of individual states in this country have created a twilight zone of jurisdiction within which some states have adopted laws or regulations that conflict with the policy and even with the international commitments of the federal government.

The nature of the United States constitutional system presented other obstacles as well to successful negotiation of nontariff barriers. Most of the US barriers that were the subject of complaints by others were contained in laws which the administration had no power to change. It was, of course, theoretically possible for the US delegation to offer modifications of these laws, subject to the approval of the Congress. The delegation did, in fact, grasp this nettle in the case of the American Selling Price issue in the chemical sector negotiations. But the unfavorable reaction of many congressmen and senators, if presented with a *fait accompli,* was predictable. In general, the US delegation understandably avoided negotiating *ad referendum* changes in US laws, even in exchange for very real benefits to American exports.

Even if the United States delegation had had greater power to negotiate, however, the nontariff barrier negotiating groups would still have had other formidable obstacles to overcome: the absence of an unambiguous line between practices that are necessary and those that are excessively protective; the diversity and unequal distribution of restrictive practices among the Kennedy Round participants; and the absence of a common denominator to use in comparing the effectiveness of different barriers in restricting trade. Because of the combination of all these difficulties, the negotiations for the most part did not progress beyond the agreement to establish negotiating groups. There were, however, two notable exceptions to this general failure: the modification of certain nontariff barriers, combined with tariff concessions, in the settlement reached in the chemical sector, which is discussed in a later chapter; and the agreement on a code of behavior in the field of antidumping practices.

The Antidumping Code

The negotiation of an antidumping code was entrusted to a Group on Antidumping Policies, which was established in July 1965 and which proceeded rapidly to a consideration of the issues. Its task was eased by the fact that all the principal participants were members of the OECD, which in 1964 had conducted a quite detailed examination of the antidumping legislation and practices of its members. Much of the necessary study and analysis having been accomplished, governments were able to exchange explicit proposals soon after the Kennedy Round group was formed.

The suggestions for a new code left the basic provisions of Article VI of the GATT (discussed in chapter V) generally intact and were designed for the most part to give them greater precision. An effort was also made to deal adequately with certain matters concerning which Article VI was silent: the application of provisional measures while a charge of antidumping is under investigation, elimination of the possibility that antidumping duties might be imposed on goods entered before the initiation of an investigation, and the adoption of standards to require disclosure of information concerning the basis of an antidumping charge and to require that interested parties be given an opportunity to present their views.

Certain proposals that would have extended the scope of Article VI obligations still further were considered but not pressed by any participant, one of these being a provision that would have required an importing country to take action against dumping when the resultant injury was not to its own producers but to those of another exporting country.

The differences between the objectives of the United States on the one hand and of Western Europe (including the United Kingdom) on the other were clear cut. The Europeans wanted, above all else, a substantial modification in the United States practice of withholding customs "appraisement" during protracted investigations. In fact, the original proposal by the United Kingdom was for the total outlawing of the withholding of appraisement, even though the imposition of a provisional duty pending completion of an investigation would have been permitted. This suggestion could have been accepted by the US delegation only had it been prepared to ask Congress to amend the US law. But the proposal was not pressed, and the United Kingdom retreated to an effort to obtain amelioration in American withholding practices: a commitment that appraisement would not be withheld without a prima facie finding of injurious dumping, and the assurance that investigations would be carried out more expeditiously.

The United States concentrated on obtaining a commitment that antidumping cases would be so conducted that the importer would know the basis for the investigation and be given adequate opportunity to present his defense. In the end, each side achieved a substantial measure of its objectives, and agreement was reached in substance well before the final phase of the Kennedy Round.

The code that emerged and that was accepted, subject only to the satisfactory settlement of the Kennedy Round as a whole, clarified and amplified the provisions of Article VI of the GATT concerning the circumstances under which antidumping action may be taken.[18] It provided for more expeditious handling of cases and for a preliminary examination of evidence both that goods were being dumped and that the dumping met the "injury" criterion of Article VI before any provisional action could be taken, whether that action consisted of the withholding of appraisement or the imposition of provisional duties. It required adequate notice to interested parties, the disclosure of all information except where its confidential nature was established, and the granting of adequate opportunity to interested parties to be heard and submit evidence. It imposed specific limits on the imposition of antidumping duties retroactively, that is, to cover imports that were entered before an investigation was completed. And, finally, by incorporating the provisions of Article VI of the GATT, it insured that all signatories, whether or not previously exempted from the application of that article under the Protocol of Provisional Application, became subject to its provisions.

Polish Accession

In May 1963, Poland, which had participated in the work of the GATT since 1959 without having achieved the status of a Contracting Party,[19] announced its desire to negotiate in the Kennedy Round as a prelude to full accession. Poland's recognition as a participant would improve the chance that products in which that country had an export interest would be included in the tariff reductions of others. But Poland had even more to gain from accession — a legal right to the benefits accorded by the General Agreement, including most favored nation treatment, which had hitherto been denied it by most European countries.[20]

The director general gave Poland's application his enthusiastic endorsement, and the ministerial meeting in May 1964 decided that the Nontariff Barrier Subcommittee should explore with Poland the kind of commitments it could undertake that would constitute a meaningful *quid pro quo* for the privileges Poland would receive as a contracting party. It was obvious that, in the absence of a competitive price economy, tariff bindings by Poland would be neither meaningful nor enforceable. Poland recognized this difficulty and proposed that its contribution to the negotiations and its "payment" for the privilege of full GATT status should be a guarantee of a specified annual increase, the amount to be negotiated, in its total purchases from the Contracting Parties as a whole. The division of this total among exporting countries would be determined by commercial considerations.

In considering Poland's proposal, the Contracting Parties were for the first time forced to confront the problem of how a system of rules designed to govern commercial relations among private-trading countries could be adapted to economic systems in which trading decisions were made by the state and in which there was no necessary relationship between internal and external prices.[21] After the Havana Conference, Wilcox had written: "As a matter of logic, it must be recognized that the fundamental problem is insoluble: complete collectivism does not fit into the pattern of free markets and multilateral trade."[22] Nevertheless, facing the prospect that the Soviet Union would become a member of the International Trade Organization, the United States had, in its original proposals for the ITO, included a provision for an annual purchase commitment by members having a complete state monopoly of foreign trade. After the Soviet Union failed to attend either the London or the Geneva preparatory meetings for the ITO, the proposal was dropped.[23] However, Poland's proposals for paying its way into the GATT and for compensating contracting parties for MFN treatment were consistent with that early American suggestion.

In the Kennedy Round the most difficult obstacle proved to be not this fundamental problem but the reluctance of the member states of the EEC, and the United Kingdom, to forego the privileged position for their exports that they had derived from their bilateral trade agreements with Poland. In those agreements they had been able to extract specific purchase commitments in exchange for granting import quotas for Polish goods. If Poland were to acquire the right to MFN treatment, they could, of course, no longer apply to Polish exports licensing requirements that were not imposed on the exports of other countries; the bilateral agreements would have to be terminated. On the other hand, the United States, which had not resorted to bilateral agreements, had no commercial advantage to lose by granting Poland MFN treatment and had something to gain from termination of Poland's bilateral agreements.

In spite of the reluctance of Poland's bilateral trading partners, the Trade Negotiations Committee, prodded by the director general, agreed in early 1965 to invite Poland to submit specific offers and, from the date of that submission, to accord it the status of a participant in the Kennedy Round. The offers were submitted in April of the same year.

In its final agreement with the Contracting Parties,[24] Poland undertook to increase the total value of its imports by not less than 7 percent each year, subject to annual review and renegotiation. Poland also undertook all the obligations of a contracting party except the requirement that it enter into a special exchange agreement with the International Monetary Fund. But the commitments of other contracting parties toward Poland were qualified in two important respects. It proved impossible to obtain agreement on the immediate dismantlement of bilateral quota agreements, and countries that, on the date of the protocol, applied such quotas to imports from Poland were given the right to continue to apply them until the expiration of a transitional period, the termination date for which was to be set during the third of the annual consultations to be held with Poland under the terms of the protocol.

The Contracting Parties as a whole protected themselves against the possibility that Poland would dump exports into their markets under conditions which would not permit the price comparisons that would enable them to apply antidumping duties. Poland agreed that, if another contracting party should find that increased imports from Poland caused or threatened serious injury to its industries, it would have the right to restrict them, subject to provisions for consultation between the parties concerned.

14

The Brink

At the beginning of 1967, some thirty-two months after the formal opening of the Kennedy Round, the negotiators finally came to grips with all of the more fundamental issues. In agriculture, the offer list of the EEC, and the counter offers of others, had at last been tabled. The Cereals Group had identified their more important causes of disagreement, and the Meat and Dairy Products Groups were finally engaged in those technical discussions that were an essential prelude to the commencement of bargaining. In one category of nontariff barriers — antidumping practices — some genuine progress had been made.

Finally, in the all-important area of industrial tariffs the open declaration of the "minimum" demands of all the participants had opened up the prospect that bilateral negotiations over exceptions lists could begin to make headway.

Any tally of the progress made up to January 1967, however, would simply have underlined how much remained to be done in the time remaining. Only six months were left before the last day on which President Johnson could sign an agreement reducing tariffs under the authority of the Trade Expansion Act, and an agreement would have to be reached in substance many weeks before June 30 if the necessary protocols were to be ready for signature. The generally accepted target for the close of bargaining was mid-April, only three and a half months away. More progress would have to be made in that time than in the years that had elapsed since the opening of the negotiations. More than two years after the exchange of exceptions lists, hundreds of millions of dollars of trade still separated the positions of the participants over linear tariff cuts, the *sine qua non* of any settlement. The chemical sector negotiations remained deadlocked over their central issue — American Selling Price — and the steel sector over the base date for tariff reductions. The aluminum and pulp and paper sectors had made no progress in closing the chasms they had revealed. Tariff negotiations in the textile sector had been repeatedly postponed as attention had concentrated on the negotiation of quotas under the Long-Term Cotton Textile Arrangement.[1] As for agriculture, the negotiation of tariffs on products not dealt with in special groups had been underway for less than six months. The only group in which any progress had been made, that dealing with cereals, still faced profound differences over the level of the proposed self-sufficiency ratio, over price levels, and over the respective shares of the participants in the fund for aid through food.

If the timetable were to be met, there would have to be drastic changes in the positions of at least some of the major participants in the weeks to follow. The locus of those changes and the form they would take would depend on why the positions had been held for so long. Was it because of a suspicion that the claims of others were tactical, leading to a determination not to yield until it could be demonstrated that the opponent would hold his ground at any cost? Or did the positions occupied by the opposing forces mark the territory they were determined to hold at any cost? In all previous dramas the heroine had been snatched from the brink just in time. Would it happen again?

The Community's Response

The central question on which the success of the Kennedy Round appeared to hinge as 1967 opened was the effect the December withdrawal exercise would have on the attitude of the European Community. Would the demonstration of its isolation bring a more flexible negotiating mandate to the commission or would it provide the more protectionist elements in the Community with an argument for a still stiffer position?

For a while it looked as if the latter was to be the answer. Some voices both within the governments of member states and in the European press cited the GATT withdrawal exercise as a further illustration of the brutal negotiating tactics of the Anglo-Saxons (the Nordics, who had presented the most massive withdrawal list, were generally exempt from criticism). The EEC was urged to meet these tactics with stiffened resistance. *Le Monde,* on January 24, commented editorially on the "blunder that the Americans have certainly committed in threatening" the EEC — a move that had resulted in "irritating Washington's best friends within the Common Market."

The EEC Council of Ministers met on January 12 to consider what to do. There was little doubt in the minds of the other participants that France would insist on a firm stand against the demands of the English-speaking delegations, perhaps because it preferred a "thin" agreement to a substantial one, perhaps because it felt that the time for compromise had not yet been reached. Germany could be counted on to favor an improvement in the Community's contribution to the Kennedy Round; the question was whether it would defend its view to the point of precipitating another crisis in the council. When the time came, Germany chose to avoid a crisis. The council's task was made easier by Jean Rey, the commissioner responsible for the negotiations, who reportedly did not ask it to do much more than reassert its earlier positions.[2] Its decisions were described at the time as "a middle way between the starting position of Germany (which wanted firm decisions on some improvement in the Community's offers) and that of France (which believed it desirable to exclude all possibility of improvement, at least until the problem of 'disparities' and 'withdrawal lists' of third countries was resolved)."[3]

The compromise within the Community was achieved when all members, as well as the commission, agreed to make an effort to appease the continental EFTA countries and, at the same time, decided to stand fast in their negotiations with others. France, and the council as a whole, recognized that the lengthy exceptions list of the EEC, while designed to help the community's bargaining power against the United States and Great Britain, had incidentally threatened to deprive its smaller European neighbors of much of the benefit they might have derived from the Kennedy Round. They agreed that the commission might engage in conversations *"with the other European countries"* in an effort to find a better balance of reciprocal offers.[4] But the EEC council showed no such tenderness toward other key countries. It instructed the commission to hold its ground on all important points, including the issues on which the negotiations almost foundered during the next few months.

Multiple Roadblocks

Not all the problems threatening the Kennedy Round involved the linear negotiations or the triangular confrontation of the EEC, the United States, and the United Kingdom. One of the most intractable issues in the grains negotiation found Japan ranged against the United States and the other cereal exporters. In the industrial sector negotiations, the Nordic countries were joined by the United States and Canada in the quest for free trade, or at least tariff harmonization, in aluminum. The search for commodity agreements in meat and dairy products found the EEC pitted against New Zealand, Argentina, and Australia. The cotton textile negotiations were threatened by a rumor, later to be proved correct, that the EEC was no longer prepared to reduce its tariffs by 50 percent, even though renewal of the LTA was already assured. Negotiations had not been joined with Australia, which had not as yet tabled an offer list. And, in the chemical sector, the United States found itself faced by a united front of other developed countries.

Accommodation — and Disappointment

Like so many deadlines in Geneva and Brussels, the mid-April target for reaching an agreement in substance had to be abandoned; and, with it, the hope of having time to record the results in an orderly manner before June 30. Nevertheless, the first four and a half months of 1967 did see the beginning of some genuine negotiation and compromise, almost the first since the Kennedy Round began. The withdrawal exercise of December did not at once result in a more flexible negotiating mandate for the EEC commission. But it began the decline of the era during which it had seemed that all negotiators would merely repeat their initial speeches until time ran out. In a new atmosphere of give-and-take, new concessions were granted, and many hitherto imperative demands were abandoned — a movement in which the Community's negotiators were able, belatedly, to join. Two of the most hotly embattled areas, however, were disputed until almost the last possible moment.

The EEC did not abandon at once its efforts to contest the withdrawal lists of others. In late March it submitted to the United States a list of "disparities" it proposed to invoke that would have resulted in the withdrawal of offers affecting some 130 positions in the Common External Tariff and about $181 million of US trade. Many of these disparities, in the US view, were not "significant in trade terms." But that criterion, like the formulas for identifying disparities, had ceased to have importance. The new list was, in effect, no more than an EEC response to the withdrawal lists of others and was quickly subsumed within the more general maneuvering for reciprocity.

The Community's effort to patch up its differences with the smaller EFTA countries had only limited success. The exploratory discussions the commission had been authorized to conduct with them ended, so far as the Scandinavian countries were concerned, in an exchange of accusations that reached the pages of the European press and with final withdrawals by them of offers affecting a half-billion dollars of EEC trade.

Renewal of the Cotton Textile Arrangement was assured when the EEC agreed to increase its import quotas, but withdrew its former linear tariff offer and substituted a general reduction of 20 percent. The evidence seems clear that this was accepted at the time by the less developed exporters but not by Japan, which was the only one to protest. It was the turn of the less developed countries to be unhappy, however, when other industrialized countries, including the United States, also reduced their cotton textile tariff offers in response to the action of the Community.

The United Kingdom helped make a steel agreement possible by an improvement in its offers which, in turn, led to a substantially improved offer by the Community.

Two potentially serious barriers to an overall settlement were removed when, to the bitter disappointment, especially of New

Zealand and Argentina, the effort to arrive at commodity agreements for meat and dairy products was abandoned and the negotiating groups disbanded.

In the field of nontariff barriers, final agreement was reached on an antidumping code, but most of the remaining requests that had not been transferred to the chemical negotiations were dropped. One exception was the US demand for general recognition that an increase in border tax adjustments might impair the value of tariff concessions, but in the end the US delegation was content to put a unilateral statement to this effect in the record.

Thus, when faced with the danger that time would be "called" before any agreement was reached, the negotiators proved willing to modify demands which they had declared irreversible at the end of the previous year. But the deadlocks over grains and chemicals persisted until well into May and threatened, until only six more weeks remained before the June 30 deadline, to endanger the entire negotiation.

The Cereals Compromise

In the Cereals Group, one more "deadline" — April 30 — had passed without agreement. Only two weeks remained before the date that all negotiators agreed was the last possible time for reaching an agreement in substance. But the grains negotiations remained on dead center. The Community had not agreed to a self-sufficiency ratio for wheat below 90 percent of consumption and would not consider means of making even that ratio self-enforcing. Then came the first genuine break in the impasse.

Late in April, the Special Representative for Trade Negotiations, William M. Roth,[5] and his deputy, W. Michael Blumenthal, who headed the US delegation, flew from Geneva to Washington to confer with President Johnson. There they obtained authority to make a completely new proposal. It was a simple one: The United States, and other exporters, would abandon the effort to obtain in the grains arrangement any assurances of access to import markets.

This was not the major concession to the EEC that it may at first appear, for any hope of truly competitive access had been abandoned long before. Even if the Community had agreed to the exporters' demand that 13 percent of EEC consumption be supplied by imports, the variable levy system would have denied them the opportunity to compete for any larger portion of that market at any price. And, in exchange for this dubious concession, the United States would have lost the "negotiating rights" which it had salvaged from the Dillon Round.[6] What the EEC would stand to lose as a result of the new American proposal was any hope of using the grains arrangement as a means of obtaining international recognition of variable levies or agreement to the "organization of markets," to which both France and the European commission were deeply attached.

The new US proposal worked. Each side abandoned the demand to which it had attached the greatest importance. And that mutual abandonment cleared the way for agreement on lesser points. A price range was agreed, which was to be implemented by a renewal of the International Wheat Agreement (IWA). The new range was about 21.5 cents per bushel above the minimum and maximum levels in the existing IWA. Finally, the arrangement was reduced in scope to one on wheat alone, as the EEC abandoned its more or less desultory effort to include coarse grains in the agreement, products in which the United States was already highly competitive and was likely to have more to lose than to gain under international regulation of prices.

The principal benefit obtained by the United States was the provision for sharing food aid. To obtain agreement, it receded to a more realistic total aid commitment by the participants. In turn, the Community raised its previous offer, and agreement was reached at four and one-half million tons of wheat to be donated by the members as a whole, of which the Community's share was about one million tons.[7]

The EEC and the United States were not the only participants who receded from their earlier positions. Australia and Canada had to be satisfied with a lower price range than they had wanted; the United Kingdom and Japan, a higher one. Finally, Japan abandoned its previous opposition to any commitment involving a contribution to the food aid fund, though the nature of its undertaking later became a new source of dispute.

Chemicals

During the first four months of 1967 there were signs that the negotiators for the European Community were gambling on an extension of the final deadline. In the corridors of the Palais des

Nations, European delegates expressed disbelief that the US administration would allow the negotiations to fail because of lack of time. There were predictions in the European press that the Congress would be asked to extend the deadline of June 30. So long as this seemed a possibility, the Community's negotiators held firm to their insistence that any tariff concessions in the chemical sector be conditioned on the abolition of ASP.

By the end of April it must have been clear that, given the glacial pace of the American legislative processes, the time remaining was too short to permit an amendment of the Trade Expansion Act. And the fact that the administration had submitted no request to Congress was convincing evidence that it had no intention of doing so. For the first time the dangerously approaching deadline seemed to have exerted its full force on the negotiations. The failure of the administration to ask for an extension was probably interpreted as a sign of strength. It had been carried close to the brink of failure and showed no sign that it was willing to compromise its position. On May 2 the commission asked the EEC Council of Ministers for carte blanche to explore with other delegations all possibilities for an agreement. The council granted this request on condition that the commission return a week later for final instructions.

Using its new freedom, the commission abandoned its total opposition to the "two-package" approach for a chemical settlement. This enabled the discussion to focus on what would be the nature and level of the offers of each side in those packages. At this point, Wyndham White — either on his own initiative or at the suggestion of one of the principals — stepped in with a detailed proposal that neither side could safely have made to the other without risking rebuff. Based on the two-package concept, it was, briefly: In the Kennedy Round settlement the United States would reduce by a full 50 percent all but its lowest chemical tariffs, and the United Kingdom and EEC would reduce most of their rates by only 20 percent. But the disparity in the depth of reductions would be balanced by the much greater volume of US exports affected by the tariff reductions to be conceded by its partners.

In the second package most of the advantages derived from the reduction of normal tariffs would go to the United States, but it would give up ASP. After abolishing that method of valuation and converting the benzenoid tariffs to rates that would yield equivalent duty under normal standards of valuation, it would reduce the converted rates so that in the two packages combined they would, generally, result in a reduction of 50 percent. For their part, the EEC and the United Kingdom would reduce their remaining chemical tariffs so as to match the US reductions in the two packages combined. As further compensation for the elimination by the United States of an onerous nontariff barrier, the EEC would eliminate the discriminatory aspect of its automobile road taxes, and the United Kingdom would reduce its tariff preference for commonwealth tobacco. The entire package was to be contingent, of course, on action by the US Congress to abolish the American Selling Price for benzenoid chemicals.

The director general's plan was not accepted in all its details, but, for the first time, it brought the positions of the two delegations within negotiating range of each other. For practical purposes the last and most intractable obstacle to agreement seemed to have been removed.

The Final Crisis

On May 15 the director general was able to announce that all major issues had been resolved, and the world's press hailed the result as the completion of the Kennedy Round.[8] It may well be that a public announcement of the success of the negotiations was essential to force the negotiators to come to grips with the formidable problems of detail that were still outstanding. In any event, the declaration that the major points of difference had been solved did release the negotiators from earlier restraints and enabled them to tackle many lesser issues that had formerly been suppressed in favor of a supreme effort to meet the May 15 deadline. These issues could no longer be ignored when it became imperative to commit the agreement to writing.

A series of disagreements immediately developed, reaching a crescendo in a major dispute betwen the United States and the EEC. On June 2, EEC Commissioner Jean Rey was reported to be "furious" over the withdrawal by the United States of offers on "several hundred million dollars of imports" that it had not specified in the "settlement" of May 15. The United States had, in fact, withdrawn offers in order to achieve reciprocity with other major participants, principally Japan. What evidently happened was that the attention of the two giant participants and of the director general had been so focused on reaching agreement between them that the remaining problems involving other negotiators had temporarily been set aside. There followed intensive discussion between Rey and Ambassador Roth in an effort to save the agreement. On June 15, Peter Dreyer reported in the *Journal of Commerce* that the trade coverage of US offers was still $250 million short of the amount the Community had understood to be firm.

But the EEC charge of surprise withdrawals by the United States was not the only cause of the threatened unraveling of the "agreement" already reached. The grains settlement came close to falling apart over a disagreement between Japan and the wheat exporters concerning the food aid commitment that Japan had made. Japan insisted that it had not agreed that its contribution would be made in the form of purchased grain, or cash earmarked for that purpose, but had reserved the right to donate the equivalent in other essentials, such as fertilizers. This moderate threat to the principal benefit the United States had expected to receive from a grains agreement was intensified when the Nordic countries refused to accept obligations that were not accepted by Japan. The EEC, whose participation in food aid was a *sine qua non,* also threatened to withdraw its commitment if Japan were excused. Argentina, too, threatened to withdraw from the arrangement for the same reason.

Even the chemical settlement threatened to dissolve. Last minute efforts by the United States to obtain compensation from Japan for the benefits the latter would receive if ASP on rubber soled footwear and canned clams were abolished made no progress and led to an exchange of further threats of withdrawal. Austria and Sweden also objected to the sector agreement on chemicals, in the negotiation of which they had not participated.

The apparent agreement concerning the depth of cuts to be made in the ECSC steel tariffs threatened to break down over the question of staging. Although it had been agreed that the final Kennedy Round reductions would bring the average level of ECSC duties to 5.7 percent, France now insisted that reductions toward this level begin at 11.4 percent, thus maintaining a consistent position that the Community's offer represented a 50 percent reduction.

The United Kingdom threatened in return to delay the staging of its own steel concessions. In mid-June, a joint meeting of the EEC council and the high authority of the ECSC failed to resolve the problem, with France holding out against the other member states, who wanted to offer to stage the reductions from 9 percent.

The misunderstandings and disagreements that threatened the Kennedy Round in these closing weeks were not all between "linear" participants. Both Australia and Argentina claimed that the EEC had failed to live up to an earlier commitment to reduce and bind the levy on frozen meat, an accusation that the Community denied. And Denmark accused the EEC of ignoring an earlier agreement concerning the entry of live cattle.

Finally, the cotton textile settlement was threatened by the Community's insistence on a reservation that would have enabled it to restore its pre-Kennedy Round duties if the LTA should be allowed to expire at the end of the three-year renewal period already established. This stipulation was consistent with, but went further than, the condition the Community had from the beginning attached to its cotton textile offers. If it were to be formalized in the final agreement, as the EEC now insisted, many delegations would have to obtain new, and in some cases extremely difficult, instructions during the few days left before the protocol concluding the Kennedy Round had to be signed.

Reciprocity to the Last

In virtually all of these misunderstandings it is easy enough to discern the part played by the universal insistence on reciprocity. In spite of the resolution of the GATT ministers, the major negotiators still insisted on reciprocity, not only in the aggregate but bilaterally. This intensified the chain reaction that was set off each time the commitment of final offers to paper revealed the omission of a concession which a participant believed had been previously agreed. The compensatory withdrawals that were then threatened often affected third parties, and their efforts to redress the balance further widened the circle of those who felt that reciprocity could be preserved only by still further withdrawals by them.

What is remarkable, under the circumstances, is that it was possible in the short time that remained to salvage an agreement that suffered relatively little from the misunderstandings, the threats, and the counterthreats that developed following the false settlement of May 15. It seems certain that, once again, the authority of the director general played an important role. As at the time of the earlier "agreement," the key to a solution lay in narrowing the difference between the Community and the United States. This was the most important task, not only because of the volume of trade conducted by them, but because for each of them something approaching a bilateral balance with the other was a political necessity. In the final settlement each had to give up some of what it thought it had obtained in mid-May in order to make an agreement possible. But most other participants were also involved in the final accommodation. Japan yielded important points on food aid. The Nordic countries receded from their insistence on qualifying their own food aid commitment, as did Argentina. The Community agreed to drop its formal cotton textile reservation and tolerated a withdrawal of concessions by Denmark designed to compensate for loss of some of the agricultural benefits the latter had understood it was to receive in the markets of the six.

These accommodations, and many others, finally permitted the Contracting Parties on June 30 — the last day possible under the President's authority — to complete and sign the protocol incorporating the results of the Kennedy Round, nearly five years after the passage of the Trade Expansion Act and more than four years after the GATT ministers had decided to conduct the first linear tariff negotiation.

Postmortem

It was, of course, no coincidence that the apparent settlement in May came at so nearly the last possible minute. The political and economic stakes of the United States in achieving maximum results were incalculable, and the American negotiators had reason to put off a final compromise until they were certain that no further concessions could be extracted from others, especially the EEC. As for other negotiators, the conviction that the United States could not afford to let the Kennedy Round fail must have encouraged the belief that the American negotiators would finally be forced either to increase their own concessions or accept a level of offers from others that they had previously rejected as inadequate. The tactics of the Community until quite close to the May 15 "settlement"

suggest that such considerations did in fact enter into their calculations. The leisurely pace of the commission in asking for, and of
the council in granting, more flexible negotiating authority could
be interpreted as a calculated tactic to force the United States to
choose between capitulation on outstanding issues and postponement of the deadline. Under either choice, the United States could
have been expected to lose. Postponement on US initiative would
simply have confirmed the impression that the one outcome the
United States administration could not accept was breakdown.

In the days just before May 15, however, any hope that the Community or others may have had of exploiting the American need
for a successful Kennedy Round must have faded. The failure of the
US administration to ask for an extension of Trade Expansion Act
authority may have provided the most convincing evidence. And
this demonstration was reinforced when the United States began
its campaign to ensure a balanced agreement by the withdrawal of
offers that had remained on the table throughout the negotiations.

There is no evidence that delaying tactics played any part during
the six weeks that remained between the May 15 "settlement" and
the expiration of the President's authority. These were weeks in
which the negotiators ceased to stake out new positions for bargaining purposes. The most difficult problems arose out of the
many ambiguities in the false agreement so hastily reached. If the
atmosphere of the preceding three years had continued in June
1967, there would have been no chance of reaching the accommodation that was ultimately achieved. Certainly the fact that time
had all but run out was of key importance in the result. But it could
not in itself have reconciled such divergent positions unless all the
major participants had considered a breakdown of the negotiations less acceptable than compromise.

To conclude that the negotiators in these closing days were
united in the determination to reach a positive result of some sort
leaves many questions unanswered. Was it also true that the same
determination would have existed if the deadline had been
reached much earlier — in 1965 or 1966 — instead of 1967? Was
the intransigence of those years entirely a function of the time remaining? Or were the laborious processes of more than three
years an essential prelude to the compromises that were hastily
contrived in the closing fortnight? Did the exasperating delays, the

stubborn repetition of arguments, or the alternating tactics of tempting offer and disappointed withdrawal change in any degree the nature of the bargain that would be acceptable? Or did they serve only to convince each participant that no further concessions could be extracted from his opponents?

Any answers to these questions must be advanced with reserve. But it is possible in the light of the history of those years to develop some plausible hypotheses. To begin with, it should be noted that the essential work that was accomplished between May 1963 and May 1967 could not have been compressed into a few months. Only if a truly linear negotiation had proved possible could much of it have been dispensed with.

But it is equally true that much of the time that elapsed after the initial decision to negotiate made little direct contribution to the negotiating process. Many of the delays arose out of structural frictions in the internal machinery of one participant — the European Community. The Kennedy Round was a play within a play, and the denouement of many a conflict in the principal plot had to await the resolution of differences in the subsidiary play — differences among the member states of the EEC.

While the multiple personality of the Community was responsible for much loss of time, it may have enhanced the influence exerted on the final agreement by the passage of time. The "success" of all multilateral tariff negotiations, that is, their failure to terminate in disagreement, owes something to the length of time devoted to the negotiating process. After many months, even years, of valuable time and work have been expended, negotiators acquire a vested interest in success that is unrelated to the economic benefits that can be expected. A participant who might have accepted a breakdown after a few weeks of bargaining is less likely to be willing to sacrifice the investment involved in a lengthy negotiation.

Probably more important than the direct effect on participants of the cumulative psychological cost of failure is its indirect effect: the perception by each participant of the price he will have to pay in loss of goodwill if he is held responsible by the others for a breakdown. This indirect effect may well have been reinforced by the split personality of the European Community. A member state that was held to be responsible for a breakdown would incur not only the wrath of the other negotiators in the Kennedy Round but that of his Common Market partners.

However much weight is given to these speculations, one fact seems clear. Within the range of those compromises that seemed likely as time came close to running out, all of the negotiators must have preferred a positive result to failure. Whether this would have been true two or three years earlier is not nearly so certain, even if the negotiators had then been faced with the necessity of concluding in a few weeks. The nearness of the deadline must have had a decisive influence on the timing of the denouement. But the fact that agreement was reached at all must be attributed to a complex of factors: the real economic advantage that most participants saw for their own economies in a reduction of trade barriers, the psychological cost to all of them of failure, and the backlash of resentment that any participant had a right to expect if he were believed to be the party responsible for the loss of the enormous expenditures that all his partners had invested in a positive outcome.

15

The Results

In the absence of a reliable technique for forecasting the trade effects of tariff concessions, a quantitative appraisal of the results of the Kennedy Round may seem an unproductive exercise. How much it might reveal about the extent of the achievement is limited. It certainly cannot settle the question of whether reciprocity, in the sense of balanced increments of trade, was achieved. An examination of the statistics that are available does, nevertheless, make possible a rough comparison between the trade coverage of the Kennedy Round and that of previous negotiations.

A comparison of the weighted averages of tariff reductions is useful for certain purposes, but conclusions based on such a comparison are treacherous if used as a gauge to measure the degree of reciprocity obtained. What cannot be measured is the judgment of each negotiator as to the "quality" of any concession, or his estimate of its probable effect on future trade. Whether that judgment is based on a conscious effort to estimate the relevant price elasticities or on informed guesses concerning market behavior, it is an essential element in each negotiator's perception of the weight to be given any concession offered or received. It is fortunate, in fact, that these qualitative judgments by negotiators are not uniform. Without a considerable latitude for differences between them, it would be much more difficult for each negotiator to return to his capital persuaded that he had obtained at least as much as he had given, and probably more.

This chapter will rely primarily on calculations made by others and will venture only a modest addition to available quantitative analyses of the results. Its main purpose will be to provide some further insight into how the issues with which the negotiators grappled were resolved.[1]

Trade Coverage

The volume of trade affected by concessions in the Kennedy Round has been estimated at $40 billion.[2] While this represented less than a quarter of total world trade, it was a substantially larger percentage (about 40 percent) of the imports of the industrialized countries that participated and a still larger percentage (perhaps 80 percent) of the trade in products "available for concessions," that is, those not already bound free. Figures are not available to permit a direct comparison of this world trade coverage with that achieved in previous negotiations. But, leaving aside for the moment the question of the depth of tariff reductions, some idea of the dimensions of the accomplishment may nevertheless be obtained so far as United States participation is concerned. In what was by far the most important of previous multilateral tariff negotiations — Geneva in 1947 — the United States had reduced tariffs on products constituting about 54 percent of its total dutiable imports. The comparable Kennedy Round percentage was 64 percent.

The 1947 negotiations, of course, involved fewer participants. Two major trading partners of the United States — Germany and Japan — were absent, which imposed a limit on the concessions that could be granted if nonparticipants were to be denied unrequited benefits.[3] Against this fact may be set the existence in 1947 of many more tariffs at a redundantly high level, which could be reduced without fear of injury to domestic producers. Probably the decisive reason for the greater commodity coverage of US tariff concessions in the Kennedy Round was the linear method of establishing the offers from which the negotiation began, in contrast to the highly selective approach pursued in the 1947 negotiations.

The Depth of Tariff Reductions

In a study prepared shortly after the conclusion of the negotiations[4] the GATT secretariat found that a selected group of industrialized countries (the EEC, Japan, Sweden, Switzerland, the United States, and the United Kingdom) had made tariff reductions on $25.7 billion of imports out of total dutiable imports of $37 billion. Reductions on $16.4 billion were of 50 percent or more, on $21 billion were over 20 percent, and on $4.2 billion were 20 percent or less.

A rough measure of overall accomplishment in tariff negotiations is the average duty reduction weighted by imports of the items reduced, as a percentage of total dutiable imports.[5] Among its disadvantages is that it does not take account of tariff concessions in the form of the binding of existing tariff rates or duty-free treatment. But, as a result of the previous negotiations in which most major trading nations have participated, the proportion of unbound rates had declined to a point where, by the opening of the Kennedy Round, it no longer had great importance. It has been estimated that the weighted average of the Kennedy Round reductions on all dutiable nonagricultural items made by the linear countries was 35 percent of the prenegotiation rates.[6] Authoritative estimates of the contribution of the various participants to this achievement are fragmentary, but those that are available correspond reasonably well with each other and show no great differences in the respective contributions of the major linear participants.

Estimates of tariff reductions affecting nonagricultural imports, in Table 6, are taken from the official US report[7] and the British White Paper[8] issued after the Kennedy Round. The tariff reductions granted by the United States, and the EEC, on nonagricultural imports from all participants were 35 and 33 percent, respectively, of their pre-Kennedy Round levels. Comparable figures for the reductions granted by the United Kingdom and Japan are not available. But UK tariffs on dutiable nonagricultural imports from the United States were reduced by about 33 percent, and Japanese tariffs on all dutiable imports from the United States, agricultural and nonagricultural, were reduced by about 35 percent. By way of comparison, at the first GATT negotiations in 1947 the United States granted tariff reductions averaging 20 percent on all dutiable imports.[9]

Although the tariff reductions in nonagricultural products achieved in the Kennedy Round were unprecedented, they fell substantially short of the goal the GATT ministers had set: 50 percent across the board, with a bare minimum of exceptions. If, for example, it had been possible to limit exceptions to 10 percent of

Table 6. Weighted average reduction[a] by "linear" participants of tariffs on dutiable nonagricultural imports (percent).

Reduction granted by—	On imports from—				
	All participants	US	EEC	Japan	UK
All linear participants	35				
US	35	—	37	38 (41)[c]	30
EEC	33[b]	33	—	(36)	
UK		33		—	
Japan	35[b]				—

[a]These average tariff reductions do not include concessions negotiated in the *ad referendum* agreement concerning chemicals. Implementation of that agreement would increase materially the level of concessions by the EEC and the United Kingdom on imports from the United States.
[b]Including agricultural imports.
[c]Percentages in parentheses are estimates in UK White Paper.

dutiable industrial trade, and all reductions had been by a full 50 percent, the weighted average reduction would have been 45 percent. What is of interest from the viewpoint of this study is to determine where the shortfalls occurred to prevent this optimum result.

The part played by total and partial exceptions, respectively, differed widely among negotiating countries depending upon the tactics they followed. As has been seen, the EEC at the outset listed a large number of "partial exceptions" and revealed its actual offers on these only as the negotiations proceeded. At the opposite extreme, the Nordic countries originally listed no exceptions and, as was generally expected, made massive withdrawals during the later stages of the negotiations.

Nearly all the products on which the United States granted no reduction were those included in its initial exceptions — and exclusions — lists. Nearly all US reductions of less than 50 percent were on products on which original 50 percent offers were later modified in the interest of reciprocity. As shown in Table 7, these partial exceptions played an important part in the overall departure

Table 7. Distribution of principal US exceptions from 50 percent reduction (number of tariff positions in the tariff schedule of the United States on nonagricultural products with imports of $100,000 or more in 1964).

		Exceptions			
Product group	Total in group	No reduction	Less than 50 percent	Total	Percent of group
Wood and related products					
Except paper	86	13	3	16	19
Paper and products	50	0	0	0	0
Textiles and textile products	296	66	99	165	56
Chemical and related products					
Subject to ASP	27	0	0	0	0
Not subject to ASP	236	16[a]	28	44	19
Nonmetallic minerals and related products	191	31[b]	7	38	20
Metals and metal products					
Iron and steel	80	32	36	68	85
Basic aluminum	10	0	6	6	60[c]
Other	476	48	10	58	12
Miscellaneous	501	74	38	112	22

Source: *Report on United States Negotiations,* II, pts. 1 and 2.
[a]Eight of which are petroleum items.
[b]All but two of the exceptions are in the categories of ceramics, china, or glass.
[c]The six accepted items represent all but 2 percent of imports of basic aluminum.

from the 50 percent target, their number exceeding total exceptions in textiles, chemicals, iron and steel, and aluminum. Counting full and partial exceptions together, the most frequent departures from a full 50 percent cut came in three of the same sectors — textiles, iron and steel, and basic aluminum. In aluminum no reductions of 50 percent were granted.

The ASP Package

The results summarized above do not reflect the supplementary agreement reached in the chemicals sector, which could come into effect only if the Congress were to take favorable action. The chemical package, as finally agreed, included the following elements:

1. The United States would eliminate the American Selling Price as the basis for assessing duties on benzenoid chemicals. After converting the post-Kennedy Round rates on these chemicals to higher rates calculated to yield the same amount of duty at present prices under normal valuation standards, they would further reduce most of these new rates to 20 percent ad valorem in the case of many products, to 30 percent in the case of most dyes, and to 25 percent in the case of sulfa drugs. On chemicals that bore tariffs of 8 percent ad valorem or less before the Kennedy Round (on which a 20 percent reduction was granted in the main negotiation) they would reduce all tariffs by an additional 30 percent of the pre-Kennedy Round rate.

2. In return, the United States would receive from its principal negotiating partners much deeper reductions in the chemical sector than those they had granted in the Kennedy Round. Thus, in the ASP Agreement, the EEC agreed to reduce by an additional 30 percent most rates which it had already reduced by 20 percent in the Kennedy Round, bringing its weighted average reduction on imports from the United States to 26 percent for the ASP package alone and 46 percent for the two agreements combined. The United Kingdom agreed to further reductions in favor of the United States to 47 percent. For the EEC, the United Kingdom, Japan, and Switzerland combined, the weighted average reduction granted on imports from the United States would rise from 26 percent in the Kennedy Round to 49 percent upon the implementation of the ASP Agreement.[10]

The point has been made earlier that, in addition to resulting in higher import charges than those yielded by application of normal valuation standards, ASP also serves as a potent nontariff barrier because the exporter cannot be sure in advance of the price on which the tariff will be assessed. Foreign governments made much of this nontariff aspect during the Kennedy Round. In return for its elimination in the ASP package they agreed to ameliorate some of their own nontariff barriers: The EEC agreed to eliminate discrimination against US types of automobile in the road-use taxes of member states; the United Kingdom agreed to reduce by 25 percent the margin of commonwealth preference for tobacco; and Switzerland agreed to eliminate quantitative restrictions on imports of canned fruit preserved in corn syrup.

On the assumption that the relation of US prices to those of foreign exporters remains the same as that on which the conversion from ASP rates was based and, therefore, that the elimination of ASP did not in itself represent a reduction in the ad valorem incidence of tariffs on benzenoid chemicals, the United States chemical industry as a whole stood to gain from this conditional chemical package a much deeper reduction in the post-Kennedy Round tariffs impeding its exports than in the tariffs protecting its domestic markets. Furthermore, after these reductions, the resulting level of the chemical tariffs of the United States would remain substantially higher than those faced by its principal chemical exports. For an industry which, as indicated by its net export position, is well able to meet foreign competition in most products, this would have seemed to be an attractive exchange. But industries, like governments, are often prisoners of the positions they have taken in the past, and almost as soon as the results of the Kennedy Round became known, spokesmen for the chemical industry as a whole declared their opposition to congressional approval of the ASP Agreement.

Other Sectors

The results of the negotiations in those products that had been selected for application of the sector technique were generally disappointing. In the basic aluminum sector, instead of the free trade that had been the hope of most exporting countries, average tariff reductions fell short of the results for industrial products as a whole. The United States reduced its tariffs by 20 percent. The United Kingdom granted a 50 percent reduction. But the reduction of 22 percent by the EEC applied only to imports within a "tariff quota" of five thousand tons per year. Tariff reductions affecting wrought aluminum were more substantial: 24 percent by the EEC, 27 percent by the United States, and 40 percent by the United Kingdom. The reductions by major participants in both the textile and iron and steel sectors, according to one estimate, averaged about 27 percent. In spite of the decision to negotiate on pulp and paper in a multilateral group, the unresolved differences between the EEC and the Scandinavian countries meant that those negotiations did not progress beyond the bilateral stage. Nevertheless, reductions in the tariffs of importance to US exports ranged from 25 percent to a full 50 percent.

On balance, in nonagricultural tariffs the sector experiment failed to yield results as substantial as those of the overall negotiations. But this fact proves nothing about the potential usefulness of the technique, as it was used only in sectors in which one or more of the participants had exhibited more than usual resistance. If these sectors had been dealt with solely in bilateral bargaining, the results might well have been still less substantial.

Negotiations with "Special Trade Structure" Countries

The average tariff reductions conceded by those developed countries permitted to participate on a nonlinear basis fell considerably short of the estimated average cut of 35 percent in industrial tariffs by the linear participants. But the item-by-item bargaining employed yielded results that were respectable by traditional standards in some cases. The United States and Canada, for example, conceded substantial reductions in tariffs on products of interest to each other. Except that the traditional bilateral request lists were dispensed with, the techniques employed by both Canada and its negotiating partners closely resembled those of previous tariff conferences, with traditional reciprocity dominating the play. Indeed, in the view of one Canadian observer, the Canadian delegation achieved the ideal of tariff negotiators and obtained something better than a balanced agreement: "Canadian negotiators managed a remarkable 'tour de force' . . . Over three billion in Canadian exports stand to benefit . . . while Canada has agreed to reduce on some two and a half billion of imports. Nearly half Canada's present dutiable imports remain untouched."[11]

The official United States report on the negotiations, while not attempting to denigrate the ability of Canada's negotiators, presents a somewhat different picture, at least so far as Canada's negotiations with the United States were concerned. According to that report, Canada's tariff concessions covered $1.4 billion, or 60 percent, of its dutiable imports from the United States.[12] The report further claims that a good part of the $1 billion of imports on which tariffs were not reduced consisted of items on which the tariff was not significant or of products which Canada does not produce and must in any case import. On the other hand, the report places the trade coverage of US tariff reductions of value to Canada at $1.3 billion. Finally, it introduces a further consideration which the Canadian negotiators had insisted upon during the negotiations: that reductions in Canadian MFN duties have the additional value for the United States of narrowing the margins of preference accorded to other members of the British Commonwealth.[13]

In spite of the misgivings that resulted from Canada's original decision not to participate on a linear basis, the Kennedy Round made more important inroads into the barriers to trade across the border than had any previous negotiation, beginning with the first bilateral agreement with Canada concluded in 1936. In the most recent multilateral negotiation, the Dillon Round, the trade coverage of US concessions to Canada had been less than $65 million.[14]

An important volume of concessions in both directions consisted of the mutual elimination of duties on products in which there was significant two-way trade between the two countries. The United States eliminated duties on products involving $480 million of imports from Canada, while tariff eliminations by Canada covered $100 million of imports from the United States. The average preagreement rate eliminated by the United States was about 2 percent ad valorem, while the average of the Canadian rates eliminated was much higher, with individual rates ranging from 5 to 20 percent.[15]

One of the significant Canadian contributions to the Kennedy Round was its acceptance of the "antidumping code." Canadian law and practice in the field of antidumping measures had in the past deviated more than that of other major trading countries from the standards laid down in the General Agreement. Canada's acceptance of a new code therefore promised to remove a long-standing source of annoyance to American and other exporters and an irritant in US-Canadian commercial relations.

Except for Canada, the "special trade structure" countries made little more than a token contribution to the results of the negotiations. Concessions granted by New Zealand covered only about 7 percent of its imports and by South Africa only 2.7 percent. Australia was the only participating contracting party that did not conclude a negotiation with any of the major participants. But if these countries originally hoped that exemption from the linear rules would bring them a negotiating advantage, they must have been disappointed. For example, New Zealand's concessions, mostly less than 50 percent, on some $16 million of imports from the United States were matched by US reductions of 50 percent on only about $12.5 million of imports from New Zealand. And the US imports covered by these concessions were only about 8 percent of the value of all US imports from that country in 1966. The results of United States negotiations with South Africa were even more meager in both absolute and relative terms.[16] If the United States can be considered representative of the linear participants in general, it would seem that, except for Canada, the effect of the abstention of the "special trade structure" countries from the linear negotiations, combined with the continued insistence of the linear countries on receiving reciprocity, played a significant part in reducing the amount of trade on which the linear countries eventually reduced their duties by the full 50 percent.

Agricultural Negotiations

The results of the negotiations in the Grains Group were incorporated in the Memorandum of Agreement on Basic Elements for the Negotiation of a World Grains Arrangement, which, for its signatories,[17] was made an integral part of the Kennedy Round agreement. After the completion of the Kennedy Round, the participants incorporated the results in a new International Grains Arrangement (IGA), thus replacing the expired International Wheat Agreement.[18] This new agreement required the consent of the Senate for ratification by the United States. The remaining agricultural "groups" failed in their original purpose, and the negotiation of such tariff reductions as proved possible was merged with the negotiation on those products that had not been set aside for possible multilateral commodity agreements. Thus, except in the case of wheat, agricultural negotiations in the Kennedy Round differed from those in previous negotiations only in the substitution of initial multilateral offer lists for the traditional bilateral exchange of requests and offers. Bargaining was bilateral and on selected products. There was no negotiation of nontariff barriers nor any use of the linear approach.

In view of the repeated obstacles encountered in the agricultural negotiations, the results achieved fell considerably short of accomplishments in the area of nonagricultural products. They were greater than had appeared possible in the fall of 1966, however. In September of that year, as recounted earlier, the president of the Farm Bureau Federation had asked that the entire negotiation be called off because of the absence of meaningful agricultural offers by the community. Others, while not recommending so drastic a course, also saw little hope of obtaining meaningful concessions from the EEC.[19] These appraisals proved unduly pessimistic.

The statistics available to the public do not permit a complete comparison between the accomplishments of the Kennedy Round in agricultural products and those in industrial products. The official United States government report[20] does not present a weighted average of the agricultural reductions granted either by the United States or by the other participants as a whole. It does, however, provide useful information concerning the results in terms of the bilateral agricultural trade between the United States and each of its principal negotiating partners. Simply by observation of the trade coverage and of the individual tariff reductions shown in these summaries, it is possible to conclude that the results of the agricultural negotiations were far from negligible.[21]

It is difficult to describe a football game or a cricket match without implicitly accepting the standard of scoring used by the players themselves, however illogical it may seem. The problem involved in discussing whether reciprocity was or was not achieved is similar, but with the added disadvantage that there is no official scorekeeper. Nor is there any way to know all the factors that have entered into the value judgments of the players. Nevertheless, in discussing a negotiation in which all the major negotiators insisted on obtaining reciprocity from each other, there is little choice but to use the vocabulary of bargaining for reciprocity, even at the risk of seeming to concur in a scoring system in which the reduction of a tariff by one's opponent is counted as a gain and the reduction of one's own tariff is scored as a loss. In reading the following paragraphs, it should be borne in mind that such expressions as "concessions granted" or "concessions received" are used without any implication of economic loss or gain.

The volume of US exports affected by the agricultural duty reductions granted by some of the more important participants, with the comparable volume of trade affected by reductions granted by the United States, is shown in Table 8. If trade coverage alone is

Table 8. Trade between the United States and selected trading partners affected by tariff reductions on dutiable agricultural imports.

Country	US imports from others (1964)		Imports by others from US (1964)	
	Total value (millions)	Percent of dutiable imports	Total value (millions)	Percent of dutiable imports
EEC	$93.7	45	$220.4	49
United Kingdom	4.9	68	56.4	28
Canada	65.6	57	87.3	50
Japan	21.9	95	219.3	75
Denmark	62.8	14	8.0	55
Switzerland	8.1	96	20.1	58

Source: *Report on United States Negotiations*, I, pt. 1.

considered, the exchange of agricultural tariff reductions was heavily in favor of the United States in the cases of the EEC, the United Kingdom, Japan, and Switzerland. The balance with Canada was more nearly equal. Only Denmark obtained from the United States concessions on a larger volume of agricultural products than it granted in return. On balance, these comparisons confirm the impression to be derived from observation of the give-and-take that made it possible to achieve the final compromise. In spite of the original distinction between the linear negotiations in industrial products and the nonlinear negotiations in agriculture, the agricultural sector was called upon to redress any imbalance in the reciprocity achieved in the other. If the United States granted a full linear reduction on a larger percentage of its dutiable industrial imports than some of its negotiating partners, it obtained greater benefits for its agricultural exports than it conceded.

The official US report on the negotiations gives the distribution of agricultural tariff reductions according to the depth of cut. The aggregated reductions granted by the countries included in Table 8 on US imports show well over half of those concessions to have been by 50 percent or more. The same was true of United States agricultural concessions to the countries concerned. But no US reductions were greater than one-half, whereas nearly 41 percent of the concessions granted by the others to the United States were of more than 50 percent. US reductions were much more heavily concentrated in the 25 to 50 percent range than were those of the others, which was a natural result of the limitations imposed by the Trade Expansion Act.

The potential effect of tariff reductions in agriculture on future trade will depend, of course, on many variables that cannot be presently measured, including the influence of nontariff barriers. One fact that is not brought out by the aggregates summarized above is that no worthwhile concessions were obtained by the exporting countries from the EEC on those items subject to the variable levy, such as grains, flour, rice, poultry meat (other than canned), and eggs.[22] And, although the United Kingdom made deep reductions in most of the agricultural tariffs on which it granted any concessions, it was constrained from taking any action on most bulk products, both by reluctance to reduce preferential margins on products of importance to its Commonwealth partners and by reluctance to bind low rates on products that would be subject to the variable levy system should Britain obtain admission to the European Common Market.

Staging of Concessions

In view of the staging requirement in the authority granted by the Trade Expansion Act, the basic rule that was applied to tariff concessions of all participants provided that tariff reductions be put into effect in annual installments, with the final installment to be made not later than four years from the date of the first. For those countries able to make the first reduction on January 1, 1968, subsequent reductions of one-fifth of the total were to be made on the first day of each of the four following years. But some countries were not able to act with sufficient speed to meet the first date and were given the option of putting two stages of their reductions into effect on July 1, 1968, instead of January 1, 1968, and January 1, 1969. Regardless of the dates chosen for the first two installments, all signatories would put their remaining reductions into effect in uniform annual installments beginning January 1, 1970.

Among the larger participating countries, the United States and Canada chose to begin their tariff reductions on January 1, 1968, and the EEC, Japan, and the United Kingdom chose to begin with a double cut on July 1 of that year.

One of the requests made by the less developed countries was that developed countries at once put into effect their full tariff reductions on products of special interest to them. The developed countries undertook to do this "where possible." The Trade Expansion Act permitted this action in the case of concessions granted under the tropical products authority (Section 213). Accordingly, the United States on January 1, 1968, put into effect all its full tariff eliminations, amounting to $61.4 million of 1965 trade. Most other developed countries also advanced some of their tariff reductions benefiting less developed countries.[23]

Initial Negotiating Rights

There has been a good deal of emphasis in these pages on the many points at which the Kennedy Round deviated from the linear approach to tariff cutting envisioned when the Trade Expansion Act was enacted, but some of the departures from the item-by-item bilateral procedure of former negotiations are also significant. One such departure took place toward the end of the negotiation and created little stir. It may not have had much more than symbolic significance, but it did represent a further step away from bilateralism in tariff negotiations.

After every previous negotiation, pairs of negotiators had exchanged memoranda in which each designated those tariff concessions it had granted directly to the other and for which it recognized the other as an "initial negotiator." Since, by the fact of their own adherence to the GATT, all contracting parties have a contractual right to the tariff treatment that others have bound in GATT schedules,* the reason for this procedure may not be readily apparent. The agreement permits a contracting party, under special

*The one exception to this is where Article XXXIII has been invoked. See chap. iii.

circumstances, to withdraw a concession, generally after consultation and negotiation with other contracting parties with which the concession was initially negotiated and with those having a principal supplying interest.[24] A country with which a concession was initially negotiated is automatically entitled to be a party to such renegotiation, but the substantial interest of others must be determined by the Contracting Parties before their contractual rights can be converted into concrete compensatory benefits.

As has been pointed out before, the major Kennedy Round departure from the traditional form of item-by-item negotiation was the omission of the preliminary bilateral exchange of requests and offers. This would have made it difficult, without injecting a further complication into the negotiations, to identify the countries that could be said to have been most active in extracting a given concession and were therefore entitled to be recognized as the "initial negotiators."

By the time the Trade Negotiations Committee came to grips with the problem, on June 28, 1967, there was in fact no alternative to the solution it adopted, namely, to recommend to the Contracting Parties the following decision, which the latter adopted at their session in November 1967: "In respect of the concessions specified in the Schedules annexed to the Geneva (1967) Protocol, a contracting party shall, when the question arises, be deemed for the purposes of the General Agreement to be the contracting party with which a concession was initially negotiated if it had during a representative period prior to that time a principal supplying interest in the product concerned."[25]

This solution, however, was agreed to only after the expression of concern by some of the smaller countries. A country such as Finland, Norway, or Israel may be heavily dependent upon exports of a given product and yet not be the principal supplier. The Contracting Parties therefore agreed that countries might, if they wished, conduct discussions with others after the Kennedy Round in order to obtain recognition as initial negotiators of concessions on products important to them.

A Backward Glance

In spite of much backsliding, the Kennedy Round did achieve a modest step in the direction of introducing multilateralism into tariff negotiations. But it fell short of a clean break with other restraints imposed by the heritage of over thirty years of tariff bargaining. The name of the game was changed; its rules were new. But the prize — reciprocity — remained the same. Its meaning was unaffected by the seemingly radical change in emphasis and objectives implied in the adoption of the linear approach.

In the final compromise, the refusal of each major participant to contemplate any potential increase in its imports that was not offset by a predictably equal increase in its exports ran head-on into the rule of MFN and established the limits of the contribution each would make to the final result. Japan was unwilling to accept as great a measure of increased competition as the United States was ready to risk. And the resulting reduction in US offers to Japan affected concessions of interest to the EEC and brought a further reduction in the concessions which the Community had agreed upon in the false "settlement" of mid-May 1967. Still further withdrawals became a real threat, which could have forced others — the EFTA countries, for example — to pick up some of their own chips. Not only were the participants' appraisals of reciprocity involved, but the pride of negotiators was engaged, thus affecting the willingness of any of them to propose compromises that would bring the process to a halt. If the director general had not relieved them of that onus, the unraveling might have gone even further than it did.

Emphasis on how much more might have been achieved had the participants been willing to accept the full implications of a truly linear negotiation should not be allowed to obscure the unique accomplishment of the Kennedy Round. Credit has already been given to the simple effect of the passage of time — to the influence exerted on the negotiators by more than four years of labor they had invested in the enterprise. But perhaps not enough has been said about the influence of the linear method of tabling offer lists. The presumption in the industrial negotiations that a participant's failure to include an item in its exceptions list was the equivalent of an offer to reduce its tariff by 50 percent and the need to justify exceptions on grounds of overriding national interest were the clearest departures from past negotiating techniques. Even though the potential achievement was diluted by later withdrawals, these departures did much to foster the unprecedented results obtained.

It is doubtful that the shortfalls in the nonlinear sectors of the negotiation could have been avoided by different methods. If it were possible to replay the Kennedy Round with the aid of ex post facto knowledge of where it went wrong, the results in the agricultural sector and in nontariff barriers would not be greatly different — unless the environment in which the negotiations were conducted could somehow have been radically changed.

Part Five: Aftermath and Legacy

16

The Changing Climate, 1967 – 1970

The euphoria generated by the successful conclusion of the
Kennedy Round in the summer of 1967 was short lived, and it was
soon replaced by serious doubts that the agreement could withstand the forces being mobilized against it. That mobilization had
begun even before the negotiations had been concluded. The Supplementary Chemicals Agreement had come under direct fire
before its final shape was known to the negotiators themselves.
While the negotiations were still in progress, the US Senate passed
a resolution clearly designed to warn the President against tampering with ASP. This resolution declared it to be the sense of the
Congress that the President should negotiate no agreement for
which authority was not expressly provided in the Trade Expansion Act.[1]

The attack on the chemicals agreement was shortly followed by
offensives on many other fronts. Before the year was up, dozens
of bills had been introduced in one or the other house of Congress
providing for the imposition of quotas against imports. Many of
them were directed toward the protection of specific products,
such as steel, textiles, mink pelts, and strawberries. But others,
such as the Fair International Trade Bill,[2] introduced by Congressman Herlong, were designed to prevent imports of any product

that might reduce the share of the domestic market enjoyed in the recent past by American producers.

While congressional and private attacks in the United States threatened the Kennedy Round, the malfunctioning of the international monetary system led to different and more widespread threats. On three occasions within a year of the conclusion of the negotiations, a monetary crisis developed which, if not contained, could have led to a general unraveling of the Kennedy Round settlement.

In the fall of 1967, even before the first stage of tariff cuts could be put into effect, speculation against sterling forced the United Kingdom to devalue the pound and thus to reduce the value of Britain's tariff concessions.

On January 1, 1968 — the day on which the first stage of concessions by the United States became effective — President Johnson released a public statement on the crisis facing the US dollar.[3] While the President's statement refrained from recommending new barriers to US import trade and placed a substantial share of the blame for the crisis on inflation in the United States, he pointedly referred to the nontariff barriers of other countries and singled out for special attention their border tax adjustments.

On July 1, 1968, the EEC was due to put into effect the first stage of its Kennedy Round reductions. Like the United States six months earlier, it met its engagement. But, only a few weeks earlier, serious domestic disorders in France had been settled at the cost of a substantial increase in wages, thus further endangering the French balance of payments, which was already strained by a speculative flight from the franc. In the first week of July, the French government announced a series of measures designed to offset the effects of these wage increases on its trade balance: a subsidy to most exports, designed to compensate for the wage increases; a further decrease in the especially favorable rediscount rate granted to exporters; and the imposition of quotas on the importation from all sources of automobiles and certain household appliances. The US Bureau of Customs promptly announced that it was considering the imposition of countervailing duties. On August 8, it ordered a 2.5 percent charge on those imports from France that were subject to the subsidy.[4]

Protectionism in the United States —
and Foreign Reaction

Throughout the second half of 1967 and all of 1968 the explosion of protectionist sentiment in the United States appeared capable at almost any moment of undoing the results of the Kennedy Round. Foreign governments were concerned with the sensitivity of the American democratic process; they were afraid that Congress would not, or could not, withstand the intense pressure being brought to bear on it by industries and labor unions seeking protection. They also showed that they took seriously the possibility of a move by the administration itself to correct the balance of payments deficit by direct action affecting the trade balance.

There was, in fact, good reason for the latter concern. For the implications of President Johnson's message of January 1 were soon made more explicit. During the first few months of 1968, foreign capitals were hosts to a succession of official American missions, sent to explain the trade measures being considered in Washington. One possibility that was prominently brandished was the adoption by the United States of its own border tax adjustments, to be based on "estimates" — necessarily arbitrary — of the average incidence of indirect taxes (federal, state, and local) paid by producers of domestic products that were exported or that competed with imported products. An alternative that aroused equally little enthusiasm abroad was the contemplated adoption of import surcharges and export rebates, at a uniform but even more arbitrary level, unrelated to domestic taxation.

In March 1968, in an effort to forestall unilateral action by the United States, the EFTA countries offered to accelerate their Kennedy Round reductions without parallel action by the United States if the EEC would do the same. The EEC soon made an acceleration offer of its own, hedged with stiffer conditions. Finally, under the guidance of Eric Wyndham White, the two European trading blocs, together with Canada and Japan, reached agreement on a joint plan. They offered to accelerate their own Kennedy Round cuts by one stage at the end of 1968 if by that time the United States had adopted no protectionist measures and had taken the necessary action to implement the ASP Agreement. The United

States was not required to accept or reject their offer, but the administration dropped consideration of early direct action to affect the trade account and concentrated its efforts on preventing the passage of protectionist legislation.

Ways and Means Committee Hearings of 1968

Marathon public hearings held by the Ways and Means Committee of the House of Representatives in June and early July of 1968[5] recorded a climate of public and congressional opinion strikingly different from that revealed by the hearings that had preceded the passage of the Trade Expansion Act six years earlier. To some extent, this may have resulted from differences in the terms of reference of the two hearings. In 1962 the theme had been a bold and imaginative legislative proposal advanced by a popular President. In 1968, there was also, it is true, an administration bill to be considered.[6] But, except for the controversial provision to repeal the American Selling Price, it was limited to restoring the expired tariff cutting authority of the Trade Expansion Act — for "housekeeping" purposes — and to liberalizing the criteria that must be met by firms or workers seeking adjustment assistance. It was hardly calculated to arouse the ardor of the forces of freer trade.

In addition to the administration bill, the 1968 hearings had a far more lively subject — the multiplicity of quota and other protectionist bills that had been accumulating in the Ways and Means Committee's docket since the previous fall. This fact could account for the vastly greater amount of time devoted to demands for the curtailment of imports in 1968 than in 1962. But, even allowing for the difference in the content of the two hearings, there is ample evidence that in the interval between them a massive shift of alignments had occurred.

During the four weeks of hearings the committee heard scores of public witnesses and a hundred of their colleagues from the House and Senate. Of that hundred, only eight testified in favor of the administration's bill, against proposed quota bills, or in favor of freer trade. Support for the administration's position came primarily from importers and public interest groups. The national farm organizations gave general support, seasoned with some adverse comment on the results obtained for agriculture in the

Kennedy Round.[7] But the overwhelming weight of the testimony of representatives of more specialized farm groups, as well as that of industry and labor unions, was cast on the side of quota bills designed to restrict imports. In terms of the number of witnesses produced, no one industry had a clear advantage. Steel, oil, textiles, shoes, lead and zinc mining, consumer electronics, and chemicals were all strongly represented. Specialized agricultural interests were also present in force, especially in favor of stricter quotas against imports of meat, dairy products, and mink.

Perhaps the most conspicuous shift in position was that of organized labor. In the past, specialized labor unions had often joined forces with their employers in demanding higher protection, but nationally organized labor had provided some of the most powerful backing for trade agreements legislation. In 1968, the spokesman for the AFL-CIO again supported the administration's trade proposals, but much of his testimony was devoted to insistence that the United States require of its trading partners, as a condition for the continuance of a liberal trade policy, prompt action to eliminate nontariff barriers and to raise their labor standards to a level closer to that of the United States. Equally urgent in his view was the need to curtail the export of American capital which has "cost American jobs, cut into American exports and added to imports."[8]

When the Ninetieth Congress adjourned before the 1968 election, the Ways and Means Committee had failed to take action either on the administration's trade bill or on any of the quota bills before it. But the reprieve for relatively unrestricted trade was clearly only temporary. It did not reflect the prevailing sentiment of Congress. What it did reflect was the political judgment of the chairman of the Ways and Means Committee that the passage of any quota legislation would open the flood gates to dozens of competing bills. Early the following year, Chairman Mills publicly expressed both his sympathy for the claims of the domestic textile industry for special protection and his attitude toward the general use of quotas: "The Congress always has trouble approving import quota legislation affecting a single industry. However sympathetic individual Representatives or Senators are to the textile import problem, there are other industries which are seeking the same form of relief and which also have supporters in the Congress. Thus, it appears difficult, if not impossible, to work out an import quota law for one industry and prevent its extension to the products of other industries."[9]

The Ways and Means Committee hearings resulted in a draw — for the time being. No quota bill was reported out. And, in the absence of action on the administration's bill, the American Selling Price Agreement could not be implemented. As a result, the EEC, EFTA, Canada, and Japan were not called upon to make good their offer to accelerate their Kennedy Round cuts. From the point of view of American international relations, it may be well that they were not. For it is doubtful, after the French balance of payments crisis, that the EEC would have been able to keep its part of the bargain.

Though the hearings failed to result in concrete action, either favorable or unfavorable to trade liberalization, the ten volumes of testimony do suggest some of the new forces that future trade policy is going to have to take into account. Some of these represent changes in the economic environment that have occurred since 1962. Others are more subjective. But the policymakers of the 1970's can no more afford to ignore the change in popular attitudes than they can the more concrete developments that have altered the conditions of international competition. They cannot, for example, fail to take into account the almost universal belief, held by businessmen, both domestically and internationally oriented, that the nontariff barriers of foreign countries have mushroomed since the Kennedy Round and have replaced the tariff as the preferred device for strangling trade. Nor can they ignore the very real increase that has taken place in United States direct investments abroad nor the conviction of some domestic industries and of organized labor that this trend is depriving the United States of a competitive answer to the lower wage rates of the rest of the world.

Tariffs Versus Nontariff Barriers

The assumed escalation of foreign nontariff barriers colored the testimony of most public and congressional witnesses in the 1968 Ways and Means Committee hearings. A typical example is the following excerpt from the statement of Congressman Peter W. Rodino of New Jersey: "It has come to my attention and to the attention of many other Members of the Congress that many of our trading partners abroad have already increased their border taxes to levels that more than offset the current reductions which they agreed to make at Geneva, so that the net effect, once again, is all give on our part and all take on their part. Their cost of entering the US market is substantially reduced, but our cost of entering their market remains approximately the same. This tampering with border taxes cannot be ignored because it poses a serious threat to our already troublesome balance of payments and negates even the pretense of reciprocity in the Geneva agreements."[10]

These remarks were made in the context of a vigorous attack on the ASP Agreement. It is not surprising, therefore, that their author was disposed to conclude that the United States had lost the Kennedy Round. But it is difficult to dismiss as special pleading a similar view expressed by Congressman Curtis in an address generally favorable to the further expansion of international trade: "Many of us like to think that the decades since the war have been marked by a continuing movement toward freer world trade and payments. The Kennedy Round in this vision is seen by short-sighted persons as the crowning achievement of the drive forward for freer trade, but they have ignored the fact that as tariffs have been dismantled . . . quotas, licenses, embargoes and other rigid and restrictive trade barriers have been created."[11]

Charges of massive cheating by America's trading partners found fertile soil. They helped explain the unsatisfactory performance of American industry in international competition. Even those who attributed the deterioration in the US trade balance to more fundamental changes in the structure of international trade found no logical difficulty in espousing at the same time a thesis that cast doubt on the equity of the Kennedy Round settlement.

Much of the original impetus for the conviction that foreign governments were to blame, however, came from the Johnson administration itself. In order to explain the decline in the balance of payments without placing all the onus on the cost of distant adventures, terrestrial and extraterrestrial, it was natural for the administration to emphasize the responsibility of foreign governments. Also, in the fight against protectionism at home, it served the administration's immediate interest to demonstrate its vigilance by challenging the trespasses of other countries. In the complex of governmental measures affecting trade, shortcomings are never hard to find. But the efforts of the European Community to harmonize the internal taxes of the member states provided a particularly timely target.[12]

The charge that European border taxes had impaired tariff concessions granted in the Kennedy Round did, in fact, have a slight basis in fact. In its search for a means of tax harmonization, the Community decided in April 1967 to put into effect, gradually, a uniform system of indirect business taxes, for which the French tax on value added (TVA) was to serve as the model.[13] Germany made the first move to carry out this decision when, on January 1, 1968, it adopted a domestic value-added tax of 10 percent. At the same time it adopted a 10 percent tax on imports and a 10 percent rebate on exports, the latter to be put into effect gradually during a transitional period. Six months later, both were increased to 11 percent. The German action was interpreted by some American exporters as equivalent to the adoption of a tariff of 11 percent. Others complained only of the increase — averaging a bit more than 6 percent — above the level of the previous German border tax. But both complaints ignored the fact that German products at the same time became liable to the full 11 percent tax.

What, then, is the basis for the view that Germany's adoption of the TVA was restrictive of imports? The most solid basis is the fact that the previous turnover tax was, on the average, undercompensated at the border. Under the TVA, for the first time, the taxes on domestic and imported products are equal. The former average undercompensation, automatically eliminated by TVA, has been estimated at 2.4 percent ad valorem for imports and .6 percent for exports.[14]

The other, more speculative, basis for the claim that imports suffered a net disadvantage from the change is related to the doctrinal controversy over tax shifting. If any part of the increased tax on domestic production in Germany were absorbed by the producers and not shifted forward to the price of the product, the effect of an increased tax on both domestic and imported products would be a further obstacle to imports. It is impossible to attach any precise value to this factor. But if any allowance is made for it, the tariff equivalent of the change in the German tax system must range, by the end of the transition period, between a minimum of 2.4 percent ad valorem and something higher. The maximum possible effect, even under the highly unrealistic assumption that no part of the increased tax is shifted forward, would be 6.4 percent.[15]

Other than the German tax action and the less important border tax changes of other Common Market countries in preparation for the adoption of TVA, the only other significant developments to support the impression of a general escalation of nontariff barriers were the adoption by the United Kingdom and France of measures designed to check serious declines in their monetary reserves. The French measures, aimed primarily at stimulating exports, have been described above. In December 1968 the United Kingdom imposed a requirement that importers deposit with customs 50 percent of the value of the goods imported, to be returned without interest after six months.[16]

Thus, the common American belief that other developed countries have undertaken a massive escalation of their nontariff barriers since the Kennedy Round appears to rest on the incidental protective effect of a changeover in the domestic tax systems of certain European countries and upon extraordinary measures taken by the United Kingdom and France in response to monetary crises.

The Reputed Obsolescence of Tariffs

The corollary of the belief in the predominance of nontariff barriers since the Kennedy Round is the conviction that customs duties have now been reduced to negligible levels. Such facts as are available cast serious doubt on this belief as well. According to a recent calculation,[17] the weighted average level of tariffs on dutiable items in the United States, the United Kingdom, Japan, and the EEC ranges from 9 percent to less than 13 percent, with the United States tariff at the bottom of the scale, Japan's at the top, and that of the EEC averaging one percentage point above that of the United States.

These overall averages, of course, conceal the existence of higher tariff averages in particular sectors. If Chapters 25 to 99 of the Brussels Tariff Nomenclature are considered separately (that is, all the chapters other than agricultural), the average rate exceeded

15 percent in twelve chapters for the United States, five for the EEC, eight for Japan, and eleven for the United Kingdom. Within these chapters there are much higher rates on individual products. Except in the case of the EEC, which has the lowest dispersion of tariff rates of the countries compared, each of the major Kennedy Round participants still applies tariffs of over 25 percent ad valorem to more than 5 percent of its dutiable imports, after giving effect to the reductions granted in the Kennedy Round.

Some idea of the level at which a tariff is conceived by governments to be high enough to restrict trade can be obtained from observing their behavior in tariff negotiations. That observation fails to reveal any tendency to establish a floor below which a further tariff reduction is considered valueless. In the Kennedy Round, reductions of rates already below 10 percent ad valorem appear to have been as frequent as reductions of higher rates.[18] Since negotiators seldom granted unrequited concessions, no matter how little the cost to them, it is a fair conclusion that their negotiating partners must have considered reductions in these relatively low rates worth paying for. In fact, some of the most vigorous bargaining in the entire Round was over tariff levels of less than 10 percent. Few disputes in the Kennedy Round exceeded in acerbity the argument as to whether the European Community would reduce its steel tariffs to 6 rather than 7.5 percent.

These facts suggest that there is still a long way to go before tariffs cease to restrict trade, even before taking into account the difference between nominal and effective rates.[19] The fact that a tariff was reduced to a very low nominal rate in the Kennedy Round does not necessarily mean that the effective protection it affords is low. It is not even correct to assume that effective rates were automatically reduced when the corresponding nominal rates were reduced. If the tariffs on imported components were reduced more than those on the end products, the result could of course be to increase the effective rates on the latter. Melvin and Wilkinson have estimated effective rates of protection before and after the Kennedy Round, at the industry level, for thirty-two selected Canadian manufacturing industries and have concluded that nearly a third of those industries were protected by higher effective rates after the Kennedy Round than before.[20]

In spite of the fact that both the increase in the incidence of nontariff barriers and the decline in the incidence of tariffs remaining after the Kennedy Round have been greatly exaggerated, there are persuasive reasons for believing that the focus of attention in future trade negotiations will have to be very different from that of the past. The relative importance of nontariff barriers has unquestionably increased as a result of the Kennedy Round reductions in tariffs. Furthermore, the fact that the great majority of the tariffs maintained by the major trading nations are now bound against increase intensifies the temptation to introduce new or more restrictive nontariff barriers, especially those that are not prohibited by present GATT rules.

The fact that nontariff barriers are widely perceived as instruments that foreign countries are able to use to nullify tariff concessions makes it unlikely that any American administration could obtain authority from the Congress to engage in a major trade negotiation that did not promise to achieve their substantial curtailment. To this reason for predicting a qualitative change in the character of trade negotiations must be added another factor — the growth of the multinational corporation and the related revolution in the international mobility of production factors.

The Revolution in Factor Mobility

Since the beginning of the decade of the 1960's, one of the most striking developments affecting international economic relations has been the growth of the multinational corporation. The direct investments of US corporations overseas have multiplied in the last ten years. In 1967 they were over $60 billion. Annual sales by US affiliates abroad are now over three times the value of total US exports.[21]

However this phenomenon is viewed, it has opened up new territories that will have to be explored and conquered in future international negotiations. Both the threat and the challenge that American direct investment implies to the host country have been popularized by Jean Jacques Servan-Schreiber in *Le Défi Américain*.[22] To the investing country multinationalization poses both general problems related to national jurisdiction over foreign subsidiaries and, in the case of the United States, special problems concerning the future application of US antitrust and other regulatory legislation.[23] The aspect that attracts most of the attention of the US Treasury is the flow of capital exports, which is the most immediate effect. The flow can be temporarily shut off when the country's balance of payments needs correction, but at an indeterminate longer-term cost in the form of the sacrifice of dividends and of potential exports that would have been generated if the investment had been permitted.

In the United States, the internationalization of American enterprises has furnished domestically oriented business and organized labor with reason for genuine concern and with arguments for higher tariffs and import quotas. In the past, the contention that the United States cannot compete on even terms with low-wage producers abroad has been blunted both by the existence of a large US trade surplus and by the demonstrable fact that US labor, in combination with other productive factors available to it, was the most productive in the world. But, in 1968, advocates of import restrictions were able to point to the rapid decline in the US trade surplus and to offer a superficially plausible explanation for it: capital, technology, and management were no longer a peculiarly American endowment. Through the medium of the multinational enterprise they had become as mobile as merchandise.[24]

To organized labor the new mobility of productive factors added up, quite simply, to the export of American jobs; US companies established production abroad either in order to produce goods for foreign markets that could otherwise have been exported from the United States or in order to satisfy American demand through foreign low-wage production. The course proposed by the AFL-CIO was that "the export of U.S. capital and its effect on international trade should be thoroughly investigated, and appropriate supervision and necessary controls should be instituted by Government authorities."[25] In this proposal it was implicit that if capital controls were not imposed organized labor might turn to the support of trade restrictions. "AFL-CIO support for the expansion of trade does not extend to the promotion of private greed at public expense, or the undercutting of U.S. wages and working conditions."[26]

A favorite subject for dispute between internationally oriented businesses and their critics is whether the exports generated by foreign investment — in the form of shipments of capital goods and components and of merchandise to fill out the lines produced abroad — are greater or less than the exports that would have been possible had the capital stayed at home. But, to the policy maker, it should make little difference who has the better of this debate. The arguments for permitting the freest possible international trade in goods apply equally to the need for maximizing, within the limits imposed by time and space, the mobility of the factors of production. If governments should seriously interfere with that mobility, the result would be to stifle the growth in economic welfare that is otherwise possible.

There are, however, severe limits to the extent to which any one country can permanently prevent others from sharing the fruits of economic and scientific advance. If the United States could pre-empt the lion's share of capital, technology, and managerial skills, it is theoretically possible that it might benefit. But this is no more a practical possibility than that a country can permanently improve its terms of trade by means of a tariff. What is required is that others stand still, which they will not do. At most, rigid controls over capital exports, communication, and the movements of persons might impede, but could not stop, foreign countries from applying more capital and improved technology to their production. The probable result of an effort by the United States to slow this development would simply be that it would obtain a smaller share of the global benefits.

Trade and Investment Policy

The increased mobility of productive factors, nevertheless, is creating both domestic and international problems that will need to be dealt with. Domestically, it may require an acceleration in the rate at which innovations in product design and production methods are introduced if the United States is not to lose its competitive position.[27] And to avoid undue hardships to firms and workers, as well as to facilitate this acceleration, it may require that governmental assistance to firms and workers be made more readily accessible and more effective than that provided by the Trade Expansion Act of 1962.

Internationally, if the United States is going to benefit to the maximum from increased factor mobility, it will probably have to take positive steps to ensure that its own willingness to permit investment capital to flow from the United States is not frustrated by the refusal of others to admit American firms.

An example of factor protectionism has been the refusal of Japan to permit American automobile companies to establish affiliates in that country. In 1968 negotiations with the Japanese government led to a nominal relaxation of this restriction, but no American company has yet found it worthwhile to comply with the conditions attached by Japan.

At least during the decade of the 1960's few impediments were erected to prevent US-based enterprises from participating in the phenomenal economic growth of Western Europe. In fact, American affiliates were often quicker than their European competitors to take advantage of the creation of a new and unified market comparable in size to that of the United States. The existence of that market acted as a check on the latent opposition in any one member state toward permitting American direct investment. For, if one member refused the American company access to its territory, another member was likely to welcome it, and the product of American capital and technology would flow freely within the Common Market.

There is no assurance that this European tolerance of American investment will endure. The EEC is engaged in a search for some means of reducing existing barriers to capital mobility and cross-boundary mergers within the Community, possibly by the establishment of a unified company law. It may be necessary for the United States to negotiate with the EEC in order to ensure equal treatment of American-based enterprises under whatever Community rules emerge. In exchange, the United States will almost certainly have to cooperate by removing the irritation caused by the conflict of jurisdiction over the affiliates of American-based multinational corporations.

Restrictive Business Practices

A by-product of greater factor mobility may be an intensification of private practices that restrict the freedom both of trade in goods and in the right to do business across international boundaries. As enterprises extend their interests across national frontiers, their increasing size and the declining importance of the frontiers themselves may increase both the incentives and the opportunities to repress competition.

The member states of the European Economic Community recognized this possibility when they drew up the Treaty of Rome. They could not escape the logical contradiction between the creation of a common market and a continued toleration of cartels. Article 85 of the Treaty of Rome prohibits "agreements between enterprises, decisions by associations of enterprises and any concerted practices" which prevent, restrict, or distort competition within the Common Market. Enforcement has been less than complete, a result which is hardly surprising in countries in which combinations in restraint of trade have traditionally been accepted as a normal, and sometimes beneficial, way of life.

Both the GATT and the OECD have made tentative efforts to come to grips with what may eventually have as great importance as the nontariff barriers erected by governments. But private restrictive practices, while sharing the complexity of nontariff barriers, are even more difficult to deal with because of the difficulty of ascertaining the facts. It is hard to see how governments will be able to avoid the problem in future negotiations. But it is equally hard to visualize either the method of approach or its end result. It may be, as Vernon has suggested,[28] that the only practical method will be to deal with restrictive business practices, one industry at a time, in the context of sector negotiations, directed toward the removal of trade barriers in general.

The Future of Reciprocity

From whatever angle future negotiations are viewed, one conclusion emerges: the reciprocity of Cordell Hull and of the early GATT negotiations has lost its relevance to the problems of the late 1960's and the 1970's. Even the efforts of the Kennedy Round to abandon it in substance, while continuing to make ritual obeisance to it, offer no satisfactory guide to the future negotiation of industrial tariffs.

Under the Luxembourg Compromise of January 1966, in spite of the provisions of Article 111, 3, of the Treaty of Rome, a change in a tariff rate still requires unanimous agreement among the member states of the European Community. If the object of a negotiation were solely to obtain a maximum reduction of industrial tariffs, the experience of the Kennedy Round suggests that the chances would be greatly improved under an automatic formula, or at least a formula much more nearly automatic than the quasi-linear approach used in the Kennedy Round.

The negotiation of tariff reductions by formula, however, encounters two obstacles that under today's conditions appear almost insuperable. On the one hand, so long as the policies of governments are dominated by concern with short-run balance of payments effects, some deficit country whose participation is a key to success is almost sure to insist on the right to accept or reject the results in light of its appraisal of the net effect on its trade balance. On the other hand, and only indirectly related to the problem of balance of payments, it is becoming increasingly unlikely that any major country, least of all the United States, will be prepared to enter a negotiation directed only toward the reduction of industrial tariffs. And it is all but impossible to visualize a way in which nontariff barriers, agricultural policies affecting trade, rules governing international direct investment, and restrictive business practices could be reconciled with an automatic approach to the reduction of industrial tariffs.

While these complications cast serious doubt on the feasibility of an automatic formula, they nevertheless help drive the final nails into the coffin of traditional reciprocity. The dismantlement of agricultural protectionism cannot be much more rapid than the progress of governments in the elimination of domestic price supports; domestic agricultural policies will have to be the object of negotiation and progressive change.

There is no common gauge for measuring the incidence of non-tariff barriers that is nearly so useful an aid to tariff bargaining as the unsatisfactory yardstick provided by nominal rates in the case of tariffs. The indirect effects of investment restraints on commodity trade are even farther from the reach of existing techniques of measurement, while it is difficult to see how the balance of advantages that has formed the basis of tariff negotiations is relevant at all to the direct welfare effects of a free flow of capital and technology. There will no longer be even ritual significance to the time-honored yardstick — trade coverage times depth of tariff cut

— that has served negotiators in the past as a rough gauge for approximating a negotiating balance.

All this is not to say that the word "reciprocity" will disappear from the language of commercial policy. But its meaning will have to change. One possibility is that it will come to mean simply that a negotiator will be expected to make a contribution that is related in some immeasurable way to the stock of antisocial practices with which it enters the negotiation. This concept, while entirely lacking in precision, would be philosophically consistent with that of traditional reciprocity. What seems a more probable interpretation, however, and one that can be applied with much more precision, would be one based on equality of result rather than equality of contribution. "Reciprocity" may well come to mean: the adoption by all participants of uniform levels of, or even the abolition of, restraints against the free flow of goods and the factors of production.

A New Free-trade Area

A realization of some of these complexities must have motivated the many free-trade area proposals that have been published since the end of the Kennedy Round.[29] In each of these, a free-trade area, "Atlantic" or "multilateral," would have as a nucleus the United States, Canada, and the EFTA countries. To this charter membership, some blueprints would add Japan and the rest of the independent Commonwealth. The proponents of all of them attempt to meet the charge that such an area would be a divisive force within the elusive Atlantic partnership by proposing that the door be kept open to the EEC for its adherence when it should be ready.

A critique of these proposals will not be attempted here, other than to say that they do not seem to offer, in the near future, a realistic alternative to negotiations based on the MFN principle.[30] But if they were feasible they would offer a way to cut through many of the complexities of future trade negotiations. An international agreement to achieve the goal of total free trade within a fixed timetable would remove the most powerful incentive for demanding reciprocity — the need to preserve bargaining power. Similarly, while not removing all problems concerning agriculture

— witness the many struggles within the EEC — the adoption of the goal of free trade would at least predispose the participants to submit their domestic policies to negotiation. And, as both the EEC and EFTA have found, it would be easier to achieve uniformity in the use of nontariff barriers, in rules to govern restrictive business practices, and in the application of measures affecting the international mobility of capital and labor.

Sector Negotiations

Another approach to future liberalization that has respectable backing in trade circles is the multipurpose negotiation limited to a particular industrial sector.[31] In spite of the very modest accomplishments of the experiment with sector negotiations in the Kennedy Round, there is a very persuasive argument in their favor. They would divide into smaller bites the indigestible mass of detail that would inevitably be involved in a negotiation involving tariffs and nontariff barriers, international investment, and restrictive business practices. Their disadvantage is likely to lie in the asymmetry of benefits and sacrifices. This asymmetry would be likely to raise demands for reciprocity that could rarely be met if the negotiation in any one sector is self-contained.

In a few industrial sectors, however, the process of industrial internationalization may already have been carried to a point at which all the countries whose participation is essential could agree on the objective of total freedom of trade and the removal of remaining impediments to the flow of capital and technology. If the fear of rising Japanese competition could be allayed, the automobile industry might be a candidate for such industrial disarmament. But, with a few such exceptions, at the present stage in the growth of multinational enterprises it does not seem likely that sectoral negotiations can be successfully concluded in watertight compartments. What is more probable is that they will prove a useful technique for dividing a more general negotiation into manageable segments, a negotiation in which each participant will reserve the right to reject all the results if the negotiations in all sectors, taken together, do not yield satisfaction.

To the future policy maker, this conclusion is bound to be disappointing. It offers no easy way to avoid the exhausting confrontations of the Kennedy Round. And, it implies prolonged preparatory work before a general trade and investment negotiation can safely be launched or the necessary legislative authority can be asked of the Congress.

Perhaps its greatest disadvantage is that it does not offer opponents of protection a simple and dramatic program about which they can rally and which would divert the fire of their adversaries.

These disadvantages should not, in themselves, be insurmountable. But they are serious enough to suggest that the negotiators of another round would need a solid institutional framework on which to build and a healthy climate in which to work. If these conditions should reappear in the 1970's, the first step should be an intensive discussion of ways and means among the prospective negotiating partners. The negotiations of the future can at least avoid the total blackout that came perilously close when preparations for the Kennedy Round, in the United States and abroad, got seriously out of phase.

17

The Twilight of the GATT?

In the preceding chapter there was an implicit assumption that the institutional and legal framework that has facilitated the conduct of multilateral trade negotiations since World War II will continue to exist. But developments of the 1960's raise sober doubts as to the permanence of GATT, and this last chapter explores the grounds for these doubts.

The present threats to the survival of the GATT, if they really are threats, are not the direct result of the Kennedy Round itself. For nearly five years, however, the negotiations did provide a buffer against pressures for protection against imports and a truce in trade controversies. Only in the aftermath of the Kennedy Round did some of the differences between the GATT of the 1950's and that of the 1960's and 1970's become obvious, and it is in this sense that the Kennedy Round may emerge in the perspective of history as the twilight of the GATT.

The GATT Credo

When the GATT was drawn up in 1947, its charter members incorporated in its text some of the lessons they had learned from the depression. The foundation of the structure was nondiscrimination. Almost equal to it in importance was the prohibition against quantitative trade restrictions, which was based on the belief that, in a world where some protection of domestic producers was inevitable, a system of stable but negotiable tariffs would do the least damage to a multilateral trading system and to the optimum allocation of resources.

Finally, in translating these principles into their program for the postwar world, the GATT founders acted upon the conviction that no country could apply them in isolation. Unless jointly bound by a set of unambiguous rules all countries would, like lemmings, rush into the sea of bilateralism and trade paralysis that had engulfed them during the depression.

By the end of the 1960's these articles of belief continued to set the tone for the publicly displayed policies of GATT governments. There were also, however, solid bases for questioning whether they exerted nearly so decisive an influence as they had during the first decade of the General Agreement.

Nondiscrimination

During and after the Kennedy Round the tendency, already apparent in the first half of the 1960's, for countries to join together in preferential trading blocs gathered new momentum. Between 1963 and 1969 new notifications to the GATT of "interim" customs union or free-trade area agreements[1] included: the Arab Common Market; the Central African Economic and Customs Union; the New Zealand/Australia Free Trade Agreement; the Association between the EEC and the African and Malagasy States; the Nigeria Association with EEC; and the Caribbean Free Trade Agreement.

In addition, one new preferential area that was neither regional nor made any pretense of meeting the requirement of GATT Article XXIV was created: the Trade Expansion and Economic Cooperation Agreement between India, the United Arab Republic and Yugoslavia.[2]

By the beginning of 1969 the list of regional arrangements claiming GATT cover under Article XXIV, together with preferential agreements submitted to the Contracting Parties for their concurrence, had swelled to seventeen and involved more than eighty member countries. During 1969 and early 1970, however, the proliferation of regional preferences began to look less like a trend than a nuclear explosion as the effects of the association agreements already concluded by the European Economic Community began to be felt by a widening circle of its neighbors. The preferences granted by the EEC to Greece and Turkey threatened the traditional European markets of other countries in the Mediterranean basin. Those who had been left out demanded some form of association that would entitle them to equal treatment, and the Community found this insistence irresistible — if, in fact, it was disposed to resist. In late 1969 and early 1970 the EEC concluded preferential agreements with Spain, Israel, Tunisia, and Morocco and held preliminary negotiations with Malta, the United Arab Republic, Algeria, and Lebanon.

What really shook the complaisance of the trading world outside of Europe and Africa, however, was the renewed prospect of a bridge between the Common Market six and the EFTA seven. De Gaulle's departure from power had removed the most serious obstacle, and by the beginning of 1970 it appeared almost certain that the United Kingdom, Norway, Denmark, and Ireland would achieve full membership and that some form of association would be worked out for the EFTA neutrals. One result, of course, would be a quantum jump in discrimination as regional free trade spread throughout most of Western Europe. But it was also certain that the acceding countries would have to assimilate those preferential and association agreements previously negotiated by the Community with peripheral countries; hence, the increasing urgency with which those Mediterranean countries that were still unassociated pressed their own suits for some form of liaison.

Three years after the Kennedy Round the structure of international trade was very different from the prospects that faced negotiators in 1962. The share of world trade to which MFN duties applied had already diminished noticeably, and the impending enlargement of the Community promised a further drastic contraction.

Generalized Preferences for Less Developed Countries

As the decade of the 1970's opens, the prospect of the spread of trade discrimination is not confined to regional preferences. Although the major developed countries have not yet reached agreement on the details of a "generalized" preference scheme for the benefit of less developed countries, they have agreed "in principle."

When these commitments are carried out, a further portion of world trade will be outside the orbit of MFN. It does not necessarily follow, however, that the change will be all in the direction of trade diversion and away from the optimum allocation of world resources. Those less developed countries that previously enjoyed preferential entry to particular developed countries — for example, the British colonies or the EEC's African associates — would have to compete with the other less developed countries on equal terms, at least to the extent that export products of the latter are not excepted from the new scheme. This broadened discrimination in favor of all less developed countries might even turn out to be a net gain for trade competition, but it will represent a further step away from the universal nondiscrimination that was a key objective of the founders of the GATT.

Quantitative Restrictions

The second basic principle that helped shape the rules of GATT — the outlawing of quantitative restrictions — has suffered less obvious damage. But it, too, has been shaken, if we class, along with import licensing systems and quotas, other measures that have the same effect. The "voluntary" limitation of exports at the request of an importing country does not technically come under the GATT ban. But most readers will find it hard to see any real distinction if the exporter is coerced into volunteering by the threat that, if he stands on his GATT rights, even more damaging measures will be used against him.

When the United States proposed the "Long-Term Arrangement" substituting regulation for competition in the trade in cotton textiles, it argued that the circumstances of that industry were unique and that the cotton textiles arrangement would not be a precedent for other products. But in the 1968 presidential campaign Richard Nixon made essentially the same pledge to the synthetic and wool textile industries that John Kennedy had made, during his campaign, to the cotton industry.

Nixon's administration, during its first year and a half in office, proved less successful in fulfilling its pledge than did Kennedy's. But this was not because it failed to use similar tactics. Japan was left in no doubt that the alternative to a voluntary agreement would be unilaterally imposed quotas. Members of Congress joined in the clamor for action. Other American industries wishing protection can hardly be blamed for assuming that voluntary restraint agreements, extracted from exporting countries on pain of something worse, are a settled feature of the commercial policy of the United States. In fact, the sponsors of some of the quota bills introduced in the Ninety-first Congress made it clear that their purpose was to provide the President with bargaining power with which to extract voluntary agreements from exporting countries.

Evasion of GATT commitments by coercion appears to have been largely an American invention although, in the case of cotton textiles, the United Kingdom and the EEC did not let principle keep them from sharing in the spoils. The EEC also provided its own contribution to the popular game of frustrating the original expectations of the drafters of the GATT. No one has yet produced a convincing brief that the Community's variable import levies violate any explicit provision of the GATT, but it is clear that they have insulated one of the world's two most important agricultural markets from the price competition contemplated by the GATT founders. The price EFTA countries will have to pay for admission to membership in the EEC will be the extension of the variable levy system to their own agricultural imports, which will then remove the important British agricultural market as well from the reach of GATT.

Such ingenious and quasi-legal devices for frustrating the purposes of the ban on quantitative restrictions have been supplemented by more open derogations of the GATT and by strained interpretations of the exceptions with which the General Agreement is already generously endowed. The US "Oil Import Program" is an undisguised system of oil import quotas. Although the official rationale is that these restrictions are necessary in order to encourage domestic exploration, and that they are, therefore, justified under the national security exception of the GATT, their most aggressive proponents are domestic oil companies that appear more interested in securing a peacetime market for their already developed reserves than in hoarding oil underground against a possible national emergency.

Japan, for its part, has not found it necessary to invent new forms of restriction. There has been nothing subtle about her long-delayed and fractional compliance with her obligation to discontinue quantitative restrictions that were originally justified by balance of payments difficulties. Even where quotas have been formally removed, licensing requirements and administrative pressures to discourage prospective importers have generally been effective in protecting domestic producers from inconvenient competition. The deliberate pace with which Japan has responded to US pressures for compliance with GATT obligations has, in its turn, provided a plausible justification to those American businessmen and members of Congress who demand the erection of new barriers against the products of Japan's efficient and progressive industries.

The Score Board

The point was made earlier that there is no reliable means of measuring the amount of trade that is diverted from its natural channels by discrimination. It is equally difficult to gauge the potential trade that is entirely prevented by quantitative restrictions. But even in the absence of statistical proof it is apparent that, simply in terms of the amount of trade affected, the departures in 1970 from a multilaterally competitive trading system are less serious than those that existed when the GATT was founded. This static comparison would suggest that progress has been made and that the state of the GATT's health is good. But this conclusion could well be different if the direction of recent change is considered.

In the early and mid-1950's, most of the larger GATT countries were engaged in removing the discriminatory element from their quantitative restrictions, or in dismantling those restrictions altogether. The 1960's, on the other hand, witnessed a change in this direction. The omen for the 1970's is for still further departures from the original GATT model for world trade.

The changes that have taken place in governmental attitudes are even more significant. Until fairly late in the decade of the 1950's, the universal expectation of those dealing with foreign trade policies was that GATT obligations would be observed whenever

possible; in no case would they be ignored. Where discrimination, or the imposition of quotas not explicitly sanctioned by a
GATT exception, was unavoidable, the contracting party responsible sought, as a matter of course, the approval of the others as
provided in the General Agreement. Thus, the United Kingdom
asked for and obtained a waiver so that it might be free to raise an
unbound rate of duty without being required to impose a duty
against those dependent territories that had traditionally enjoyed
duty-free entry.[3] Similarly, the United States obtained a waiver
to permit the imposition of agricultural quotas that Congress had
made mandatory in an amendment to Section 22 of the Agricultural Adjustment Act.[4]

Anyone conversant with the GATT of the late 1960's and early
1970's will recognize the contrast between these cases and recent
practice. When Canada,[5] and later the United Kingdom,[6] imposed surcharges for balance of payments reasons, instead of the
quotas sanctioned for that purpose, they refused to request
waivers; their actions were nevertheless tacitly condoned by the
Contracting Parties. The latter could not bring themselves to
agree that the preferential agreement with the former French colonies (the Yaoundé Convention) established eighteen separate
free-trade areas, as claimed.[7] But they took no action to outlaw it.
The EEC, in notifying the GATT of its recent preferential agreements with Tunisia and Morocco, claimed that they were in full
accord with Article XXIV in spite of the absence of any commitment to achieve a customs union or free-trade area within a stated
period. When members of the working party that considered the
agreements offered to give them legal cover by means of a waiver,
the offer was refused. The agreements — and the discrimination —
remained.

In a still more recent but almost certainly not final example,
the EEC concluded agreements with both Spain and Israel that
from the first were openly called "preferential" by community
spokesmen. By mid-1970 the EEC had not yet revealed whether it
intended to seek a waiver. But even if it should, the contrast with
the attitude that prevailed during the early years of the GATT
would remain. It would be hard to find anyone in GATT circles
who believes that, if the Contracting Parties should disapprove,
the Community and its partners would abandon their agreements.

The Outlook

There is, of course, a possibility that the falling tide of expectations in the GATT will turn and that somehow the perception of a common interest that inspired the original signers of the agreement may be reborn. Perhaps a precondition for this is that the GATT be renegotiated to take into consideration the realities of today.

If the GATT were to be written *ab initio* in 1970, a number of its provisions would probably be quite different in detail, if not in intent, from the 1947 text. An obvious example is Article XXIV, which limits the sanction provided for regional trading arrangements to cases where the participants are prepared to commit themselves to virtually unlimited competition within the region. If the purpose of the original drafters had been to encourage regional economic integration instead of to accept it only where it was inevitable, some less heroic safeguards against abuse might have sufficed. They might, for example, have avoided the danger of selective preferential agreements disguised as free-trade areas by providing that any exchange of tariff preferences involve an equal percentage reduction for all products or, in the case of a quasi-customs union, that the members adopt a common *internal* tariff.

Another area in which the GATT rules have proved unrealistic is that of the trade adjustments permitted for the correction of balance of payment difficulties. The drafters were motivated by the conviction that payments disequilibriums should normally be corrected by fiscal and monetary means and that trade measures should be avoided except in extreme cases. What they accomplished, however, by specifying quantitative controls as the sole trade measure permitted was not to discourage the use of trade measures but to ensure that the GATT rules would be disregarded. Countries that have suffered renewed monetary disequilibrium since the liberalization of their postwar controls have typically resorted to other devices, such as prior import deposits or import surcharges, rather than invite the headaches of quota administration.

There are other instances in which the GATT rules might benefit from modernization. But we must ask whether this would restore its effectiveness as an international code of trade behavior, or whether, in fact, it is possible to re-create the perception of mutual interest on which the GATT was founded.

Probably the only way to be sure of the answer is to try. But the environment in which such an effort would have to be made in 1970 is certain to be less congenial than it was in 1947. Not only have some of the earlier incentives become dulled, but new and formidable obstacles have arisen. In the immediate postwar period nobody wanted to cling permanently to wartime controls. Since prewar bilateral trading commitments were casualties of the war, the founders of GATT could begin with a nearly clean slate. The war also provided the United States with the prestige and financial power to exploit and direct this mood. Finally, and of decisive importance, few American industries felt any pressure from foreign competition, so there was no effective opposition to the administration's plans for committing the country to a regime of liberal and multilateral trade.

In 1970 the United States no longer holds the helm; nor is there the unanimity of 1947 regarding the direction in which it should steer. Some of the country's traditionally most self-confident industries have acquired strongly protectionist views. There have even been signs recently that the automobile industry is becoming more concerned with preserving its domestic market than with its sales abroad. Nationally organized labor, which, since the days of Cordell Hull, consistently supported the renewal of trade agreements legislation, has crossed the aisle.

True, the present wave of protectionism in the United States is a by-product of the war in Indochina and the accompanying inflation and could prove transitory. But we would still have to look to the climate in those other countries whose active participation in the rejuvenation of the GATT would be essential. Here, even more fundamental changes have occurred since 1947. The roster of participants itself has drastically altered, the most important change being the numerical preponderance of less developed countries whose enthusiasm for free and multilateral trade, if any, is subordinate to their insistence on having the unimpeded right to develop their infant and unborn industries and to their desire for preferential access to the markets of rich countries. But a fundamental change has also taken place among the countries that led the fight for multilateral trade in the 1940's and 1950's. Almost any issue that involved a threat to the GATT system once found the United Kingdom, Benelux, Switzerland, the Scandinavian countries, and, later, Germany arrayed on the side of global multilateral trade. In 1970 they still see their interests tied up with multilateral trade. But, as an alternative to global multilateralism, there is the new prospect of membership in a more limited but vast and growing area of regional free trade. Even though some of them — Germany and the United Kingdom, for example — would probably prefer to combine the benefits of both systems, they will be preoccupied for perhaps another decade with the effort to perfect their enlarged common market. Suppose the United States, freed of the millstone of Indochina, were to attempt to re-create the spirit of the original GATT. This time it would probably find its natural partners with their minds on closer, and perhaps even greener, pastures.

To suggest attainable goals for the United States under these circumstances, or the strategy to be used in pursuing them, would require a self-confidence unjustified by present knowledge. Two conclusions do seem safe, however. Of the actors on the stage of world trade in the 1970's, only two — the United States and the EEC — come close to having the economic power required to lead the world toward the revival of a genuine multilateral trading system. Of these, the EEC, whether or not enlarged, is unlikely to have the necessary incentive for a long time to come, and the United States is certain to have neither the will nor the power until it has conquered the causes of inflation and domestic strife.

Bibliography

The following bibliography omits many of the sources referred to in the text and footnotes of this volume. Nor does it purport to be an exhaustive inventory of the more important works in the field of commercial policy and trade negotiations. The criteria used in its selection have been, in part, the frequency of citation and in part the degree of relevance to those aspects of commercial policy that have received the greatest emphasis in this volume. These criteria have necessarily resulted in the omission of many works that would deserve a place in any complete survey of the development of trade theory and international institutions dealing with trade.

The bibliography is divided into: a general section, devoted to books and periodicals; a section providing references to the texts of a very few of the international treaties and agreements referred to in the volume; a section listing the GATT publications on which I have most depended; and a very limited selection of US laws, US government publications, and congressional hearings.

As will be clear from the footnotes, I have made frequent use of mimeographed GATT documents, most of which are not generally available in libraries other than that of the GATT headquarters in Geneva. These as well as the much smaller number of documents of the OECD and UNCTAD, referred to in the volume, have been omitted from the bibliography, as have newspapers and the various excellent reporting bulletins of the EEC and EFTA.

Books and Periodicals

Balassa, Bela A. "Tariff Protection in Industrial Countries: An Evaluation," *Journal of Political Economy,* LXXIII (Dec. 1965), pp. 573-594.

Basevi, Giorgio. "The United States Tariff Structure: Estimates of Effective Rates of Protection of United States Industries and Industrial Labor," *Review of Economics and Statistics,* XLVIII (May 1966), pp. 147-160.

Bauer, Raymond A., Ithiel de Sola Pool, and Lewis Anthony Dexter. *American Business and Public Policy: The Politics of Foreign Trade.* New York: Atherton Press for the Massachusetts Institute of Technology, 1967.

Benedict, Murray R., and Oscar C. Stine. *The Agricultural Commodity Program.* New York: Twentieth Century Fund, 1956.

Benoit, Emile. *Europe at Sixes and Sevens: The Common Market, the Free Trade Association and the United States.* New York: Columbia University Press, 1961.

Bertrand, Raymond. "Comparaison de Niveau des Tariffs Douanier," *Cahiers de l'Institut de Science Economique Appliquée,* Series R, No. 2 (Feb. 1958).

Camps, Miriam. *Britain and the European Community, 1955-1963.* London: Oxford University Press, 1964.

———— *European Unification in the Sixties: From the Veto to the Crisis.* New York: McGraw-Hill Book Co. for the Council on Foreign Relations, 1966.

———— *What Kind of Europe? The Community since de Gaulle's Veto.* Chatham House Essays. London: Oxford University Press, 1965.

Cooper, Richard N. "Tariff Dispersion and Trade Negotiations." *Journal of Political Economy,* LXXII (Dec. 1964), pp. 597-603.

Coppock, John O. *North Atlantic Policy — The Agricultural Gap.* New York: Twentieth Century Fund, 1963.

Corden, W. M. *Recent Developments in the Theory of International Trade.* Special papers in International Economics, No. 7. Princeton, N.J.: Princeton University Press, 1965.

Curzon, Gerard. *Multilateral Commercial Diplomacy: The General Agreement on Tariffs and Trade and Its Impact on National Commercial Policies and Techniques.* London: Michael Joseph, 1965.

Diebold, William, Jr. *The End of the ITO.* Essays in International Finance, No. 16. Princeton, N.J.: Princeton University Press, 1952.

———— *The Schuman Plan.* New York: Frederick A. Praeger, 1959.

———— *Trade and Payments in Western Europe: A Study in Economic Cooperation.* New York: Harper and Brothers, 1952.

Evans, John W. *U. S. Trade Policy: New Legislation for the Next Round.* New York: Harper and Row for the Council on Foreign Relations, 1967.

———— "The General Agreement on Tariffs and Trade." In *The Global*

Partnership: International Agencies and Economic Development. Edited by Richard N. Gardner and Max F. Millikan. New York: Frederick A Praeger, 1968.

Frank, Isaiah. *The European Common Market: An Analysis of Commercial Policy.* London: Stevens & Sons, Ltd., 1961.

Gardner, Richard N. *Sterling-Dollar Diplomacy: The Origins and the Prospects of our International Economic Order.* New ed. New York: McGraw-Hill, 1969.

———— "The United Nations Conference on Trade and Development." In *The Global Partnership: International Agencies and Economic Development.* Edited by Richard N. Gardner and Max F. Millikan. New York: Frederick A. Praeger, 1968.

Gordon, R. T. "The Incidence of the Corporation Income Tax in U.S. Manufacturing, 1925-62."*American Economic Review,* LVII (Sept. 1967), pp. 731-758.

Haberler, Gottfried. *Theory of International Trade.* London: William Hodge and Co., 1936.

———— *Quantitative Trade Controls: Their Causes and Nature.* Geneva: League of Nations, 1943.

Hawkins, Harry C., and Janet L. Norwood. "The Legislative Basis of United States Commercial Policy." In *Studies in United States Commercial policy.* Edited by William B. Kelly, Jr., Chapel Hill: University of North Carolina Press, 1963.

Hunsberger, Warren S. *Japan and the United States in World Trade.* New York: Harper and Row for the Council on Foreign Relations, 1964.

Jackson, John H. "The General Agreement on Tariffs and Trade in United States Domestic Law." *Michigan Law Review,* LXVI (Dec. 1967), pp. 249-332.

———— *World Trade and the Law of GATT.* Indianapolis: Bobbs-Merrill Co., 1969.

Johnson, D. Gale. "Agricultural Trade and Foreign Economic Policy," *Foreign Trade and Agricultural Policy,* Volume VI, *Technical Papers.* Washington, D.C.: National Advisory Commission on Food and Fiber, Aug. 1967.

Johnson, Harry G. *Economic Policies toward Less Developed Countries.* Washington, D.C.: Brookings Institution, 1967.

Kelly, William B., Jr. "Antecedents of Present Commercial Policy." In *Studies in United States Commercial Policy.* Edited by William B. Kelly, Jr. Chapel Hill: University of North Carolina Press, 1963.

———— "The 'Expanded' Trade Agreements Escape Clause, 1955-61," *Journal of Political Economy,* LXX (Feb. 1962), pp. 37-63.

———— "Nontariff Barriers." In Bela A. Balassa et al., *Studies in Trade Liberalization: Problems and Prospects for the Industrial Countries.* Baltimore: Johns Hopkins Press, 1967.

Leddy, John M. "United States Commercial Policy and the Domestic Farm Program." In *Studies in United States Commercial Policy.*

Edited by William B. Kelly, Jr. Chapel Hill: University of North Carolina Press, 1963.

———— and Janet L. Norwood. "The Escape Clause and Peril Points Under the Trade Agreements Program." In *Studies in United States Commercial Policy.* Edited by William B. Kelly, Jr. Chapel Hill: University of North Carolina Press, 1963.

Meade, James E. *The Theory of Customs Unions.* Amsterdam: North Holland Publishing Company, 1955.

———— and H. H. Liesner and S. J. Weeks. *Case Studies in European Economic Union.* London: Oxford University Press, 1962.

Mikesell, Raymond F. *Foreign Exchange in the Postwar World.* New York: Twentieth Century Fund, 1954.

———— "The Movement toward Regional Trading Groups in Latin America." In *Latin American Issues: Essays and Comments.* Edited by A. O. Hirschman. New York: Twentieth Century Fund, 1961.

Nye, Joseph S., Jr. "Central American Regional Integration." *International Conciliation* (Carnegie Endowment for International Peace), No. 562 (Mar. 1967).

Patterson, Gardner. *Discrimination in International Trade: The Policy Issues, 1945-1965.* Princeton, N.J.: Princeton University Press, 1966.

Preeg, Ernest H. *Traders and Diplomats: An Analysis of the Kennedy Round of Negotiations under the General Agreement on Tariffs and Trade.* Washington: Brookings Institution, 1970.

Sullivan, Clara K. *The Search for Tax Principles in the European Economic Community.* Cambridge, Mass.: Law School of Harvard University, 1963.

Svennilson, Ingvar. *Growth and Stagnation in the European Economy.* Geneva: UN Economic Commission for Europe, 1954.

Vanek, Jaroslav. *General Equilibrium of International Discrimination: The Case of Customs Unions.* Cambridge, Mass.: Harvard University Press, 1965.

Vernon, Raymond. "Antitrust and International Business." *Harvard Business Review,* XLVII (Sept.-Oct. 1968), pp. 78-87.

———— "International Business and International Trade in the Product Cycle." *Quarterly Journal of Economics,* LXXX (May 1966), pp. 190-207.

Viner, Jacob. *The Customs Union Issue.* New York: Carnegie Endowment for International Peace, 1950.

———— *Dumping: A Problem in International Trade.* Chicago: University of Chicago Press, 1923.

Weintraub, Sidney. "Border Tax Adjustments and the GATT." *Tax Executive,* XVII (July 1965), pp. 304-320.

Wilcox, Clair. *A Charter for World Trade.* New York: Macmillan Co., 1949.

Yates, P. Lamartine. *Food Production in Western Europe.* London: Macmillan, 1940.

Zaglits, Oscar. "Agricultural Trade and Trade Policy." In *Foreign Trade and Agricultural Policy*. Volume VI, *Technical Papers*. Washington, D.C.: National Advisory Commission on Food and Fiber, 1967.

International Treaties and Agreements (in chronological order)

United Nations Conference on Trade and Employment. *Havana Charter for an International Trade Organization* (Havana Charter). *Final Act and Related Documents*, Mar. 24, 1948, UN Doc. E/Conf. 2/78. It is also reproduced in Department of State Publication 3117, Commercial Policy Series 113.

The General Agreement on Tariffs and Trade (GATT). 55 United Nations Treaty Series (UNTS), Reg. 814, p. 187. Made effective for initial Contracting Parties on January 1, 1948, by the Protocol of Provisional Application. 55 UNTS 308. Dates and citations for subsequent protocols of accession, supplementary concessions, and amendments are listed in GATT. *Basic Instruments and Selected Documents* (BISD), Volume IV. Geneva, 1969, pp. 81-88. (See GATT Publications, below). The same volume contains the text of the Protocol of Provisional Application (pp. 77-78) and the text of the GATT in force on March 1, 1969.

Treaty Constituting the European Coal and Steel Community. Entered into force May 1, 1953. 471 UNTS 296. (Also in the *United States Treaty Series* (UST) 2672)

Treaty Establishing the European Economic Community (Treaty of Rome). Signed at Rome on March 25, 1957. 298 UNTS (English text).

Convention Establishing the European Free Trade Association (Stockholm Convention). Signed at Stockholm on January 4, 1960. 370 UNTS 3.

Agreement setting up an Association between the European Economic Community and Greece (with Protocol and Annexes). Signed at Athens, July 9, 1961. For text, see European Yearbook, IX, (1961), pp. 452-499, and GATT Doc. L/1601/Add. 1, Dec. 7, 1961.

Convention of Association between the European Economic Community and African and Malagasy States (with Protocol). Signed at Yaoundé, July 20, 1963 (Yaoundé Convention). For text, see European Yearbook, XI (1963), p. 2, pp. 622-673; and GATT Doc. L/2160/Add. 1, Apr. 7, 1964.

US-Canada Automotive Agreement, Jan. 1965. For text, see 17 UST 1372. Also reproduced in 89th Cong., 1st sess. *House Report No. 537*, Jan. 1, 1965.

Treaty Establishing a Single Council and a Single Commission of the European Communities (with Protocol, Final Act, and Annexes). Signed at Brussels on April 8, 1966, effective July 1, 1967. For text, see *Legal Materials* (American Society of International Law), IV (July 1965), p. 776.

International Grains Arrangement. Signed at Rome, Aug. 18, 1967. For text, see US Department of State TIAS 6537.

GATT Publications

The Contracting Parties to the General Agreement on Tariffs and Trade, *Basic Instruments and Selected Documents.* Volume I (containing the original text) and Volume II (containing principal decisions of the Contracting Parties) dated Geneva, May 1952. Volume I, revised, containing text of amendments drawn up at the Review Conference, 1955-56; Volume III, Geneva, Nov. 1958, contains the revised text in force in 1958. Volume IV, Geneva, 1969, contains the text in force on March 1, 1969. Supplements begin in 1953 and have been published at approximately yearly intervals thereafter, the latest being the *Sixteenth Supplement,* published in April 1969. The supplements contain the texts of decisions and reports adopted subsequent to Volume II. The *Sixteenth Supplement* contains a cumulative index to all volumes and the supplements.
——— General Agreement on Tariffs and Trade. *Analytical Index* (2d rev.). Geneva, Feb. 1966. "Notes on the drafting, interpretation and application of the articles of the General Agreement."
——— *International Trade, 1952.* Geneva, June 1953. And annual volumes with the same title, *mutatis mutandis,* for the years 1956 through 1968. Contain descriptions of principal developments in international trade for the years covered, with text and tables.
——— *Legal Instruments Embodying the Results of the 1964-1967 Trade Conference.* Geneva, 1967.
——— *Trends in International Trade: Report by a Panel of Experts.* (Haberler Report) Geneva, 1958.

US Congress (in chronological order)

Joint Economic Committee. *Hearings before the Subcommittee on Foreign Economic Policy of the Joint Economic Committee.* 2 vols. 87th Cong., 1st sess., Dec. 4-14, 1961.
House, Committee on Ways and Means. *Trade Expansion Act of 1962, Hearings before the Committee on Ways and Means.* 6 vols. 87th Con., 2d sess., 1962.
Senate, Committee on Financing. *Hearings on the Trade Expansion Act of 1962, before the Committee on Finance.* 2 vols. 87th Cong., 2d sess., 1962.
House, Committee on Ways and Means. *Foreign Trade and Tariff Proposals, Hearings.* 10 vols. 90th Cong., 2d sess., 1968.

US Government Publications

Office of the Special Representative for Trade Negotiations. *1964-67 Trade Conference: Report on United States Negotiations.* 2 vols. Washington, D.C.: Government Printing Office (1968).
_____ *Future United States Trade Policy: Report to the President.* Washington, D.C.: Government Printing Office, 1969.
Tariff Commission. *Operation of the Trade Agreements Program, June 1934-April 1948.* 2d Ser., No. 160, 5 Pts. Washington, D.C.: Government Printing Office, 1949. This report is followed by annual reports in the same series covering the period from April 1948-March 1949 to July 1957-June 1958.
Treasury Department. *Maintaining the Strength of the United States Dollar in a Strong Free World.* Washington, D.C.: Government Printing Office, 1968.

Notes

Introduction

1. Trade Expansion Act of 1962, as amended, PL 87-794, Oct. 11, 1962, 76 Stat. 872 [Hereafter cited as Trade Expansion Act].

Chapter 1

1. US Tariff Commission, *Operation of the Trade Agreements Program, June 1934-April 1948*, (Washington, D.C.: Government Printing Office, 1949), pt. II, pp. 7-8.

2. See Harry C. Hawkins and Janet L. Norwood, "The Legislative Basis of United States Commercial Policy," in *Studies in United States Commercial Policy*, ed. William B. Kelly, Jr., (Chapel Hill: University of North Carolina Press, 1963), p. 70.

3. *Ibid.*, pp. 71-73.

4. Cordell Hull, *Memoirs*, (2 vols., New York: The Macmillan Co., 1948), I, p.356.

5. See Hawkins and Norwood, "Legislative Basis of United States Commercial Policy," p. 75.

6. John M. Leddy and Janet L. Norwood, "The Escape Clause and Peril Points under the Trade Agreements Program," in *Studies in United States Commercial Policy*, ed. Kelly, p. 124.

7. US Tariff Commission, *Operation of the Trade Agreements Program, June 1934-April 1948*, pt. II, pp. 10-14.

8. *Ibid.,* pt. III, p. 12.

9. *Ibid.,* pt. IV, p. 8.

10. *Ibid.,* pt. III, Table 3, and pt. IV, Table 6.

11. Fifteen of the twenty-seven countries involved were in Latin America and presumably benefited from the Good Neighbor Policy of the Roosevelt administration.

12. US Tariff Commission, *Operation of the Trade Agreements Program, June 1934-April 1948,* pt. II, p. 14.

13. Trade Agreements Extension Act of 1945, 59 Stat. 410, July 5, 1945, 19 USC 1351-1354.

14. For a contemporary account of the negotiation of the International Trade Organization (ITO) Charter, see Clair Wilcox, *A Charter for World Trade* (New York: The Macmillan Co., 1939). An excellent account of the events leading to United States failure to ratify the charter is contained in William Diebold, *The End of the ITO* (Princeton, N.J.: Princeton University Press, 1952).

15. Geneva negotiators with whom bilateral agreements with the United States were already in effect were: Belgium and Luxembourg, Brazil, Canada, Ceylon, Cuba, France, the Netherlands, Newfoundland, and the United Kingdom.

16. The term "contracting parties" is used to designate full participants in the GATT. When the words are spelled with initial capital letters, they designate the participants acting together as an organization.

17. But the enforcement of those rights is more nearly automatic in the case of a contracting party with which a concession was "initially negotiated." See General Agreement on Tariffs and Trade [hereafter cited as GATT], 55 United Nations Treaty Series [hereafter cited as UNTS], Reg. 814, p. 187, Article XXVIII. Subsequent protocols are reproduced in 55-61 UNTS, Reg. 814. Except where otherwise specified, references to the GATT text in this volume are to the text in force in 1969. It is reproduced in The Contracting Parties to the General Agreement on Tariffs and Trade, *Basic Instruments and Selected Documents* (GATT, BISD), Volume IV, *Text of the General Agreement* (Geneva: GATT, 1969); it also appears as Department of State Publication 8468, distributed by the Government Printing Office, Washington, D.C.

18. US Tariff Commission, *Operation of the Trade Agreements Program, June 1934-April 1948,* pt. III, Table 3.

19. *Ibid.,* pt. IV, Table 6.

20. *Ibid.,* Table 7.

21. Trade for 1947. US, Tariff Commission, *Trade Agreements Program, Third Report* (Washington, D.C.: Government Printing Office, 1951), Tables 2 and 7.

22. US Tariff Commission, *Trade Agreements Program, Fourth Report* (Washington, D.C., 1952), Tables 1 and 2.

23. US Tariff Commission, *Trade Agreements Program, Ninth Report*

(Washington, D.C.: Government Printing Office, 1957), Table 1.

24. Treaty Establishing the European Economic Community, signed March 25, 1957, 298 UNTS 11 (English text), [hereafter cited as the Treaty of Rome].

25. Benelux (the Customs Union of Belgium, the Netherlands, and Luxembourg) had a common tariff on the base date.

26. Both progress toward internal free trade and adjustment of the tariffs of member states to the Common External Tariff (CXT) were to be accomplished in stages and completed by the end of the "transitional period," originally set at twelve years from when the treaty entered into force.

27. European Free Trade Association: Austria, Denmark, Norway, Portugal, Sweden, Switzerland, and the United Kingdom.

28. US Tariff Commission, *Trade Agreements Program, Fourteenth Report* (Washington, D.C.: Government Printing Office, 1962), Table 1 and p. 19.

29. An excellent and much more complete account of the changes in United States legislation in the postwar period will be found in Hawkins and Norwood, "Legislative Basis for United States Commercial Policy," pp. 104-114; and Leddy and Norwood, "Escape Clause and Peril Points," pp. 128-143.

30. Trade Agreements Extension Act of 1958, P.L. 85-686, Aug. 20, 1958, 72 Stat. 673.

31. See US Tariff Commission, *Trade Agreements Program, Fourth Report*, pp. 31-32.

32. See William B. Kelly, Jr., "The 'Expanded' Trade Agreements Escape Clause, 1955-61," *Journal of Political Economy*, LXX (Feb. 1962), pp. 37-38.

33. See Leddy and Norwood, "Escape Clause and Peril Points," p. 140.

34. US Tariff Commission, *Trade Agreements Program, Fourth Report*, p. 30.

35. See Leddy and Norwood, "Escape Clause and Peril Points," p. 131.

36. *Ibid.*, pp. 145-146.

Chapter 2

1. Hawkins and Norwood, "The Legislative Basis of United States Commercial Policy," p. 70. The authors make clear, nevertheless, that they did not consider such strict application appropriate in 1934, when a persistent export surplus by the United States was resulting in a depletion of the gold reserves of other countries and causing those countries to continue exchange controls and quantitative trade restrictions.

2. See, for example, Harry G. Johnson, "An Economic Theory of

Protectionism, Tariff Bargaining, and the Formation of Customs Unions," *Journal of Political Economy,* LXXIII (June 1965), pp. 256-282.

3. The Organization for European Economic Cooperation (OEEC), of which only Western European countries were full members, was later replaced by the Organization for European Cooperation and Development (OECD), with the added membership of the United States and Canada.

4. See Gerard Curzon, *Multilateral Commercial Diplomacy: The General Agreement on Tariffs and Trade and Its Impact on National Commercial Policies and Techniques* (London: Michael Joseph, 1965), p. 87; and Isaiah Frank, *The European Common Market: An Analysis of Commercial Policy* (London: Stevens and Sons, Ltd., 1961), p. 16.

5. GATT/CPS/5, April 2, 1951.

6. GATT, BISD, Suppl. 2, pp. 68-92. Dates and citations for subsequent protocols of accession, supplementary concessions, and amendments are listed in GATT, BISD, IV, pp. 81-88.

7. See Curzon, *Multilateral Commercial Diplomacy,* p.93.

8. *UN, Conference on Trade and Employment, Havana Charter for an International Trade Organization,* UN Doc. E/Conf..2/78, Article 17, 2 (d) [hereafter cited as the Havana Charter]. Similar language was incorporated in the negotiating rules for various tariff rounds and in the text of the GATT in 1956 in Article XXVIII, bis, 2 (a).

9. See, for example, US Tariff Commission, *Operation of the Trade Agreements Program, June 1934-April 1948,* pt. IV, pp. 9-10.

10. US, Congress, House, Committee on Ways and Means, *Hearings on H. R. 2652,* 79th Cong., 1st sess., 1945, I, rev., p. 15.

11. *Ibid.,* Testimony of Edward R. Stettinius, p. 12.

12. Kelly, "The 'Expanded' Trade Agreements Escape Clause," p. 14.

13. For a discussion of the fallacy behind the low-wage argument, see US, Congress, House, Joint Economic Committee, *Hearings before the Subcommittee on Foreign Economic Policy of the Joint Economic Committee,* 87th Cong., 1st sess., Dec. 4-14, 1961, testimony of Professor Raymond Vernon, pp. 281-284.

14. Gottfried Haberler, *Theory of International Trade* (London: William Hodge and Co., 1936), pp. 278-284.

15. For a brief summary and bibliography of the terms-of-trade theory, see W. M. Corden, *Recent Developments in the Theory of International Trade,* Special Papers in International Economics, No. 7 (Princeton, N.J.: Princeton University Press, 1965), pp. 42-48.

16. Corden traces the development of the theory from Fleming and Meade, through Linsey, Lancaster, Johnson, etc., *ibid.,* pp. 46-49.

17. *Ibid.*

18. The use of charges other than statutory customs duties as a counter to balance of payment difficulties, however, has been common. A number of less-developed countries have obtained GATT waivers to permit them to apply temporary import fees above their bound tariff

rates. Also, in 1962 and in 1963, Canada and the United Kingdom, respectively, adopted temporary import surcharges for this reason.

19. Most American farm interests opposed the proposal of Secretary of Agriculture Charles F. Brannan to replace agricultural price supports with direct income subsidies to farmers.

20. Such an attitude would be consistent with what has been called "the collective preference for [domestic] industrial production." See H. G. Johnson, "An Economic Theory of Protectionism," pp. 256-282.

21. Raymond A. Bauer, Ithiel de Sola Pool, and Lewis Anthony Dexter, *American Business and Public Policy: The Politics of Foreign Trade* (New York: Atherton Press, 1963), p. 147.

22. For example, see GATT, BISD, II, p. 216, for statement by E. Sveinbjornsson to the Contracting Parties on October 27, 1951.

23. Italics added.

24. Frank W. Taussig, "Necessary Changes in our Commercial Policy," *Foreign Affairs,* II (Apr. 1933), pp. 402-403.

Chapter 3

1. William B. Kelly, Jr., "Antecedents of Present Commercial Policy," in *Studies in United States Commercial Policy,* ed. Kelly, p. 34. Kelly's study contains a useful short summary of the history of the most favored nation commitment in US commercial policy. This and other matters dealt with in the present chapter have been explored in considerably greater detail in Gardner Patterson, *Discrimination in International Trade: The Policy Issues, 1945-1965* (Princeton, N.J.: Princeton University Press, 1966). Professor Patterson's researches in the archives of GATT have considerably eased my task.

2. Kelly, "Antecedents of Present Commercial Policy," p. 34.

3. Cordell Hull, *Memoirs,* (2 vols., New York: The Macmillan Co., 1948), pp. 371-374.

4. Don D. Humphrey, "The United Kingdom, the Commonwealth, the Common Market, and the United States," in *Studies in United States Commercial Policy,* ed. Kelly, p. 227.

5. Wilcox, *A Charter for World Trade,* p. 27.

6. For a summary of US practice until 1923, see Kelly, "Antecedents of Present Commercial Policy," pp. 33-38; and for the post-1923 record, see Hawkins and Norwood, "The Legislative Basis of United States Commercial Policy," pp. 90-99.

7. However, the Cuban "reciprocity" treaty of 1902, proclaimed on December 17, 1903, granted preferential treatment to Cuba. Before 1890 seven reciprocity treaties calling for preferential treatment were negotiated, but only two entered into force. The treaty with Canada (1854) was abrogated in 1865. The treaty with Hawaii was in force from 1875 until the annexation of Hawaii in 1898. Under the provisions of

the Tariff Act of 1890 reciprocity agreements were made with six American states, Austria-Hungary, Germany, Great Britain (for the West Indies), and Spain (for Cuba and Puerto Rico). These were terminated when the Tariff Act of 1894 came into force. See US, Tariff Commission, *Reciprocity and Commercial Treaties* (Washington, D.C.: Government Printing Office, 1919).

8. Kelly, "Antecedents of Present Commercial Policy," pp. 51-52.

9. *Ibid.,* pp. 48-53.

10. GATT, 55 UNTS, Reg. 814, Article I, 1.

11. *Ibid.,* Article XI.

12. *Ibid.,* Article XIV. The general rule applying MFN to quantitative restrictions is contained in Article XII, which aims at approximating nondiscrimination by requiring unallocated quotas or, if quotas are allocated, distribution in accordance with shares of trade in a representative period.

13. The ITO Charter had also contained a provision obligating members of preferential systems to negotiate for their elimination (Article 17). This provision, however, was not carried over into the GATT.

14. Free-trade areas were introduced into the dispensation provided by Article XXIV only toward the end of the negotiation, on the insistence of Syria and Lebanon. See Wilcox, *A Charter for World Trade,* p. 71.

15. *Ibid.,* p. 70.

16. The first important work in this series was Jacob Viner's *The Customs Union Issue* (New York: Carnegie Endowment for International Peace, 1950). This study was extended and refined by James E. Meade in *The Theory of Customs Unions* (Amsterdam: North Holland Publishing Co., 1955). Further refinements have been added by a number of economists. For a survey of this literature, see Corden, *Recent Developments in the Theory of International Trade,* pp. 52-55.

17. Jaroslav Vanek, *General Equilibrium of International Discrimination: The Case of Customs Unions* (Cambridge, Mass.: Harvard University Press, 1965), p. 9.

18. Jacob Viner has pointed out that Cordell Hull had a similar objective in mind when, in 1933, he proposed to the League of Nations Monetery and Economic Conference criteria for exceptions to unconditional MFN treatment. Preferential agreements were to be permitted, provided, *inter alia,* they were accomplished by a uniform percentage reduction in all tariff rates "or by some other formula of equally broad application." See also Patterson, *Discrimination in International Trade,* pp. 124-125.

19. See Raymond F. Mikesell, *Foreign Exchange in the Postwar World* (New York: Twentieth Century Fund, 1954), pp. 37-38.

20. See Wilcox, *A Charter for World Trade,* p. 19.

21. GATT, *International Trade* (Geneva, 1961), Table I, following p. 134.

22. Not all of this decline is attributable to the reduction of MFN rates of duty; the decline in the ad valorem equivalents of specific rates also affected the ad valorem margins of preference. Patterson, *Discrimination in International Trade*, p. 232,n.

23. *Treaty Establishing the European Economic Community* [hereafter cited as Treaty of Rome], 298 UNTS, Articles 131-133.

24. Convention of Association between the European Economic Community and African and Malagasy States (with Protocol), signed at Yaoundé on July 20, 1963 [hereafter cited as Yaoundé Convention]. For text, see *European Yearbook, XI* (1963), pt. 2, p. 622, and GATT Doc. L/2160/Add. 1, Apr. 7, 1964.

25. Patterson, *Discrimination in International Trade*, p. 254,n.

26. *Ibid.*, p. 257.

27. Treaty for East African Cooperation (with Annexes), signed at Kampala, June 6, 1967. For text, see the American Society of International Law, *Legal Materials*, VI (Sept. 1967), p. 932.

28. GATT, BISD, suppl. 6, pp. 89-110. See also Curzon, *Multilateral Commercial Diplomacy*, pp. 276-282.

29. Edward Dana Wilgress, *A New Attempt at Internationalism*, University of Geneva, Institut Universitaire de Hautes Etudes Internationales (Paris: Société d'Editions d'Enseignement Supérieur 1949), p. 139.

30. Mikesell, *Foreign Exchange in the Postwar World*, p. 37. See also summary description of bilateral agreement in the same source, chaps. x and xi and appendix 5.

31. *Ibid.*, p. 579.

32. See Patterson, *Discrimination in International Trade*, esp. chaps. ii and iii.

33. Accounts of these consultations may be found in GATT, BISD, suppls. 3-10.

34. "Recent international financial developments have established an environment favorable to the elimination of discrimination for balance-of-payments reasons. There has been a substantial improvement in the reserve positions of the industrial countries in particular and widespread moves to external convertibility have taken place. Under these circumstances the Fund considers that there is no longer any balance-of-payments justification for discrimination by members whose currency receipts are largely in externally convertible currencies." GATT, BISD, suppl. 8, p. 72.

35. However, most European countries continued to conduct their trade with Communist countries under bilateral agreements.

36. For an account of the early stages of the European Payments Union (EPU) and the OEEC Code, see Mikesell, *Foreign Exchange in the Postwar World*, pp. 112-135. Patterson, in *Discrimination in International Trade*, pp. 91-119, continues the account up to the dissolution of these arrangements.

37. OEEC, *Code of the Liberalization of Trade*, entered into force on

September 19, 1950. For the text, including later amendments, see OEEC, *Code of Liberalization,* new ed. (Paris, May 1, 1958).

38. Patterson reviews the arguments in his *Discrimination in International Trade,* pp. 93-95. See also William Diebold, Jr., *Trade and Payments in Western Europe: A Study in Economic Co-operation* (New York: Harper and Brothers, 1952) and Robert Triffin, *Europe and the Money Muddle* (New Haven, Conn.: Yale University Press, 1957).

39. GATT, BISD, suppl. 3, p. 178.

40. See Patterson, *Discrimination in International Trade,* p. 106.

41. GATT, BISD, suppl. 3, p. 178.

42. GATT, BISD, suppl. 5, pp. 62-63.

43. *Ibid.*

44. *Ibid.,* suppl. 9, p. 63.

45. In 1957, following a review of the GATT articles, the text of the General Agreement had been amended to provide, *inter alia,* more lenient criteria for determining whether an underdeveloped country was permitted to resort to the use of quantitative restrictions. Thereafter, the maintenance of such restrictions by such countries was dealt with under the new provisions of Section B of Article XVIII of the GATT.

46. An incidental but important effect of quantitative restrictions applied for balance-of-payments reasons in the postwar period was the protection against import competition they afforded domestic producers. Industries that had flourished under this protection naturally resisted liberalization, and governments found it difficult to dismantle their quantitative restrictions as quickly as their monetary reserves and payment balances would have justified. To permit the more gradual elimination of those residual restrictions that were proving most difficult to eradicate, the Contracting Parties adopted the so-called "Hard-Core Waiver," which permitted them to be dismantled gradually within a period approved by the Contracting Parties. See Decision of March 5, 1955, GATT, BISD, suppl. 3, p. 38.

47. Australia, Austria, Belgium, Brazil, Cuba, France, Haiti, India, Luxembourg, the Netherlands, New Zealand, the Federation of Rhodesia and Nyasaland, the Union of South Africa, and the United Kingdom were the countries involved.

48. See report of the review of Article XXXV, GATT, BISD, suppl. 10, pp. 69-74.

49. See Warren S. Hunsberger, *Japan and the United States in World Trade* (New York: Harper and Row, 1964), pp. 322-323.

50. Patterson, *Discrimination in International Trade,* p. 296.

51. For text, see 471 UNTS 296. (Also in *United States Treaty Series,* 13 UST 2672.)

52. Treaty Instituting the European Coal and Steel Community, 261 UNTS 140.

53. GATT, Decision of Nov. 10, 1952, in GATT, BISD, suppl. 1, pp. 17-22.

54. For text of United States-Canadian Automotive Agreement, see 17 UST 1372. It is also annexed to US Congress, House, Report No. 537, *Report of the Committee on Ways and Means, House of Representatives to Accompany H.R. 9042,* 89th Cong., 1st sess., Jan. 1, 1965.

55. United States—Imports of Automotive Products. Decision of Dec. 20, 1965, in GATT, BISD, suppl. 14, pp. 37-42.

56. The following sources are suggested for information about these arrangements: for the *ECSC,* William Diebold, *The Schuman Plan* (New York: Frederick A. Praeger, Inc., 1959); James E. Meade, H. H. Liesner, and S. J. Weeks, *Case Studies in European Economic Union* (London: Oxford University Press, 1962); for the *EEC,* Miriam Camps, *Britain and the European Common Market, 1955-1963* (London: Oxford University Press, 1964) also her *European Unification in the Sixties: From the Veto to the Crisis* (New York: McGraw-Hill Book Co., 1966), and Isaiah Frank, *The European Common Market;* for *EFTA,* the same works by Miriam Camps and the various information bulletins issued by the European Free Trade Association, Geneva; for Latin American customs unions and free-trade areas, see Raymond F. Mikesell, "The Movement toward Regional Trading Groups in Latin America," in *Latin American Issues: Essays and Comments,* ed. Albert O. Hirschman (New York: Twentieth Century Fund, 1961), and Joseph S. Nye, Jr., "Central American Regional Integration," *International Conciliation,* No. 562 (Mar. 1967).

57. For text of the Treaty of Rome, see 298 UNTS 11.

58. *Treaty Establishing a Single Council and a Single Commission of the European Communities* (with Protocol, Final Act, and Annexes), signed at Brussels, Apr. 8, 1966, effective July 1, 1967. For text, see the American Society of International Law, *Legal Materials,* IV (July 1965), p. 776.

59. For text, see *Convention Establishing the European Free Trade Association* (Stockholm Convention), signed Jan. 4, 1960, 370 UNTS 3.

60. *General Treaty on Central American Economic Integration,* signed at Managua, Dec. 13, 1960, 455 UNTS 2.

61. The Caribbean Free Trade Association was founded in 1967 by Antigua, Barbados, British Guiana, and Trinidad and Tobago. In 1968, Dominica, Grenada, St. Kitts-Nevis-Anguilla, St. Lucia, St. Vincent, Jamaica, and Montserrat were added. See *Agreement Establishing the Caribbean Free Trade Association,* as it appeared in the American Society of International Law, *Legal Materials,* VII (Sept. 1968), p. 935.

62. For text, see *Economic Community of East Africa: Terms of Association, ibid.,* V (July 1966), p. 633; also UN Doc. E. CN. 14/352.

63. The United States and other contracting parties have frequently attacked both the legality and desirability of the "reverse preferences" that the EEC extracted from its African associates.

64. See Curzon, *Multilateral Commercial Diplomacy,* pp. 283-286.

65. Patterson, *Discrimination in International Trade,* p. 225,n.

66. *Agreement Setting up an Association between the European Eco-*

nomic Community and Greece (with Protocol and Annexes), signed at Athens, July 9, 1961. For text, see *European Yearbook,* IX (1961), p. 452; and GATT Doc. L/1601/ Add. 1, Dec. 7, 1961.

67. Patterson, *Discrimination in International Trade,* pp. 250-251.

68. See *ibid.,* chap. viii, for a development of this view.

Chapter 4

1. Oscar Zaglits, "Agricultural Trade and Trade Policy," in *Foreign Trade and Agricultural Policy,* Volume VI, *Technical Papers* (Washington, D. C.: National Advisory Commission on Food and Fiber, 1967), p. 138.

2. Quoted in Kelly, "Antecedents of Present Commercial Policy," p. 7.

3. It is not the intention to suggest that the American system of price support was developed as a direct reaction to the European. But the sharp drop in international prices to which European restrictions contributed was a major factor in the distress of American farmers and led not only to such domestic measures as the refinancing of farm indebtedness but also to the adoption of price-support programs.

4. The account that follows is based primarily on Professor Haberler's study of quantitative restrictions prepared for the League of Nations in 1943, entitled *Quantitative Trade Controls: Their Causes and Nature* (Geneva: League of Nations, 1943), Ingvar Svennilson's *Growth and Stagnation in the European Economy* (Geneva: UN Economic Commission for Europe, 1954), pp. 89-101, and P. Lamartine Yates's *Food Production in Western Europe* (London: Macmillan, 1940). Useful material on national agricultural programs from the early 1930's until the mid 1950's is contained in Murray R. Benedict and Oscar C. Stine, *The Agricultural Commodity Program* (New York: Twentieth Century Fund, 1956).

5. Haberler, *Quantitative Trade Controls,* p. 16.

6. Svennilson, *Growth and Stagnation,* p. 90.

7. Yates, *Food Production in Western Europe,* p. 234.

8. *Ibid.,* p. 311.

9. *Ibid.,* Table 101, p. 532.

10. This section has drawn heavily on the detailed account by John M. Leddy, "United States Commercial Policy and the Domestic Farm Program," in *Studies in United States Commercial Policy,* ed. Kelly, pp. 174-191.

11. *Ibid.,* p. 181.

12. Agricultural Adjustment Act of 1933, in 48 Stat. 31, and in 7 USC 601-605, 607-623.

13. United States v. Butler et al., Receivers of Hoosac Mills Corporation, 297 US 1 (1936).

14. See The Soil Conservation and Domestic Allotment Act of 1936, 49 Stat. 163, chap. 85; and 16 USC 590h(b).

15. In the period before World War II, this was the only authority providing for export subsidies. Not until 1944 was the Commodity Credit Corporation (CCC) authorized to resell its accumulated stocks at a loss.

16. Leddy, "United States Commercial Policy and the Domestic Farm Program," p. 182.

17. Ibid., p. 188.

18. Reciprocal Trade Agreement Between the United States and Canada, US Executive Agreement Series, No. 149, Article 10. Note that it was not necessary to make special provision for Section 32; bilateral agreements contained no restraints on the use of subsidies, as the agreements were entirely concerned with the bilateral trading relationships between the signatories and not with competition between them for third markets.

19. US Tariff Commission, Operation of the Trade Agreements Program, June 1934-April 1948, pt. IV, Table 33.

20. See Section 4 of the Commodity Credit Corporation Appropriation Act of July 1, 1941, 55 Stat. 498, as amended, 56 Stat. 768; see also 15 USC 713 a-8.

21. In the Stabilization Act of 1942, 56 Stat. 765, ch. 578; and 15 USC 713 a-8,n.

22. For the Surplus Property Act of 1944, see 58 Stat. 765, and 50 USC 1622, 1641 (Appropriation sections).

23. This is not to say that the GATT, as an executive agreement, does not have the force of domestic law. (See John H. Jackson, "The General Agreement on Tariffs and Trade in United States Domestic Law," Michigan Law Review, LXVI [Dec. 1967], p. 249.) But the administration's relations with Congress would not have been happy if those GATT obligations that conflicted with existing law had been accepted without qualification and without congressional approval.

24. For countries acceding later, the date was, of course, a later one. The Protocol of Provisional Application is reproduced in 55 UNTS 308; and also in GATT, BISD, volume IV, p. 77.

25. Section 104 of the Defense Production Act. For a fuller account of this and other legislative developments, see Leddy, "United States Commercial Policy and the Domestic Farm Program," pp. 202-221.

26. See Jackson, "General Agreement on Tariffs and Trade in United States Domestic Law," p. 268.

27. Waiver Granted to the United States in Connection with Import Restrictions Imposed under Section 22 of the United States Agricultural Adjustment Act (of 1933) as Amended, March 5, 1955, GATT, BISD, suppl. 3, June 1955, pp. 32-38. This waiver legalized not only the quotas already in force but any action "required to be taken . . . under Section 22."

28. Ibid., pp. 38-41. This decision came to be known as the "Hard

Core Waiver."
29. GATT, *Trends in International Trade: Report by a Panel of Experts* ("Haberler Report") (Geneva, 1958), pp. 80-89.
30. *Ibid.,* p. 87.
31. Named after Professor Gottfried Haberler, chairman.
32. Dean D. Gale Johnson of the University of Chicago has commented that this prediction is excessively optimistic and that it makes insufficient allowance for the political power of the secondary beneficiaries of farm supports, those who furnish the growing volume of the farmers' purchased inputs. It is certainly true that this offset to the declining power of the farmer must be taken into account. And it may be decisive so long as the best customers for fertilizers and farm machinery —the large-scale farmers—continue to prefer price supports, with curtailed production, to the freedom to compete. Perhaps the only real hope that agriculture will break out of its squirrel cage lies in the possibility that the present tendency of large farmers to identify their own interests with those of marginal farmers will not last forever.
33. See Zaglits, "Agricultural Trade and Trade Policy," p. 196.
34. John A. Schnittger, "Farm Policy—Today's Direction," *Journal of Farm Economics,* XLVIII (Dec. 1966), p. 1094.
35. *Ibid.,* p. 1096.
36. D. Gale Johnson, "Agricultural Trade and Foreign Economic Policy," in *Foreign Trade and Agricultural Policy,* Volume VI, *Technical Papers,* p. 8.
37. Zaglits, "Agricultural Trade and Trade Policy," pp. 151-152.
38. HR 10864. See PL 90-475, secs. 4, 6, Aug. 11, 1968, 82 Stat. 701-702; see also 7 USC 1347, as amended.
39. Zaglits, "Agricultural Trade and Trade Policy," p. 157.
40. The complete list is contained in Annex II of the Treaty of Rome.
41. Treaty of Rome, Title II.
42. Contracting Parties, Twenty-second Session, *Report of Committee II on the Consultation with the European Economic Community,* GATT Doc. L/2389, Mar. 13, 1965.
43. See chap. viii, n. 38.
44. See John O. Coppock, *North Atlantic Policy: The Agricultural Gap* (New York: Twentieth Century Fund, 1963), p. 11.
45. Zaglits, "Agricultural Trade and Trade Policy," p. 178.
46. Commission des Communautés Européennes, *Memorandum sur la réforme de l'agriculture dans la Communauté Economique Européenne,* Doc. Com. (68) 1000, Dec. 18, 1968, Part A, and annexes, Parts B-F.
47. Dean D. Gale Johnson has suggested to me that the effective protection resulting from the existing level of agricultural tariff rates is increasing as a result of the rising ratio of purchased inputs to the value added by the farmer, the lower rates of protection on those inputs than on the farmer's output, and the fact that some inputs are subsidized.

Even if the essential conditions for this conclusion are not met in all cases, Dean Johnson's conclusion seems certain to be borne out for many farm products both in the United States and in other developed countries.

Chapter 5

1. This chapter has profited at many points from facts derived from a chapter by William B. Kelly, Jr., entitled "Nontariff Barriers," in Bela Balassa et al., *Studies in Trade Liberalization: Problems and Prospects for the Industrial Countries* (Baltimore: Johns Hopkins Press, 1967), pp. 265-314.

2. For examples of some of these, see Mark S. Massel, *Non-Tariff Barriers as an Obstacle to World Trade,* Brookings Reprint No. 97 (Washington, D. C.: Brookings Institution, 1965), pp. 63-65.

3. For the *Protocol of Provisional Application,* see 55 UNTS 308. (Also reproduced in GATT, BISD, Volume IV, pp. 77-78. For example, Canada was under no obligation to apply the limitations specified in Article VI in assessing antidumping duties, and the United States was relieved of the obligation to apply the injury requirement in assessing countervailing duties against subsidized imports; both resulted from conflict between those GATT provisions and mandatory legislation existing before their acceptance of the GATT. For a further discussion of the *Protocol of Provisional Application,* see chap. iv.

4. Quantitative trade restrictions, though among the most important of nontariff barriers, are not discussed in this chapter. The contractual commitments in GATT concerning their use are so precise as to leave little scope for negotiation. Mention has been made of such restrictions where appropriate, however, as in the chapters dealing with discrimination, agriculture, and the Kennedy Round negotiations.

5. Valuation can also affect the level of a "specific" duty where the rate differs as between various "value brackets."

6. GATT, Article X, 1.

7. *Ibid.,* Article VII, 2(a).

8. GATT, BISD, suppl. 3, pp. 103-126.

9. Kelly, "Nontariff Barriers," p. 287. In the same essay (pp. 287-293), the author presents a useful summary of the various bases for valuation prescribed by US law.

10. *Convention on the Valuation of Goods for Customs Purposes,* drawn up by the Customs Cooperation Council in 1952, 157 UNTS 129.

11. This is not to be confused with "American Selling Price."

12. This is known as "Constructed Value."

13. US Tariff Commission, *Products Subject to Duty on the American Selling Price Basis of Valuation: Conversion of Rates of Duty on Such Products to Rates Based on Values Determined by Conventional Valua-*

tion Methods, Publication 181 (Washington, D. C.: Government Printing Office, 1966).

14. Kelly, "Nontariff Barriers," p. 291.

15. The additional protection afforded by uncertainty, and the high potential protection afforded to products not presently produced domestically, explain why the benzenoid chemical industry has consistently resisted the substitution for ASP of higher *rates* estimated to yield under normal valuation standards the same protection as that currently afforded by ASP.

16. GATT, BISD, suppl. 1, decision of Nov. 7, 1952, pp. 23-24.

17. *Ibid.,* recommendation of Nov. 7, 1952, pp. 25-26.

18. *Ibid.,* suppl. 3, pp. 91-94.

19. *Ibid.,* suppl. 5, pp. 102-108.

20. GATT, Article III, paragraphs 1 and 2.

21. GATT, BISD, II, pp. 183-188; suppl. 2, pp. 25-26, and suppl. 4, pp. 21-22.

22. *Ibid.,* suppl. 5, pp. 124-125.

23. This standard (the "Wine Gallon Assessment") also applies to the customs tariff and has an effect similar to an arbitrary valuation for customs purposes.

24. Because the standard for collection of the tax was horsepower rather than size or value, most European automobiles, including those in the luxury category, avoided the effects of this discontinuity of rates. Except for two models of the Facel Vega, all French automobiles were rated as less than twelve fiscal horsepower.

25. Kelly, "Nontariff Barriers," p. 302.

26. GATT, Article III, 2. Emphasis added.

27. Interpretive note to Article XVI.

28. These conclusions, in turn, derived from the theory that the schedule of producers' offering prices is determined by the cost to the producer of the most costly unit. Since there is no profit on the marginal unit, it cannot give rise to an income tax. But a tax imposed on the product, applicable to all producers and all units produced, will be fully reflected in marginal cost and therefore in supply price. To say that the GATT provisions were based on this theory misrepresents, of course, the state of economic theory in existence when the GATT was drawn up. Long before, Marshall had recognized that the classical theory of tax incidence would apply fully only under conditions of perfect competition. For a fairly representative exposition of the argument against the existing GATT rules, but one which acknowledges this qualification by Marshall and others, see Helen Junz, "Issues and Objectives of U. S. Foreign Trade Policy," in *A Compendium of Statements Submitted to the Subcommittee on Foreign Economic Policy of the Joint Economic Committee, Congress of the United States,* 90th Cong., 1st sess., 1967, pp. 31-40.

29. See *ibid.,* pp. 731-758. For a recent empirical study concluding

that direct corporate taxes are not shifted forward, see R. T. Gordon, "The Incidence of the Corporation Income Tax in U.S. Manufacturing, 1925-62," *American Economic Review*, LVII (Sept. 1967), pp. 731-758.

30. See Sidney Weintraub, "Border Tax Adjustments and the GATT," *Tax Executive*, XVII (July 1965), pp. 304-320.

31. An excellent description and analysis is contained in Clara K. Sullivan, *The Search for Tax Principles in the European Economic Community* (Cambridge: Harvard Law School 1963).

32. See GATT, Articles II, 4, and interpretive note; III, 4 and 8(a); XVII; and the interpretive note entitled "Ad Articles XI, XII, XIII, XIV, and XVIII."

33. *Ibid.*, Article XVII, 1(b).

34. *Ibid.*, Article II, 4.

35. ITO (Havana) Charter, Article 31, 5, incorporated in the GATT through the interpretative note to Article II, 4. For text of the *Havana Charter for an International Trade Organization*, see UN Doc. E/Conf. 2/78. (It is also reproduced in Department of State Publication 3117, Commercial Policy Series 113.)

36. Treaty of Rome, Article 37.

37. GATT, BISD, II, p. 36.

38. *Ibid.*, suppl. 8, pp. 17-20.

39. *Ibid.*, suppl. 10, pp. 62-63.

40. GATT, Article III, 8(a).

41. GATT, Article XVII, 2.

42. OECD, Working Party of the Trade Committee, *Inquiry into Government Purchasing Procedures*, Aug. 4, 1965.

43. The "Buy American Act" of 1933, 41 USC 10a-d requires that purchases by the federal government for use on US territory must be made from domestic sources unless the procurement agency should decide that to do so is not in the national interest or that the cost of domestic purchase is "unreasonable."

44. Under Executive Order No. 10,582 of 1954, 3 CFR Comp., Dec. 17, 1954, the President laid down as a general guideline a 6 percent price margin in favor of domestic production, and 12 percent in the case of goods produced in depressed areas or by small businesses.

45. A summary of dumping theory cannot be undertaken here. The reader is referred to Jacob Viner, *Dumping: A Problem in International Trade* (Chicago: University of Chicago Press, 1923), and Gottfried Haberler, *Theory of International Trade*, pp. 247 ff.

46. GATT, Article VI. This article also permits the imposition of "countervailing duties" to offset export subsidization by other countries.

47. According to James P. Hendrick, Deputy Assistant Secretary of the Treasury, out of 356 antidumping cases concluded from 1955 through the first ten months of 1966, only 11 resulted in the imposition of an antidumping duty. (Address to the Customs Seminar of the Synthetic Organic Chemical Manufacturers Association, New York, Nov.

10, 1966.)

48. See GATT, *Anti-Dumping and Countervailing Duties* (Geneva, July 1958).

Chapter 6

1. The United Nations Conference on Trade and Development (UNCTAD). See Richard N. Gardner, "The United Nations Conference on Trade and Development," in *The Global Partnership: International Agencies and Economic Development*, ed. Richard N. Gardner and Max F. Millikan (New York: Frederick A. Praeger, 1968), pp. 99-130.

This chapter includes portions of my essay, "The General Agreement on Tariffs and Trade," which also appears in the volume edited by Gardner and Millikan (pp. 72-98) and is reproduced by permission of the World Peace Foundation.

2. GATT, Article XVIII, in its 1947 version, provided that less-developed countries and countries engaged in postwar reconstruction could be released from the relevant obligations of the GATT in order to provide special protection to "particular industries" but only in accordance with specified criteria and procedures. Different criteria and procedures were specified for dealing with requests for release from the obligation not to increase tariffs that had been "bound" and the obligation not to use quantitative restrictions (quotas) for protecting a domestic industry against competition.

3. Clair Wilcox, *A Charter for World Trade*, pp. 48-49.

4. Ambassador K. B. Lall of India, in address before the Seventh World Conference of the Society for International Development, Washington, D. C., Mar. 1965. Reproduced in the society's publication, *International Development* (New York, 1965), pp. 174-179.

5. US Tariff Commission, *Operation of the Trade Agreements Program, June 1934-April 1948*, pt. III, Tables 33, 34, 36.

6. *Ibid.*, pt. IV, Table 7.

7. *Ibid.*, Table 33.

8. GATT, BISD, II, pp. 21-27.

9. *Ibid.*, p. 20.

10. *Ibid.*, p. 26.

11. The details of these cases, including the factors taken into account, are set forth in *ibid.*, II and suppls. 1-4.

12. Previously referred to in chap. IV.

13. GATT, BISD, suppl. 7, pp. 27-29.

14. GATT, Committee on the Legal and Institutional Framework, "Proposed Chapter on Trade and Development: Comparative Provisions of Five Submissions," Feb. 24, 1964 [mimeo].

15. GATT, Article XXXVII.

16. *Ibid.*, Article XXXVI.

17. Readers who wish a mathematical presentation of these relationships are referred to: Bela A. Balassa, "Tariff Protection in Industrial Countries: An Evaluation," *Journal of Political Economy,* LXXIII (Dec. 1965), pp. 573-594; or Giorgio Basevi, "The United States Tariff Structure: Estimates of Effective Rates of Protection of United States Industries and Industrial Labor," *Review of Economics and Statistics,* XLVIII (May 1966), pp. 147-160.

18. GATT Doc. COM. TD/W/74, June 25, 1968.

19. *Ibid.,* p. 3.

20. See, for example, H. G. Johnson, *Economic Policies toward Less-Developed Countries* (Washington, D. C.: Brookings Institution, 1967), p. 96.

21. Balassa, "Tariff Protection in Industrial Countries," p. 591.

22. Johnson, *Economic Policies toward Less-Developed Countries,* Tables 4 and 5.

Chapter 7

1. See Camps, *Britain and the European Community,* pp. 356-366.

2. *International Financial Statistics* (International Monetary Fund), XIV (Dec. 1961), pp. 264-265.

3. *Ibid.,* Belgium-Luxembourg, pp. 54-55; France, pp. 122-123; Germany, pp. 126-127; Italy, pp. 172-173; the Netherlands, pp. 192-193.

4. The "transition period" before the full application of the Common Market had originally been expected to require from twelve to fifteen years from the entry into force of the Treaty of Rome on January 1, 1958 (Article 8).

5. Camps, *Britain and the European Community,* pp. 253-264.

6. *Ibid.,* pp. 235-244. For a sympathetic account of US intervention in the negotiations for an all-Europe Free Trade Area, see Emile Benoit, *Europe at Sixes and Sevens* (New York: Columbia University Press, 1961).

7. See Curzon, *Multilateral Commercial Diplomacy,* p. 280.

8. Treaty of Rome, Preamble and Article 110.

9. See Frank, *The European Common Market,* pp. 159 and 189 and 189n.

10. *New York Times,* Feb. 7, 1961.

11. See chap. ii; see also Leddy and Norwood, "Escape Clause and Peril Points under the Trade Agreements Program," p. 145.

12. See *New York Times,* May 17, 1961.

13. See Camps, *Britain and the European Community,* pp. 352-353.

14. *Ibid.,* p. 336.

15. *Ibid.,* p. 237.

16. *Ibid.*

17. For an authoritative and detailed account of the efforts at bridge building and the role played by the United States, see *ibid.,* pp. 232-273.

18. *New York Times,* Jan. 8, 1962.

19. See testimony of George Ball, US, Congress, House, Committee on Ways and Means, *Trade Expansion Act of 1962, Hearings before the Committee on Ways and Means,* 87th Cong., 2d sess., 1962, p. 673 [hereafter cited as *House Hearings*].

20. Trade Expansion Act of 1962, Oct. 11, 1962, P.L. 87-794, 76 Stat. 872.

21. *New York Times,* Oct. 7, 1961.

22. *Ibid.,* Nov. 2, 1961.

23. *Ibid.*

24. *New York Times,* Nov. 9, 1961.

25. *Ibid.,* Dec. 7, 1961.

26. US, Congress, House, Joint Economic Committee of the Congress, *Foreign Economic Policy, Hearings before the Subcommittee on Foreign Economic Policy of the Joint Economic Committee,* 87th Cong., 1st sess., Dec. 4-14, 1961 [hereafter cited as *Boggs Hearings*].

27. *Ibid.,* pp. 284-308.

28. *House Hearings,* pp. 1-9.

29. A more complete summary, prepared by the administration, as well as the full text of the bill, are reproduced in *ibid.,* pp. 11-31.

30. *Ibid.,* p. 60.

31. The only precedents, neither of which permitted a reduction to zero, had been the authority in the 1955 Extension Act to reduce very high rates to 50 percent and, in the 1958 Act, the additional authority to reduce very low rates by 2 percentage points.

32. See Camps, *Britain and the European Community,* pp. 267-268.

33. See testimony of Carl J. Gilbert, chairman of the Committee for a National Trade Policy, *House Hearings,* pp. 1871-1878; and testimony of J. K. Southerland, on behalf of the US poultry industry, *ibid.,* pp. 1959-1966.

34. Testimony of Irving B. Kravis, *Boggs Hearings,* p. 322; testimony of Charles W. Engelhard, *ibid.,* p. 384; testimony of Luther Hodges, *ibid.,* p. 62.

35. Reproduced in *House Hearings,* p. 113.

36. For example, the influence of European postwar modernization and the stimulating effect of American capital seeking a protected base within the enlarged European market.

37. Statement of Representative James B. Utt, *House Hearings,* p. 2571.

38. *Ibid.,* p. 1349.

39. *Ibid.,* p. 120.

40. *Ibid.,* p. 4.

41. The UK and some other Europeans, of course, were expected to become EEC members.

42. See Camps, *Britain and the European Community,* pp. 390-393.

43. See testimony of Charles B. Shuman, *House Hearings,* pp. 3209-

3221; testimony of Herschel D. Newsom, *ibid.,* pp. 2656-2660.
44. Testimony of Orville L. Freeman, *ibid.,* p. 1963.
45. *Ibid.,* p. 843.
46. *Ibid.,* p. 641.
47. Testimony of Theodore Geiger, *Boggs Hearings,* p. 83; see also the testimony of Jacob Viner, *ibid.,* p. 25.
48. For explicit expressions of this view, see testimony of Viner, *ibid.,* p. 18; testimony of Morris C. Dobrow, *ibid.,* p. 225.
49. See, for example, testimony of Henry Wallich, *Boggs Hearings,* p. 51. (The belief that the EEC tariff was higher than that of the US will be discussed in a subsequent chapter.)
50. *House Hearings,* p. 818.
51. See, for example, testimony of Alfred C. Neal, *Boggs Hearings,* p. 16; testimony of Theodore V. Houser, *ibid.,* p. 253.
52. Testimony of Morris Dobrow, *ibid.,* pp. 225-226.
53. Testimony of Alfred C. Neal, *ibid.,* p. 16.
54. Statement of Congressman Byrnes, *House Hearings,* pp. 3844-3845.
55. Testimony of Leon E. Hickman, *ibid.,* p. 2538; testimony of William C. Babbitt, *ibid.,* pp. 2941-2949; testimony of Harold O. Toor, *ibid.,* pp. 3186-3188.
56. *Ibid.,* p. 3845.
57. "Export Trade" (April 1962), reproduced in *House Hearings,* p. 3960.
58. Raymond Vernon, *Trade Policy in Crisis,* Essays in International Finance, No. 29 (Princeton, N.J.: Princeton University Press, 1958), p. 15.
59. This proposal was essentially the same as the "French Plan," proposed in GATT in 1953 and opposed at that time by the United States. See chap. ii, p. 22. For a description of such a plan by a public witness, see testimony of Irving Kravis, *Boggs Hearings,* pp. 323-324.
60. *Ibid.,* p. 346.
61. *House Hearings,* p. 819.
62. See, for example, testimony of George Ball, *Boggs Hearings,* p. 346.
63. See testimony of Bert Seidman, *ibid.,* pp. 325-332.
64. Statement by a "spokesman of the Commission," quoted in the *Bulletin of the European Community* (Commission of the European Economic Community [hereafter cited as *EEC Bulletin*]), V (Mar. 1962), p. 35.
65. See chap. i.
66. Testimony of William R. Neblett on behalf of the National Shrimp Congress, Inc., *House Hearings,* pp. 4169-4170.
67. US, Congress, Senate, Committee on Finance, *Hearings on Trade Expansion Act of 1962, Before Committee on Finance,* 87th Cong., 2d sess., 1962. [Hereafter cited as *Senate Hearings.*]
68. Gaston Coblentz, *New York Herald Tribune,* July 29, 1962.
69. *Senate Hearings,* p. 2200.

70. The list of products that would be subject to the 80 percent tax if the Community were to include the United Kingdom is reproduced in *Senate Hearings,* pp. 44-45.

71. *Ibid.,* pp. 2259-2261.

72. PL 87-794, 87th Cong. [hereafter cited as Trade Expansion Act]. The substitute bill which the Ways and Means Committee reported out and which was voted by the House and served as the basis for the *Senate Hearings* bears the number HR 11970, in place of HR 9900. See *Trade Expansion Act of 1962, Report of the Committee on Ways and Means to Accompany H.R. 11970,* 87th Cong., 2d sess., House Report No. 1818 (1962). [Hereafter cited as *House Report No. 1818.*]

73. See *House Report No. 1818,* p. 19.

74. See Section 225(b) of the Trade Expansion Act.

75. See Section 231 of the Trade Expansion Act.

76. See *House Report No. 1818,* p. 4.

77. Italics added.

78. See Section 252 of the Trade Expansion Act.

79. Testimony of Alfred Neal, *Boggs Hearings,* p. 14; testimony of Dean Acheson, *ibid.,* p. 45; testimony of George Ball, *ibid.,* p. 343.

80. Testimony of George Ball, *Senate Hearings,* p. 2200.

81. See, for example, Senator Prescott Bush, *Boggs Hearings,* p. 105.

82. *New York Times,* Dec. 7, 1961.

Chapter 8

1. European Office of the United Nations, Press Release, GATT/65, Nov. 30, 1961.

2. *Ibid.,* p. 2.

3. *Ibid.*

4. See chap. vi.

5. Reproduced in GATT L/1733, Feb. 26, 1962.

6. Italics added.

7. Italics added.

8. Eric Wyndham White, whose title was later changed to director general.

9. Curzon, *Multilateral Commercial Diplomacy,* p. 103.

10. GATT L/1891, Nov. 2, 1962.

11. GATT L/1844, Oct. 8, 1962.

12. Recall, for example, the requirement that the President "reserve" certain items from negotiation.

13. In the language of the executive secretary, "the Working Party may recognize that, while access for many agricultural products is governed solely by the tariff, access to markets for other agricultural goods is governed by other factors." The assumption that the negotiating rules for tariffs would apply to agricultural products was obviously tactical and not naïve.

14. Wilton and velvet, or wool tapestry carpets; cylinder, crown, and sheet glass. See White House press release, Mar. 19, 1962.

15. The Swiss reaction to an increase in the duty on watches was the nearest equivalent.

16. Tariff increases for mosaic tile and baseball gloves. See White House Press Release, Mar. 19, 1962.

17. Carpets, Aug. 3, 1961; glass, May 17, 1961. US Tariff Commission, *Operations of the Trade Agreements Program, Fourteenth Report* (Washington, D. C.: Government Printing Office, 1964), p. 10.

18. *New York Times,* Mar. 24, 1962.

19. *Ibid.,* Mar. 30, 1962.

20. *Ibid.,* Mar. 23, 1962.

21. *Ibid.,* Apr. 14, 1962.

22. *EEC Bulletin,* V (June 1962), p. 12.

23. *New York Times,* Mar. 24, 1962.

24. White House press release, Mar. 30, 1962.

25. *EEC Bulletin,* V (July 1962), p. 21. Certain forms of polyethylene and polystyrene, woven fabrics of synthetic and artificial fibers, and cold-water paints.

26. *New York Times,* June 15, 1962.

27. See Camps, *Britain and the European Community,* pp. 473-476.

28. See chap. vii, p. 155.

29. See chap. vii, p. 143.

30. Camps, *Britain and the European Community,* pp. 468-471.

31. Miriam Camps, *What Kind of Europe? The Community since de Gaulle's Veto* (London: Oxford University Press, 1965), p. 3.

32. *Ibid.,* p. 1.

33. See chap. x.

34. *The Poultry and Egg Situation* (US Department of Agriculture, Economic Research Service), no. 218 (Mar. 1962), pp. 46-47.

35. *Ibid.,* no. 227 (Sept. 1963), pp. 11-15.

36. Ibid., nos. 218, 220, 222 (Mar., July, Nov. 1962); nos. 226, 227 (July, Sept. 1963).

37. *Agreement Between the United States of America and the European Economic Community, pursuant to Article XXIV: 6 of the General Agreement on Tariffs and Trade,* signed at Geneva, Mar. 7, 1962, 13 UST pt. I, 1962 (TIAS 5018), pp. 506-577.

38. The agreement stipulated that "upon adoption of the [common] agricultural policy for corn, ordinary wheat, rice and poultry, the Community undertakes to enter into negotiations with the United States on the situation of exports of these products by the United States. The negotiations . . . will take place on the basis of the negotiating rights which the United States held under the General Agreement for these products as of September 1, 1960." Department of State, *Corn, Sorghum, Ordinary Wheat, Rice and Poultry; Agreement between the United*

States of America and the European Economic Community and Member States, signed at Geneva, Mar. 7, 1962, 13 UST pt. I, 1962 (TIAS 5034), pp. 960-961.

39. *The Poultry and Egg Situation* No. 222, (Nov. 1962).

40. "We are not going to stand by and . . . allow our historical market to be taken away," *New York Times*, Nov. 17, 1962.

41. *EEC Bulletin*, VI (July 1963), p: 39.

42. *Journal Officiel des Communautés Européennes* (EEC), VI (June 1, 1963).

43. Office of the Special Representative for Trade Negotiations, press release R-13, Washington, May 31, 1963.

44. *Ibid.*, Aug. 6, 1963.

45. *EEC Bulletin*, VI (Sept./Oct. 1963), pp. 37-38.

46. *Ibid.*

47. In accordance with Article XXIV of the GATT, the "XXIV:6 negotiations" were conducted under the provisions of Article XXVIII ("Modification of Schedules"). These provisions applied, therefore, to the negotiating rights retained in the bilateral agreement.

48. Acceptance of both these points is explicit in statements issued at the time (see, for example, *EEC Bulletin*, VI (Sept./Oct. 1963), pp. 37-38. Newspaper comment, however, almost universally misunderstood the second point and assumed that the amounts involved represented the *loss* of trade resulting from the withdrawal of tariff bindings rather than the total trade in those items. (See, for example, *New York Times*, Aug. 11, 1963, Section IV, p. 2.) The fact they overlooked was that the withdrawal of a tariff binding deprives the exporting country of any assurance against imposition of a prohibitive tariff that could eliminate all imports of the product. If, on the other hand, the poultry binding had been replaced by a new binding, even at a higher level, the pertinent yardstick would have been the anticipated loss of trade involved.

49. *The Poultry and Egg Situation*, No. 218 (Mar. 1962), pp. 46-47; ibid., No. 227 (Sept. 1963), pp. 11-15.

50. *EEC Bulletin*, VI (Sept./Oct. 1963), p. 38.

51. See nn. 40 and 45.

52. To make such counterwithdrawals legally under the GATT, the EEC would have had to submit the issue under Article XXIII and to obtain a judgment from the Contracting Parties that the action was appropriate. The same procedure would also apply in the case of further, responsive US withdrawals. But given the existing state of tension, there was no assurance that the niceties of GATT procedures would have been observed.

53. Even after the GATT panel had settled the issue, a major New York poultry exporter urged the US government to reject the settlement. (*New York Times*, Nov. 27, 1962).

54. Article XXVIII of the GATT (see n. 47) makes no provision for a case in which counterwithdrawals (by the US in this case) are con-

sidered to be excessive. If the EEC considered that a new imbalance had been created, it would have had to resort to Article XXIII, which requires approval by the Contracting Parties to the General Agreement.

55. *EEC Bulletin*, VI (Nov. 1963), p. 13.

56. Eric Wyndham White, executive secretary of the GATT, chairman; Albert Weitnauer (Switzerland); Robert Campbell-Smith (Canada); Nils Montan (Sweden); F. Patrick Donovan (Australia).

57. GATT press release, "Report of the Panel on Poultry," GATT/819, Nov. 21, 1963.

58. The US brief, for example, attempted to arrive at the $46 million figure by an elaborate econometric calculation that relied on "constructed prices" and assumed elasticities of demand; it is not surprising that the panel, in its report, ignored this shaky edifice.

59. *EEC Bulletin*, VII (Jan. 1964); and Office of the Special Representative for Trade Negotiations, press release R-32, Nov. 21, 1963.

Chapter 9

1. GATT L/1844, Oct. 8, 1962.

2. GATT L/1982, Mar. 14, 1963. The working party explicitly excepted negotiations with less developed countries.

3. GATT, MIN(63)9, May 22, 1963.

4. To this problem may be added the effect of "dispersion" referred to below and the influence of tariff "structure," discussed in chap. vi.

5. See Treaty of Rome, Article 19, 1.

6. Raymond Bertrand, "Comparaison de Niveau des Tariffs Douanier," *Cahiers de l'Institut de Science Economique Appliquée*, Series R, No. 2 (Feb. 1958).

7. Richard N. Cooper, "Tariff Dispersion and Trade Negotiations," *Journal of Political Economy*, LXII (Dec. 1964), pp. 597-603.

8. See Camps, *European Unification in the Sixties*, pp. 5-6.

9. May 20, 1963.

10. May 19, 1963.

11. GATT, MIN(63)9, May 22, 1963, p. 1.

12. "Double spread."

13. GATT, SPEC/64/12, Jan. 30, 1964.

14. GATT, TN 64/15, Apr. 10, 1964.

15. The Community had not, as yet, formally accepted 50 percent as the target for linear reductions, but that depth of cut continued to be taken as a "working hypothesis" in the consideration of other aspects of the tariff negotiating plan.

16. For example, it was possible that a linear reduction by a country not able to claim a disparity would bring its rate to below the reduced rate of one able to do so, thus reversing their initial positions.

17. GATT Press Release 869, May 11, 1964.

18. *Resolution Adopted on 6 May 1964*, GATT, TN 64/27, May 11, 1964.
19. *Ibid.*
20. *Ibid.*

Chapter 10

1. Camps, *What Kind of Europe?* pp. 20-30.
2. In the transition to a Common Agricultural Policy, "Member States had to discontinue the use of their national instruments of support and protection and in their place had to use the instruments and techniques provided for in the relevant CAP regulation, as in particular the import levies." Zaglits, "Agricultural Trade and Trade Policy," p. 180.
3. The "Baumgartner Plan." See Camps, *Britain and the European Community*, p. 405n.
4. "Organization of the market."
5. The United States favored lower world prices than those desired by other exporters, especially Australia. In his opening speech John McEwen, Australia's Deputy Prime Minister, asked *inter alia* for higher world prices and comprehensive commodity agreements for bulk commodities, a position that had some resemblance to the "Baumgartner Plan." (GATT Press Release 794, May 18, 1963.)
6. GATT Press Release 751, May 17, 1963.
7. GATT, MIN(63)9, May 22, 1963.
8. Camps, *What Kind of Europe?* pp. 21-24.
9. *Le Monde,* June 8, 1963.
10. See chap. viii.
11. After Dr. Sico Mansholt, the commissioner specializing in agricultural policy.
12. Camps, *What Kind of Europe?* p. 27.
13. *Ibid.*
14. *Ibid.,* p. 30.
15. GATT, TN 64/AGR/1, Feb. 19, 1964.
16. *Ibid.,* p. 5.
17. Some of these elements were concealed by ambiguity in the February 1964 submission and did not emerge clearly until after several months of discussion in the Committee on Agriculture. The reader wishing to verify them will need to examine both the original submission *(ibid.)* and the supplementary paper submitted by the commission on August 3, 1964 *(ibid.,* TN 64/AGR/5) in response to the written objections of the US delegation *(ibid.,* 64/AGR/4, June 17, 1964).
18. *Ibid.,* TN 64/AGR/5, p. 3.
19. *Ibid.,* p. 5.
20. GATT, TN 64/27, May 11, 1964.
21. *Ibid.*

22. Italics added.
23. GATT, TN 64/AGR/5, Aug. 3, 1964, p. 3.
24. See Camps, *European Unification in the Sixties,* p. 12, and, for a more detailed account of the developing crisis in the community from the summer of 1964 to the De Gaulle boycott in 1965, see *ibid.,* pp. 12-80.
25. See *ibid.,* p. 17.
26. GATT, TN 64/AGR/W.1, Jan. 27, 1965.
27. GATT, TN 64/39, Mar. 13, 1965.
28. Once again, the reader is referred to the work of Mrs. Camps, *European Unification in the Sixties,* pp. 29-124.
29. See John W. Evans, *U. S. Trade Policy: New Legislation for the Next Round* (New York: Harper and Row, 1967), pp. 76-82.
30. See Camps, *European Unification in the Sixties,* pp. 104-115, for details of the "Luxembourg Compromise."

Chapter 11

1. GATT, Press Release 906, Nov. 17, 1964.
2. See, for example, *Financial Times,* London, Feb. 12, 1965; and *Frankfurter Algemeine Zeitung,* Feb. 15, 1965.
3. See *Europe,* Feb. 10, 1965.
3. Whether such "exclusions" should be treated like other exceptions was an issue over which there was still disagreement at the time the lists were tabled.
5. A similar observation was made by Eric Wyndham White, GATT's director general, in an address in Paris on June 2, 1965, before the Union of French Export Industries (GATT INT (65) 168, June 1, 1965).
6. Until the merger of the communities in 1967, the ECSC, although consisting of the same member states as the EEC, had an independent institutional structure and separate jurisdiction over products representing about 85 percent of imports in the sector.
7. GATT, BISD, suppl. 1, Mar. 1953, pp. 17-22.
8. *Ibid.,* p. 18.
9. ECSC, High Authority Press Release, Luxembourg, Nov. 16, 1964.
10. These and further relevant details concerning the steel sector negotiations may be found in a useful report by Congressman Thomas B. Curtis of Missouri, a congressional adviser to the US Kennedy Round delegation. (*Congressional Record* [further sections of report hereafter cited as *Curtis Report*], May 31, 1966, CXII, pt. 9, pp. 11859-11860).
11. For a more detailed discussion of the problems in the chemicals sector, see *ibid.,* pp. 11861-11866.
12. See chap. v.
13. W. M. Blumenthal, in an address to the Centre Européen des Fédérations de l'Industrie Shimique, Kronberg, Dec. 8, 1966.
14. "Pulp and paper prices in Scandinavia are said to be set by five

producers' cartels headquartered in Stockholm." *Curtis Report,* July 24, 1967, CXIII, pt. 15, p. 19931.
15. *Ibid.*
16. *Ibid.*
17. For previous reference, see chap. iii.
18. This is an unofficial summary. The full text is reproduced in GATT, BISD, suppl. 11, pp. 25-36.
19. The facts in this section are largely derived from unpublished GATT documents and from the *Curtis Report,* July 24, 1967, CXIII, pt. 15, pp. 19931-19932.
20. See Camps, *European Unification in the Sixties,* pp. 47-48.
21. See *ibid.,* pp. 29-124.

Chapter 12

1. See Zaglits, "Agricultural Trade and Trade Policy," p. 226.
2. Quoted in *ibid.,* p. 227.
3. As reported by Edwin L. Dale in the *New York Times,* Sept. 16, 1966.
4. See chap. x.
5. TN 64/20, Apr. 27, 1964.
6. See chap. x, n.30.
7. See Zaglits, "Agricultural Trade and Trade Policy," p. 196.

Chapter 13

1. In referring to "secondary" rings, it is not the intention to suggest that these aspects of the negotiations were unimportant. They did, however, have less impact on the final results.
2. GATT, MIN(63)9, May 22, 1963, p. 2; see also chap. vi.
3. GATT, TN 64/LDC/22, Nov. 25, 1964.
4. See, for example, Committee III, Nov. 16, 1962, in GATT, BISD, suppl. 11, pp. 168-176.
5. Some of this section is reproduced, with permission of the publishers, from John W. Evans, "The General Agreement on Tariffs and Trade," in *The Global Partnership: International Agencies and Economic Development,* ed. Richard N. Gardner and Max F. Millikan (New York: Frederick A. Praeger, 1968), pp. 72-98.
6. Joint statement by the Developing Participating Countries in the Kennedy Round Negotiations, GATT, Press Release, GATT/994, June 30, 1967.
7. EEC, Japan, Sweden, Switzerland, UK, and US; GATT Doc. COM. TD/48/Rev. 1, Nov. 21, 1967.
8. See Office of the Special Representative for Trade Negotiations,

1964-1967 Trade Conference: Report on United States Negotiations [hereafter cited as *Report on United States Negotiations*] (2 vols., Washington, D.C.: Government Printing Office, [1968]), I, pt. 1, p. 131.

9. Based on 1964 trade.

10. GATT, Doc. COM./TD/48, p. 44.

11. UNCTAD, TD/6/suppl. 2, Sept. 4, 1967.

12. Argentina, Brazil, Chile, Dominican Republic, India, Jamaica, Korea, Peru, and Trinidad and Tobago.

13. A number of the less developed countries negotiated, however, in the context of liberalization measures, including tariff reductions that they had already adopted or similar measures not affecting tariffs which they proposed to adopt. See *Report on United States Negotiations,* I, pt. 1, pp. 132-164.

14. GATT, MIN(63)9, May 22, 1963, p. 1.

15. GATT, TNC/4/NTB/8, Nov. 15, 1963.

16. Most of the nontariff barriers referred to in the following paragraphs have been discussed at greater length in chap. v.

17. Most quantitative restrictions were omitted because, as measures that were illegal under the GATT, they were not considered appropriate for negotiation.

18. GATT, *Legal Instruments Embodying the Results of the 1964-1967 Trade Conference* (5 vols., Geneva, 1967), V, p. 3693.

19. GATT, BISD, suppl. 8, p. 11.

20. It will be recalled that the provision of the Trade Expansion Act of 1962 that required the President to deny MFN treatment to Poland and Yugoslavia had been repealed in 1963; see chap. VII.

21. It had been possible for the Contracting Parties to ignore the problem in the case of Czechoslovakia because that country had not come under Communist control until after it had become a contracting party.

22. Wilcox, *Charter for World Trade,* p. 97.

23. *Ibid.,* p. 101.

24. Protocol for the Accession of Poland to the General Agreement on Tariffs and Trade, June 30, 1967, GATT, BISD, suppl. 15, pp. 46-52.

Chapter 14

1. For text, see 471 UNTS 296.

2. See Europe, *Bulletin Quotidien* (Brussels), no. 2598 (Jan 12, 1967).

3. *Ibid.*

4. *Ibid.* Italics added.

5. Successor to Christian Herter, who had died early in January.

6. These retained negotiating rights are explained in the discussion of the background to the "Chicken War," chap. viii.

7. *Report on United States Negotiations,* I, pt. 2, p. 171.

8. See *New York Times,* May 16, 1967.

Chapter 15

1. The reader wishing a more complete statistical appraisal of the results of the Kennedy Round will find a number of informative tables in Ernest H. Preeg, *Traders and Diplomats* (Washington, D.C.: (The Brookings Institution, 1970), chap. xiii. The conclusions of the present chapter are consistent with those of Mr. Preeg, though arrived at without the benefit of his more detailed estimates. One of the difficulties involved in calculating the Kennedy Round results has been the unavailability of trade data at the level of disaggregation of individual tariff rates and the lack of a concordance between tariff items in the Brussels Tariff Nomenclature and the tariffs of countries not using that nomenclature. The GATT secretariat, with the aid of the major participants in the Kennedy Round, has been engaged in the preparation of such a concordance and of computer tapes combining tariff and trade data for those participants. This work is expected to be completed before the end of 1970, when it should be possible to calculate definitive weighted averages of tariff levels and Kennedy Round reductions.

2. On the basis of 1964 statistics. *Report on United States Negotiations,* I, pt. 1, p. i. Parts 1 and 2 of Volume I, as well as Volumes II and III, are the principal sources for information contained in the present chapter.

3. For example, in the 1947 negotiations the United States granted a substantial tariff reduction on decorated bone china, of which the United Kingdom was principal supplier, but they did not make a similar reduction in the duty on cheaper china, of which Japan was the principal supplier.

4. GATT, Press Release, GATT/922, June 30, 1967.

5. Preeg, *Traders and Diplomats,* Appendix A, includes a useful discussion of various methods of averaging duties and duty reductions.

6. *Report on United States Negotiations,* I, pt. 1, p. v.

7. *Ibid.*

8. President of the Board of Trade, *The Kennedy Round of Trade Negotiations, 1964-1967,* Cmnd. 3347 (London: Her Majesty's Stationery Office, 1967).

9. US Tariff Commission, *Operations of the Trade Agreements Program, June 1934-April 1948,* pt. III, Table 3.

10. These calculations and the details of the chemical concessions are contained in testimony by William M. Roth, reproduced in US, Congress, House, Committee on Ways and Means, *Hearings before the Committee on Ways and Means on Tariffs and Trade Proposals,* 90th Cong., 2d sess., 1968, pp. 501-508, 521-546.

11. Norman Vickery, Address to the Annual Convention of the Insti-

tute of Associate Executives, Ottawa, Aug. 18, 1967.

12. *Report on United States Negotiations*, I, pt. 1, p.20.

13. *Ibid.*, p. 21.

14. *Analysis of United States Negotiations, 1960-1961 Tariff Conference*, Department of State Publication 7349, Commercial Policy Ser. 186, (4 vols., Washington, D.C.: Government Printing Office, 1962), I, p. 203.

15. *Report on United States Negotiations*, I, pt. 1, pp. 25-33.

16. *Ibid.*, pp. 100, 107.

17. United States, Argentina, Australia, Canada, Denmark, Finland, Japan, Norway, Sweden, Switzerland, the United Kingdom, and the EEC.

18. The International Wheat Agreement (444 UNTS 3; and Department of State, TIAS 5115) had been in existence, with amendment as to details, since 1949. Its substantive provisions, principally minimum and maximum prices, were allowed to expire on July 31, 1967, in anticipation of a new agreement, but its governing body, the International Wheat Council, was continued until July 1, 1968. The immediate outcome of the work of the Cereals Group in the Kennedy Round was a Memorandum of Agreement on Basic Elements for the Negotiation of a World Grains Arrangement. See GATT, *Legal Instruments Embodying the Results of the 1964-1967 Trade Conference*, V, pp. 3677-3691. On August 18, 1967, at Rome, the signatories to this memorandum agreed to the text of the International Grains Arrangement (IGA), US Department of State, *TIAS 6537*. (Also reproduced in US, Congress, House, Committee on Ways and Means, *Foreign Trade and Tariff Proposals, Hearings*, 90th Cong., 2d sess., 1968, pt. 1, pp. 394-437.) After receiving the necessary ratifications, the IGA entered into force on July 1, 1968. Except with respect to food aid, the new agreement is limited to wheat in spite of its more inclusive title.

19. I was among the skeptics. See Evans, *U. S. Trade Policy*, p. 45.

20. *Report on United States Negotiations.*

21. The discussion of US negotiations with each participant contained in the report includes a table showing the trade coverage of agricultural concessions exchanged, broken down to show the distribution in accordance with the depth of cut.

22. Zaglits, "Agricultural Trade and Trade Policy," p. 236.

23. GATT, L/2862/Rev. 1, Feb. 2, 1968.

24. GATT, Article XXVIII: 1.

25. GATT, L/2867, Oct. 13, 1967.

Chapter 16

1. US, Congress, Senate, *Senate Concurrent Resolution 100*, 90th Cong., 2d sess. (1967).

2. US, Congress, House, *HR 16936*, 90th Cong., 2d sess. (1968).

3. Reproduced in US Treasury Department, *Maintaining the Strength*

of the United States Dollar in a Strong Free World (Washington, D.C.: Government Printing Office, 1968), pp. iii-xviii.

4. By a decision of August 10, 1968, effective September 13, 1968, the US Treasury ordered a 2.5 percent countervailing duty to be applied to most imports from France (TD 68-192). This decision was modified by a decision of October 25, 1968 (TD 68-270), which reduced the duty to 1.5 percent, effective November 1, 1968. It was revoked by a decision of January 24, 1969 (TD 69-41), effective for goods exported from France on or after February 1, 1970.

5. US, Congress, House, Committee on Ways and Means, *Foreign Trade and Tariff Proposals, Hearings,* 90th Cong., 2d sess. (1968), pts. 1-10 [hereafter cited as *Ways and Means Committee Hearings (1968)*].

6. US, Congress, House, *HR 17551,* 90th Cong., 2d sess. (1968), reproduced in *ibid.,* pt. 1, pp. 5-12.

7. See, for example, testimony of John C. Lynn, of the American Farm Bureau Federation, in *ibid.,* pt. 3, pp. 1215-1224.

8. See testimony of Andrew J. Biemiller, AFL-CIO, *ibid.,* pt. 3, p. 1093.

9. Remarks of Wilbur D. Mills before the Annual Meeting of the National Cotton Council of America, Hot Springs, Arkansas, Jan. 27, 1969.

10. See *Ways and Means Committee Hearings (1968),* pt. 10, p. 4670.

11. Speech by Congressman Thomas B. Curtis to the National Foreign Trade Convention, New York City, Nov. 19, 1968.

12. For the background of the border tax issue, see chap. v.

13. *Journal Officiel des Communautés Européenes* (EEC), X (Apr. 14, 1967), pp. 1301/67-1312/67.

14. Compensation at the border will continue to be incomplete during a transitional period ending in 1972. The estimates in this paragraph are derived from unpublished documents submitted by the Federal Republic of Germany to the OECD in October 1967 and May 1968.

15. In late November 1968, partly in response to the French monetary crisis and demands that the mark be revalued, Germany reduced its border tax adjustments affecting trade with third countries as well as the community, by 4 percent *ad valorem.* It thus offset most if not all of the protective effect that could have resulted from its adoption of the TVA.

16. Her Majesty's Government, Customs (Import Deposits) Act, 1968 (chap. lxxiv), Dec. 5, 1968.

17. The data used in this section are derived from unofficial and unpublished data compiled within the US government.

18. See GATT, *Legal Instruments Embodying the Results of the 1964-1967 Trade Conference,* II and IV; and *Report on United States Negotiations,* II, pts. 1 and 2.

19. See the discussion of effective tariff rates in chap. vi.

20. James R. Melvin and Bruce W. Wilkinson, *Effective Protection in the Canadian Economy,* prepared for the Economic Council of Canada (Ottawa: Queen's Printer, 1968), p. 56 and Table 3.

21. See *New Directions for U. S. International Economic Policy* (New York: United States Council of the International Chamber of Commerce, 1969), p. 6.

22. Jean Jacques Servan-Schreiber, *Le Défi Américain* (Paris:Denoël, 1967).

23. See Raymond Vernon, "Antitrust and International Business," *Harvard Business Review,* XLVII (Sept.-Oct. 1968), pp. 78-87.

24. See, for example, testimony of James M. Ashley for the Trade Relations Council of the United States, Inc., *Ways and Means Committee Hearings (1968),* pt. 3, pp. 1162-1163.

25. Testimony of Andrew J. Biemiller, *ibid.,* p. 1093.

26. *Ibid.*

27. See Raymond Vernon, "International Investment and International Trade in the Product Cycle," *Quarterly Journal of Economics,* LXXX (May 1966), pp. 190-207.

28. In an unpublished manuscript.

29. For a summary of these proposals, see David Robertson, *Scope for New Trade Strategy* (London: Atlantic Trade Study, 1968).

30. For my own views see John W. Evans, *U.S. Trade Policy,* pp. 76-82. For a more recent criticism, with which I agree, see Special Representative for Trade Negotiations, *Future United States Trade Policy, Report to the President* (Washington, D.C.: Government Printing Office, 1969), pp. 10-11.

31. See, for example, Special Representative for Trade Negotiations, *Future United States Trade Policy,* pp. 18-19.

Chapter 17

1. John H. Jackson, in *World Trade and the Law of GATT* (New York: Bobbs-Merrill, 1969), lists all agreements notified to GATT under Article XXIV to January 1, 1969, with the action, if any, taken by the Contracting Parties.

2. GATT, BISD, suppl. 16, p. 17.

3. *Ibid.,* suppl. 2, p. 20.

4. *Ibid.,* suppl. 3, p. 32.

5. *Ibid.,* suppl. 11, pp. 57-58.

6. GATT, Doc. C/50 (1964).

7. GATT, BISD, suppl. 14, pp. 22, 100.

Index

Publications Written under the Auspices of the Center for International Affairs, Harvard University

Created in 1958, the Center for International Affairs fosters advanced study of basic world problems by scholars from various disciplines and senior officials from many countries. The research at the Center focuses on economic, social, and political development, the management of force in the modern world, and the evolving roles of Western Europe and the Communist bloc. The published results appear here in the order in which they have been issued. The research programs are supervised by Professors Robert R. Bowie (Director of the Center), Hollis B. Chenery, Samuel P. Huntington, Alex Inkeles, Henry A. Kissinger, Seymour Martin Lipset, Edward S. Mason, Gustav F. Papanek, Thomas C. Schelling, and Raymond Vernon.

Books

The Soviet Bloc, by Zbigniew K. Brzezinski (jointly with the Russian Research Center), 1960. Harvard University Press. Revised edition, 1967.

The Necessity for Choice, by Henry A. Kissinger, 1961. Harper & Bros.

Strategy and Arms Control, by Thomas C. Schelling and Morton H. Halperin, 1961. Twentieth Century Fund.

Rift and Revolt in Hungary, by Ferenc A. Váli, 1961. Harvard University Press.

United States Manufacturing Investment in Brazil, by Lincoln Gordon and Engelbert L. Grommers, 1962. Harvard Business School.

The Economy of Cyprus, by A. J. Meyer, with Simos Vassiliou (jointly with the Center for Middle Eastern Studies), 1962. Harvard University Press.

Entrepreneurs of Lebanon, by Yusif A. Sayigh (jointly with the Center for Middle Eastern Studies), 1962. Harvard University Press.

Communist China 1955–1959: Policy Documents with Analysis, with a foreword by Robert R. Bowie and John K. Fairbank (jointly with the East Asian Research Center), 1962. Harvard University Press.

In Search of France, by Stanley Hoffman, Charles P. Kindleberger, Laurence Wylie, Jesse R. Pitts, Jean-Baptiste Duroselle, and François Goguel, 1963. Harvard University Press.

Somali Nationalism, by Saadia Touval, 1963. Harvard University Press.

The Dilemma of Mexico's Development, by Raymond Vernon, 1963. Harvard University Press.

Limited War in the Nuclear Age, by Morton H. Halperin, 1963. John Wiley & Sons.

The Arms Debate, by Robert A. Levine, 1963. Harvard University Press.

Africans on the Land, by Montague Yudelman, 1964. Harvard University Press.

Counterinsurgency Warfare, by David Galula, 1964. Frederick A. Praeger, Inc.

People and Policy in the Middle East, by Max Weston Thornburg, 1964. W. W. Norton & Co.

Shaping the Future, by Robert R. Bowie, 1964. Columbia University Press.

Foreign Aid and Foreign Policy, by Edward S. Mason (jointly with the Council on Foreign Relations), 1964. Harper & Row.

Public Policy and Private Enterprise in Mexico, by M. S. Wionczek, D. H. Shelton, C. P. Blair, and R. Izquierdo, ed. Raymond Vernon, 1964. Harvard University Press.

How Nations Negotiate, by Fred Charles Iklé, 1964. Harper & Row.

China and the Bomb, by Morton H. Halperin (jointly with the East Asian Research Center), 1965. Frederick A. Praeger, Inc.

Democracy in Germany, by Fritz Erler (Jodidi Lectures), 1965. Harvard University Press.

The Troubled Partnership, by Henry A. Kissinger (jointly with the Council on Foreign Relations), 1965. McGraw-Hill Book Co.

The Rise of Nationalism in Central Africa, by Robert I. Rotberg, 1965. Harvard University Press.

Pan-Africanism and East African Integration, by Joseph S. Nye, Jr., 1965. Harvard University Press.

Communist China and Arms Control, by Morton H. Halperin and Dwight H. Perkins (jointly with the East Asian Research Center), 1965. Frederick A. Praeger, Inc.

Problems of National Strategy, ed. Henry Kissinger, 1965. Frederick A. Praeger, Inc.

Deterrence before Hiroshima: The Airpower Background of Modern Strategy, by George H. Quester, 1966. John Wiley & Sons.

Containing the Arms Race, by Jeremy J. Stone, 1966. M.I.T. Press.

Germany and the Atlantic Alliance: The Interaction of Strategy and Politics, by James L. Richardson, 1966. Harvard University Press.

Arms and Influence, by Thomas C. Schelling, 1966. Yale University Press.

Political Change in a West African State, by Martin Kilson, 1966. Harvard University Press.

Planning without Facts: Lessons in Resource Allocation from Nigeria's Development, by Wolfgang F. Stolper, 1966. Harvard University Press.

Export Instability and Economic Development, by Alasdair I. MacBean, 1966. Harvard University Press.

Foreign Policy and Democratic Politics, by Kenneth N. Waltz (jointly with the Institute of War and Peace Studies, Columbia University), 1967. Little, Brown & Co.

Contemporary Military Strategy, by Morton H. Halperin, 1967. Little, Brown & Co.

Sino-Soviet Relations and Arms Control, ed. Morton H. Halperin (jointly with the East Asian Research Center), 1967. M.I.T. Press.

Africa and United States Policy, by Rupert Emerson, 1967. Prentice-Hall.

Elites in Latin America, edited by Seymour M. Lipset and Aldo Solari, 1967. Oxford University Press.

Europe's Postwar Growth, by Charles P. Kindleberger, 1967. Harvard University Press.

The Rise and Decline of the Cold War, by Paul Seabury, 1967. Basic Books.

Student Politics, ed. S. M. Lipset, 1967. Basic Books.

Pakistan's Development: Social Goals and Private Incentives, by Gustav F. Papanek, 1967. Harvard University Press.

Strike a Blow and Die: A Narrative of Race Relations in Colonial Africa, by George Simeon Mwase, ed. Robert I. Rotberg, 1967. Harvard University Press.

Party Systems and Voter Alignments, edited by Seymour M. Lipset and Stein Rokkan, 1967. Free Press.

Agrarian Socialism, by Seymour M. Lipset, revised edition, 1968. Doubleday Anchor.

Aid, Influence, and Foreign Policy, by Joan M. Nelson, 1968. The Macmillan Company.

International Regionalism, by Joseph S. Nye, 1968. Little, Brown & Co.

Revolution and Counterrevolution, by Seymour M. Lipset, 1968. Basic Books.

Development Policy: Theory and Practice, edited by Gustav F. Papanek, 1968. Harvard University Press.

Political Order in Changing Societies, by Samuel P. Huntington, 1968. Yale University Press.

The TFX Tangle: The Politics of Innovation, by Robert J. Art, 1968. Little, Brown & Co.

Korea: The Politics of the Vortex, by Gregory Henderson, 1968. Harvard University Press.

Political Development in Latin America, by Martin Needler, 1968. Random House.

The Precarious Republic, by Michael Hudson, 1968. Random House.

The Brazilian Capital Goods Industry, 1929—1964 (jointly with the Center for Studies in Education and Development), by Nathaniel H. Leff, 1968. Harvard University Press.

Economic Policy-Making and Development in Brazil, 1947–1964, by Nathaniel H. Leff, 1968. John Wiley & Sons.

German Foreign Policy in Transition, by Karl Kaiser, 1968. Oxford University Press.

Protest and Power in Black Africa, edited by Robert I. Rotberg, 1969. Oxford University Press.

Peace in Europe, by Karl E. Birnbaum, 1969. Oxford University Press.

The Process of Modernization: An Annotated Bibliography on the Sociocultural Aspects of Development, by John Brode, 1969. Harvard University Press.

Taxation and Development: Lessons from Colombian Experience, by Richard M. Bird, 1970. Harvard University Press.

Lord and Peasant in Peru: A Paradigm of Political and Social Change, by F. LaMond Tullis, 1970. Harvard University Press.

The Kennedy Round in American Trade Policy: The Twilight of the GATT? by John W. Evans, 1971. Harvard University Press.

Occasional Papers, Published by the Center for International Affairs

1. *A Plan for Planning: The Need for a Better Method of Assisting Underdeveloped Countries on Their Economic Policies,* by Gustav F. Papanek, 1961.
2. *The Flow of Resources from Rich to Poor,* by Alan D. Neale, 1961.*
3. *Limited War: An Essay on the Development of the Theory and an Annotated Bibliography,* by Morton H. Halperin, 1962.*
4. *Reflections on the Failure of the First West Indian Federation,* by Hugh W. Springer, 1962.*
5. *On the Interaction of Opposing Forces under Possible Arms Agreements,* by Glenn A. Kent, 1963.
6. *Europe's Northern Cap and the Soviet Union,* by Nils Orvik, 1963.
7. *Civil Administration in the Punjab: An Analysis of a State Government in India,* by E. N. Mangat Rai, 1963.
8. *On the Appropriate Size of a Development Program,* by Edward S. Mason, 1964.
9. *Self-Determination Revisited in the Era of Decolonization,* by Rupert Emerson, 1964.
10. *The Planning and Execution of Economic Development in Southeast Asia,* by Clair Wilcox, 1965.
11. *Pan-Africanism in Action,* by Albert Tevoedjre, 1965.
12. *Is China Turning In?* by Morton H. Halperin, 1965.
13. *Economic Development in India and Pakistan,* by Edward S. Mason, 1966.
14. *The Role of the Military in Recent Turkish Politics,* by Ergun Ozbudun, 1966.

15. *Economic Development and Individual Change: A Social-Psychological Study of the Comilla Experiment in Pakistan,* by Howard Schuman, 1967.
16. *A Select Bibliography on Students, Politics, and Higher Education,* by Philip Altbach, 1967.
17. *Europe's Political Puzzle: A Study of the Fouchet Negotiations and the 1963 Veto,* by Alessandro Silj, 1967.
18. *The Cap and the Straits: Problems of Nordic Security,* by Jan Klenberg, 1968.
19. *Cyprus: The Law and Politics of Civil Strife,* by Linda B. Miller, 1968.
20. *East and West Pakistan: A Problem in the Political Economy of Regional Planning,* by Md. Anisur Rahman, 1968.
21. *Internal War and International Systems: Perspectives on Method,* by George A. Kelly and Linda B. Miller, 1969.
22. *Migrants, Urban Poverty, and Instability in New Nations,* by Joan M. Nelson, 1969.
23. *Growth and Development in Pakistan, 1955–1969,* by Joseph J. Stern and Walter P. Falcon, 1970.
24. *Higher Education in Developing Countries: A Select Bibliography,* by Philip G. Altbach, 1970.
25. *Anatomy of Political Institutionalization: The Case of Israel and Some Comparative Analyses,* by Amos Perlmutter, 1970.
26. *The German Democratic Republic from the 1960s to the 1970s,* by Peter Christian Ludz, 1970.

* Out of print.